HAPPINESS
#1

SHUZO OSHIMI

HAPPINESS #1 CONTENTS

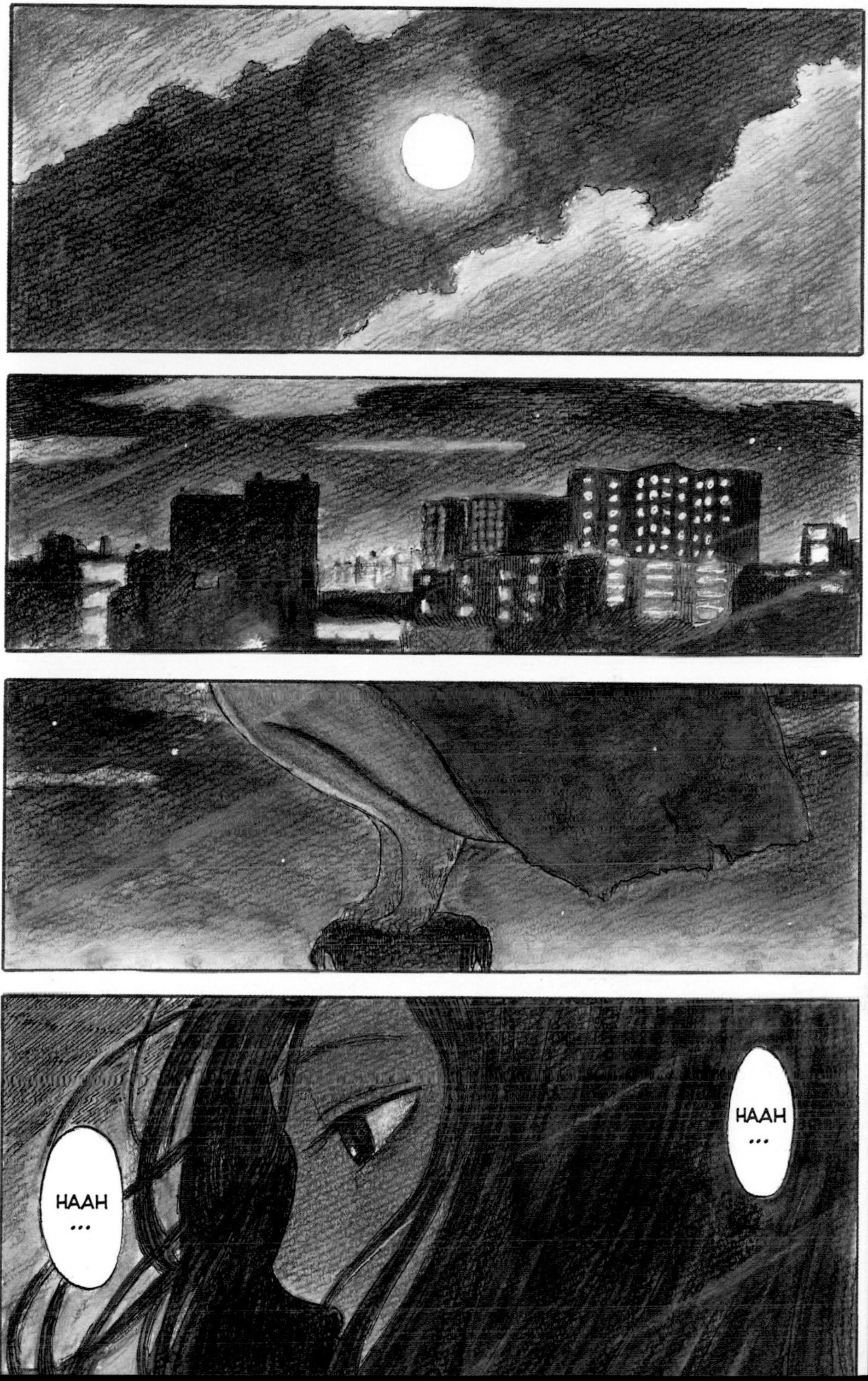
HAAH ...
HAAH ...

Chapter 1: Nora

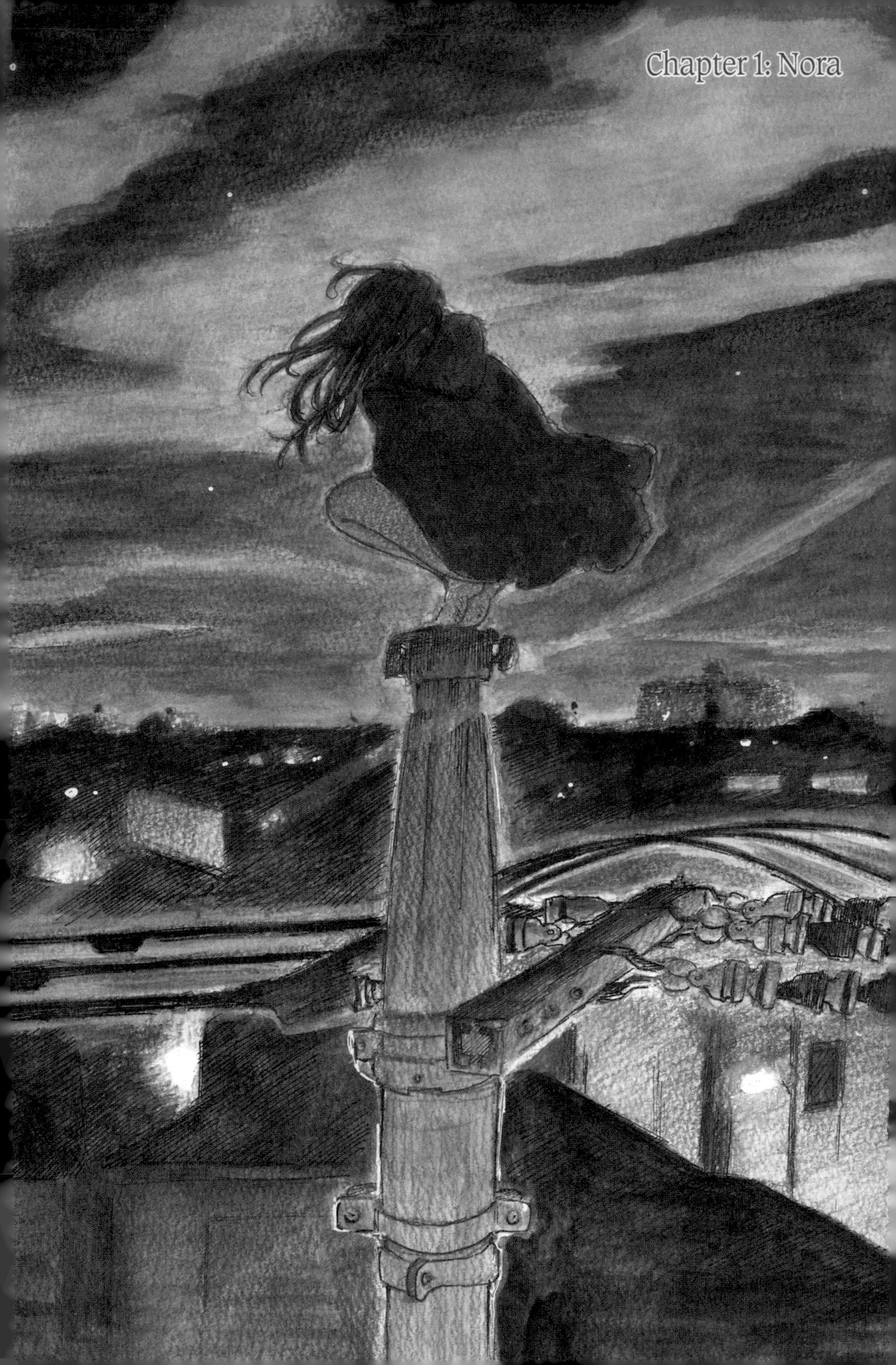

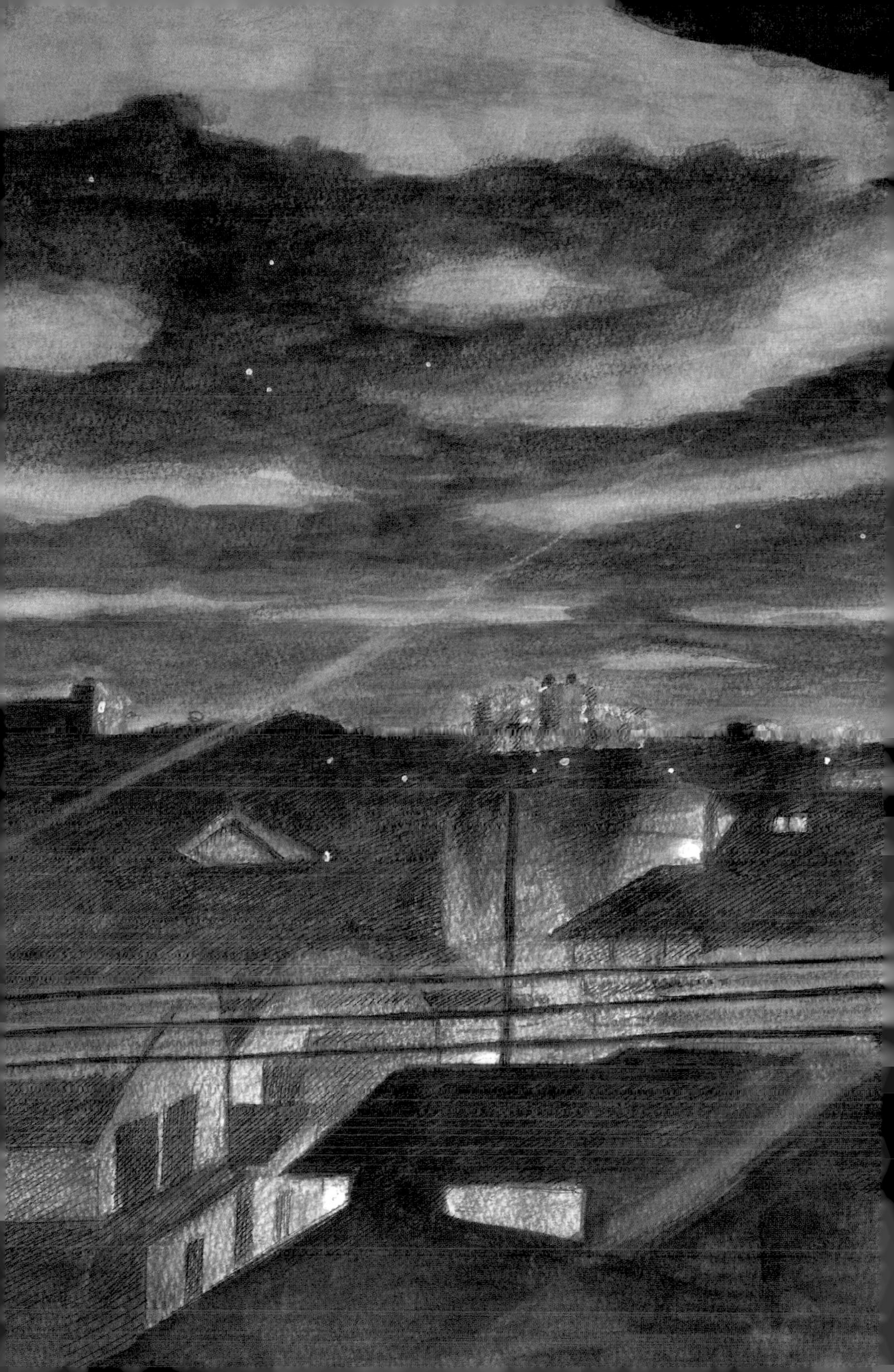

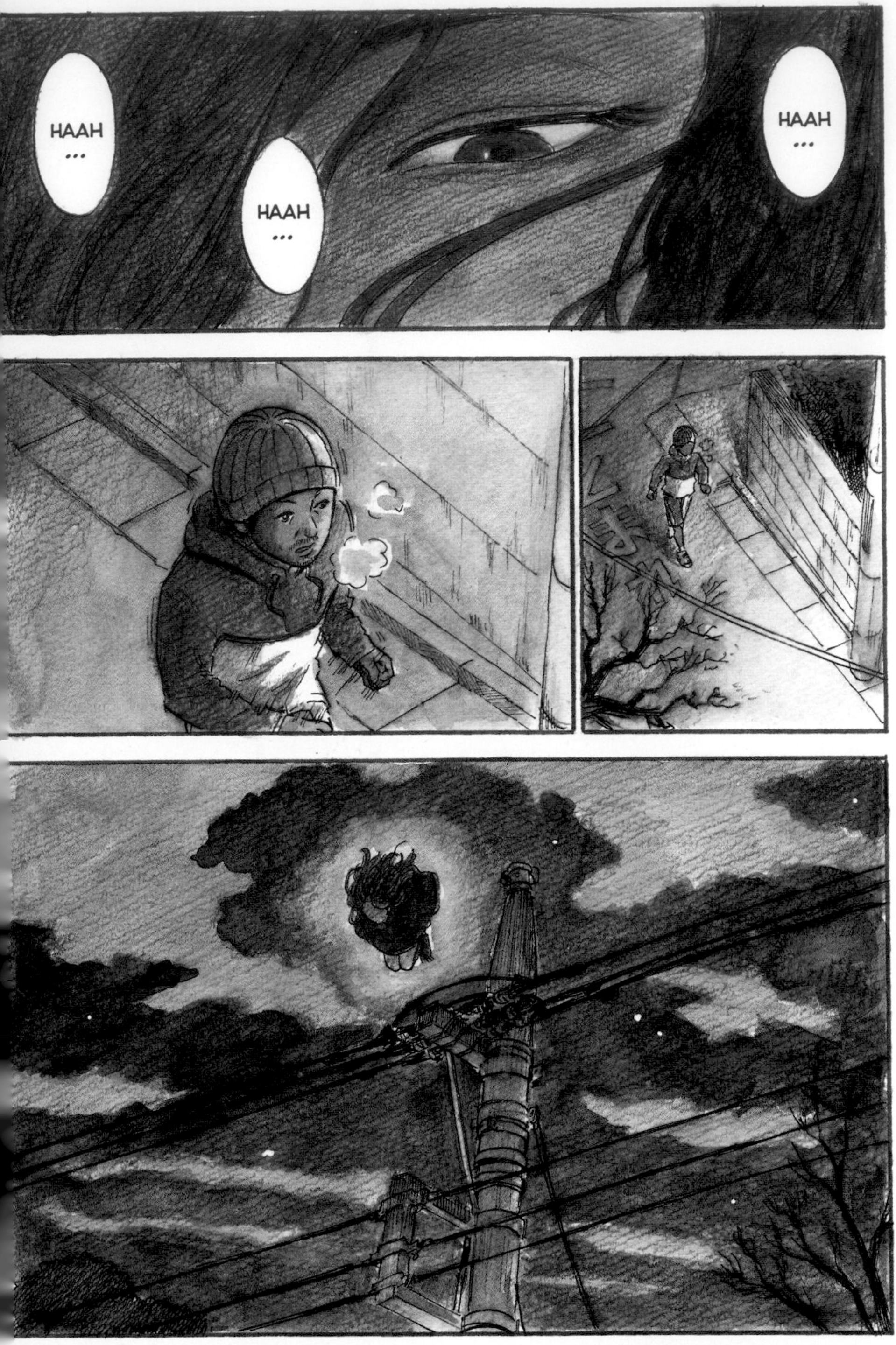
HAAH ...
HAAH ...
HAAH ...

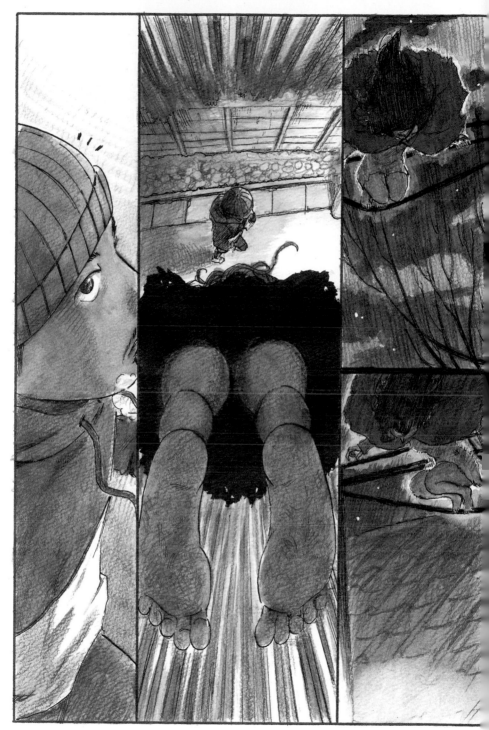

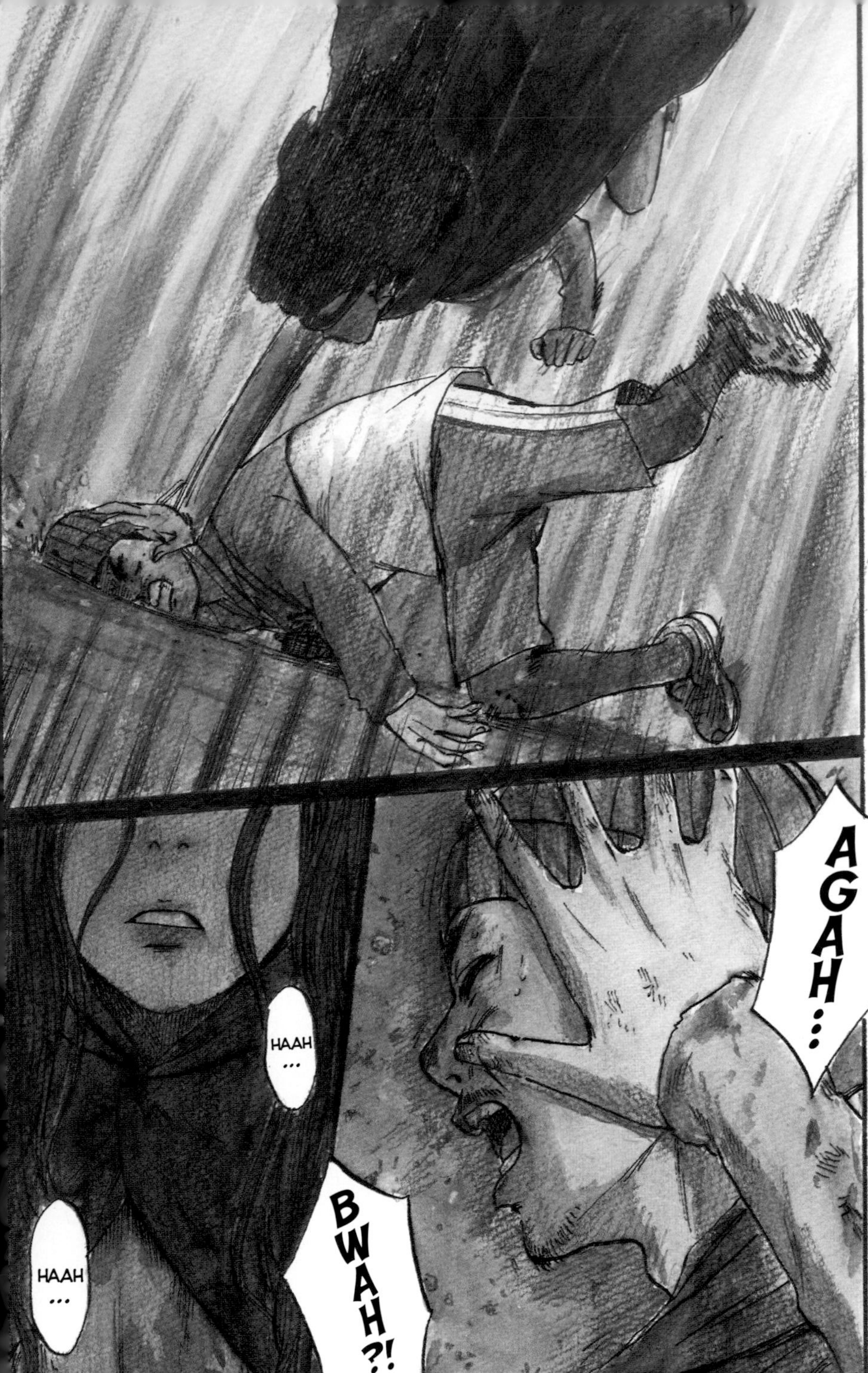
AGAH…
BWAH?!
HAAH…
HAAH…

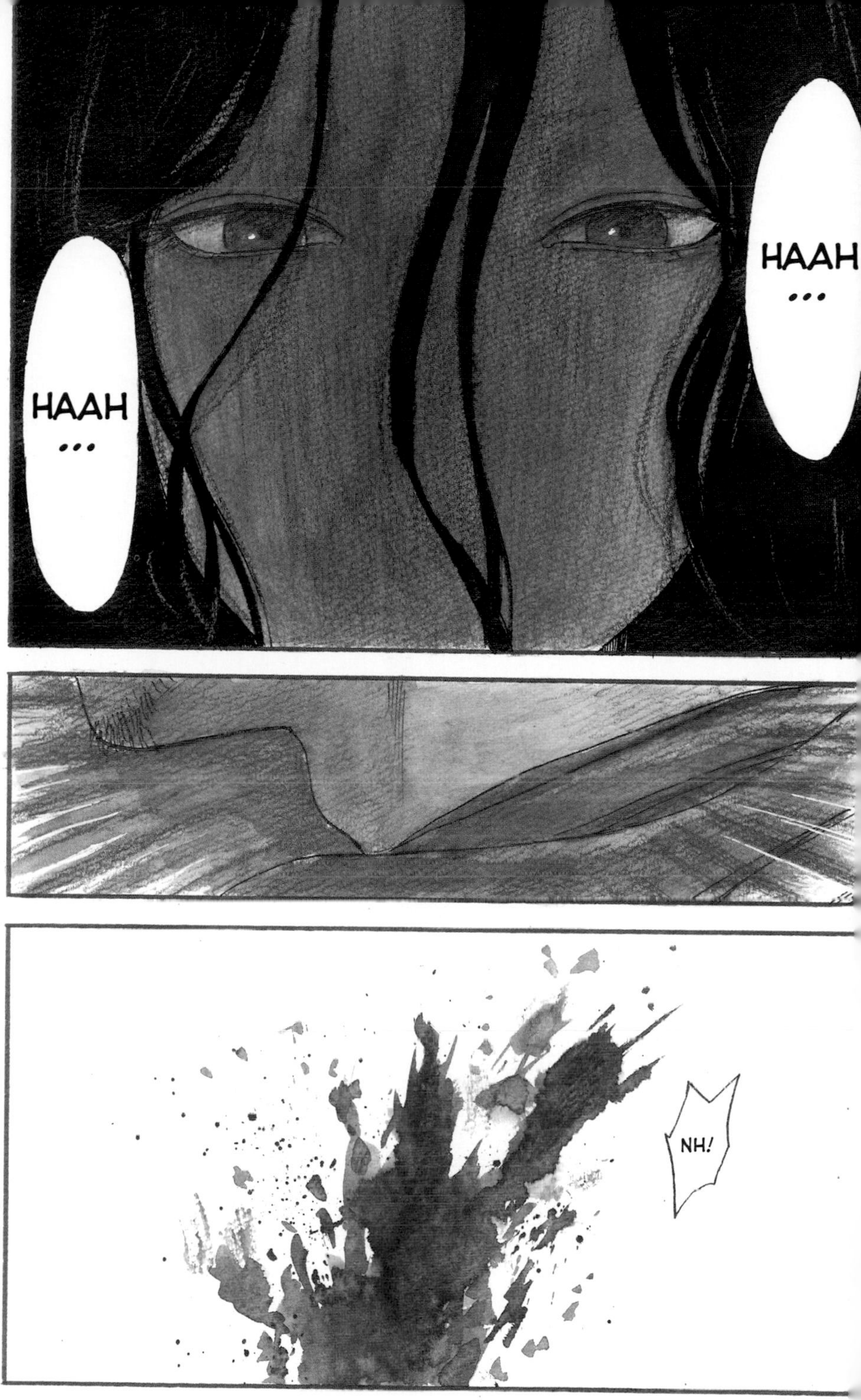
HAAH ...
HAAH ...
NH!

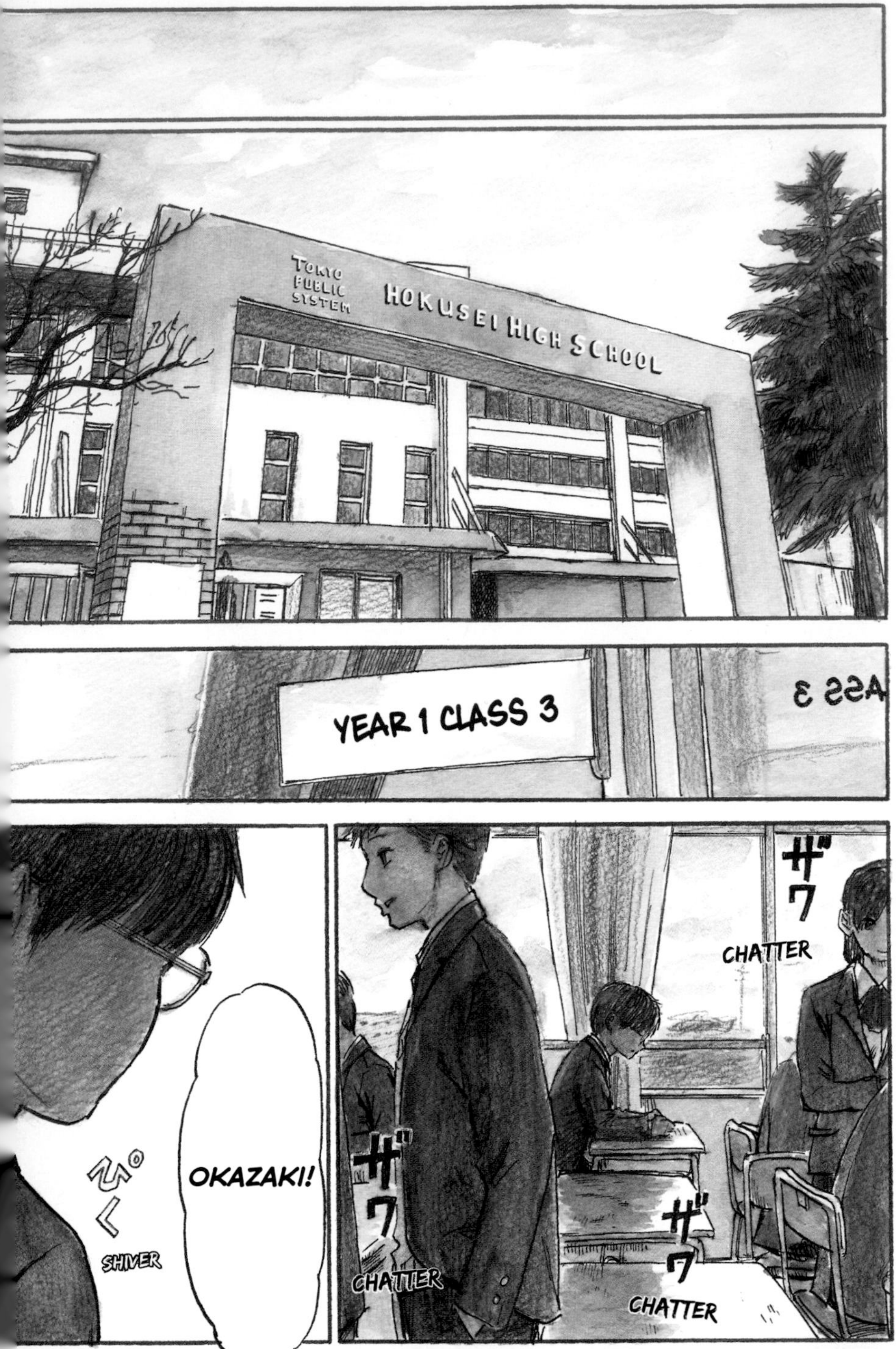
TOKYO PUBLIC SYSTEM
HOKUSEI HIGH SCHOOL
YEAR 1 CLASS 3
ザワ
CHATTER
ザワ
CHATTER
ザワ
CHATTER
OKAZAKI!
SHIVER

TOMARE!

[STOP!]

You're going the wrong way!

Manga is a completely different type of reading experience.

To start at the *beginning*, go to the *end*!

That's right! Authentic manga is read the traditional Japanese way—from right to left. Exactly the *opposite* of how American books are read. It's easy to follow: Just go to the other end of the book, and read each page—and each panel—from right side to left side, starting at the top right. Now you're experiencing manga as it was meant to be!

Kodansha Comics Trade Paperback Original.

ppiness volume 1 copyright © 2015 Shuzo Oshimi
glish translation copyright © 2016 Shuzo Oshimi

rights reserved.

lished in the United States by Kodansha Comics, an imprint of Kodansha USA
lishing, LLC, New York.

lication rights for this English edition arranged through Kodansha Ltd., Tokyo.

t published in Japan in 2015 by Kodansha Ltd., Tokyo, as *Hapinesu* volume 1.

N 978-1-63236-363-3

ted in the United States of America.

w.kodanshacomics.com

7 6 5 4 3 2

slation: Kevin Gifford
ering: David Yoo
ing: Paul Starr
ansha Comics edition cover design by Phil Balsman

Based on the critically acclaimed classic horror manga

The first new *Parasyte* manga in over 20 years!

NEO PARASYTE f

BY ASUMIKO NAKAMURA, EMA TOYAMA, MIKI RINNO, LALAKO KOJIMA, KAORI YUKI BANKO KUZE, YUUKI OBATA, KASHIO, YUI KUROE, ASIA WATANABE, MIKIMAKI HIKARU SURUGA, HAJIME SHINJO, RENJURO KINDAICHI, AND YURI NARUSHIMA

A collection of chilling new *Parasyte* stories from Japan's top shojo artists

Parasites: shape-shifting aliens whose only purpose is to assimilate with and consum the human race... but do these monsters have a different side? A parasite becomes prince to save his romance-obsessed female host from a dangerous stalker. Anothe hosts a cooking show, in which the real monsters are revealed. These and 13 more stories, from some of the greatest shojo manga artists alive today, together make up a chilling, funny, and entertaining tribute to one of manga's horror classics!

KC KODANSHA COMICS

"I'm pleasantly surprised to find modern shojo using cross-dressing as a dramatic device to deliver social commentary... Recommended."

-Otaku USA Magazine

The prince in his dark days

By **Hico Yamanaka**

drunkard for a father, a household of poverty... For 17-year-old Atsuko, isfortune is all she knows and believes in. Until one day, a chance counter with Itaru-the wealthy heir of a huge corporation-changes erything. The two look identical, uncannily so. When Itaru curiously es missing, Atsuko is roped into being his stand-in. There, in his shoes, suko must parade like a prince in a palace. She encounters many new periences, but at what cost…?

KC

KODANSHA COMICS

Japan's most powerful spirit medium delves into the ghost world's greatest mysteries!

Story by Kyo Shirodaira, famed author of mystery fiction and creator of *Spiral*, *Blast of Tempest*, and *The Record of a Fallen Vampire*.

Both touched by spirits called yôkai, Kotoko and Kurô have gained unique superhuman powers. But to gain her powers Kotoko has given up an eye and a leg, and Kurô's personal life is in shambles. So when Kotoko suggests they team up to deal with renegades from the spirit world, Kurô doesn't have many other choices, but Kotoko might just have a few ulterior motives...

IN/SPECTRE

STORY BY **KYO SHIRODAIRA**
ART BY **CHASHIBA KATASE**

KC
KODANSHA
COMICS

New action series from Hiroyuki Takei, creator of the classic shonen franchise Shaman King!

In medieval Japan, a bell hanging on the collar is a sign that a cat has a master. Norachiyo's bell hangs from his katana sheath, but he is nonetheless a stray — a ronin. This one-eyed cat samurai travels across a dishonest world, cutting through pretense and deception with his blade.

NEKOGAHARA

STRAY CAT SAMURAI

By

Hiroyuki Takei

KC KODANSHA COMICS

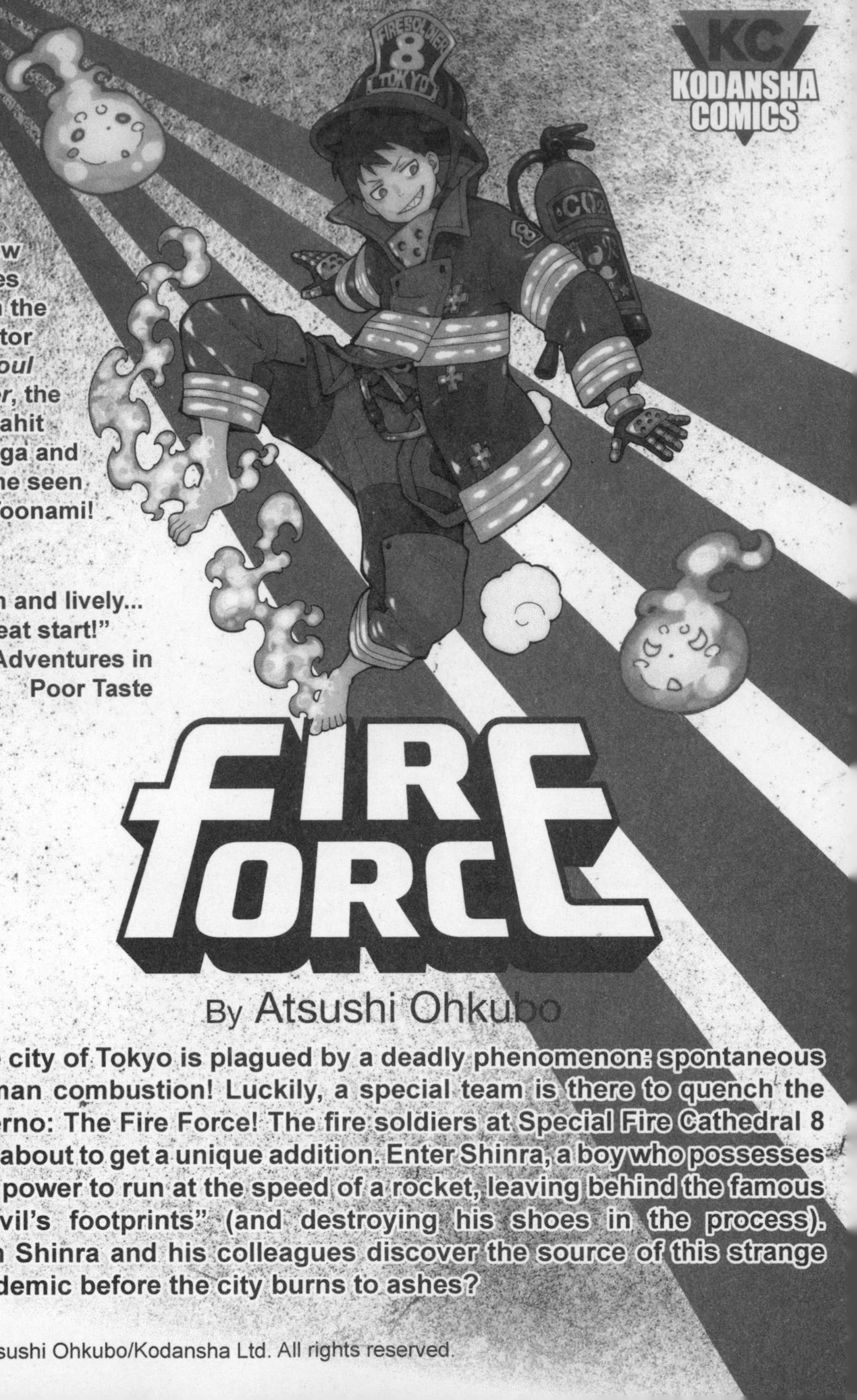

FIRE SOLDIER 8 TOKYO

A new series from the creator of *Soul Eater*, the megahit manga and anime seen on Toonami!

"Fun and lively... a great start!"
-Adventures in Poor Taste

FIRE FORCE

By Atsushi Ohkubo

The city of Tokyo is plagued by a deadly phenomenon: spontaneous human combustion! Luckily, a special team is there to quench the inferno: The Fire Force! The fire soldiers at Special Fire Cathedral 8 are about to get a unique addition. Enter Shinra, a boy who possesses the power to run at the speed of a rocket, leaving behind the famous "devil's footprints" (and destroying his shoes in the process). Can Shinra and his colleagues discover the source of this strange epidemic before the city burns to ashes?

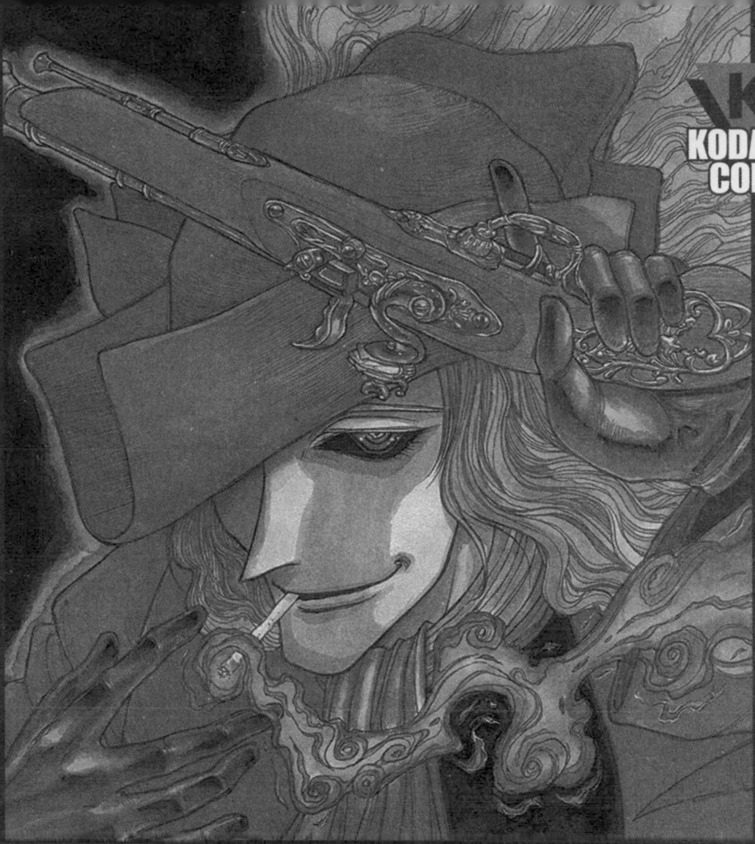

KODANSHA COMICS

The Black Museum The Ghost and the Lady

By Kazuhiro Fujita

Deep in Scotland Yard in London sits an evidence room dedicated to the greatest mysteries of British history. In this "Black Museum" sits a misshapen hunk of lead—two bullets fused together—the key to a wartime encounter between Florence Nightingale, the mother of modern nursing, and a supernatural Man in Grey. This story is unknown to most scholars of history, but a special guest of the museum will tell the tale of The Ghost and the Lady...

Praise for Kazuhiro Fujita's *Ushio and Tora*

"A charming revival that combines a classic look with modern depth and pacing... **Essential viewing both for curmudgeons and new fans alike.**" — Anime News Network

"**GREAT!** The first episode of Ushio and Tora captures the essence of '90s anime." — IGN

Page 19
"Tatsuya" is a reference to Tsutaya, a national video and music rental chain. Media rented at Tsutaya is given to the customer in a distinctive blue fabric envelope with the store's name on it, which is what catches Okazaki's eye in this scene.

TATSUYA

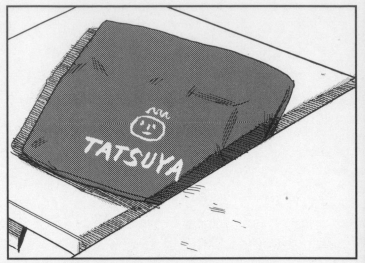

Page 146
LINE is Japan's most popular social media and text messaging app. It's largely replaced other forms of text messaging for most smartphone users, and is widely used throughout southeast Asia as well. It's notable for its popularization of the use of virtual stickers in text messaging, and the LINE cast of sticker characters have become extremely popular in their own right.

...
OH, OKA-ZAKI-KUN ...
ARE YOU ON *LINE* OR ANY-THING?

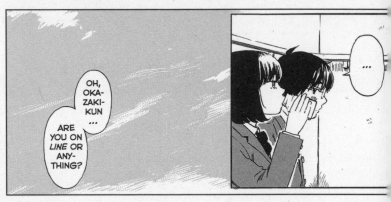

Translation Notes

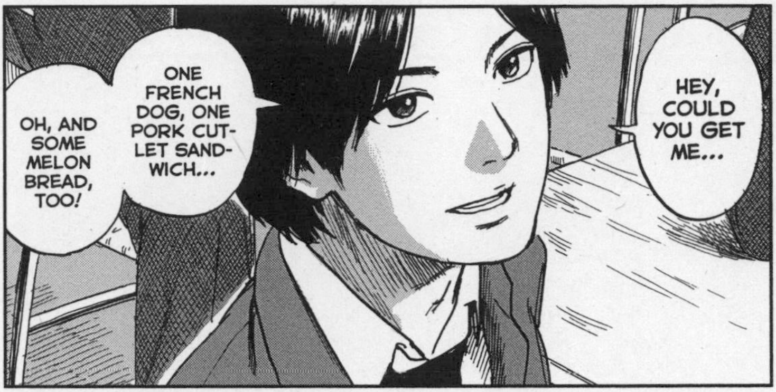
HEY, COULD YOU GET ME...
ONE FRENCH DOG, ONE PORK CUT-LET SAND-WICH...
OH, AND SOME MELON BREAD, TOO!

Page 11
A French dog is a bit of American-inspired Japanese cuisine invented in Hokkaido. It's basically a corn dog, except with fish sausage and an exterior that's often coated in candy sugar. Melon bread is a type of sweet bun with a crispy cookie-dough top which when baked, looks like the skin of a muskmelon. Despite the name, they usually don't taste much like melon.

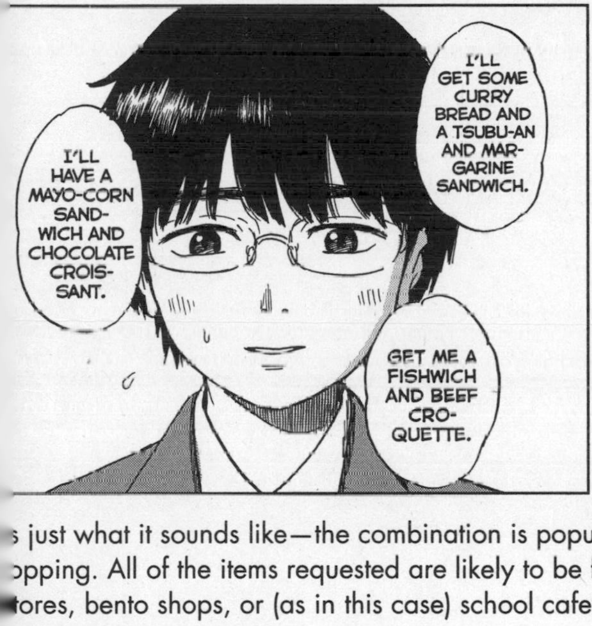
I'LL GET SOME CURRY BREAD AND A TSUBU-AN AND MAR-GARINE SANDWICH.
I'LL HAVE A MAYO-CORN SAND-WICH AND CHOCOLATE CROIS-SANT.
GET ME A FISHWICH AND BEEF CRO-QUETTE.

Page 12
Curry bread is a fried dough bun with curry inside. Tsubu-an is a coarsely ground Japanese bean paste, often mixed with margarine and put in a sandwich. Mayo-corn s just what it sounds like—the combination is popular in sandwiches and as a pizza opping. All of the items requested are likely to be found in Japanese convenience tores, bento shops, or (as in this case) school cafeterias.

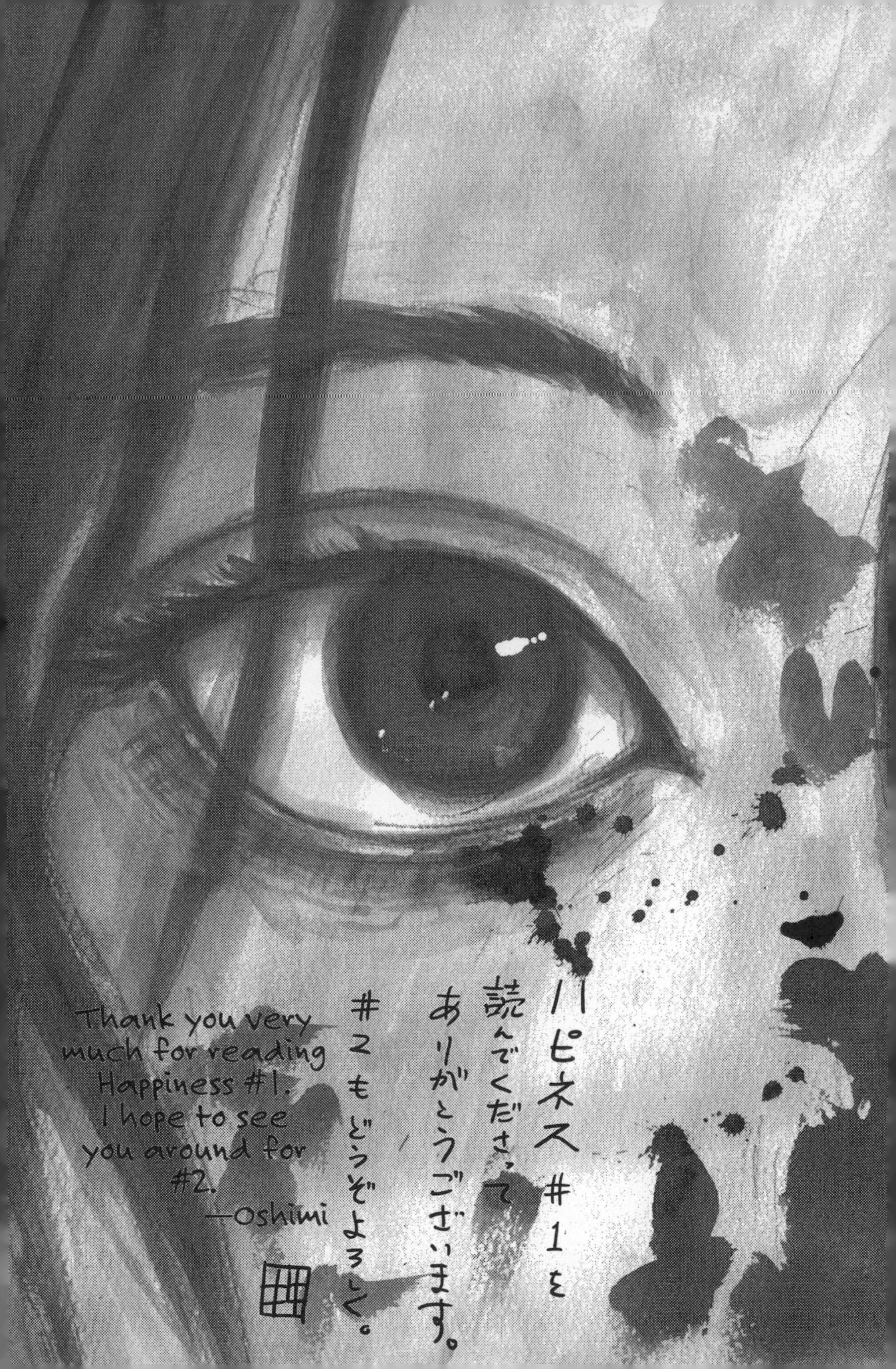
ハピネス＃1を
読んでくださって
ありがとうございます。
＃2もどうぞよろしく。
Thank you very much for reading Happiness #1. I hope to see you around for #2.
—Oshimi

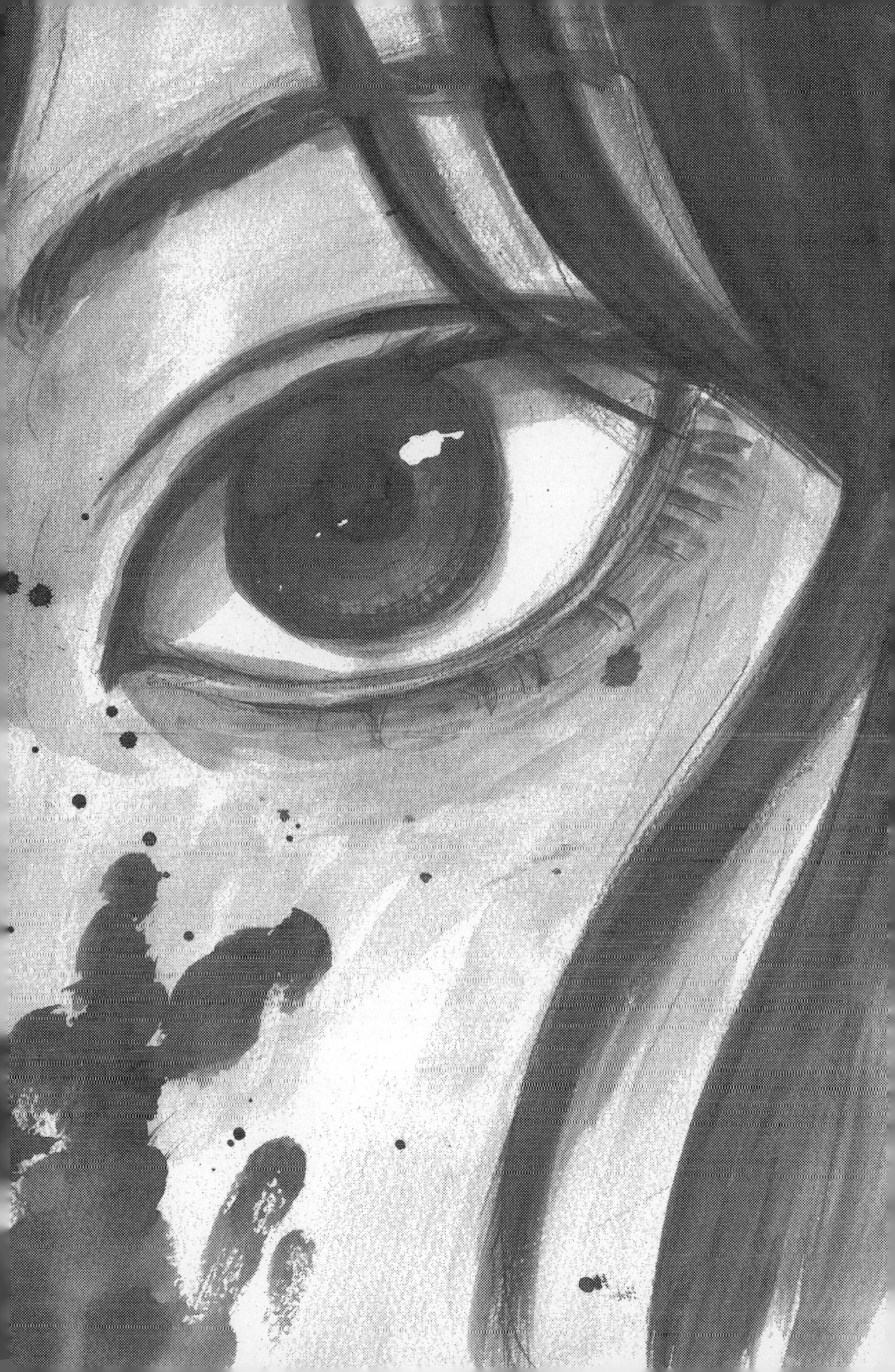

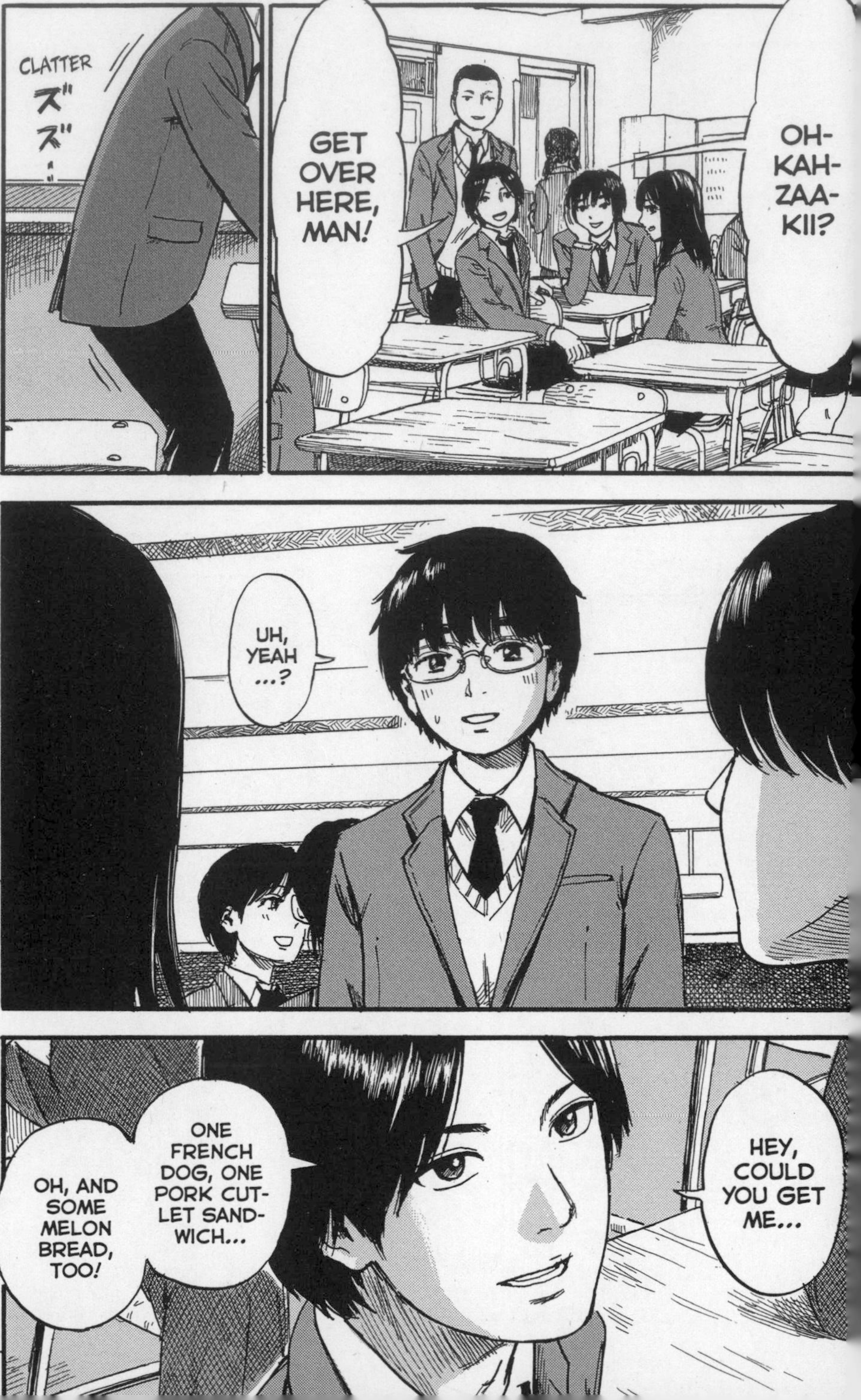
OH-KAH-ZAA-KII?
GET OVER HERE, MAN!
CLATTER
ズズ…
UH, YEAH ...?
HEY, COULD YOU GET ME...
ONE FRENCH DOG, ONE PORK CUT-LET SAND-WICH...
OH, AND SOME MELON BREAD, TOO!

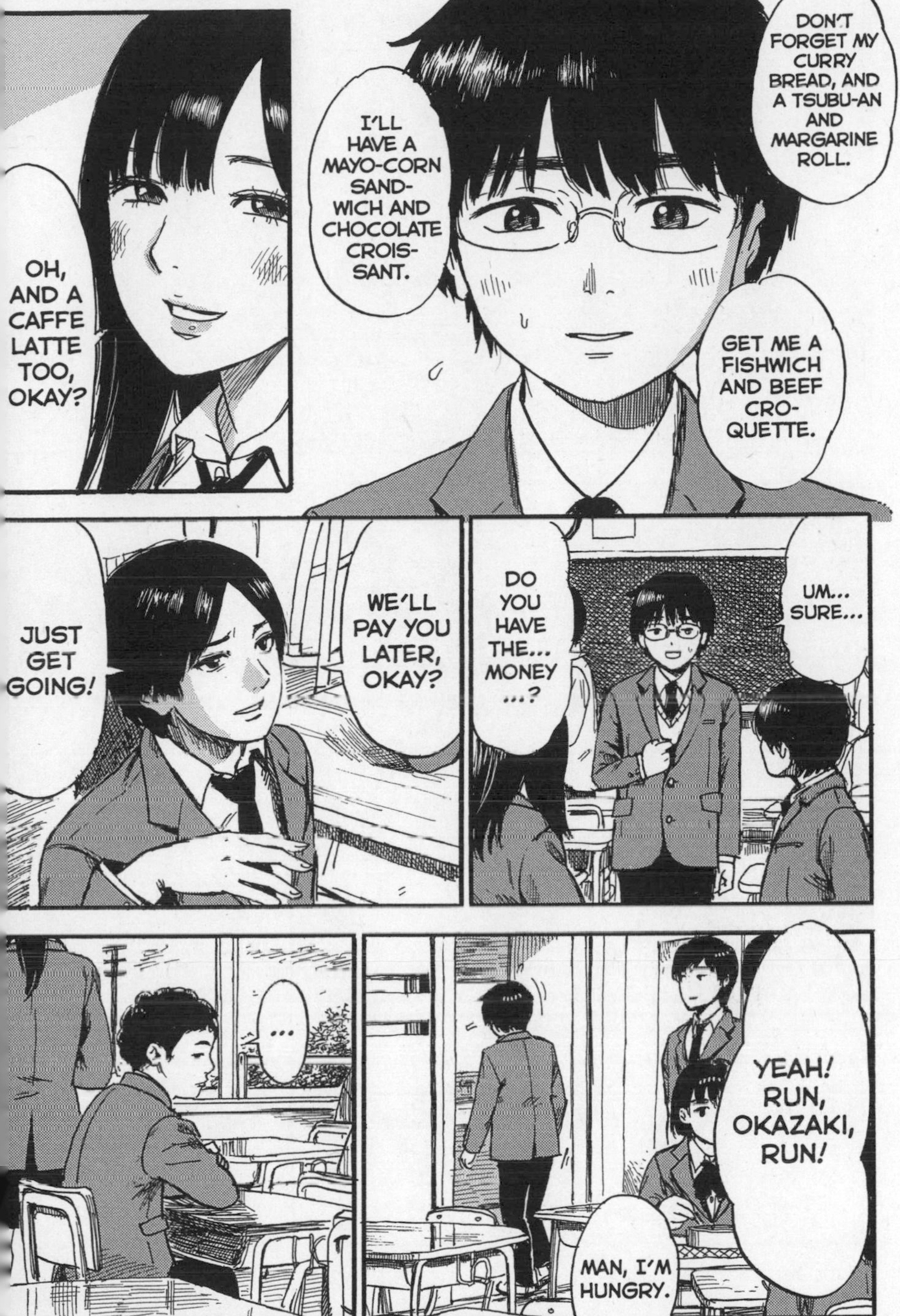
DON'T FORGET MY CURRY BREAD, AND A TSUBU-AN AND MARGARINE ROLL.
I'LL HAVE A MAYO-CORN SAND-WICH AND CHOCOLATE CROIS-SANT.
GET ME A FISHWICH AND BEEF CRO-QUETTE.
OH, AND A CAFFE LATTE TOO, OKAY?
UM... SURE...
DO YOU HAVE THE... MONEY ...?
WE'LL PAY YOU LATER, OKAY?
JUST GET GOING!
YEAH! RUN, OKAZAKI, RUN!
MAN, I'M HUNGRY.
...

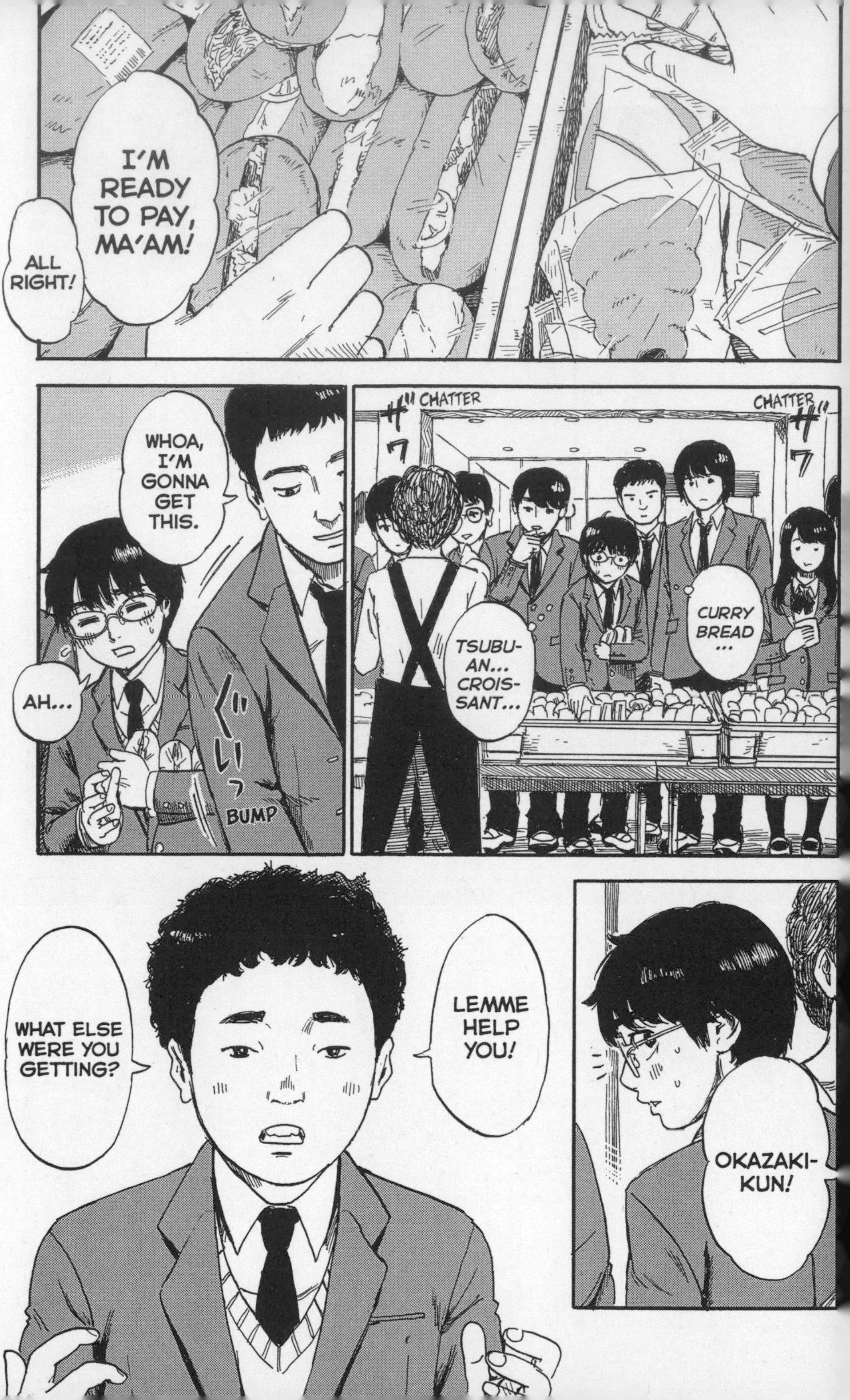
I'M READY TO PAY, MA'AM!
ALL RIGHT!
ザワ
CHATTER
ザワ
CHATTER
CURRY BREAD...
TSUBU-AN... CROIS-SANT...
WHOA, I'M GONNA GET THIS.
ぐいっ
BUMP
AH...
OKAZAKI-KUN!
LEMME HELP YOU!
WHAT ELSE WERE YOU GETTING?

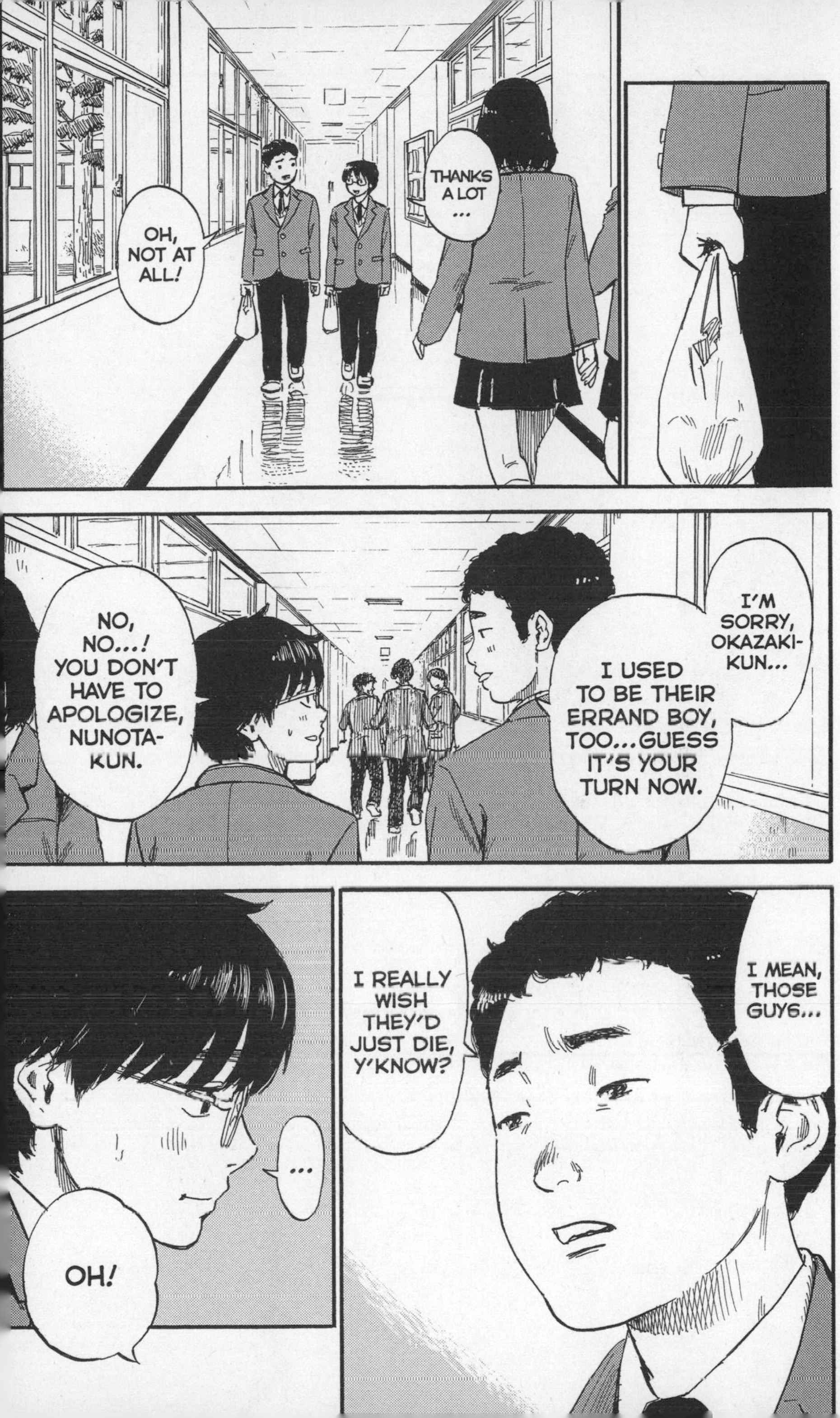
THANKS A LOT ...
OH, NOT AT ALL!
I'M SORRY, OKAZAKI-KUN...
I USED TO BE THEIR ERRAND BOY, TOO...GUESS IT'S YOUR TURN NOW.
NO, NO...! YOU DON'T HAVE TO APOLOGIZE, NUNOTA-KUN.
I MEAN, THOSE GUYS...
I REALLY WISH THEY'D JUST DIE, Y'KNOW?
...
OH!

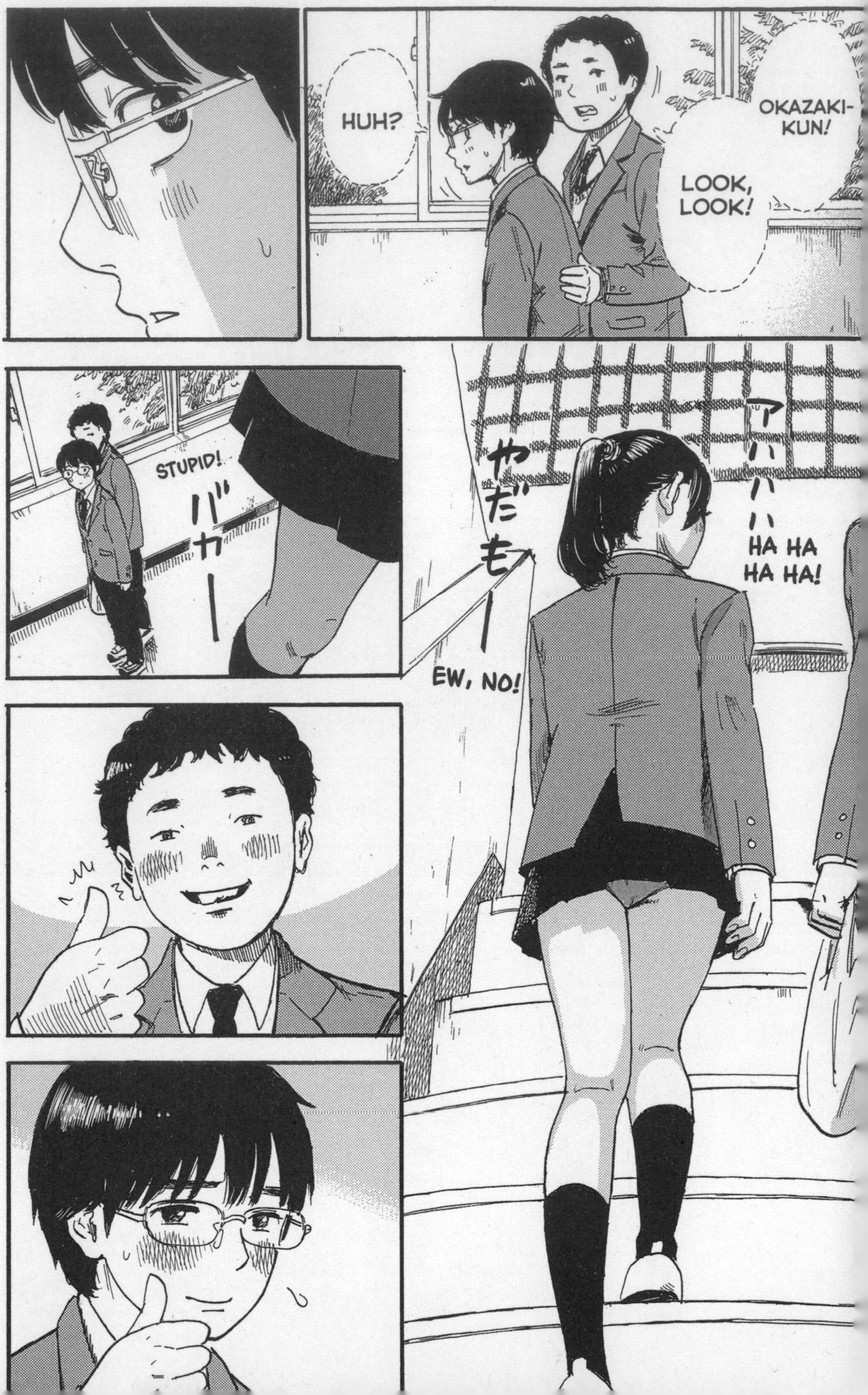
OKAZAKI-KUN!
LOOK, LOOK!
HUH?
アハハハ
HA HA HA HA!
やだもー
EW, NO!
STUPID!
バカー

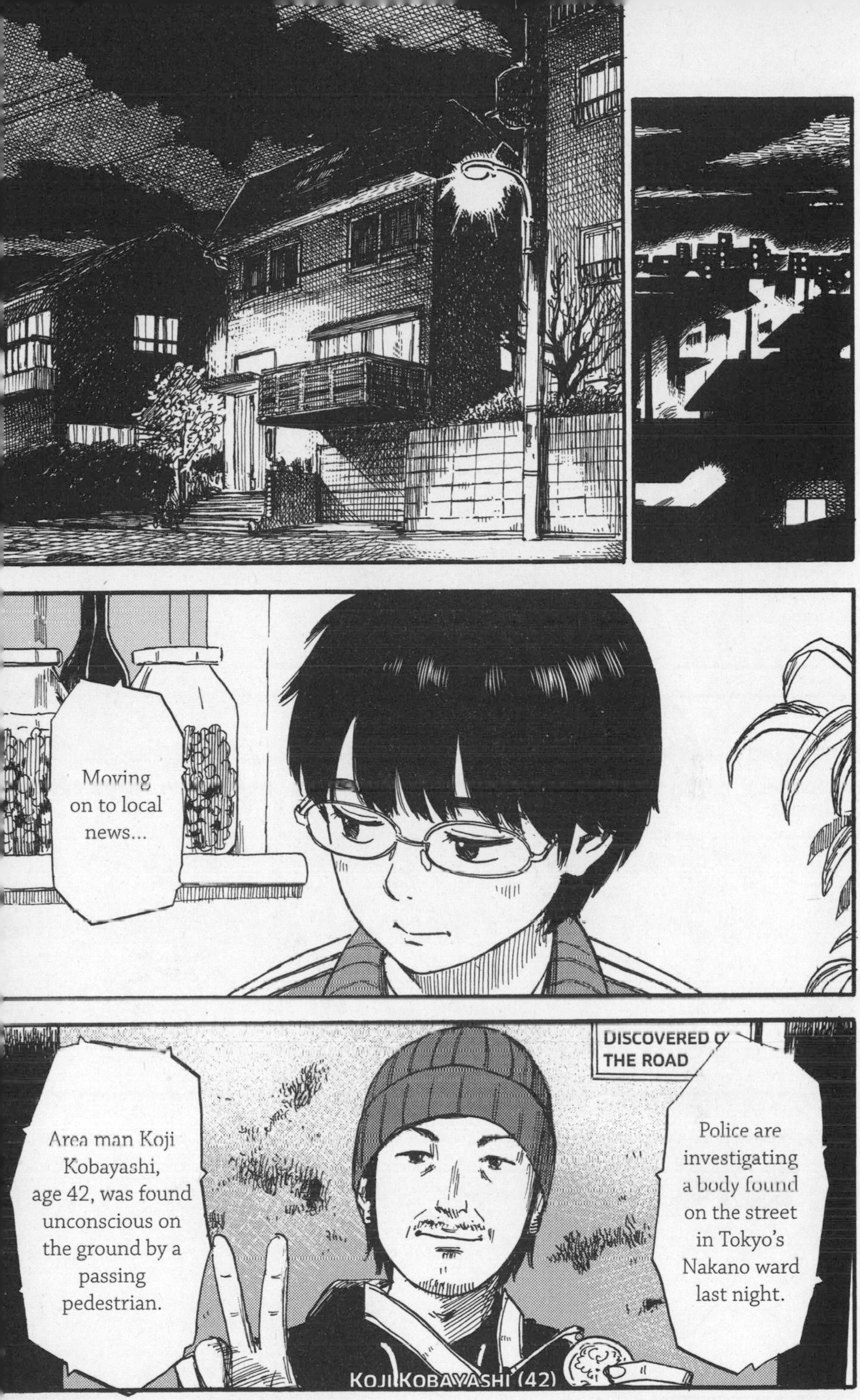
Moving on to local news...
DISCOVERED
THE ROAD
Police are investigating a body found on the street in Tokyo's Nakano ward last night.
Area man Koji Kobayashi, age 42, was found unconscious on the ground by a passing pedestrian.
KOJI KOBAYASHI (42)

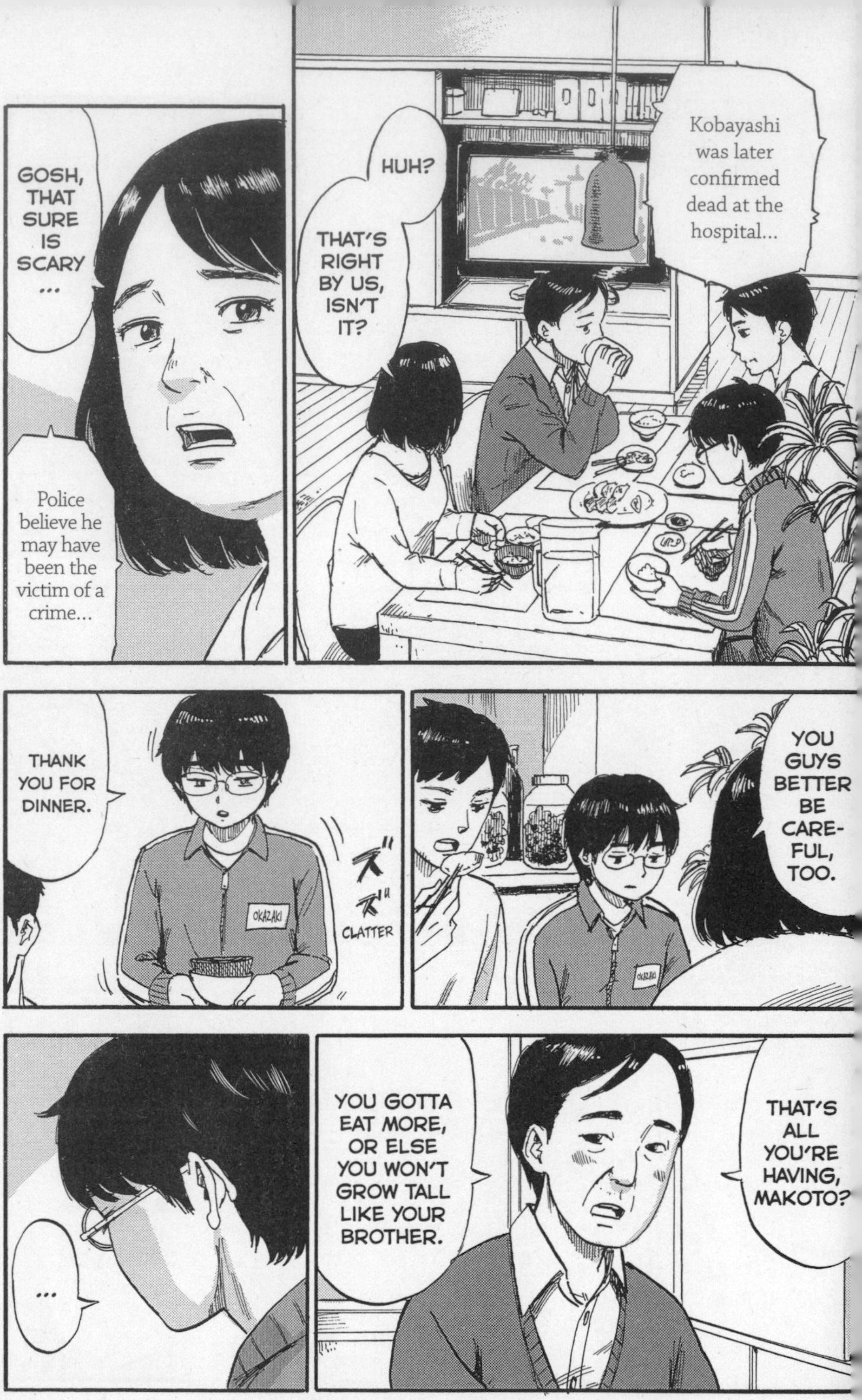
Kobayashi was later confirmed dead at the hospital...
HUH?
THAT'S RIGHT BY US, ISN'T IT?
GOSH, THAT SURE IS SCARY...
Police believe he may have been the victim of a crime...
YOU GUYS BETTER BE CARE-FUL, TOO.
OKAZAKI
THANK YOU FOR DINNER.
CLATTER
OKAZAKI
THAT'S ALL YOU'RE HAVING, MAKOTO?
YOU GOTTA EAT MORE, OR ELSE YOU WON'T GROW TALL LIKE YOUR BROTHER.
...

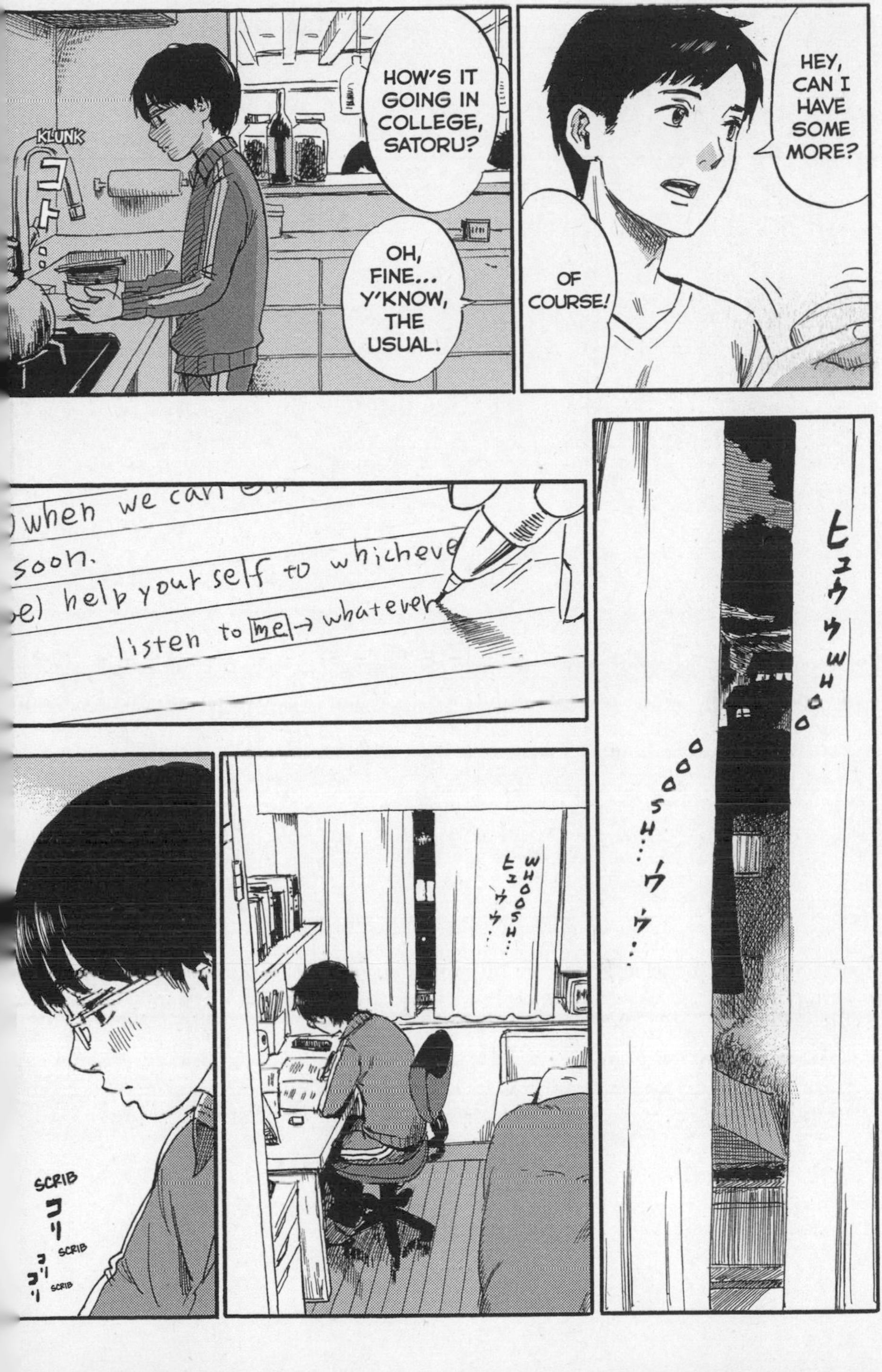
HEY, CAN I HAVE SOME MORE?
OF COURSE!
HOW'S IT GOING IN COLLEGE, SATORU?
OH, FINE... Y'KNOW, THE USUAL.
KLUNK
コト
WHOOOOOOSH...
ヒュウゥゥ...
when we can
soon.
help your self to whicheve
listen to me → whatever
WHOOSH...
ヒュゥゥ...
SCRIB
コリ
SCRIB
コリ
SCRIB

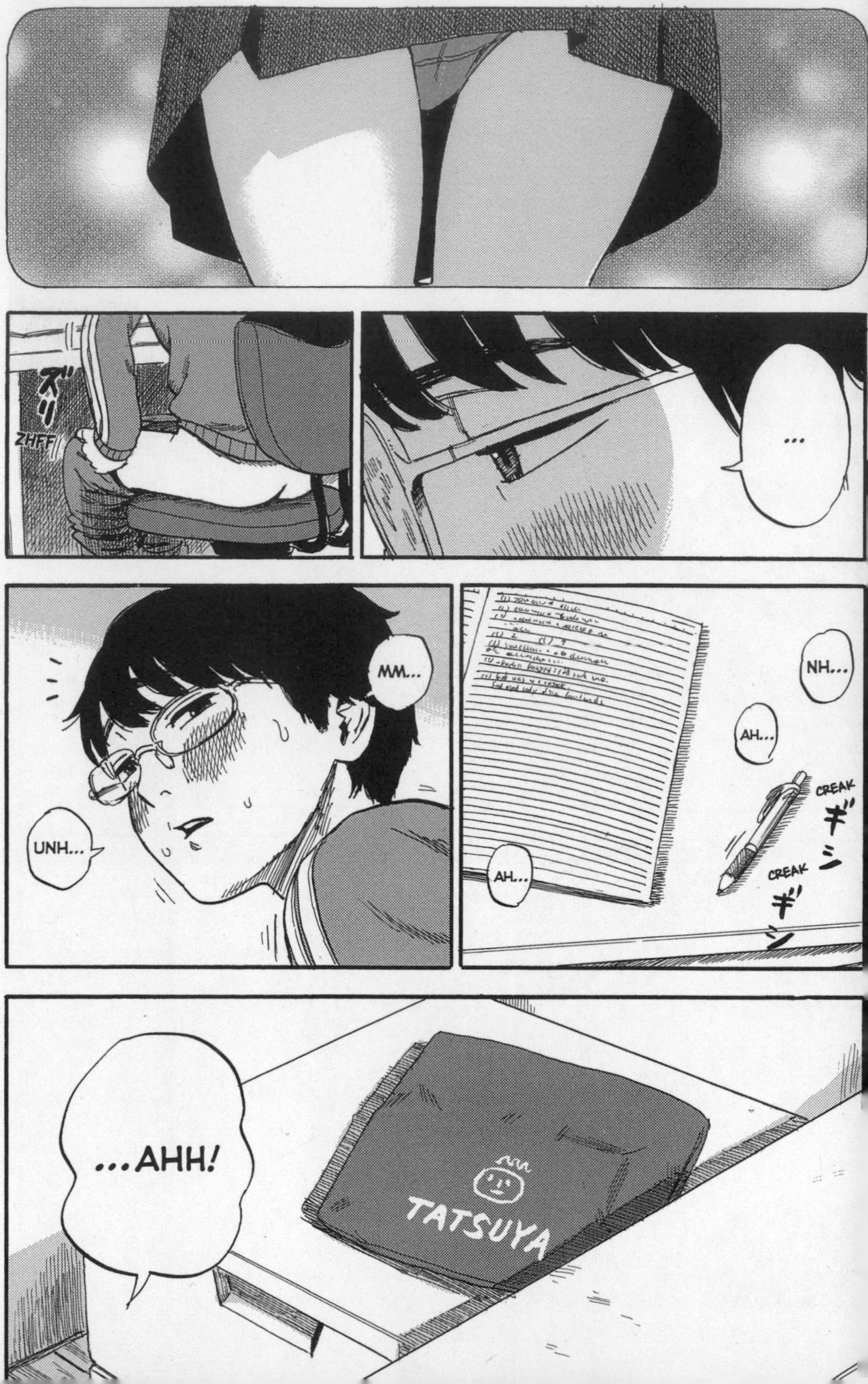
...
ズリ
ZHFF
NH...
AH...
CREAK
ギシ
CREAK
ギシ
AH...
MM...
UNH...
...AHH!
TATSUYA

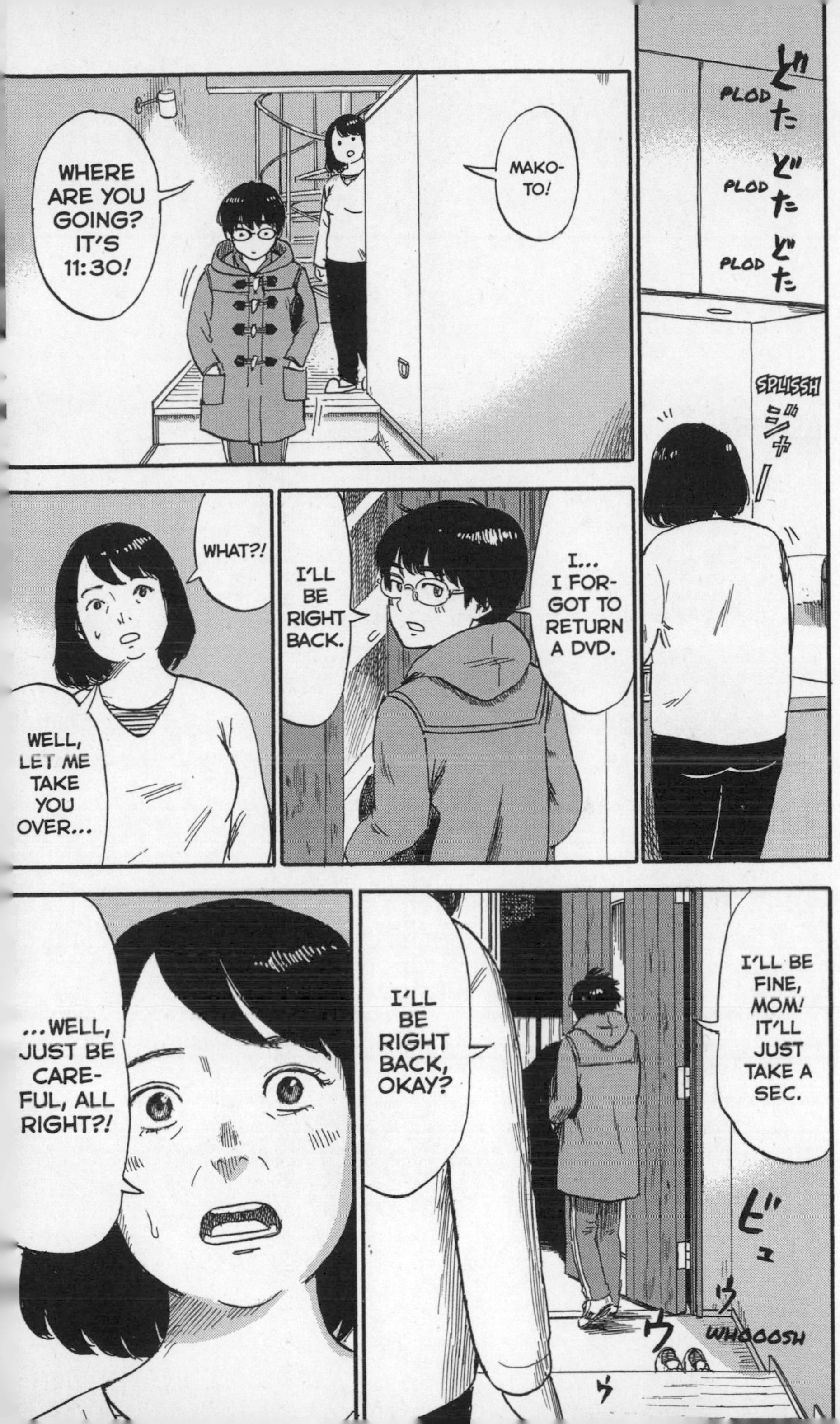
PLOD どた
PLOD どた
PLOD どた
SPLISSH ジャ
MAKO-TO!
WHERE ARE YOU GOING? IT'S 11:30!
I... I FOR-GOT TO RETURN A DVD.
I'LL BE RIGHT BACK.
WHAT?!
WELL, LET ME TAKE YOU OVER...
I'LL BE FINE, MOM! IT'LL JUST TAKE A SEC.
I'LL BE RIGHT BACK, OKAY?
ビュ
WHOOOSH
...WELL, JUST BE CARE-FUL, ALL RIGHT?!

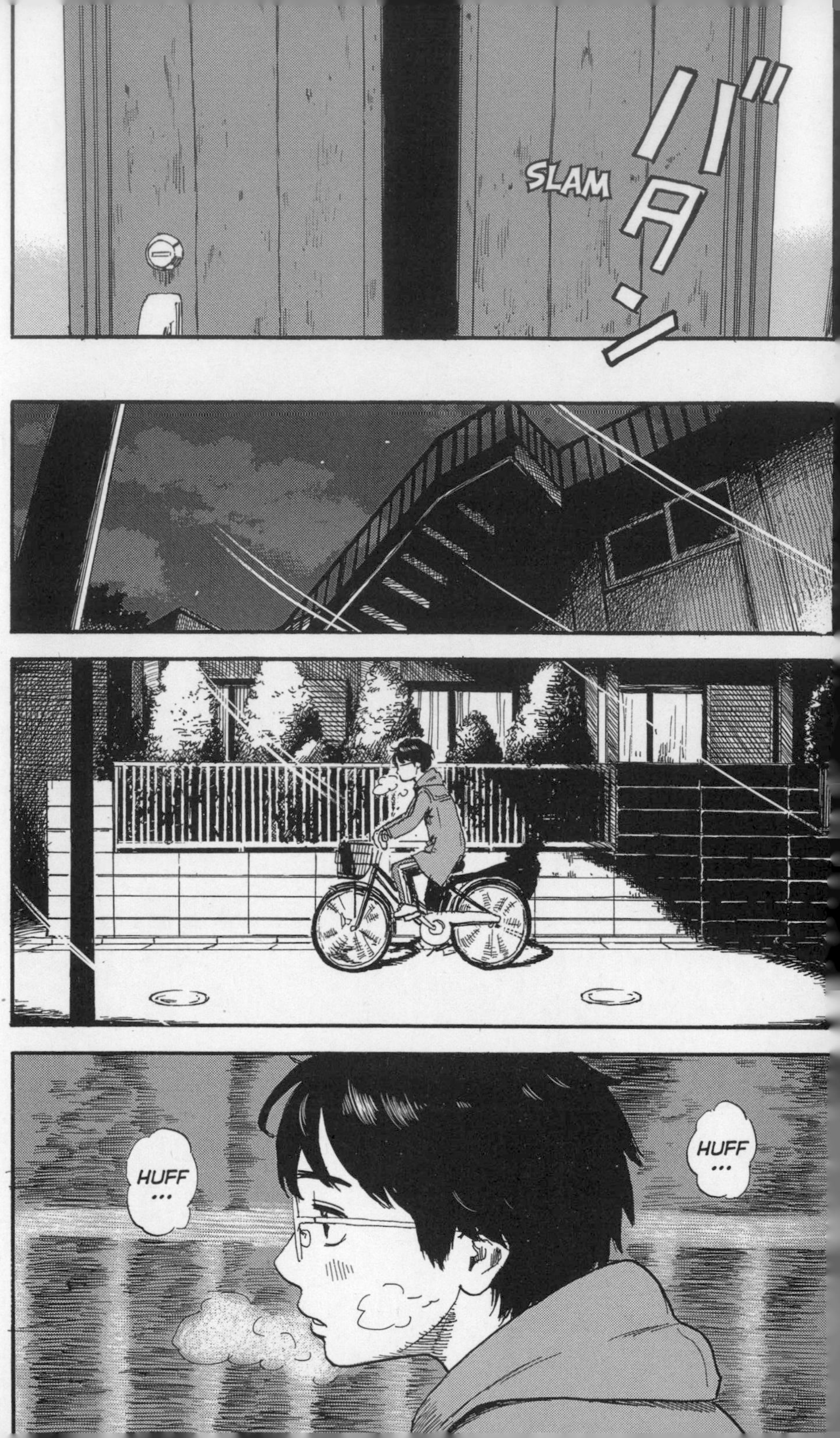
バタン
SLAM
HUFF ...
HUFF ...

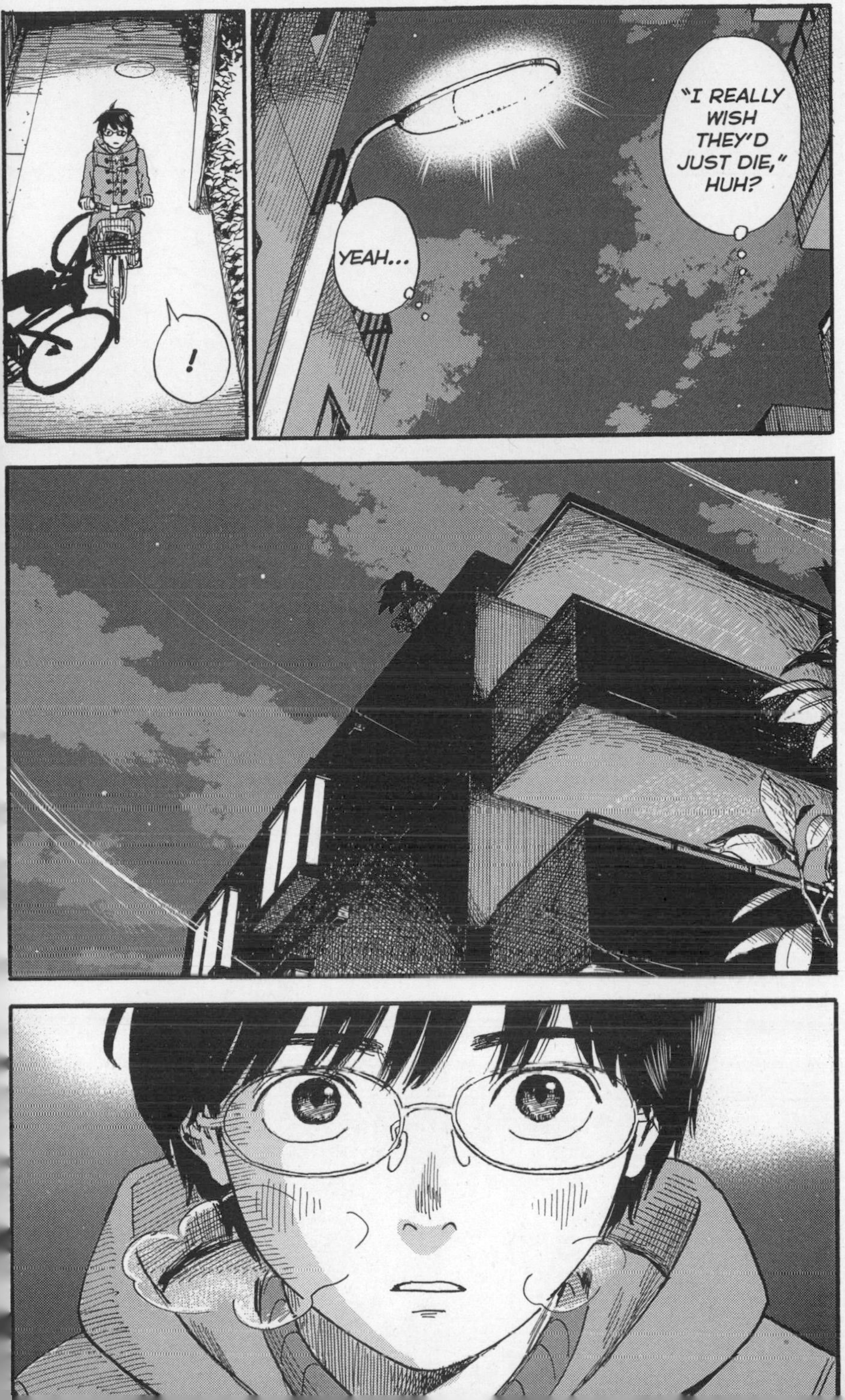
"I REALLY WISH THEY'D JUST DIE," HUH?
YEAH...
!

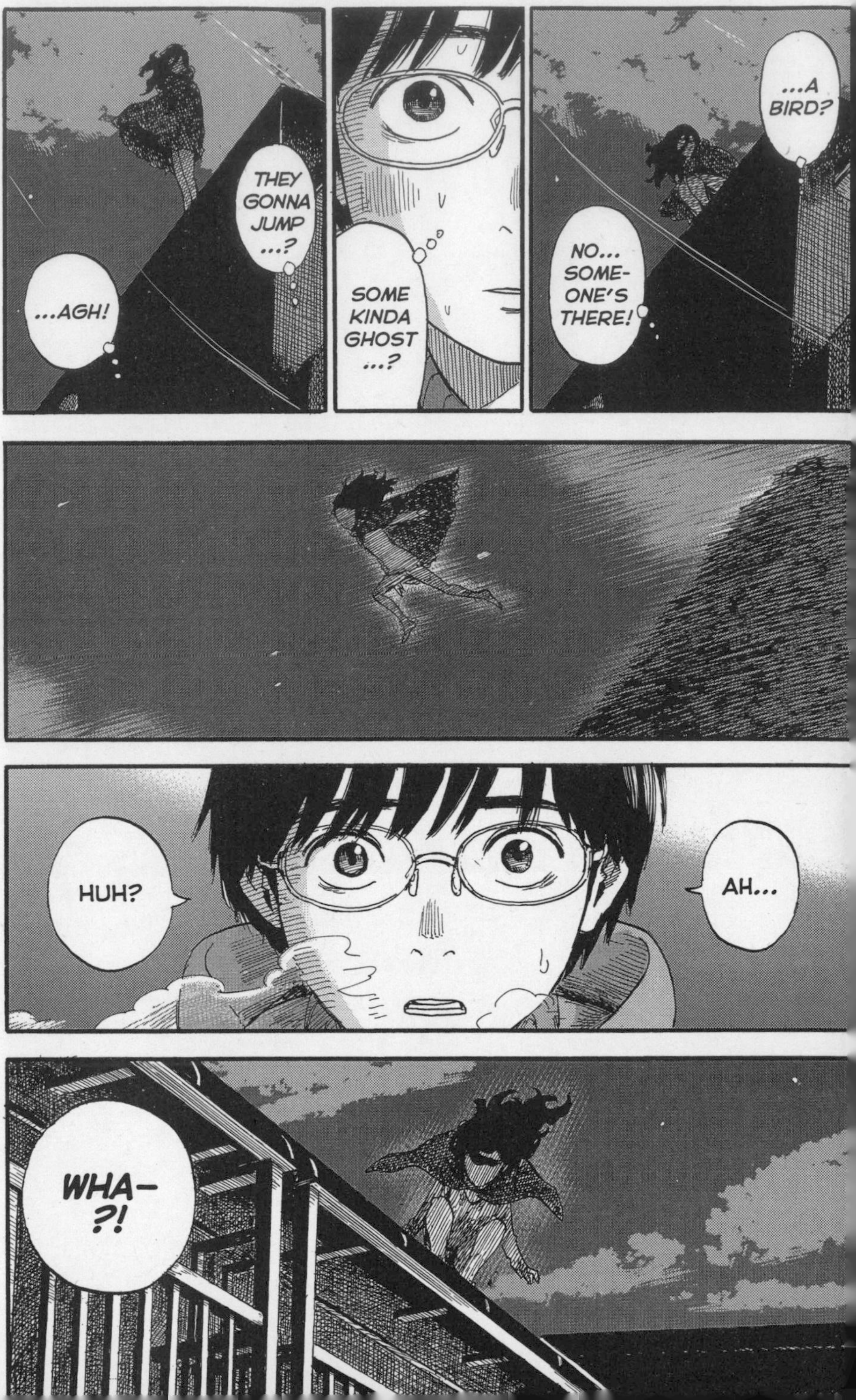
...A BIRD?
NO... SOME-ONE'S THERE!
SOME KINDA GHOST ...?
THEY GONNA JUMP ...?
...AGH!
AH...
HUH?
WHA-?!

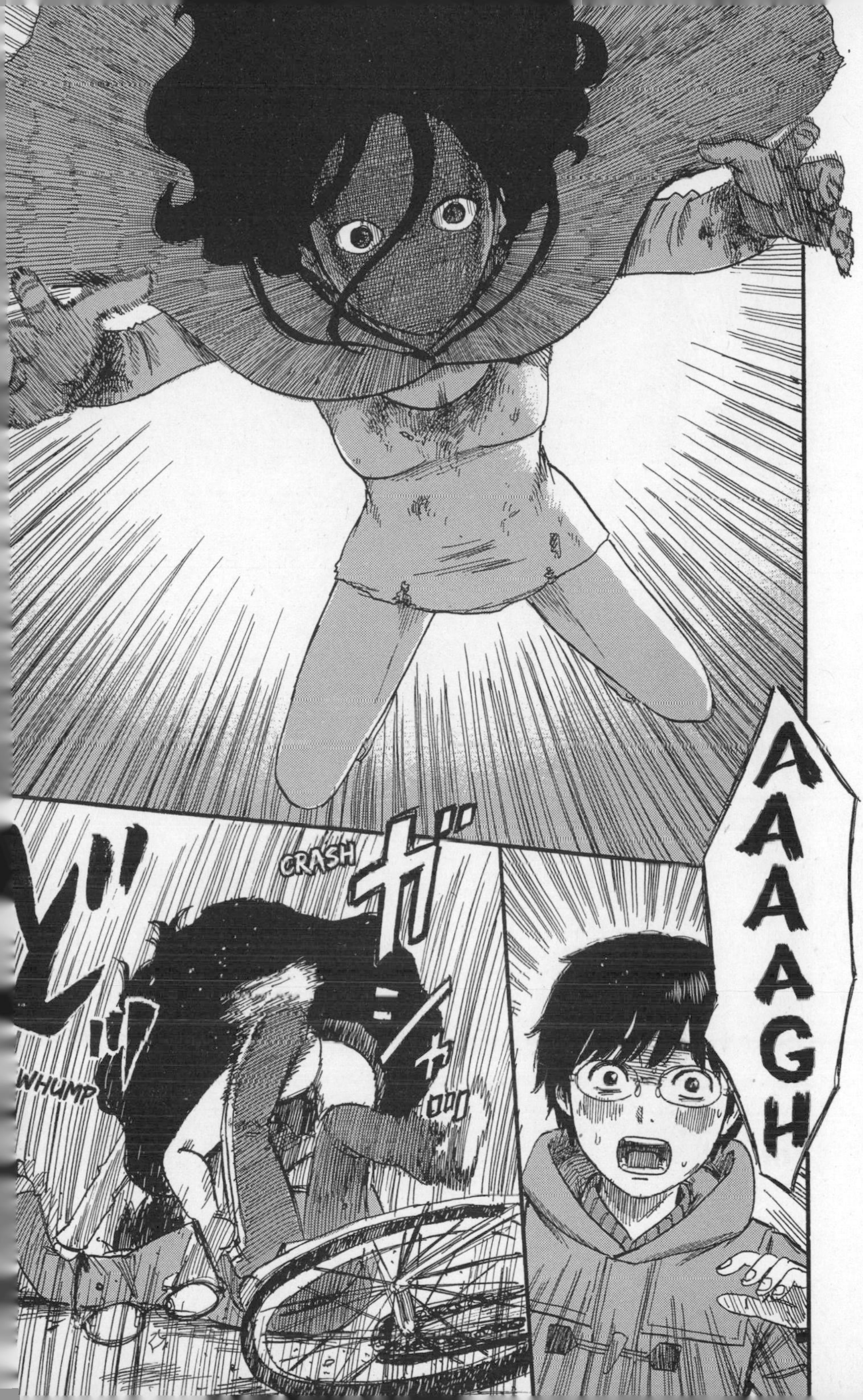
AAAAGH
CRASH
WHUMP

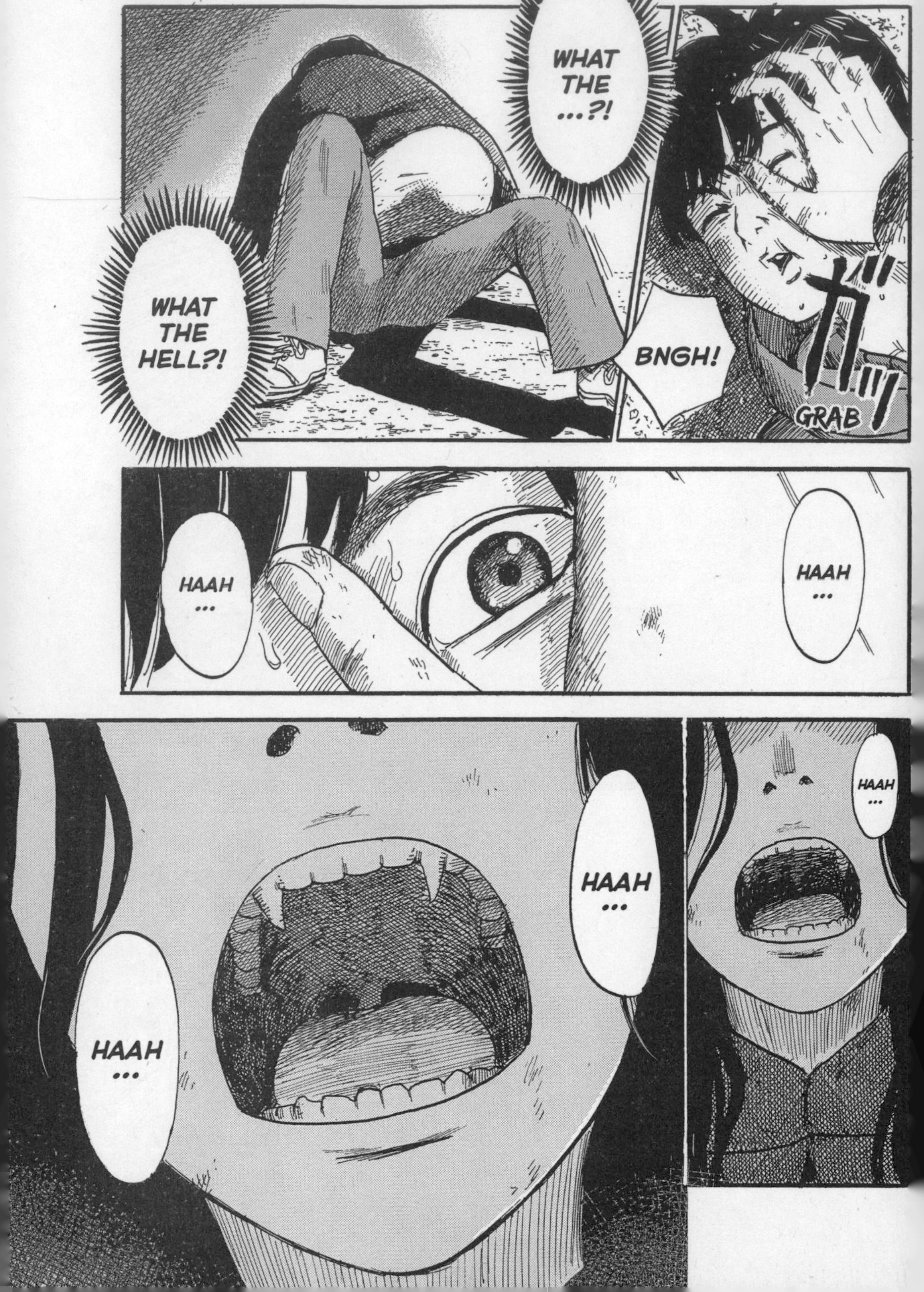

GRAB
ガッ
BNGH!
WHAT THE ...?!
WHAT THE HELL?!
HAAH ...
HAAH ...
HAAH ...
HAAH ...
HAAH ...

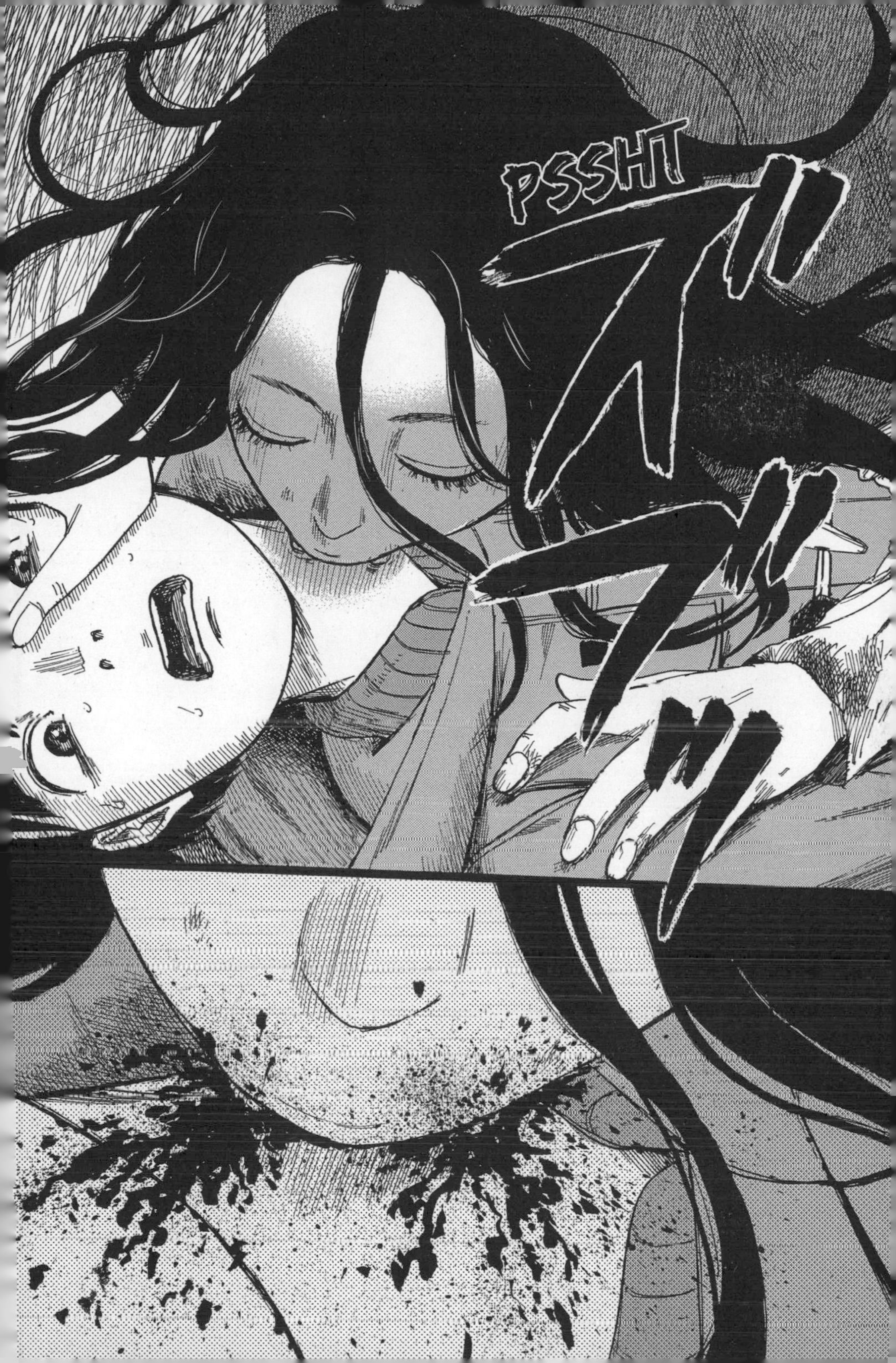
PSSHT

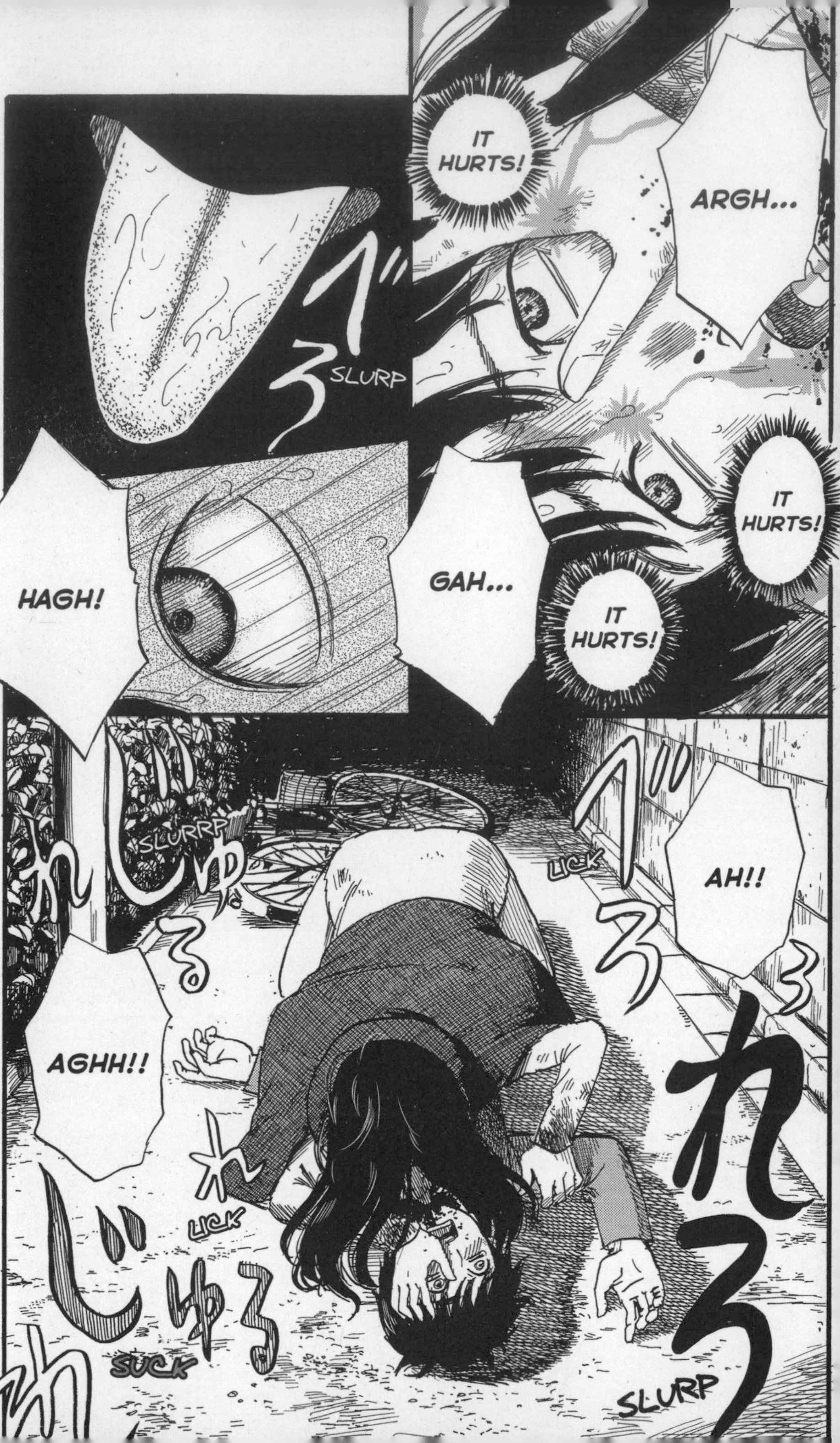
ARGH...
IT HURTS!
IT HURTS!
IT HURTS!
GAH...
SLURP
HAGH!
AH!!
LICK
SLURRP
AGHH!!
SLURP
LICK
SUCK

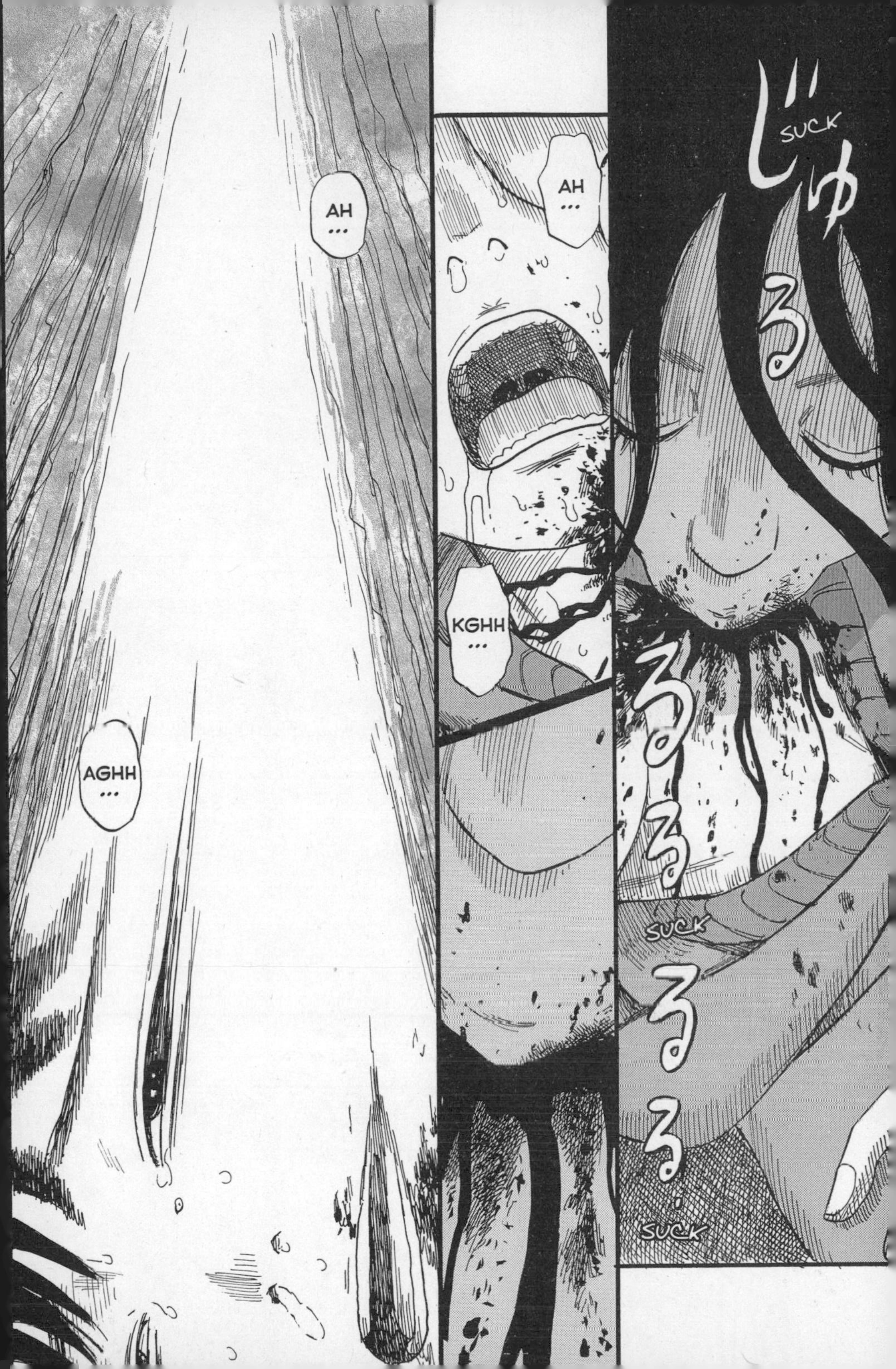
じゅる
SUCK
SUCK
SUCK
AH ...
KGHH ...
AH ...
AGHH ...

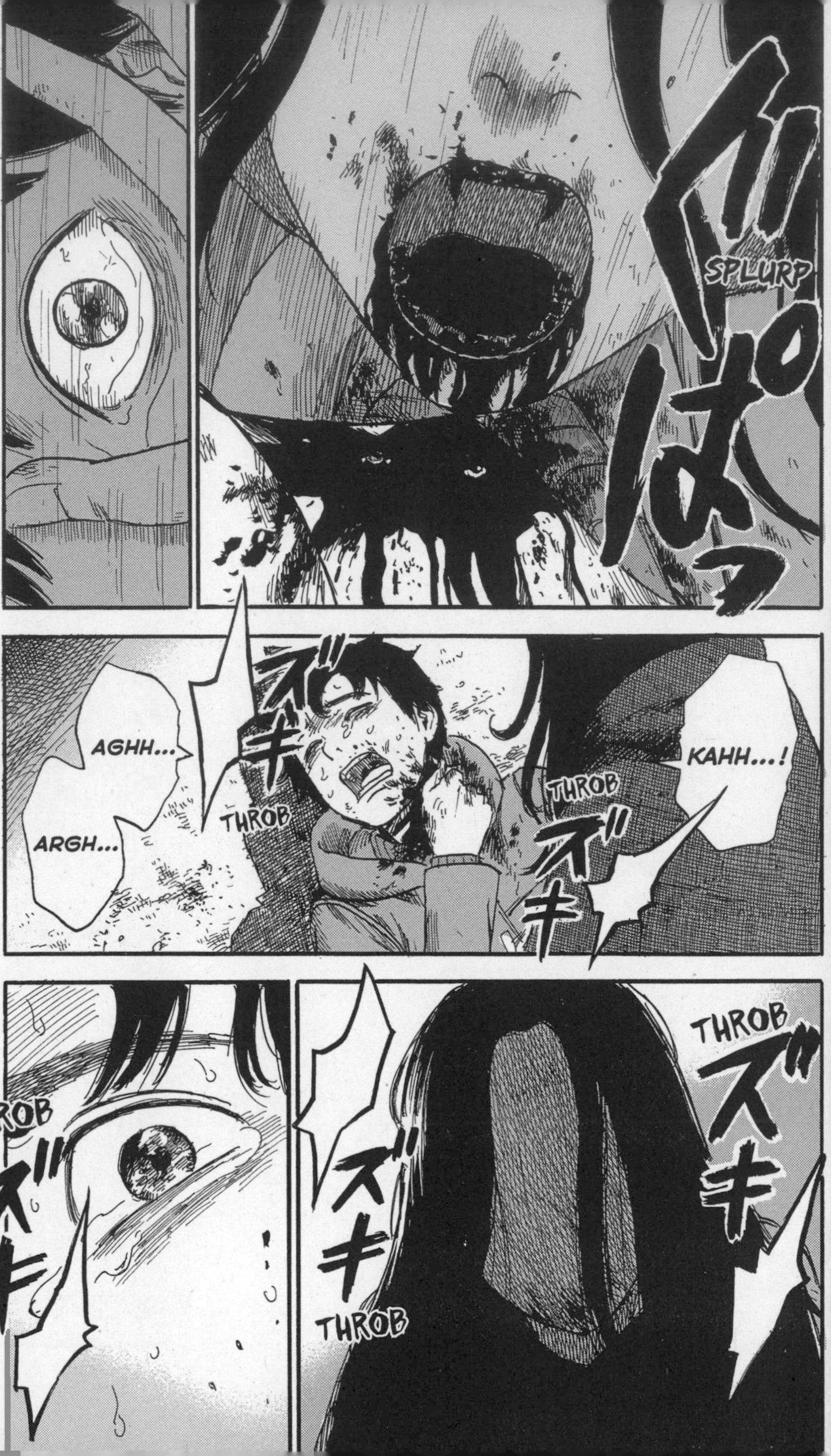
くぱっ
SPLURP
KAHH...!
ズキ
THROB
ズキ
THROB
AGHH...
ARGH...
THROB
ズキ
ズキ
THROB
THROB
ズキ

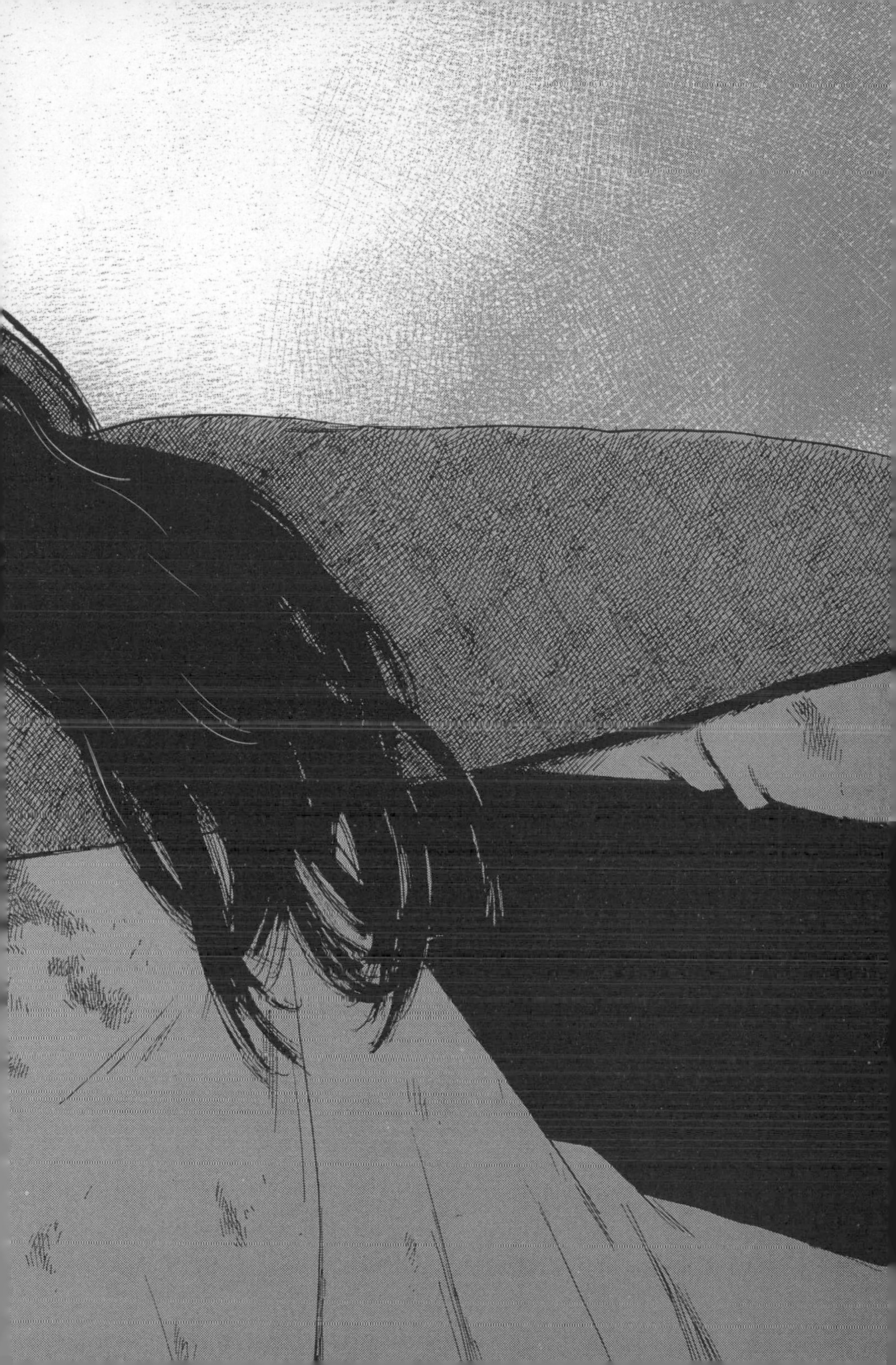

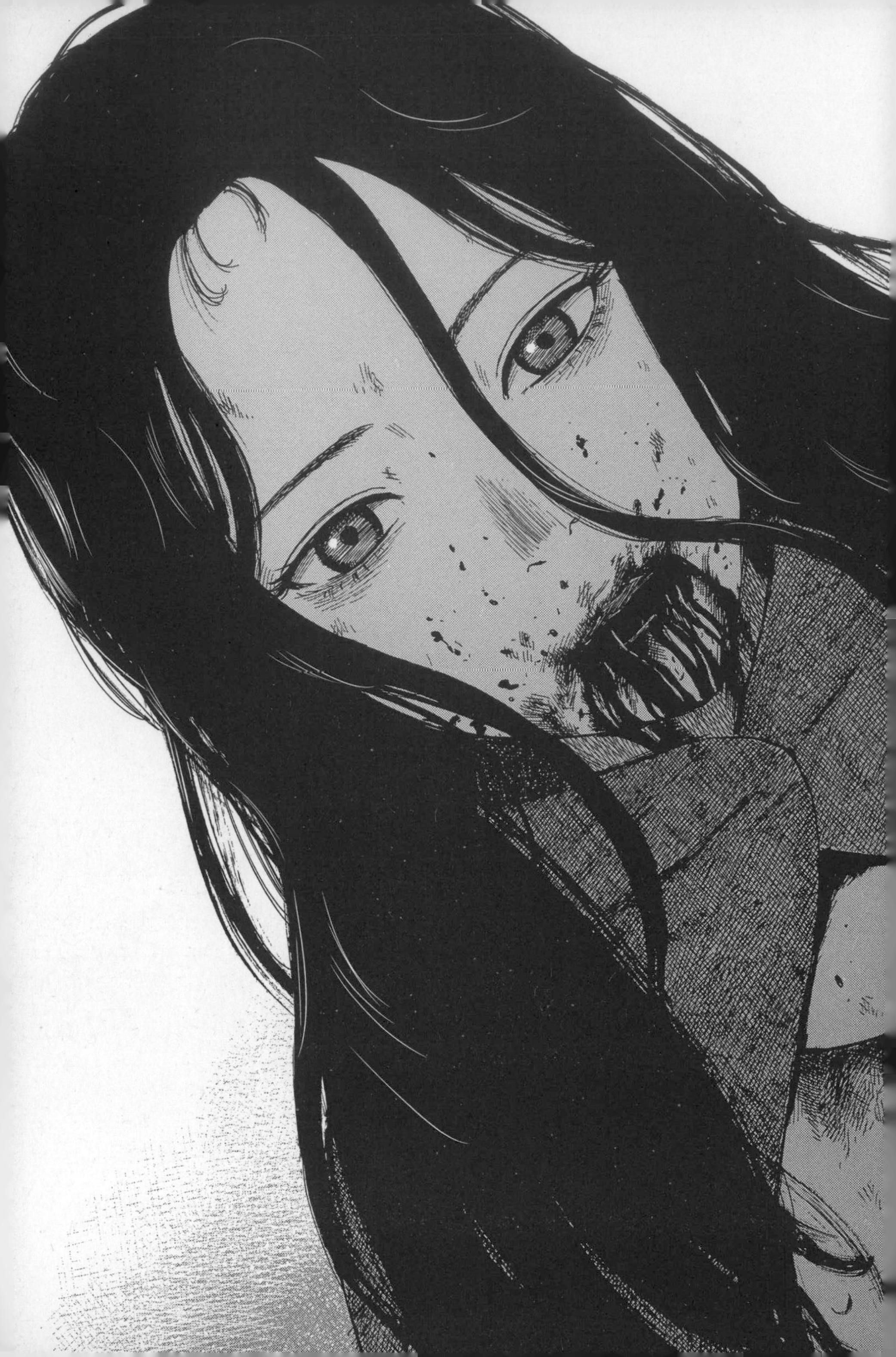

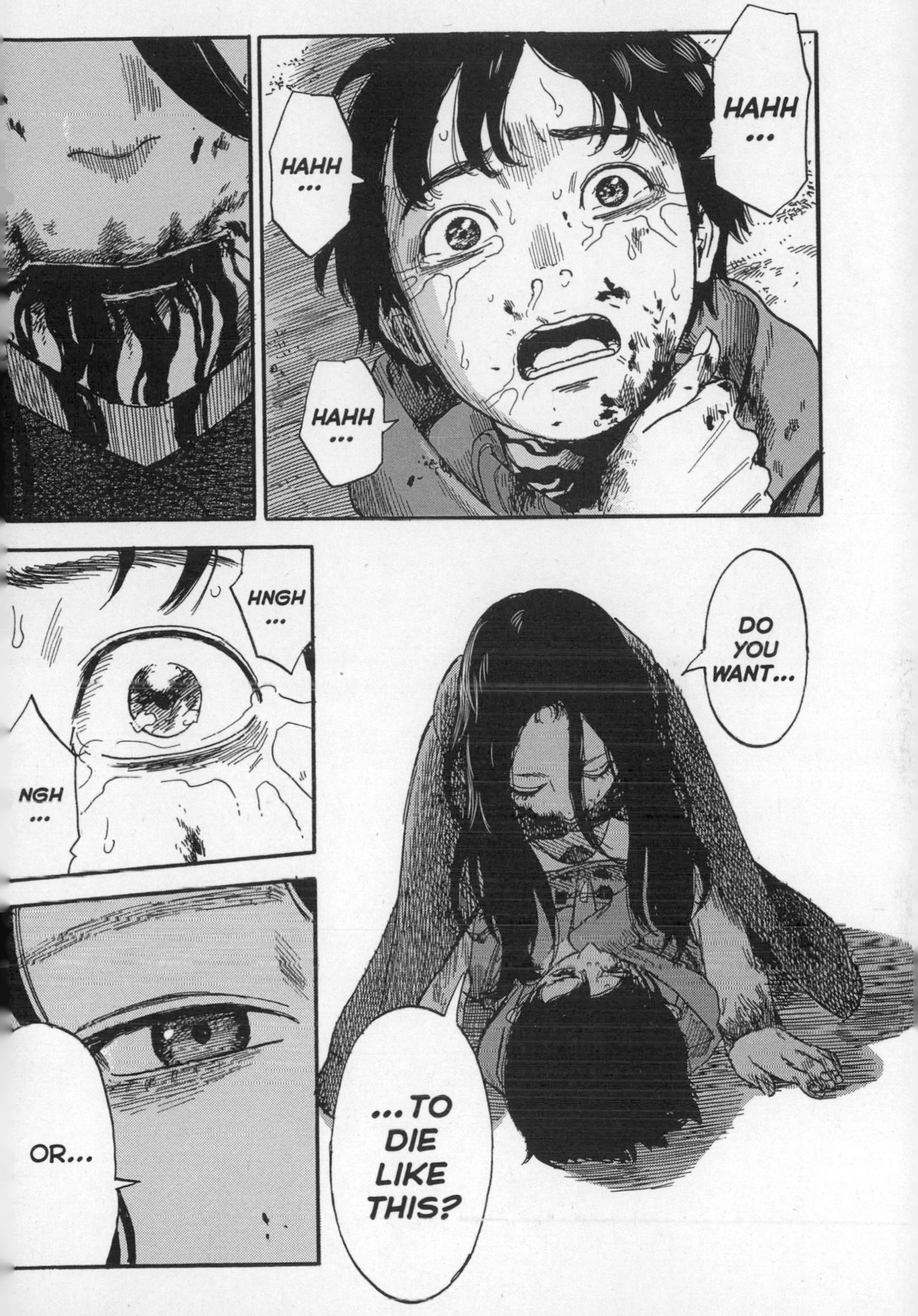
HAHH ...
HAHH ...
HAHH ...
DO YOU WANT...
...TO DIE LIKE THIS?
HNGH ...
NGH ...
OR...

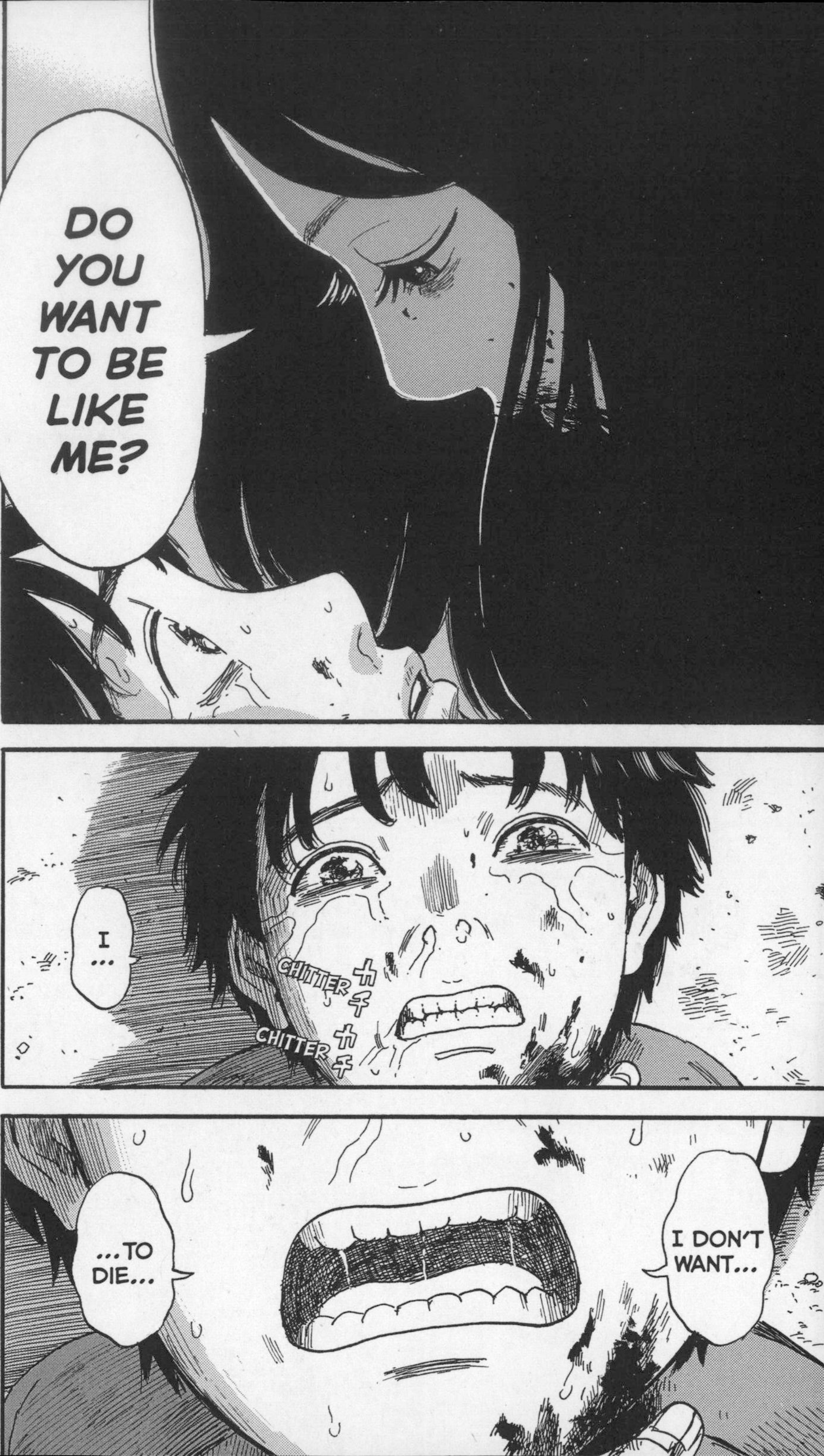
DO YOU WANT TO BE LIKE ME?
I...
CHITTER カチ
CHITTER カチ
I DON'T WANT...
...TO DIE...

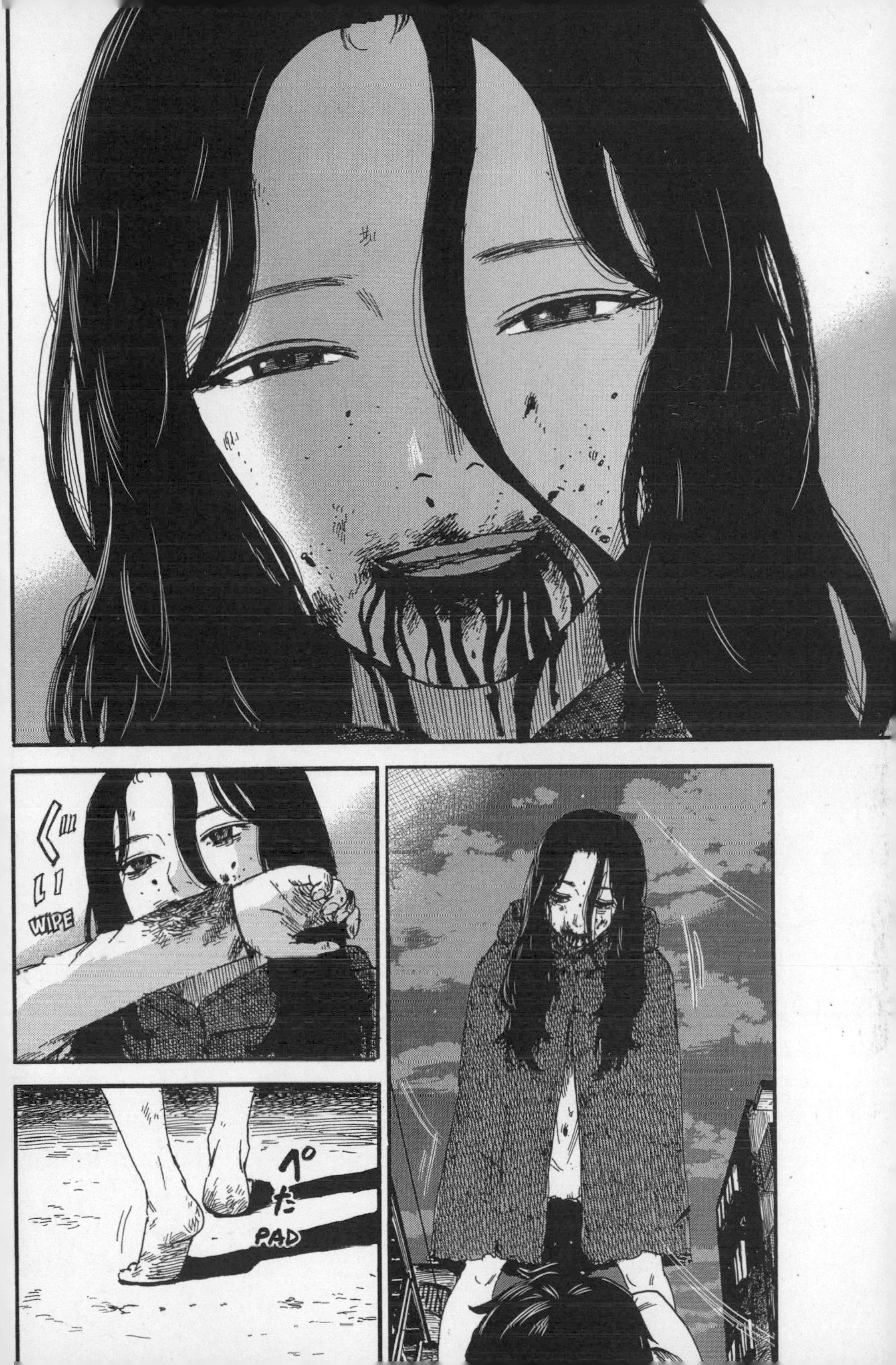
ぐい
WIPE
ぺた
PAD

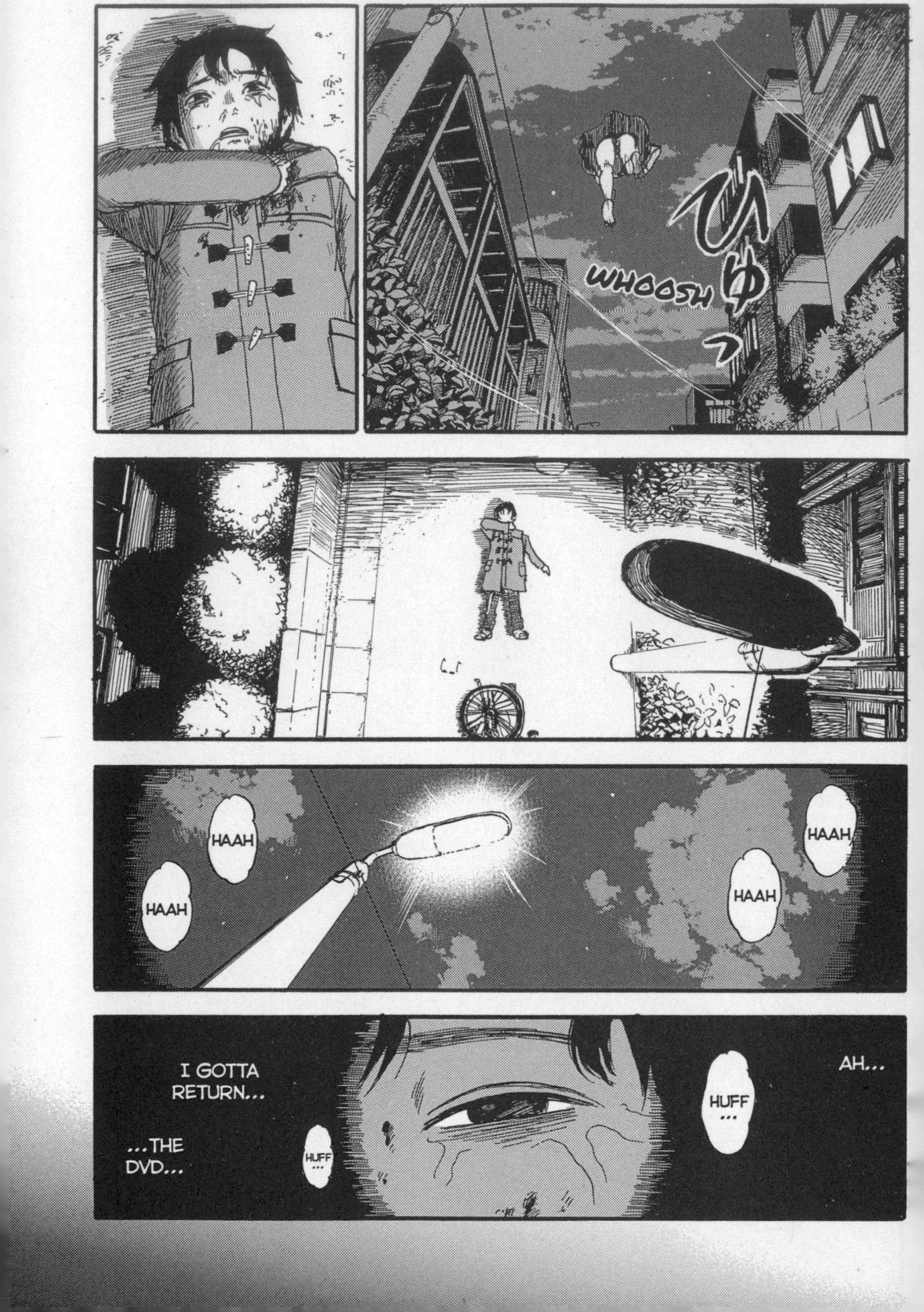
ひゅっ
WHOOSH
HAAH
HAAH
HAAH
HAAH
AH...
HUFF...
HUFF...
I GOTTA RETURN...
...THE DVD...

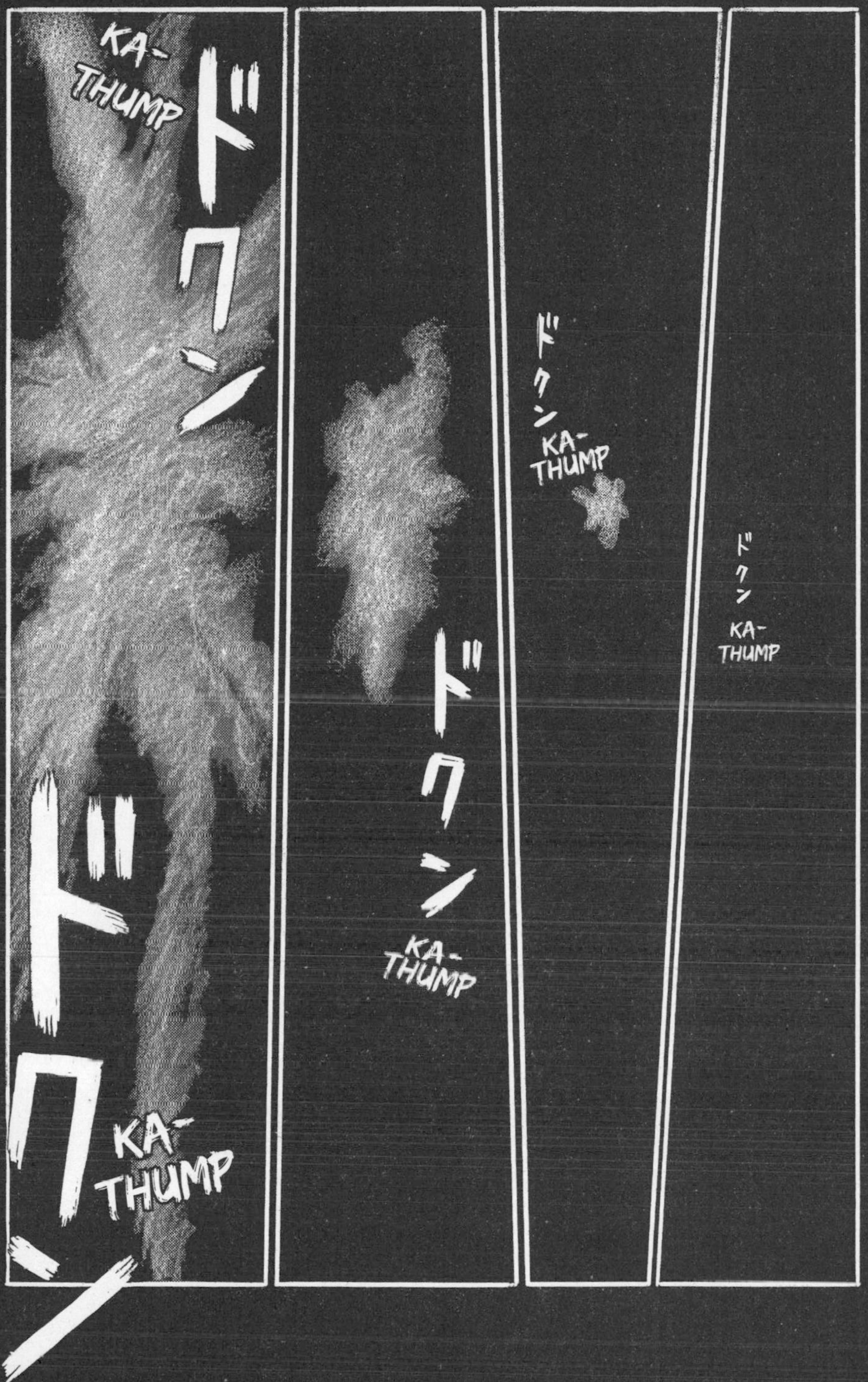
ドクン
KA-THUMP
ドクン
KA-THUMP
ドクン
KA-THUMP
ドクン
KA-THUMP
ドクン
KA-THUMP

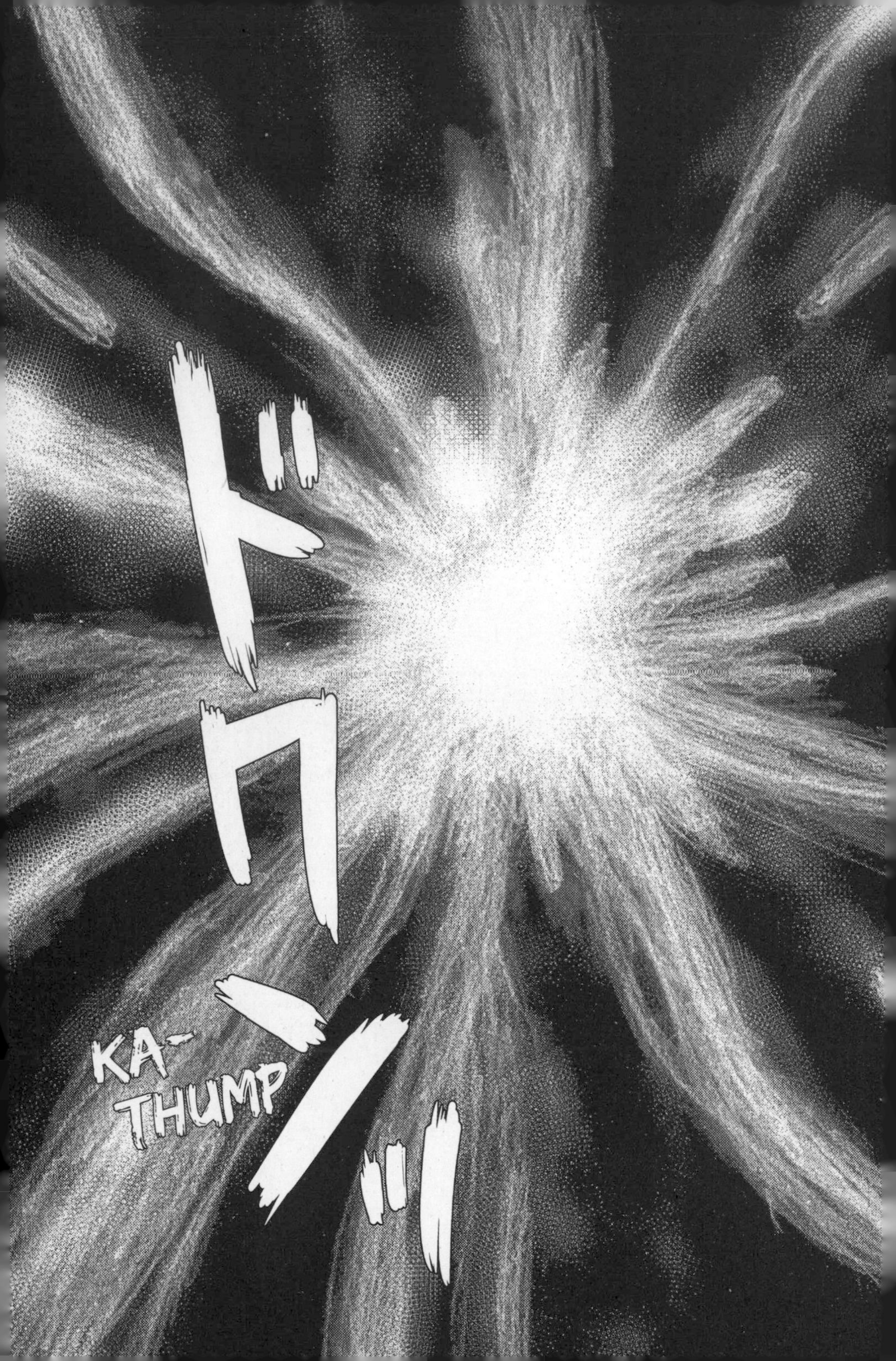
ドクン
KA-THUMP

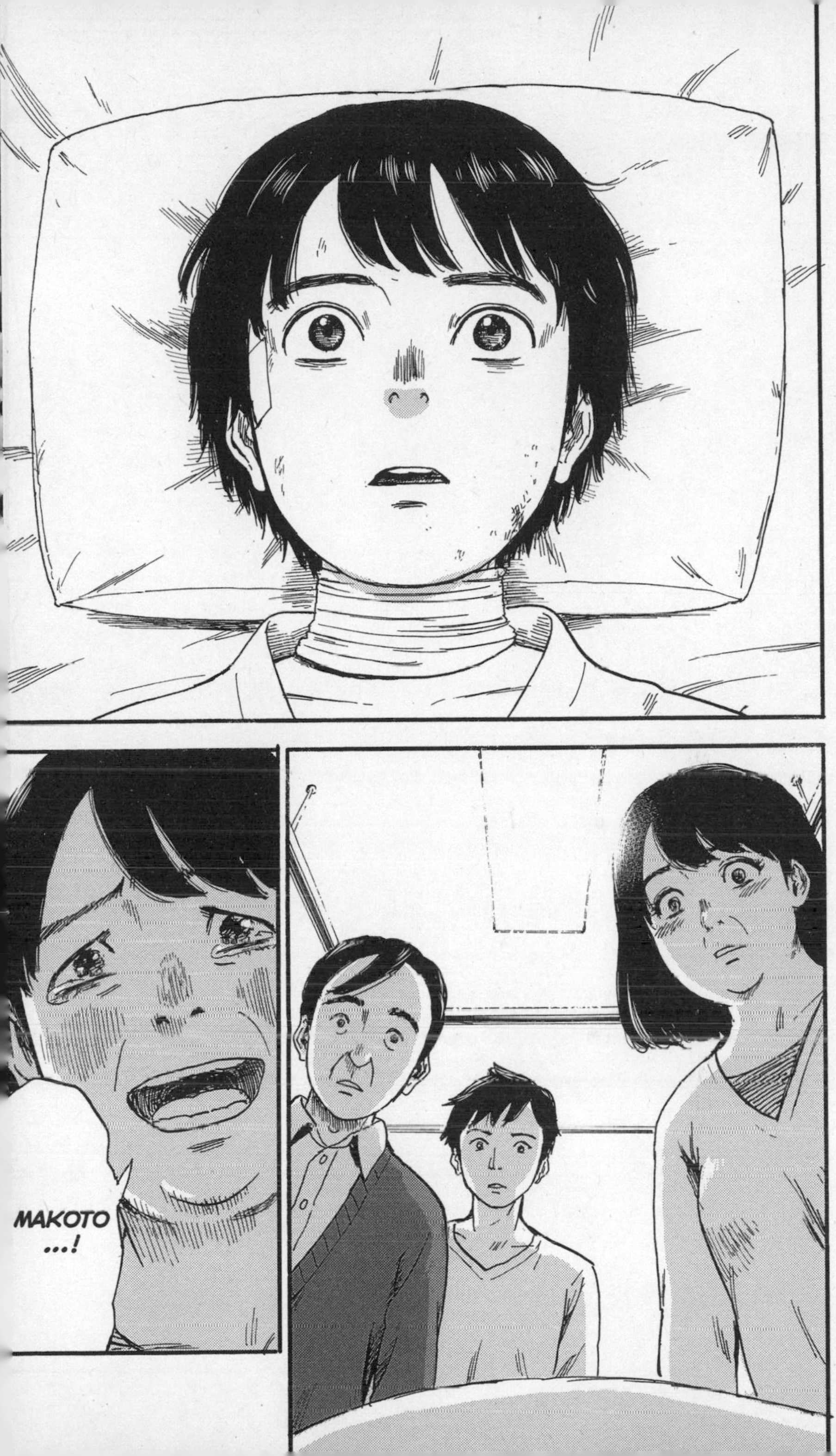
MAKOTO ...!

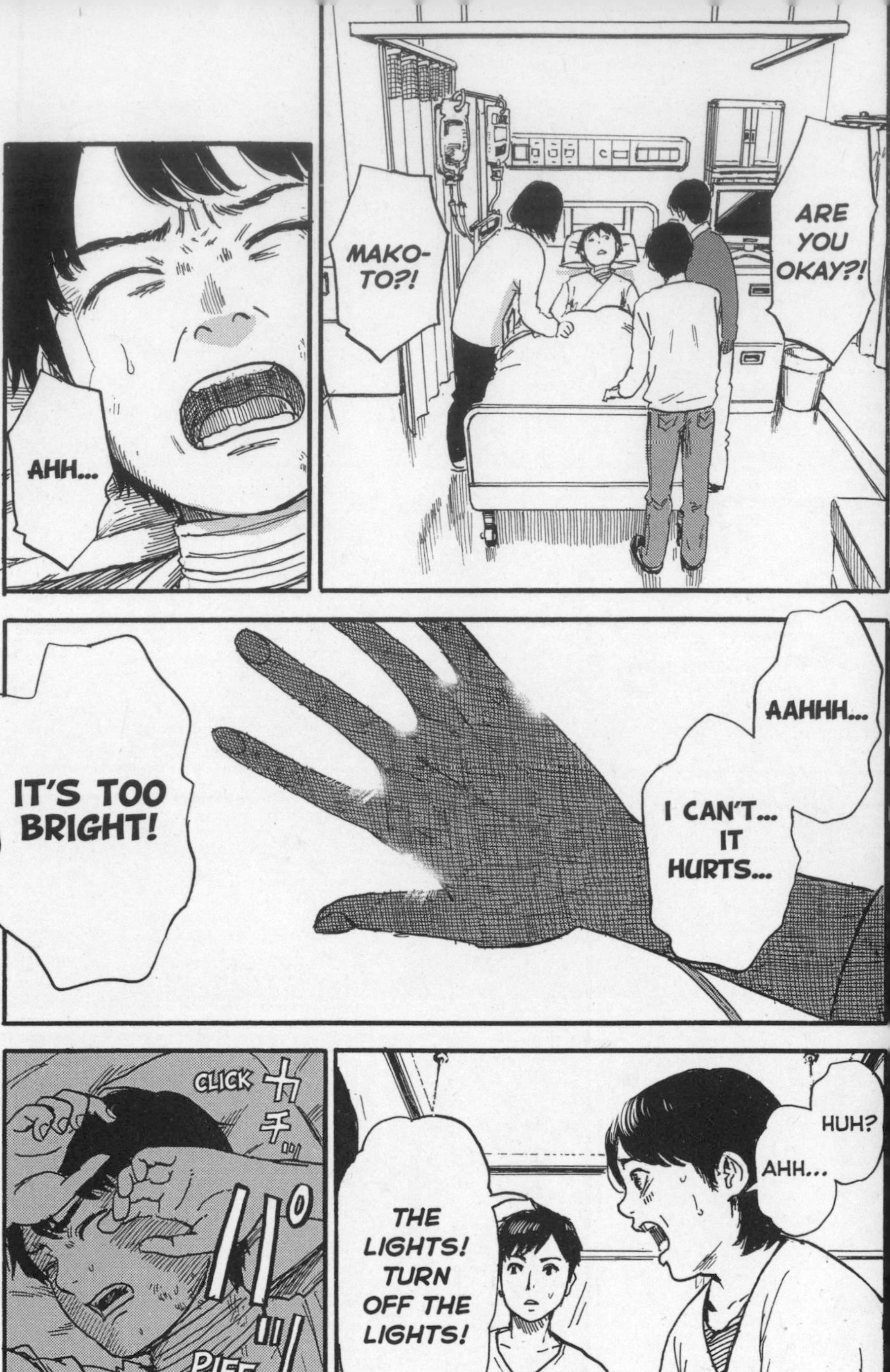
ARE YOU OKAY?!
MAKO-TO?!
AHH...
AAHHH...
I CAN'T... IT HURTS...
IT'S TOO BRIGHT!
HUH?
AHH...
THE LIGHTS! TURN OFF THE LIGHTS!
CLICK
カチッ
PIFF

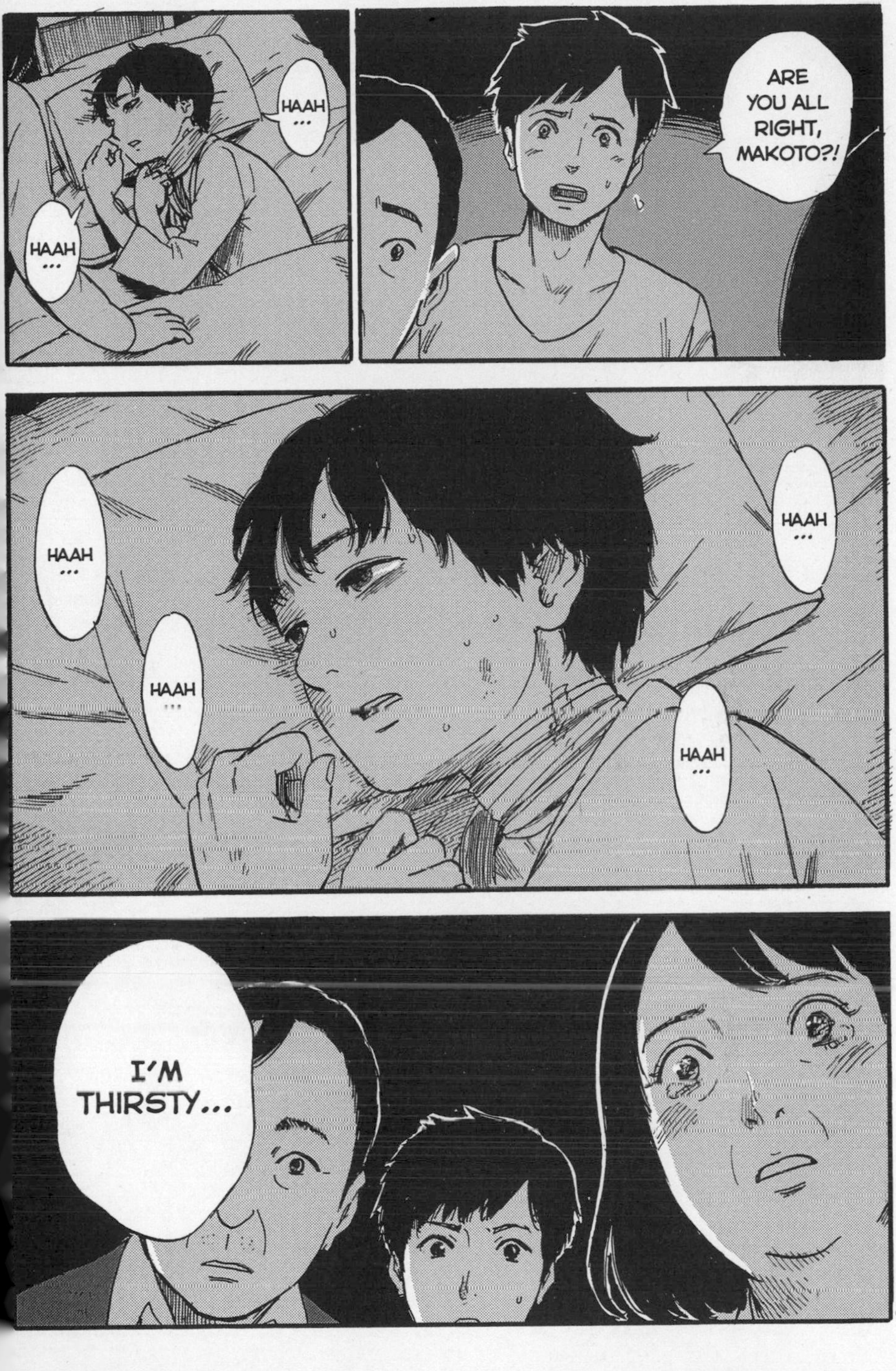
ARE YOU ALL RIGHT, MAKOTO?!
HAAH...
HAAH...
HAAH...
HAAH...
HAAH...
HAAH...
I'M THIRSTY...

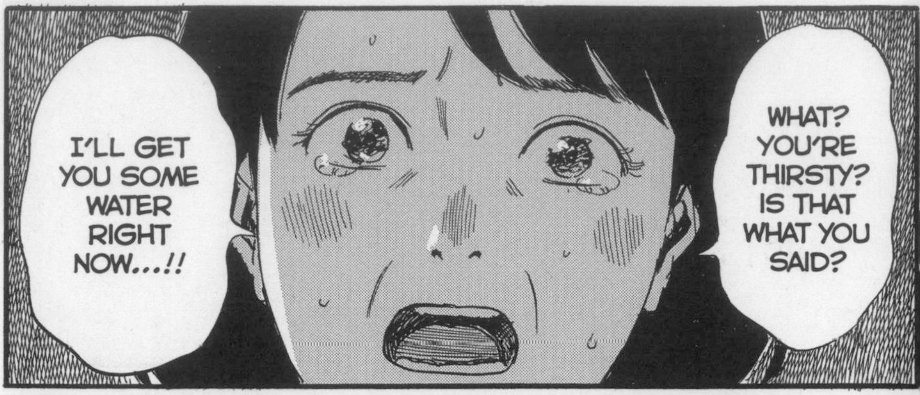
WHAT? YOU'RE THIRSTY? IS THAT WHAT YOU SAID?
I'LL GET YOU SOME WATER RIGHT NOW...!!

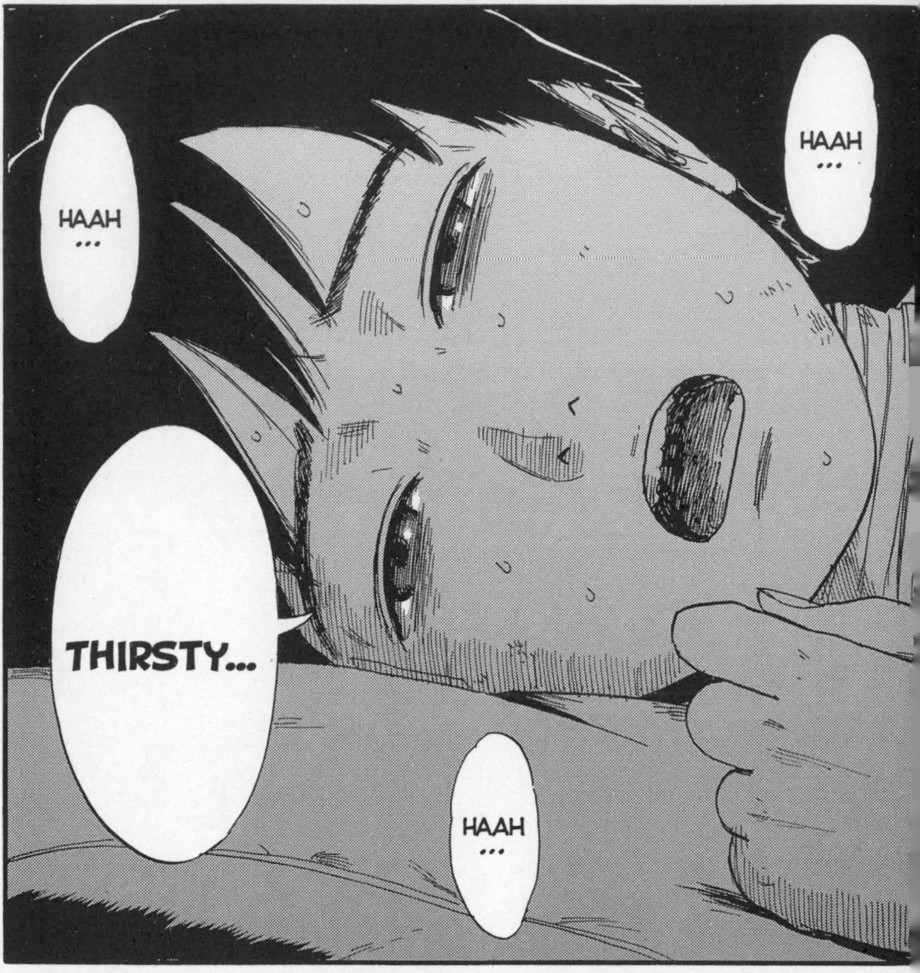
HAAH...
HAAH...
THIRSTY...
HAAH...

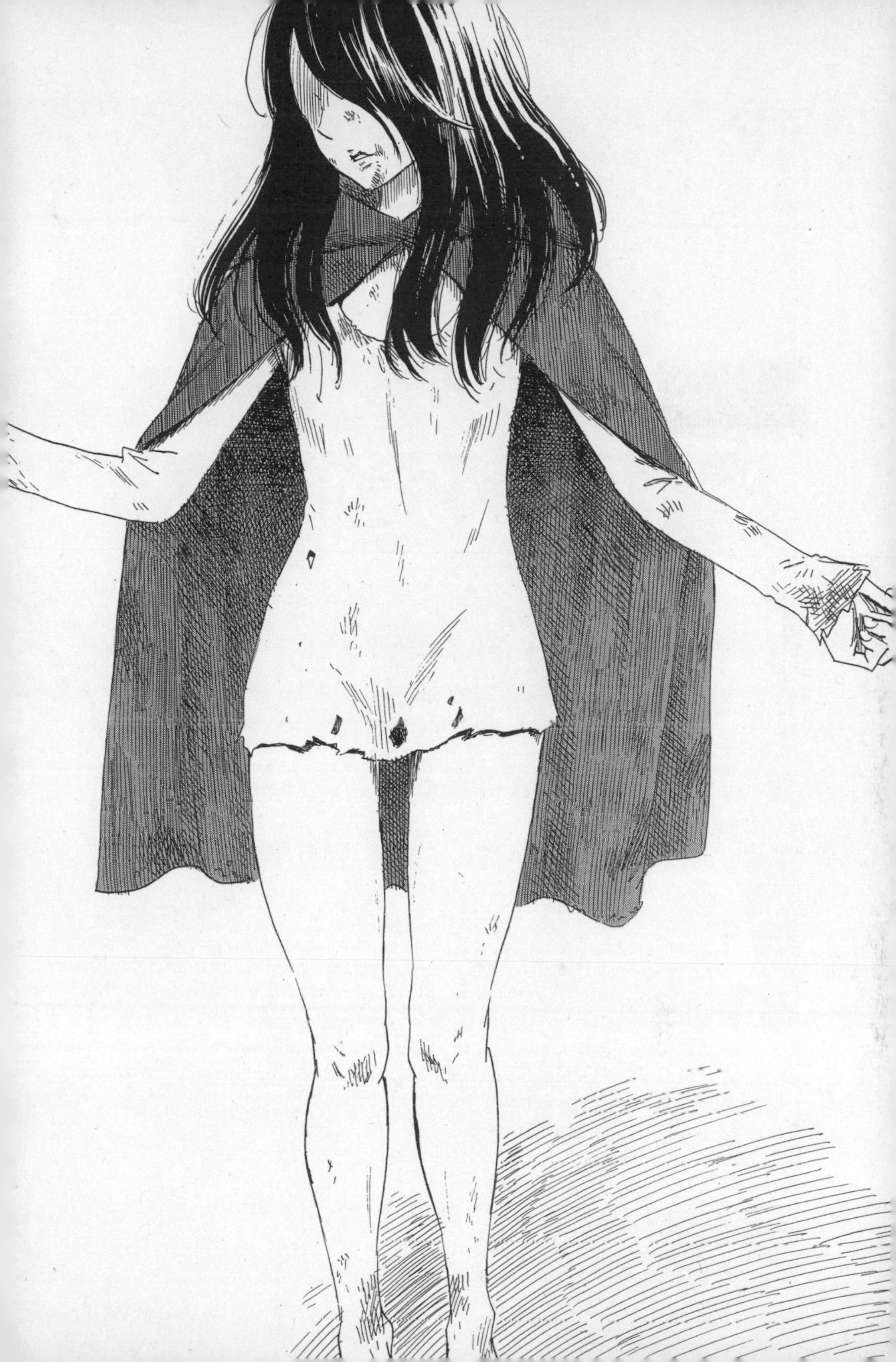

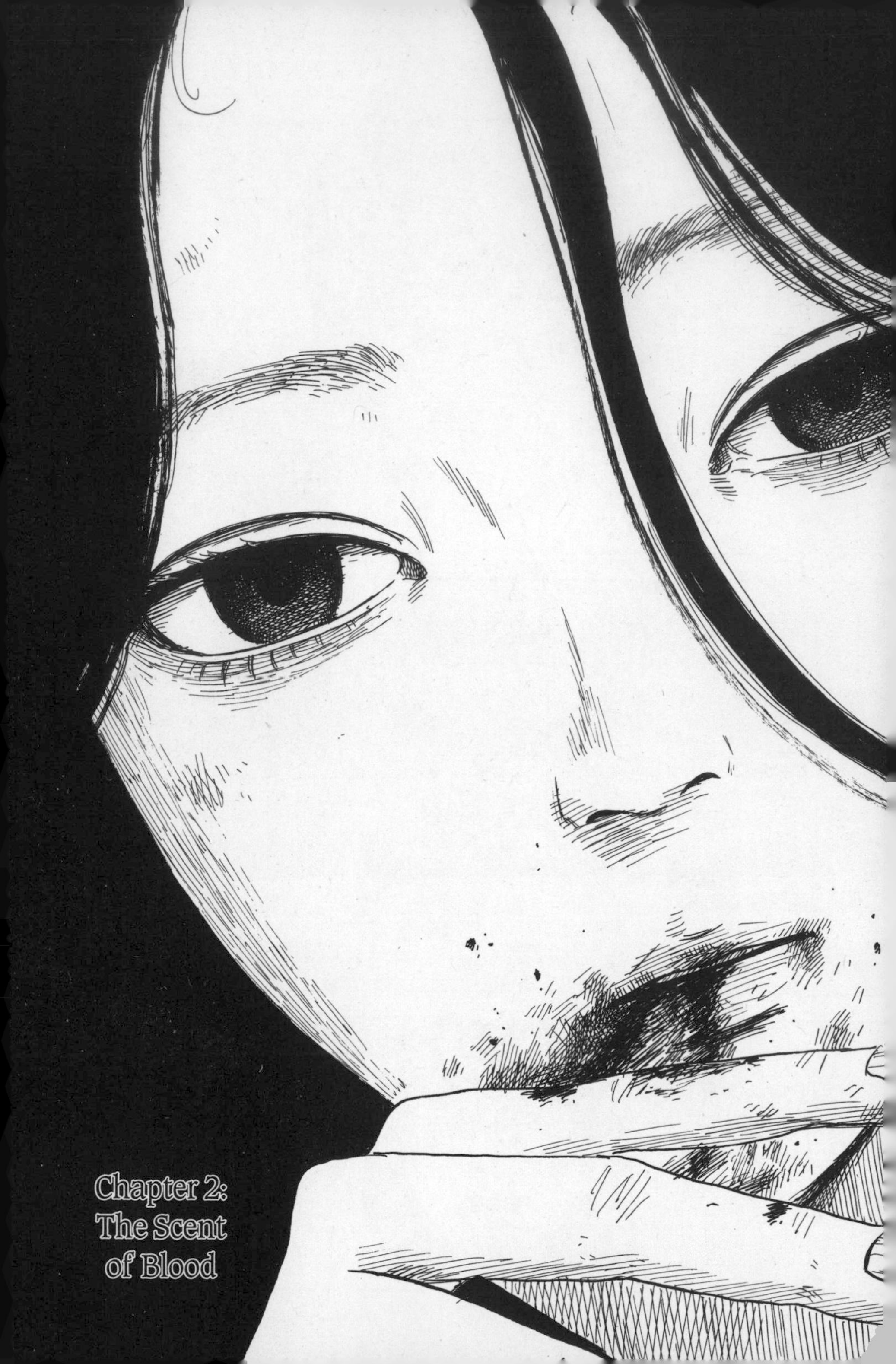

Chapter 2: The Scent of Blood

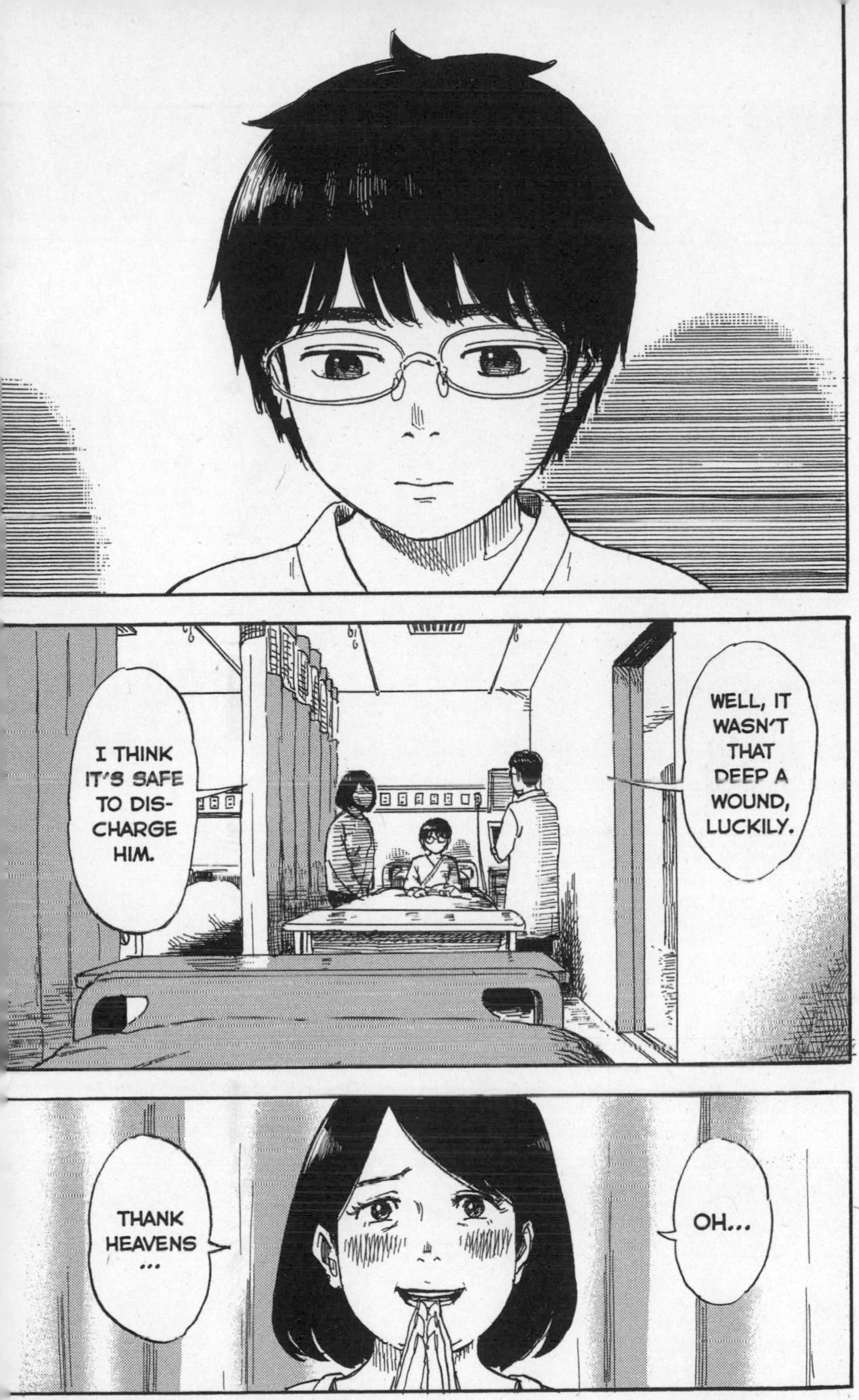
WELL, IT WASN'T THAT DEEP A WOUND, LUCKILY.
I THINK IT'S SAFE TO DIS-CHARGE HIM.
OH...
THANK HEAVENS ...

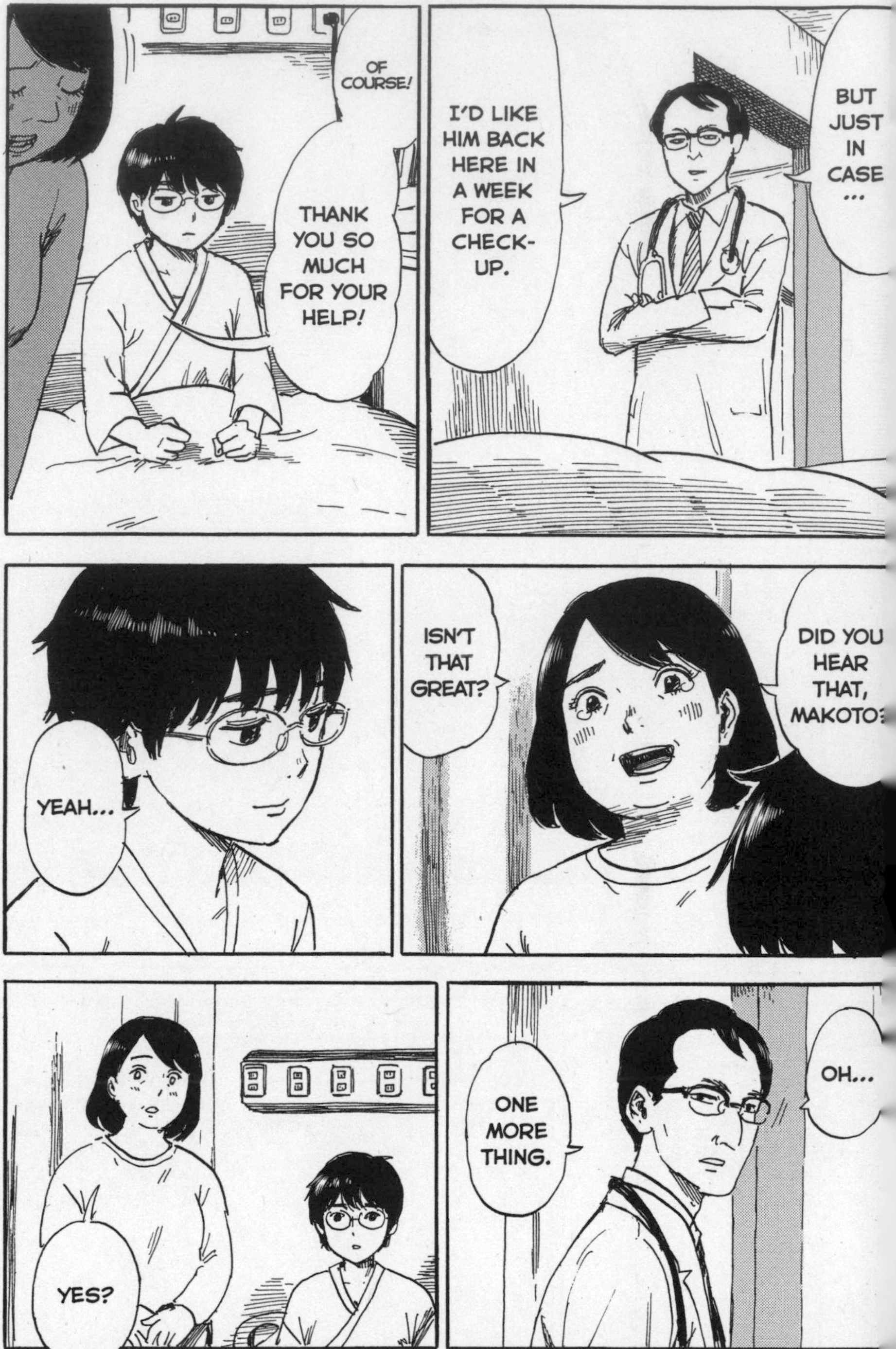
BUT JUST IN CASE...
I'D LIKE HIM BACK HERE IN A WEEK FOR A CHECK-UP.
OF COURSE!
THANK YOU SO MUCH FOR YOUR HELP!
DID YOU HEAR THAT, MAKOTO?
ISN'T THAT GREAT?
YEAH...
OH...
ONE MORE THING.
YES?

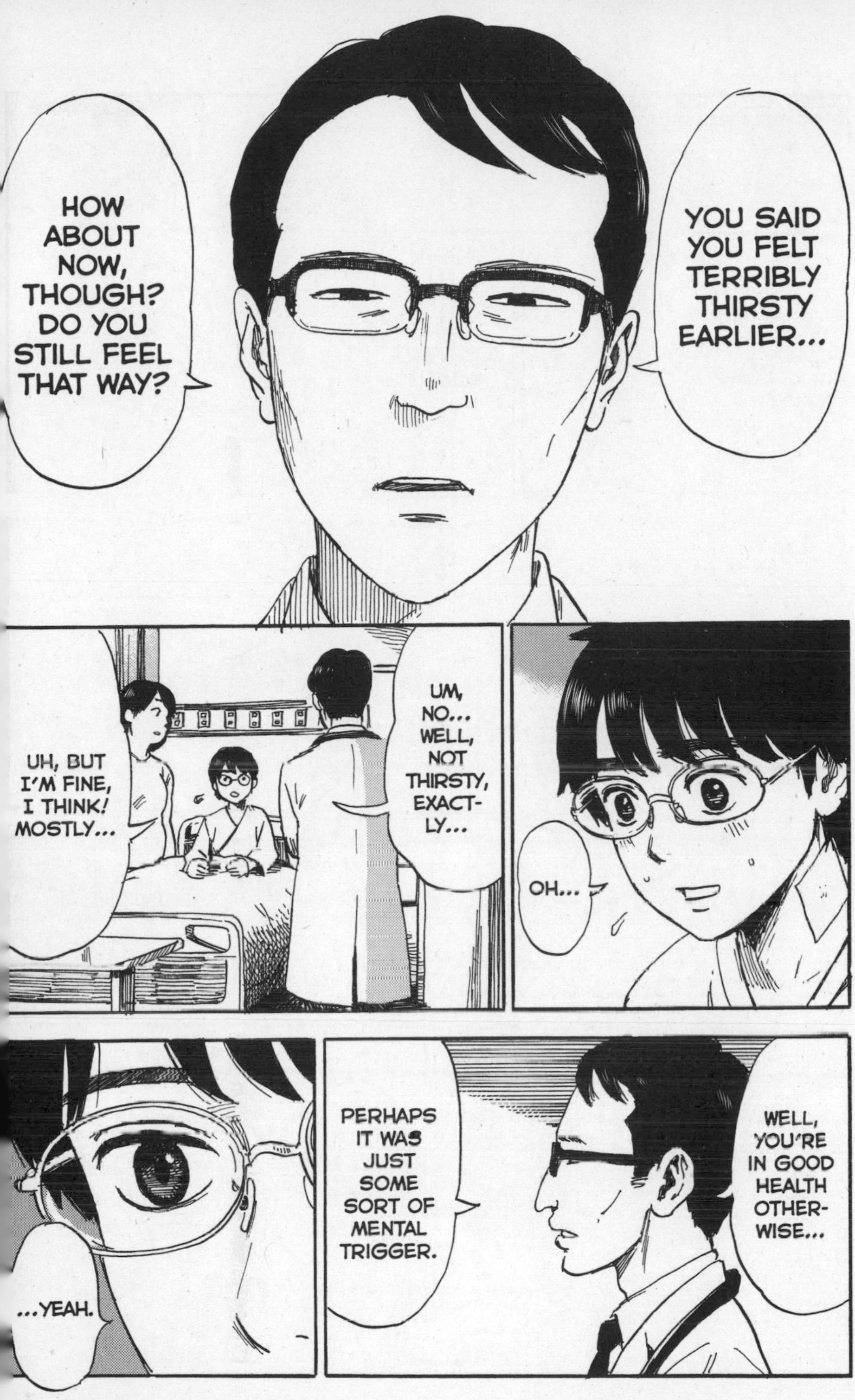
YOU SAID YOU FELT TERRIBLY THIRSTY EARLIER...
HOW ABOUT NOW, THOUGH? DO YOU STILL FEEL THAT WAY?
OH...
UM, NO... WELL, NOT THIRSTY, EXACTLY...
UH, BUT I'M FINE, I THINK! MOSTLY...
WELL, YOU'RE IN GOOD HEALTH OTHERWISE...
PERHAPS IT WAS JUST SOME SORT OF MENTAL TRIGGER.
...YEAH.

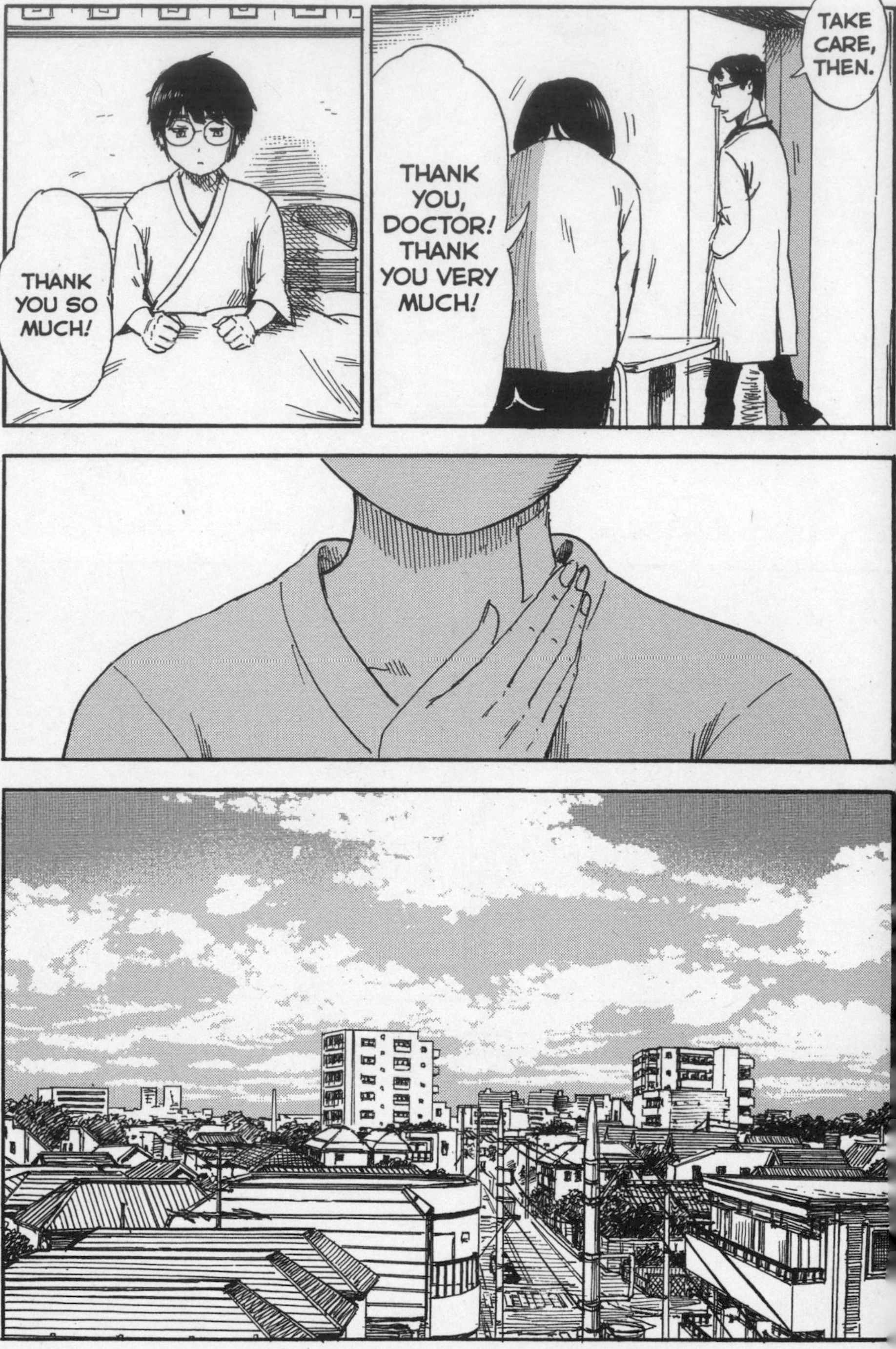
TAKE CARE, THEN.
THANK YOU, DOCTOR! THANK YOU VERY MUCH!
THANK YOU SO MUCH!

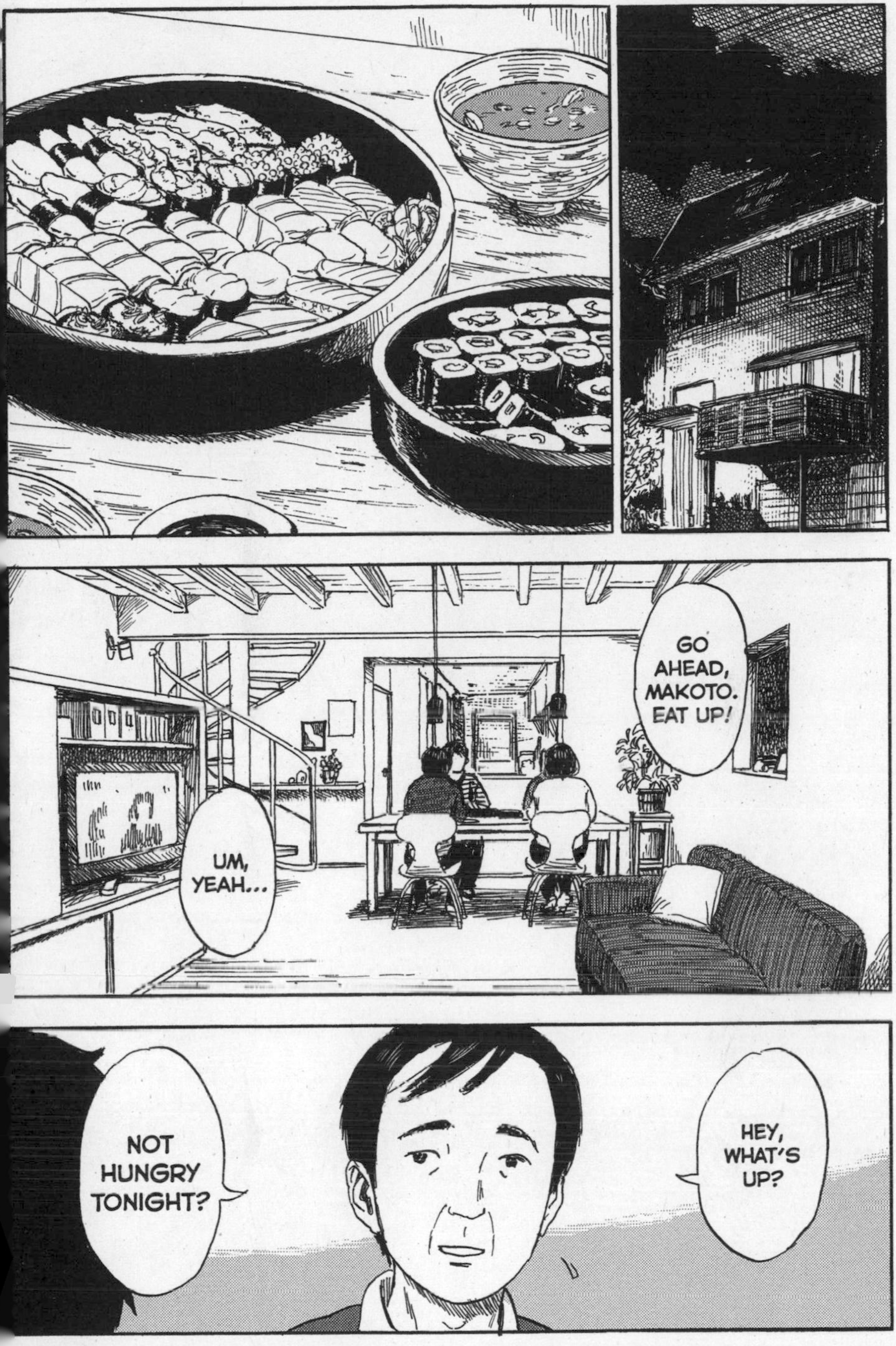
GO AHEAD, MAKOTO. EAT UP!
UM, YEAH...
HEY, WHAT'S UP?
NOT HUNGRY TONIGHT?

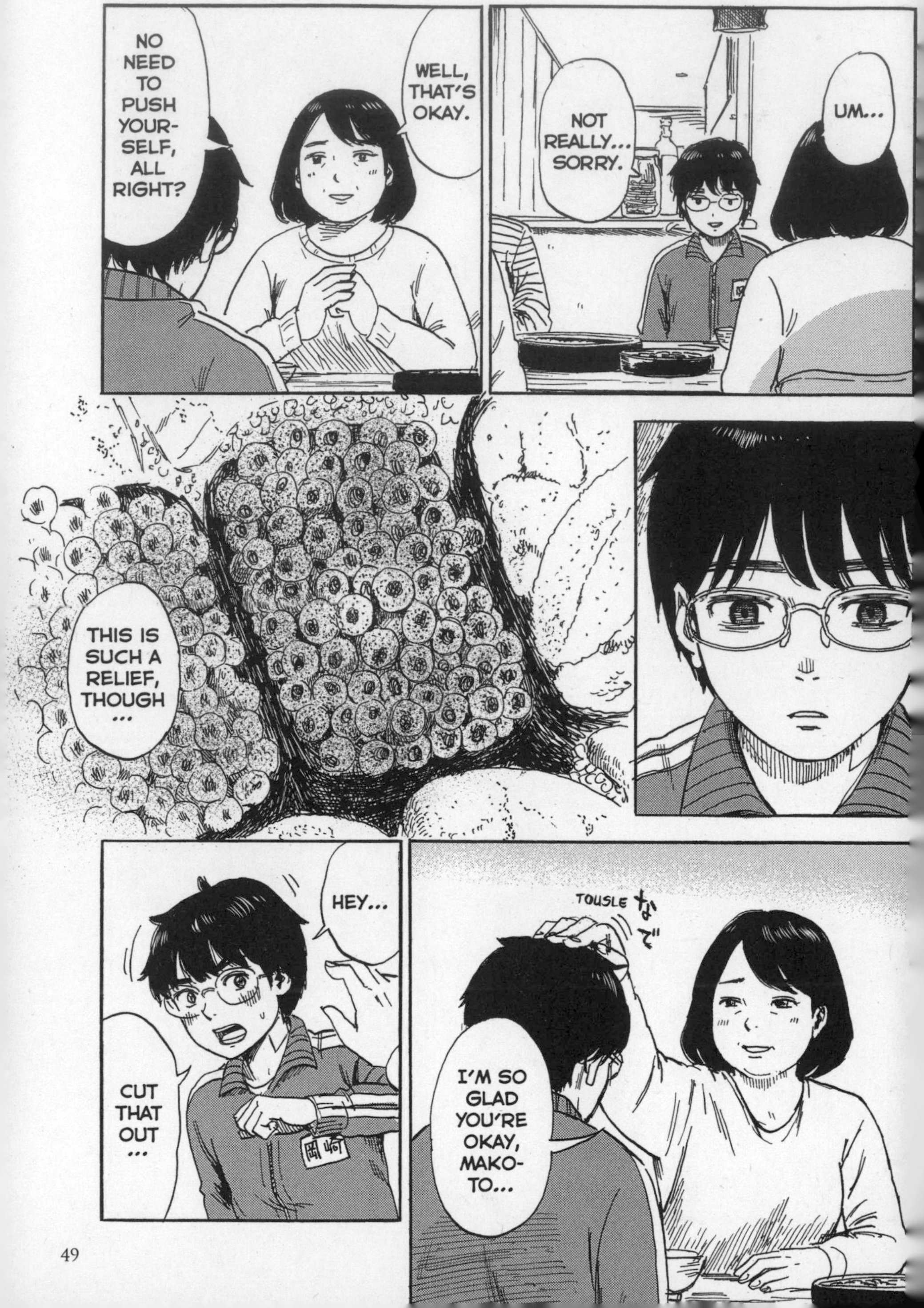
UM...
NOT REALLY... SORRY.
WELL, THAT'S OKAY.
NO NEED TO PUSH YOUR-SELF, ALL RIGHT?
THIS IS SUCH A RELIEF, THOUGH...
TOUSLE なで
I'M SO GLAD YOU'RE OKAY, MAKO-TO...
HEY...
CUT THAT OUT...
岡崎

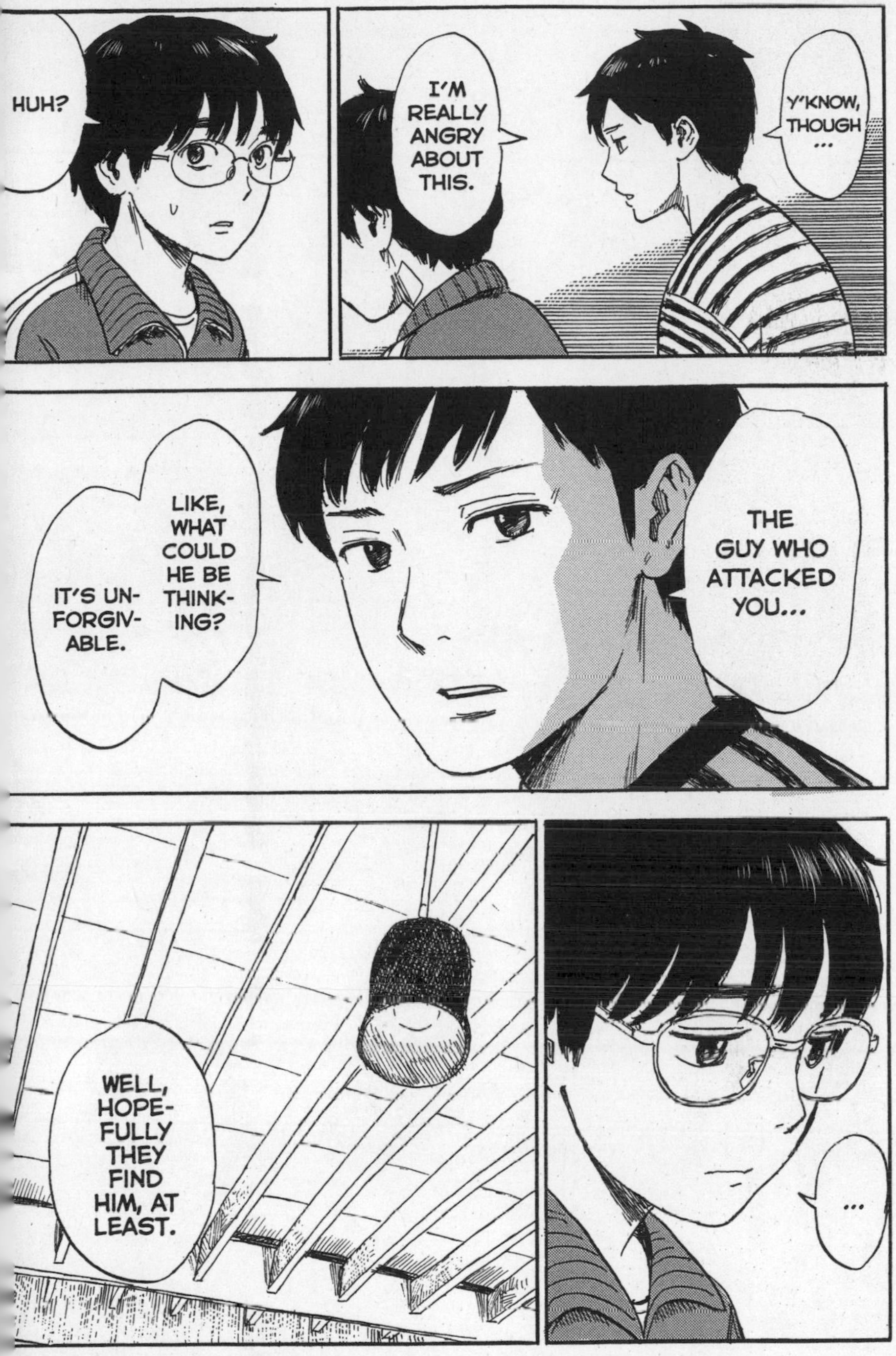
Y'KNOW, THOUGH...
I'M REALLY ANGRY ABOUT THIS.
HUH?
THE GUY WHO ATTACKED YOU...
LIKE, WHAT COULD HE BE THINKING?
IT'S UNFORGIVABLE.
...
WELL, HOPEFULLY THEY FIND HIM, AT LEAST.

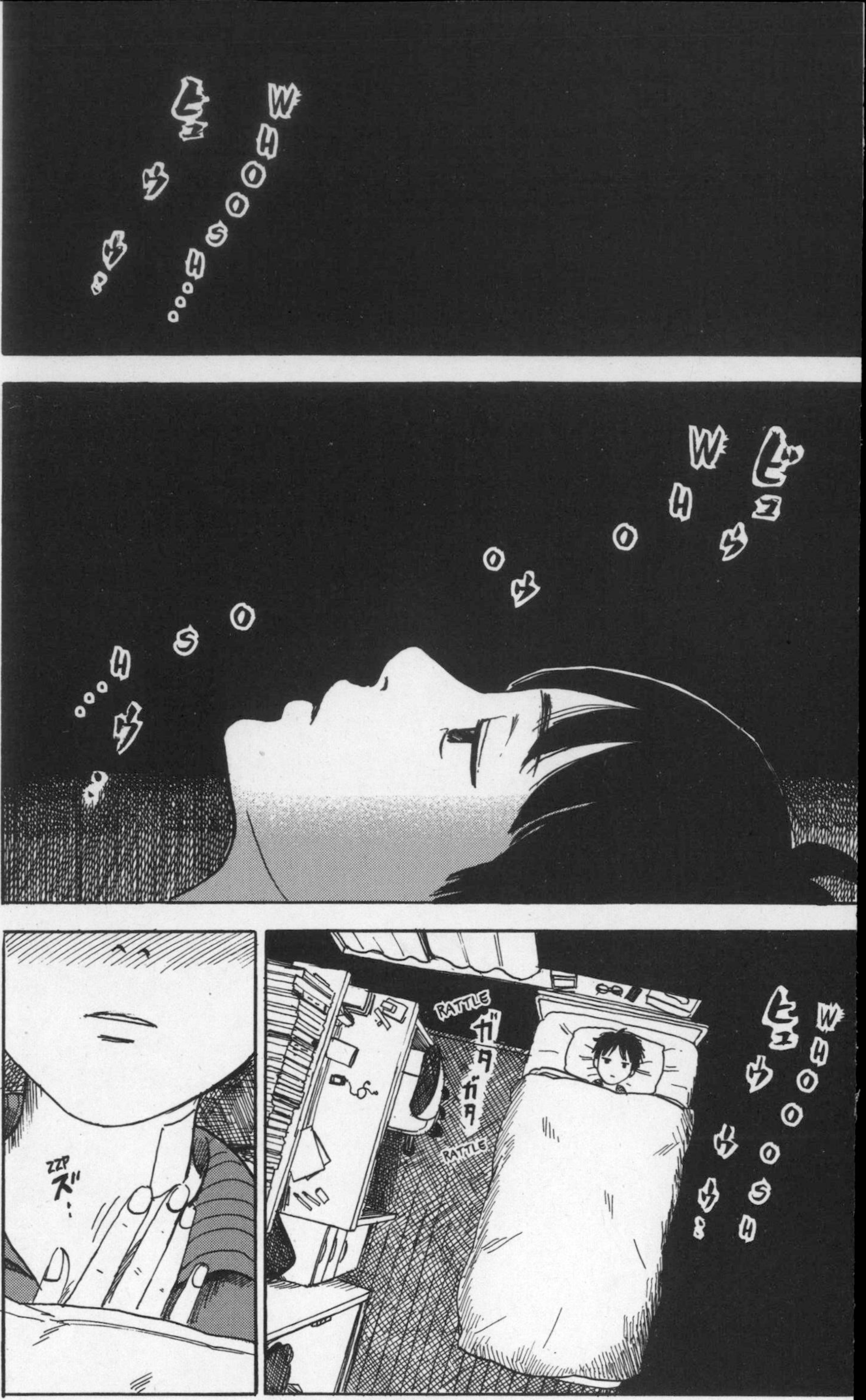
WHOOOSH...
ヒュゥゥ…
ビュゥゥゥ
WHOOOSH...
WHOOOSH
ヒュゥゥゥ…
RATTLE
ガタガタ
RATTLE
ZZP
ズ…

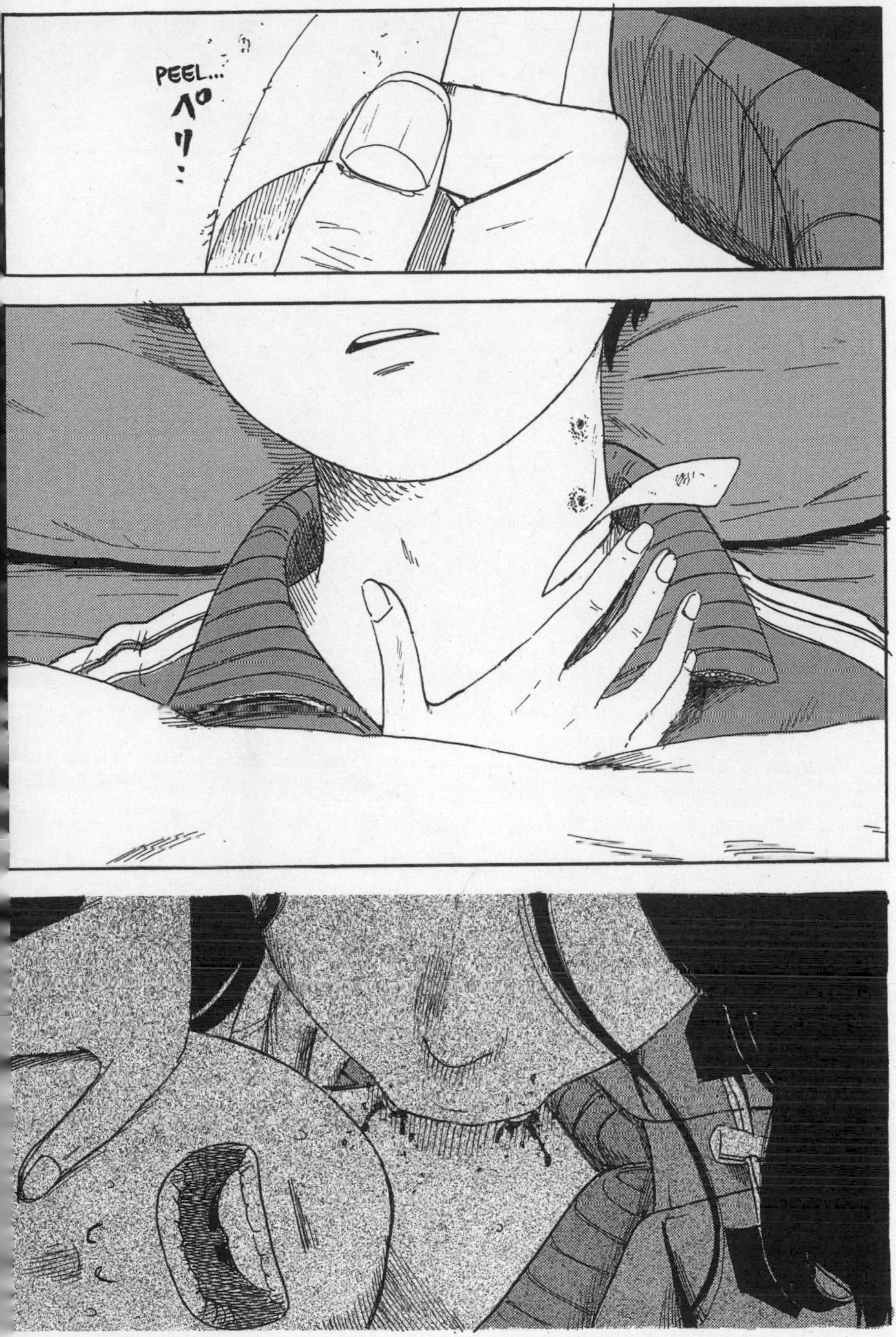
PEEL...
ペリッ

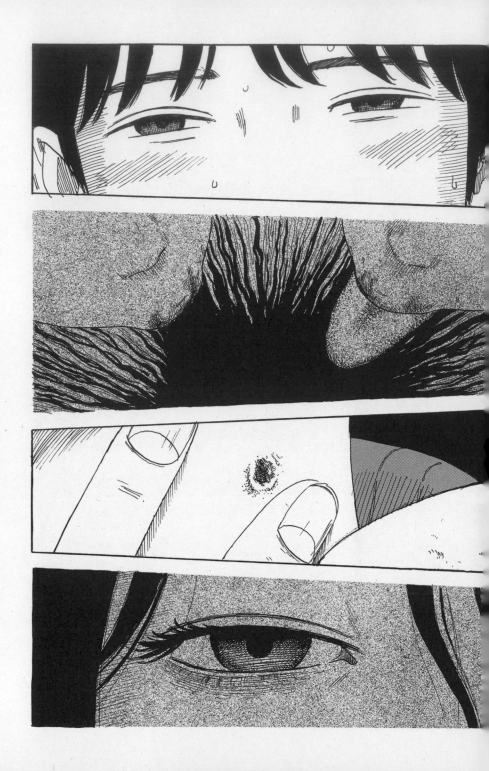

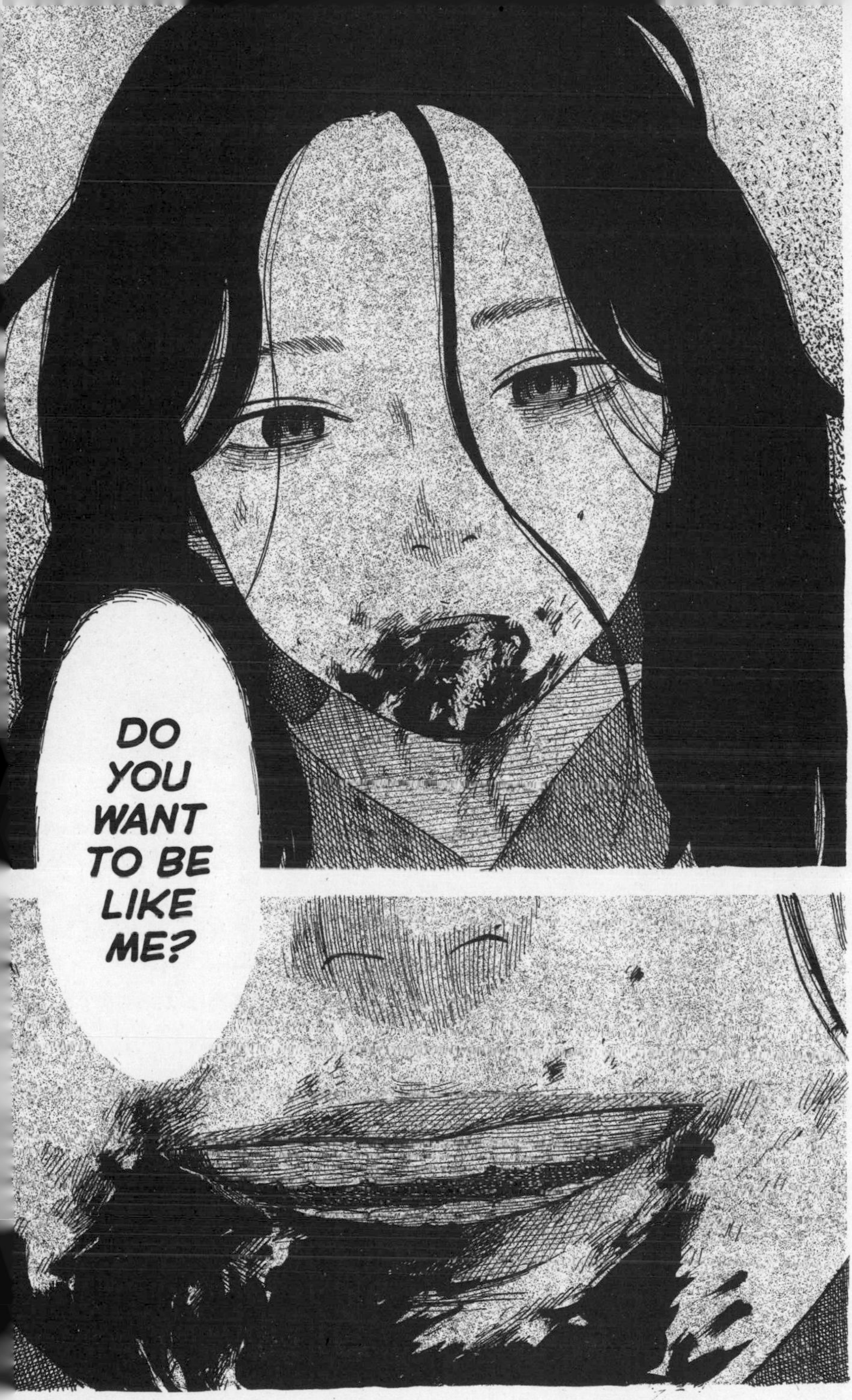
DO YOU WANT TO BE LIKE ME?

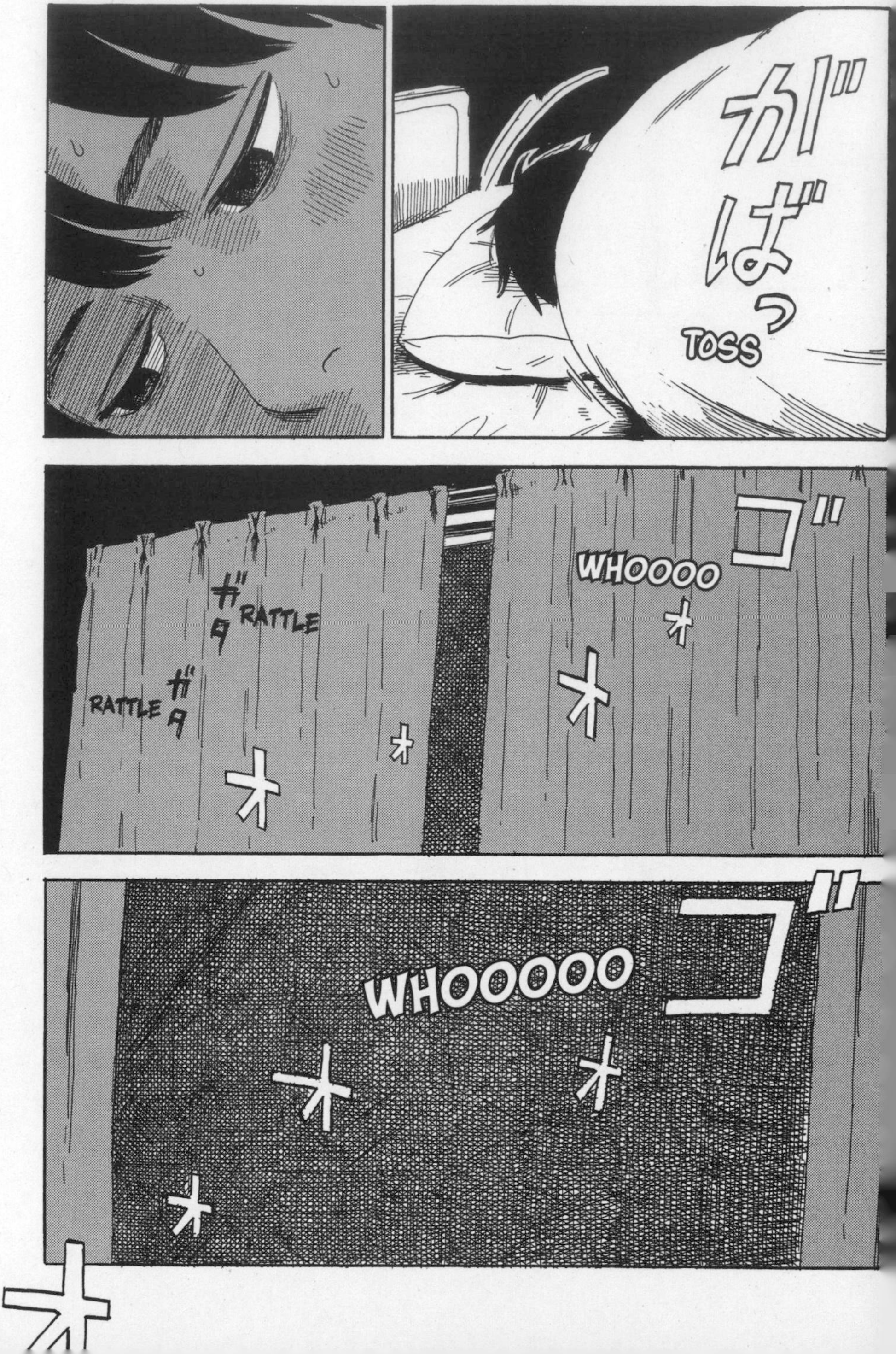

がばっ
TOSS
ゴ
WHOOOO
オ
オ
ガタ
RATTLE
ガタ
RATTLE
オ
オ
ゴ
WHOOOOO
オ
オ
オ
オ

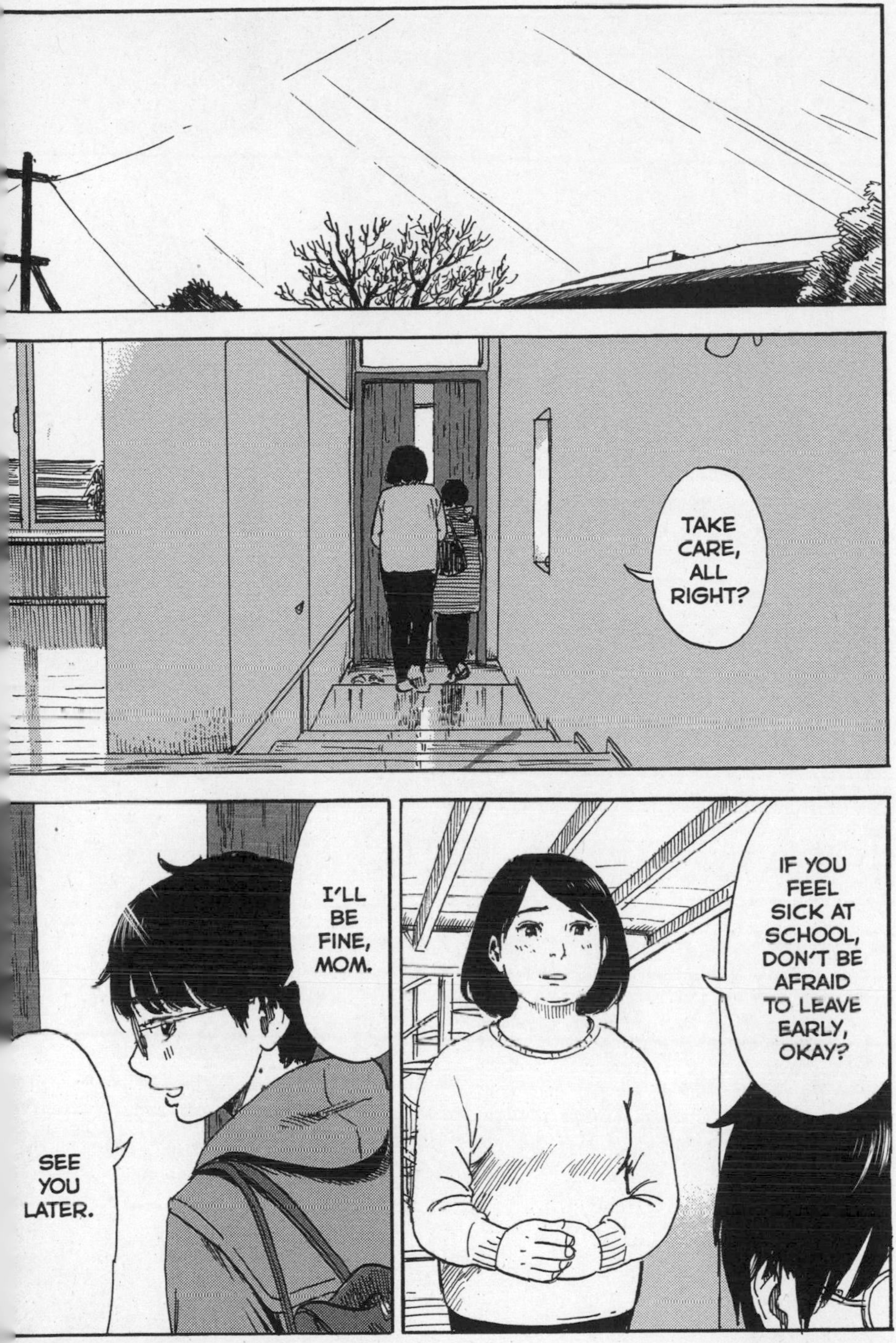
TAKE CARE, ALL RIGHT?
IF YOU FEEL SICK AT SCHOOL, DON'T BE AFRAID TO LEAVE EARLY, OKAY?
I'LL BE FINE, MOM.
SEE YOU LATER.

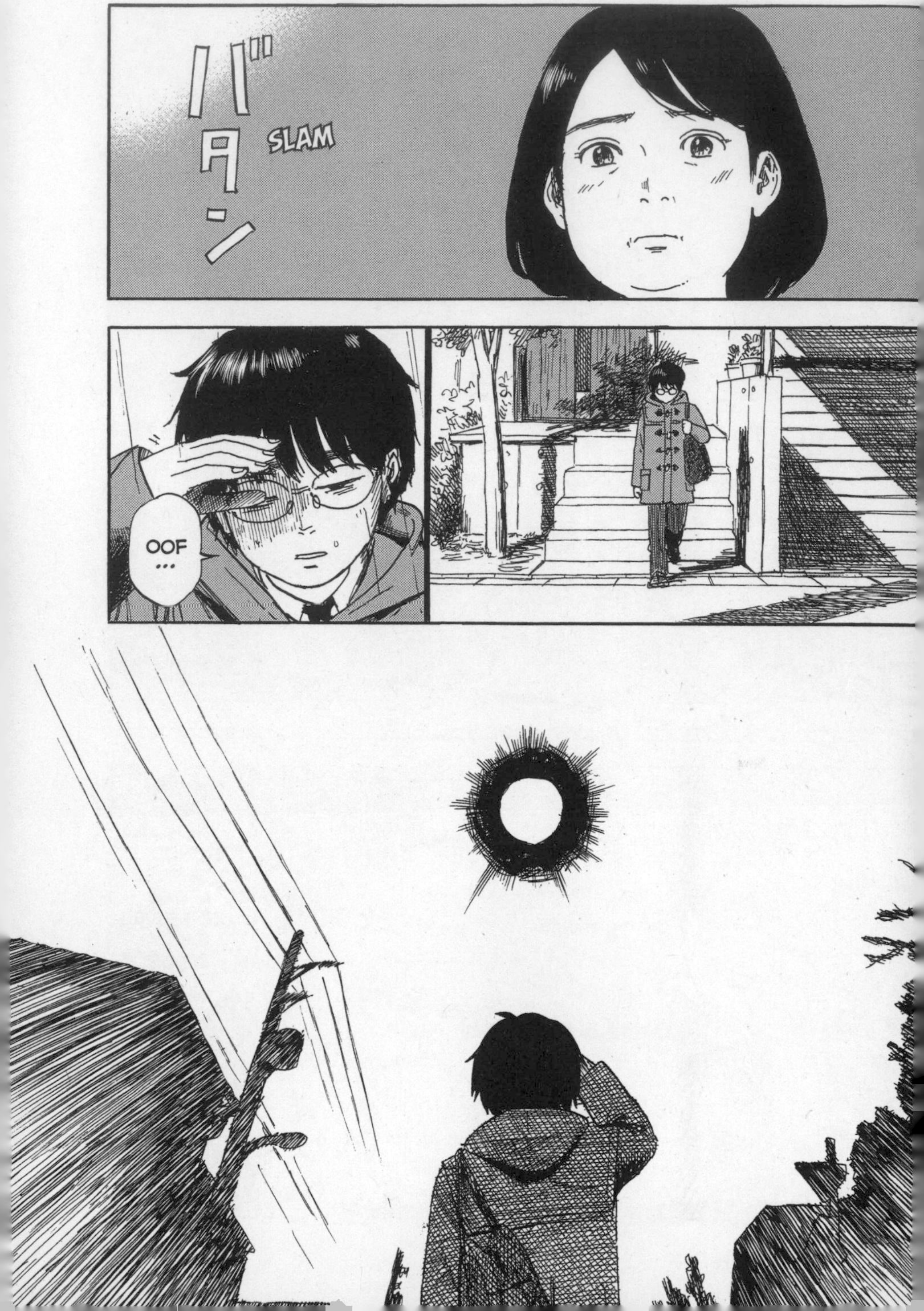
バタン
SLAM
OOF...

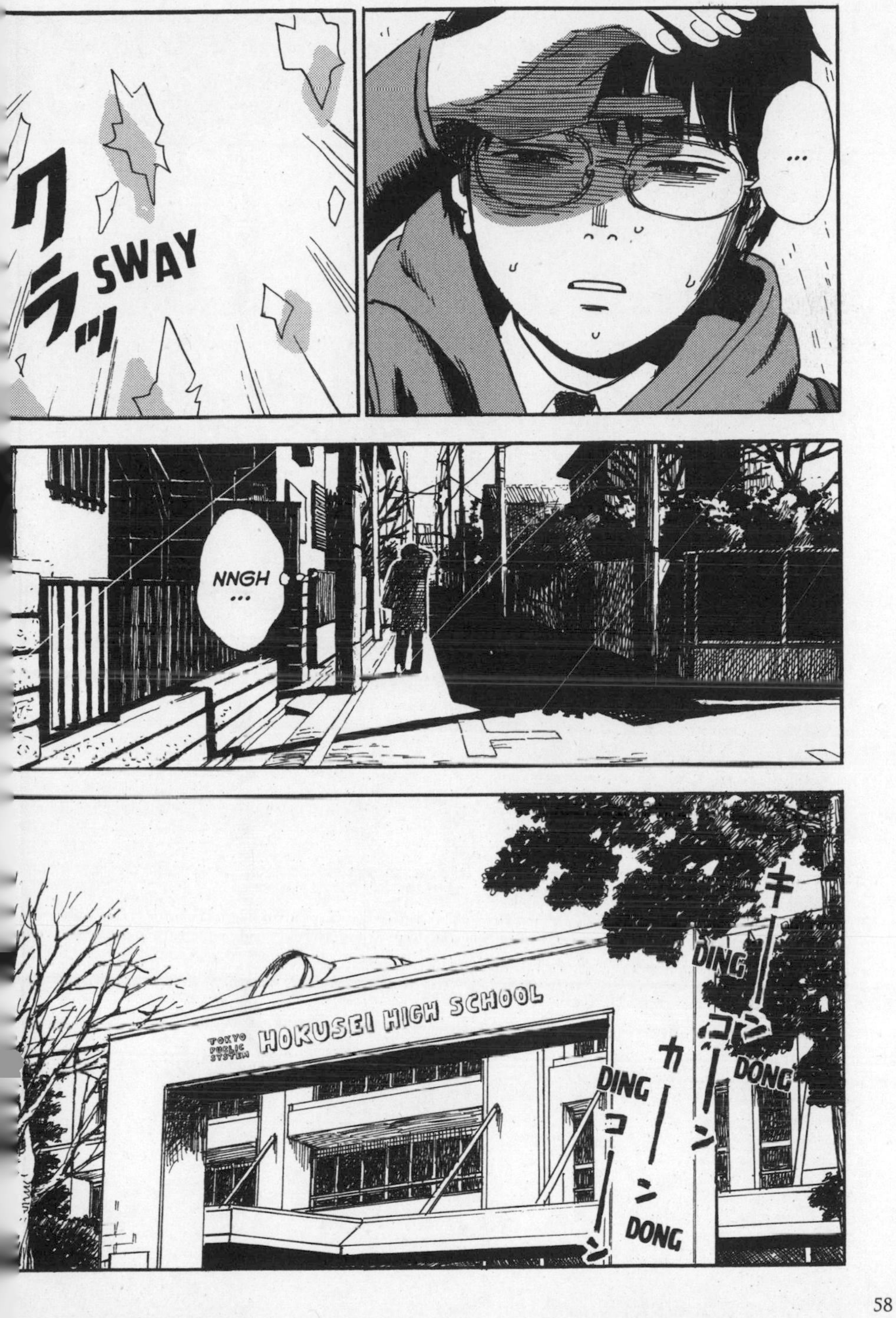
...
クラッ
SWAY
NNGH ...
TOKYO PUBLIC SYSTEM
HOKUSEI HIGH SCHOOL
キーン
DING
コーン
DONG
カーン
DING
コーン
DONG

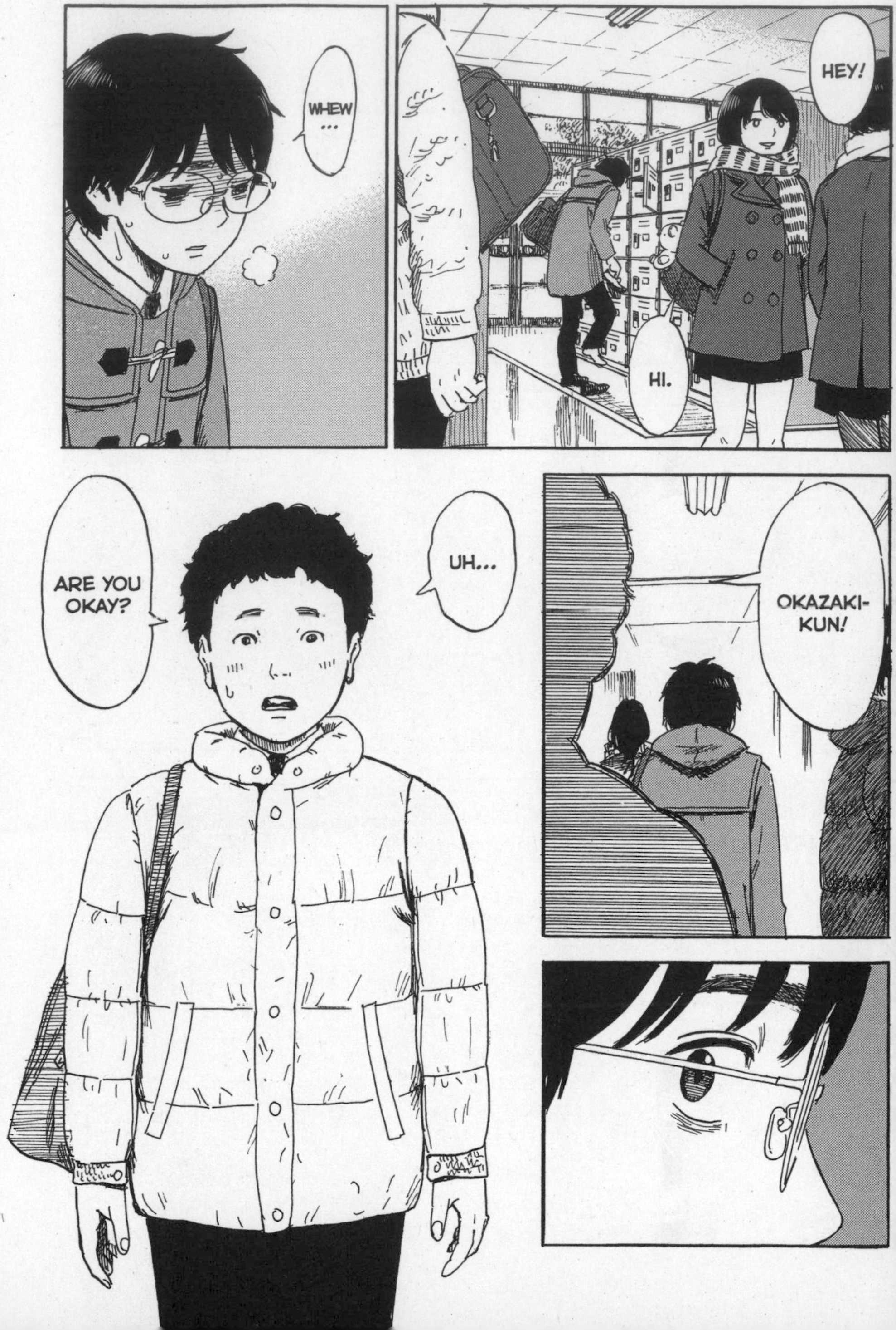
HEY!
HI.
WHEW...
OKAZAKI-KUN!
UH...
ARE YOU OKAY?

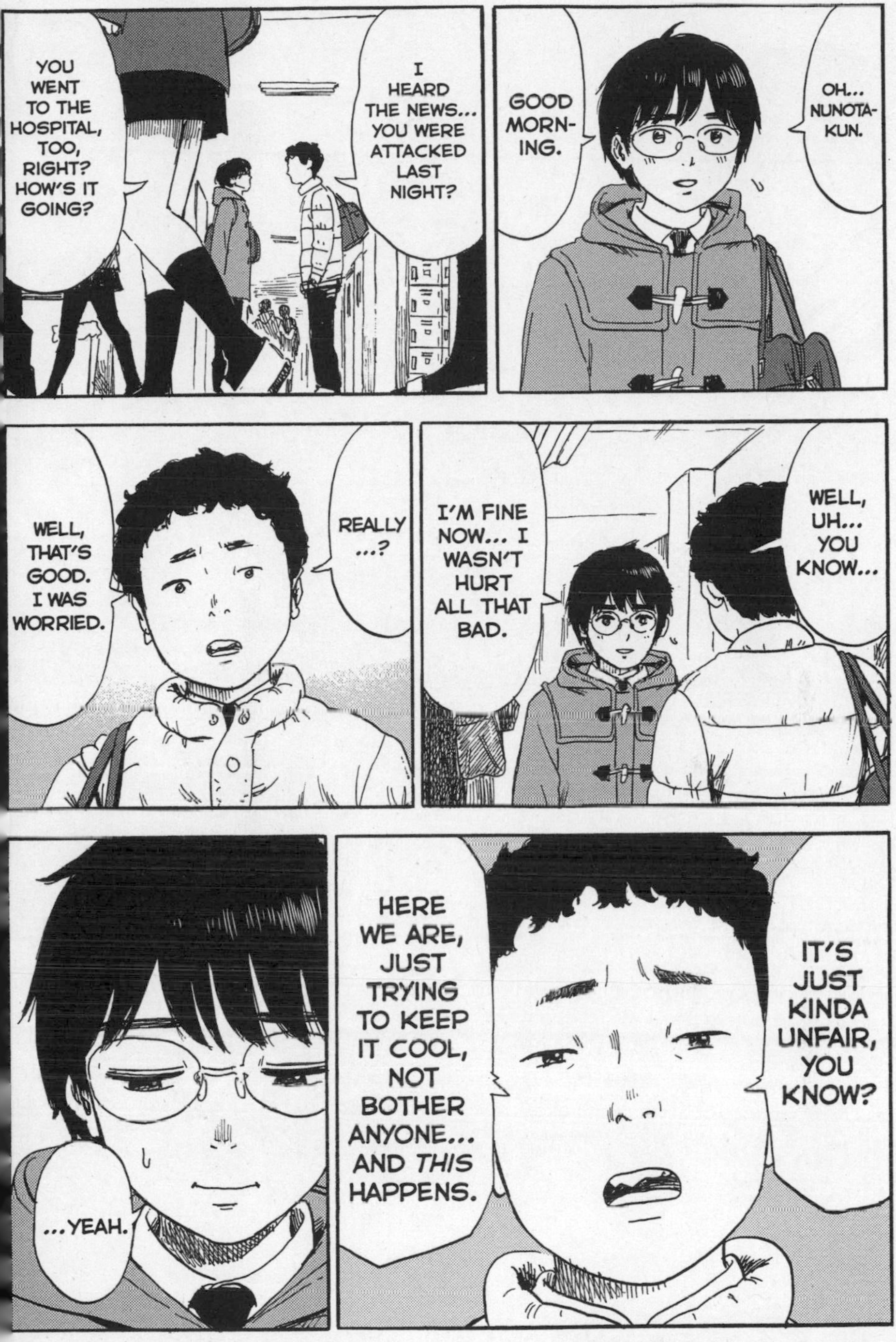
OH... NUNOTA-KUN.
GOOD MORNING.
I HEARD THE NEWS... YOU WERE ATTACKED LAST NIGHT?
YOU WENT TO THE HOSPITAL, TOO, RIGHT? HOW'S IT GOING?
WELL, UH... YOU KNOW...
I'M FINE NOW... I WASN'T HURT ALL THAT BAD.
REALLY ...?
WELL, THAT'S GOOD. I WAS WORRIED.
IT'S JUST KINDA UNFAIR, YOU KNOW?
HERE WE ARE, JUST TRYING TO KEEP IT COOL, NOT BOTHER ANYONE... AND *THIS* HAPPENS.
...YEAH.

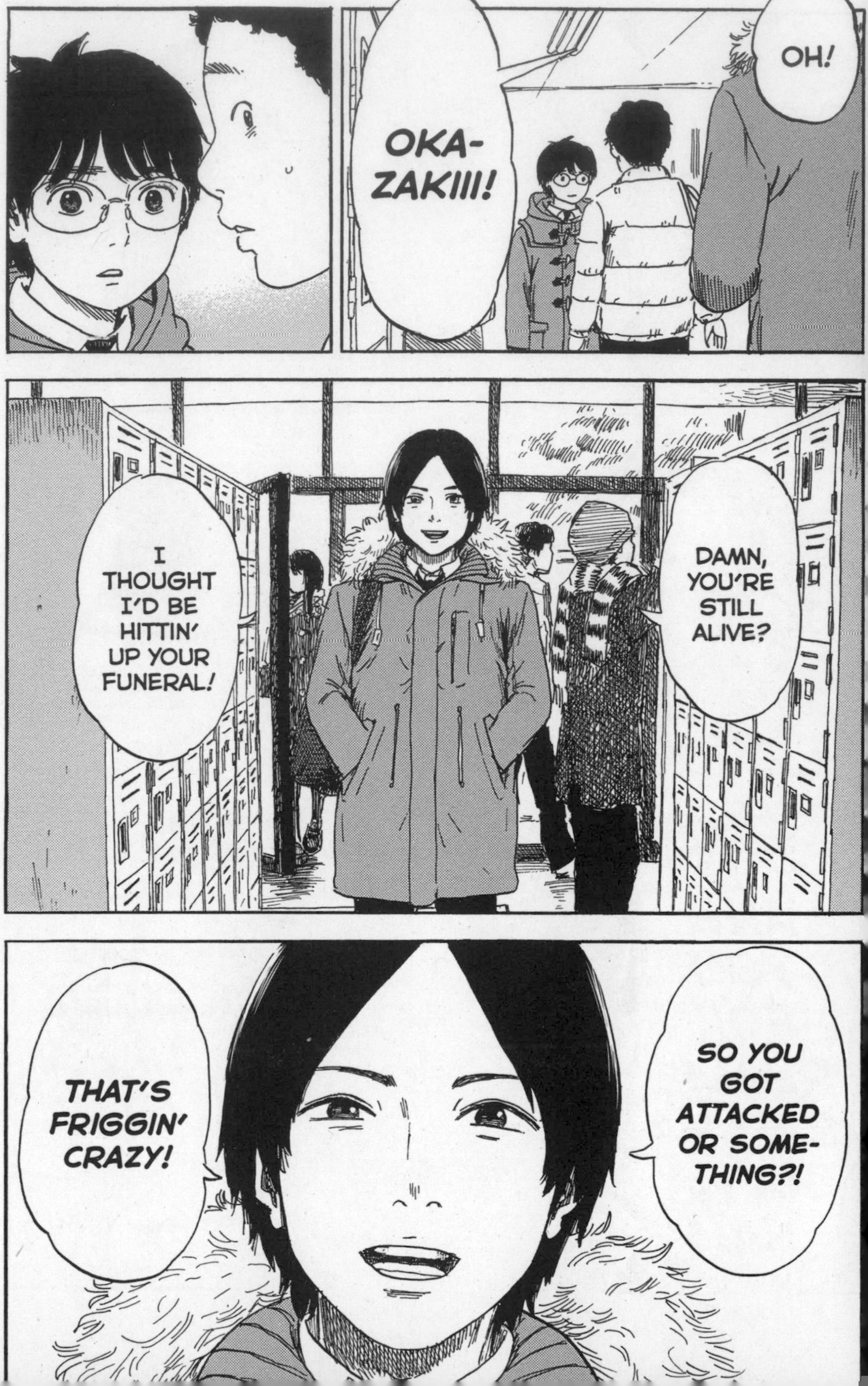
OH!
OKA-ZAKIII!
DAMN, YOU'RE STILL ALIVE?
I THOUGHT I'D BE HITTIN' UP YOUR FUNERAL!
SO YOU GOT ATTACKED OR SOME-THING?!
THAT'S FRIGGIN' CRAZY!

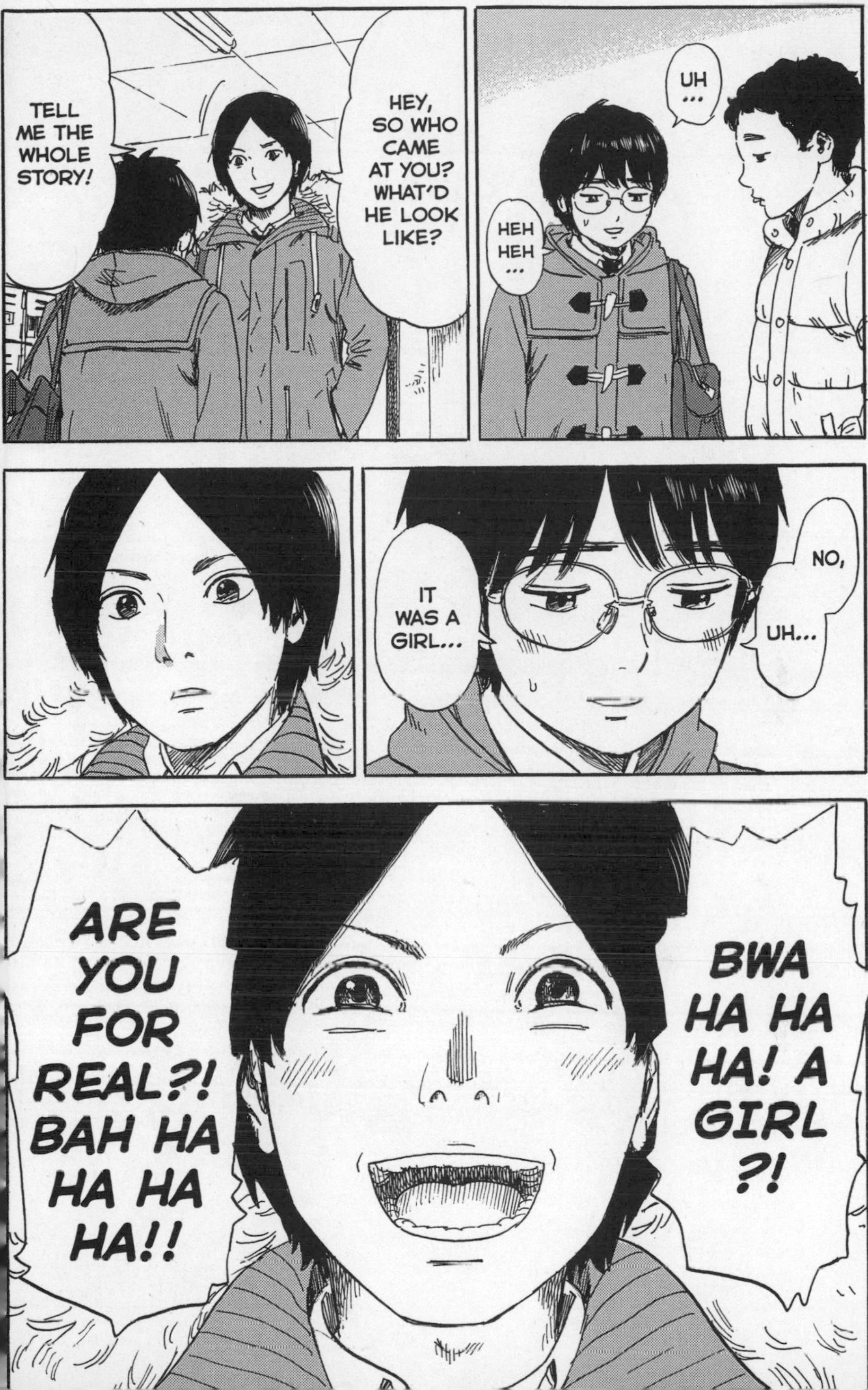

UH ...
HEH HEH ...
HEY, SO WHO CAME AT YOU? WHAT'D HE LOOK LIKE?
TELL ME THE WHOLE STORY!
NO, UH...
IT WAS A GIRL...
BWA HA HA HA! A GIRL ?!
ARE YOU FOR REAL?! BAH HA HA HA HA HA HA!!

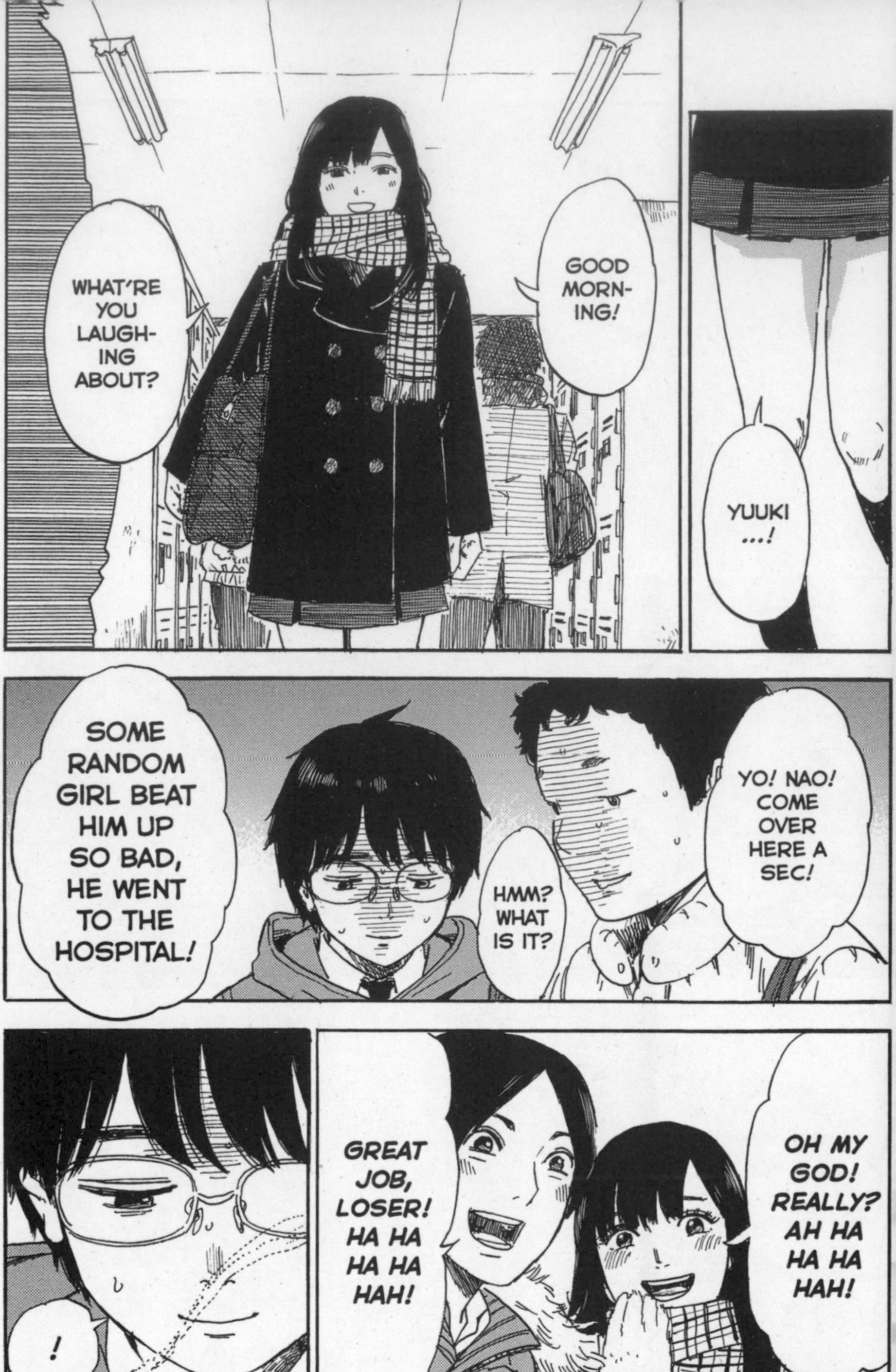
YUUKI ...!
GOOD MORNING!
WHAT'RE YOU LAUGHING ABOUT?
YO! NAO! COME OVER HERE A SEC!
HMM? WHAT IS IT?
SOME RANDOM GIRL BEAT HIM UP SO BAD, HE WENT TO THE HOSPITAL!
OH MY GOD! REALLY? AH HA HA HA HAH!
GREAT JOB, LOSER! HA HA HA HA HAH!
!

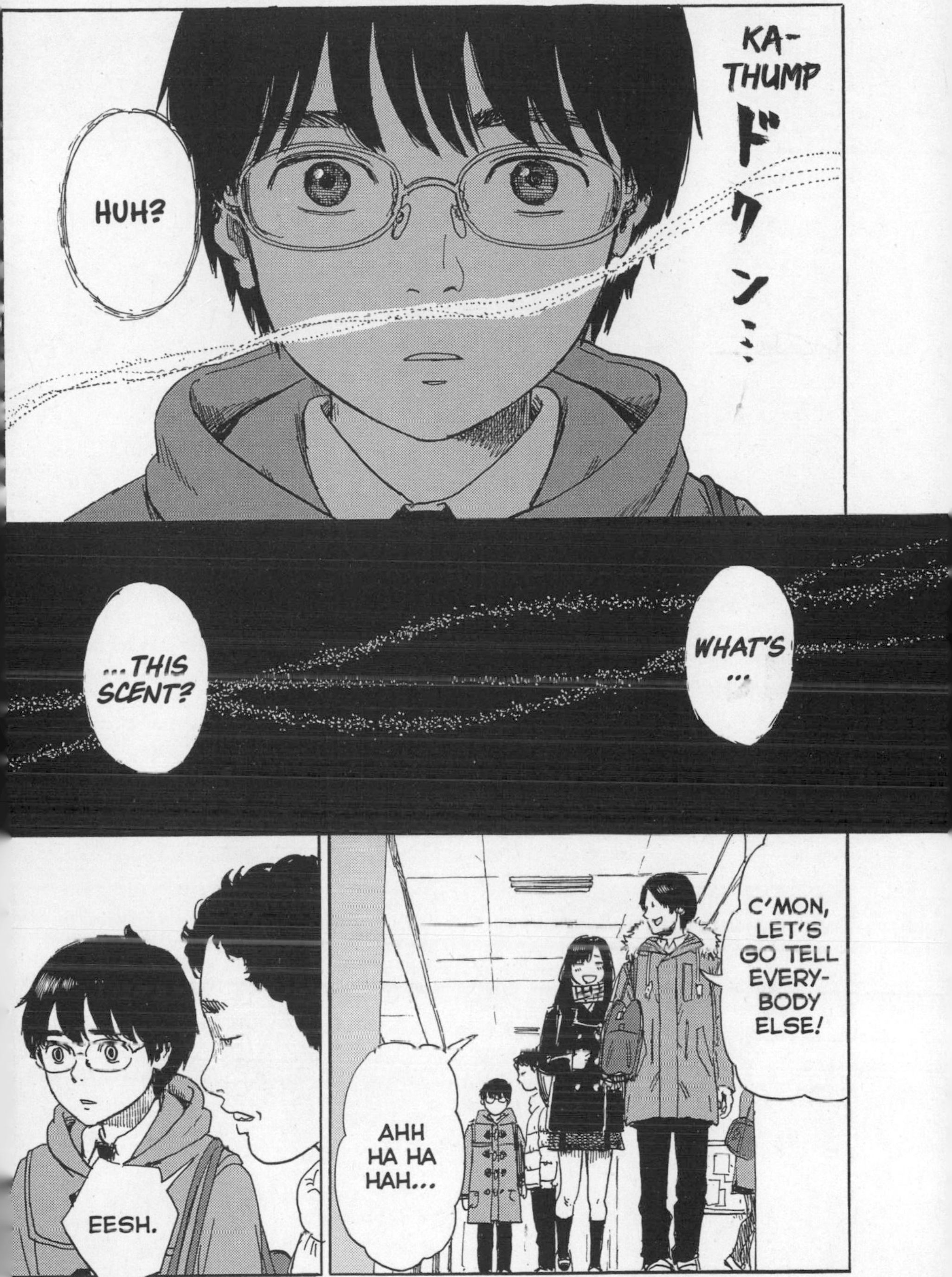
KA-THUMP
ドクン…
HUH?
WHAT'S...
...THIS SCENT?
C'MON, LET'S GO TELL EVERY-BODY ELSE!
AHH HA HA HAH...
EESH.

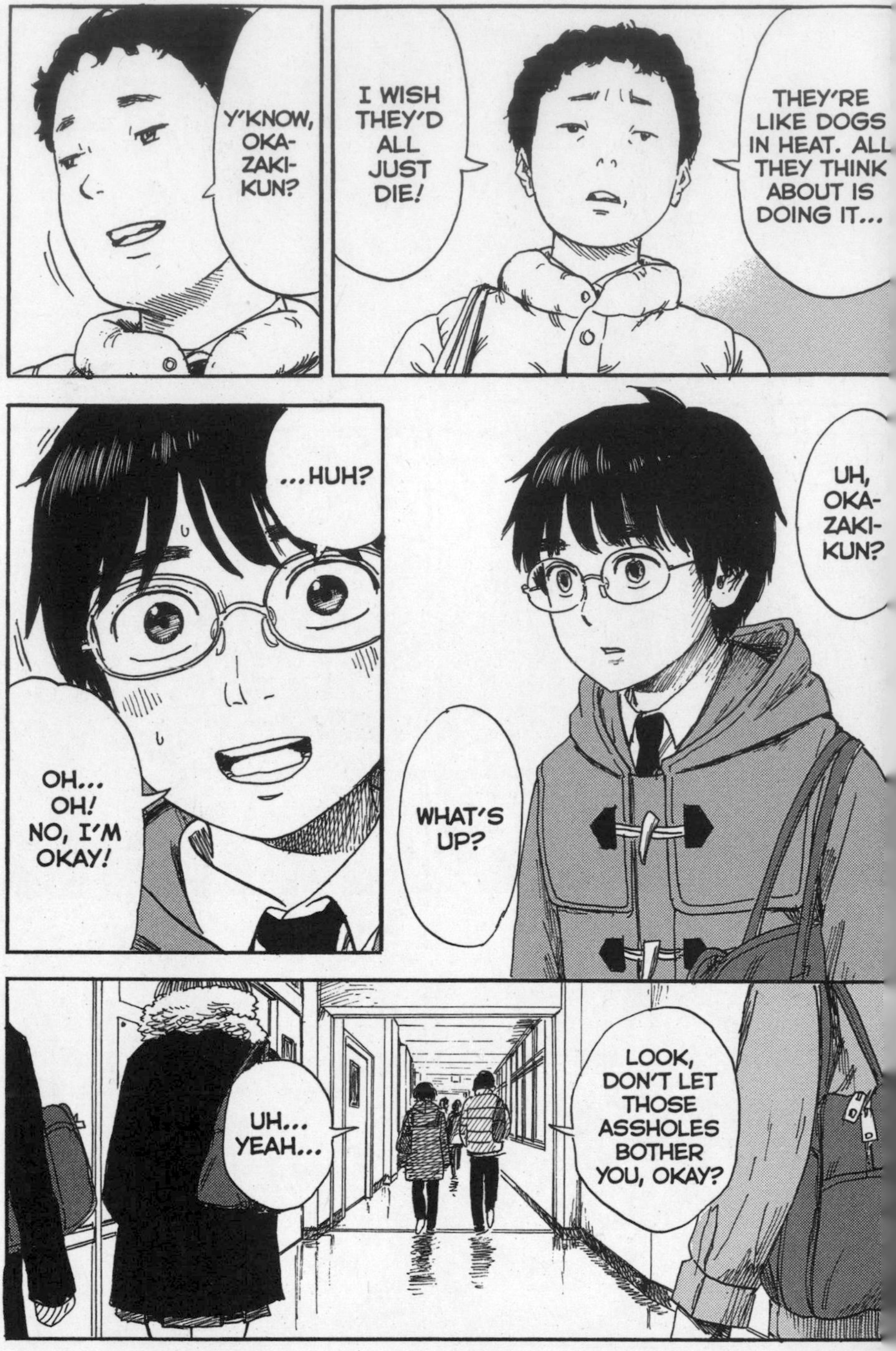
THEY'RE LIKE DOGS IN HEAT. ALL THEY THINK ABOUT IS DOING IT...
I WISH THEY'D ALL JUST DIE!
Y'KNOW, OKA-ZAKI-KUN?
UH, OKA-ZAKI-KUN?
WHAT'S UP?
...HUH?
OH... OH! NO, I'M OKAY!
LOOK, DON'T LET THOSE ASSHOLES BOTHER YOU, OKAY?
UH... YEAH...

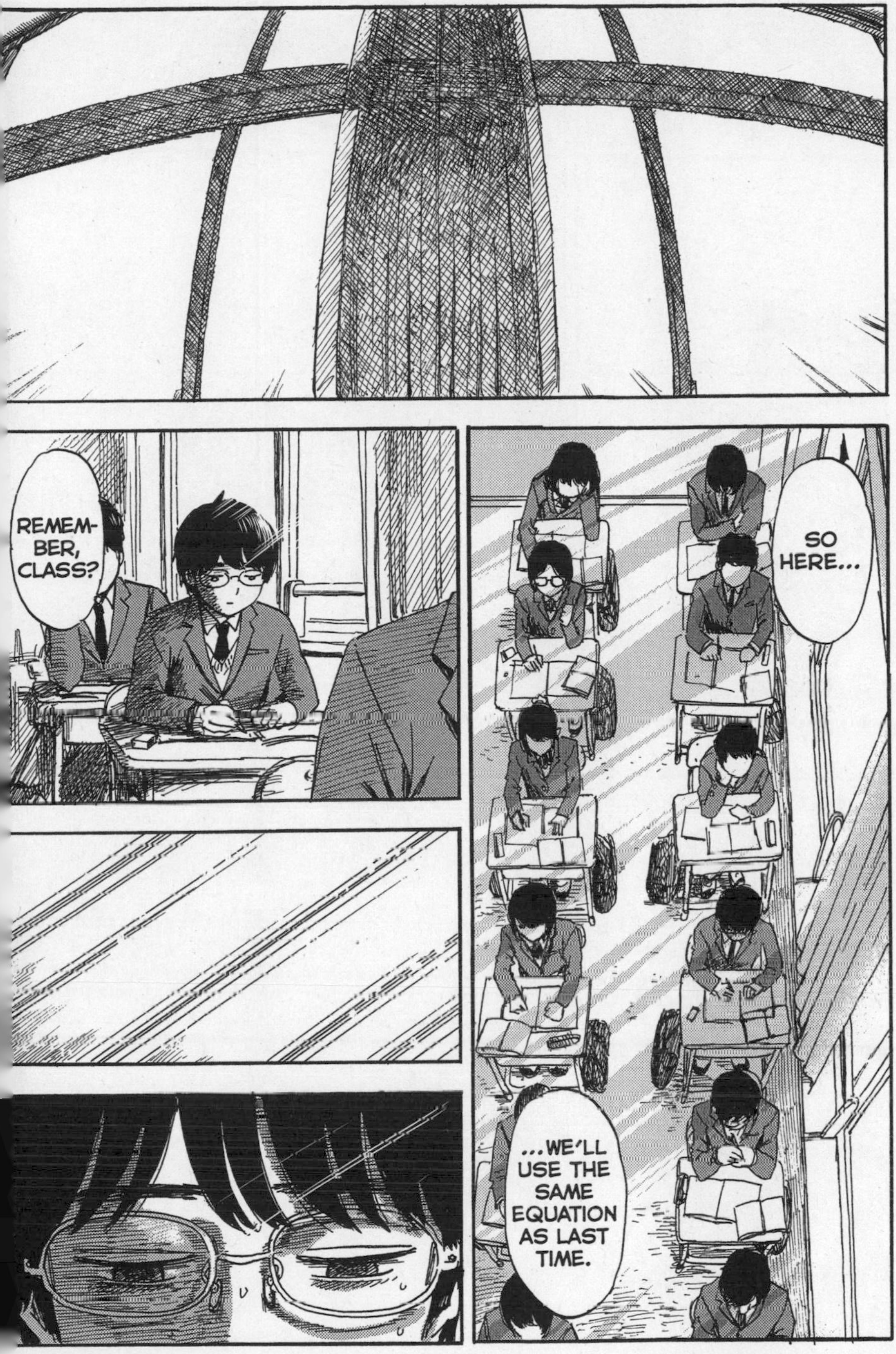
SO HERE...
...WE'LL USE THE SAME EQUATION AS LAST TIME.
REMEMBER, CLASS?

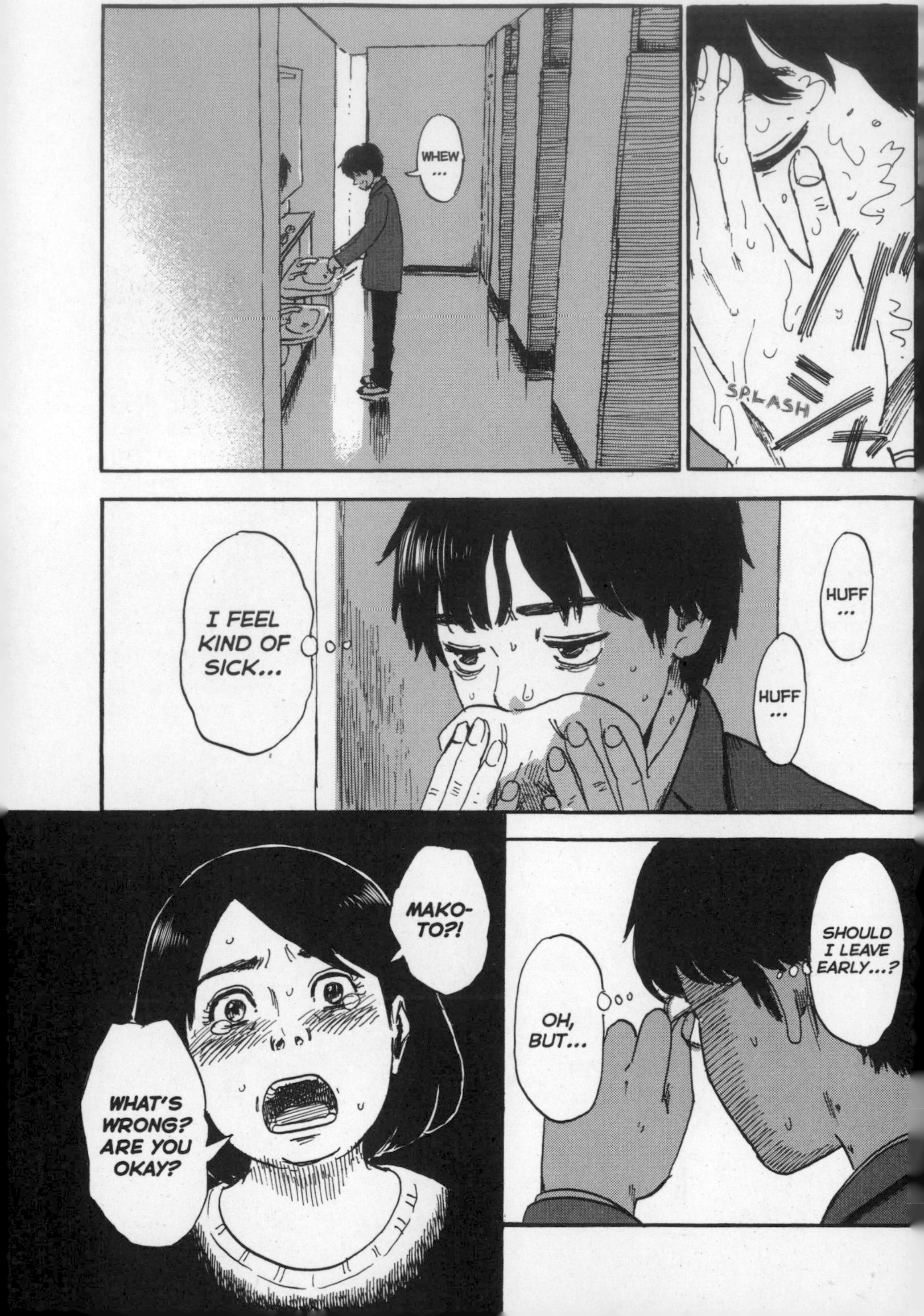
SPLASH
WHEW...
HUFF...
HUFF...
I FEEL KIND OF SICK...
SHOULD I LEAVE EARLY...?
OH, BUT...
MAKO-TO?!
WHAT'S WRONG? ARE YOU OKAY?

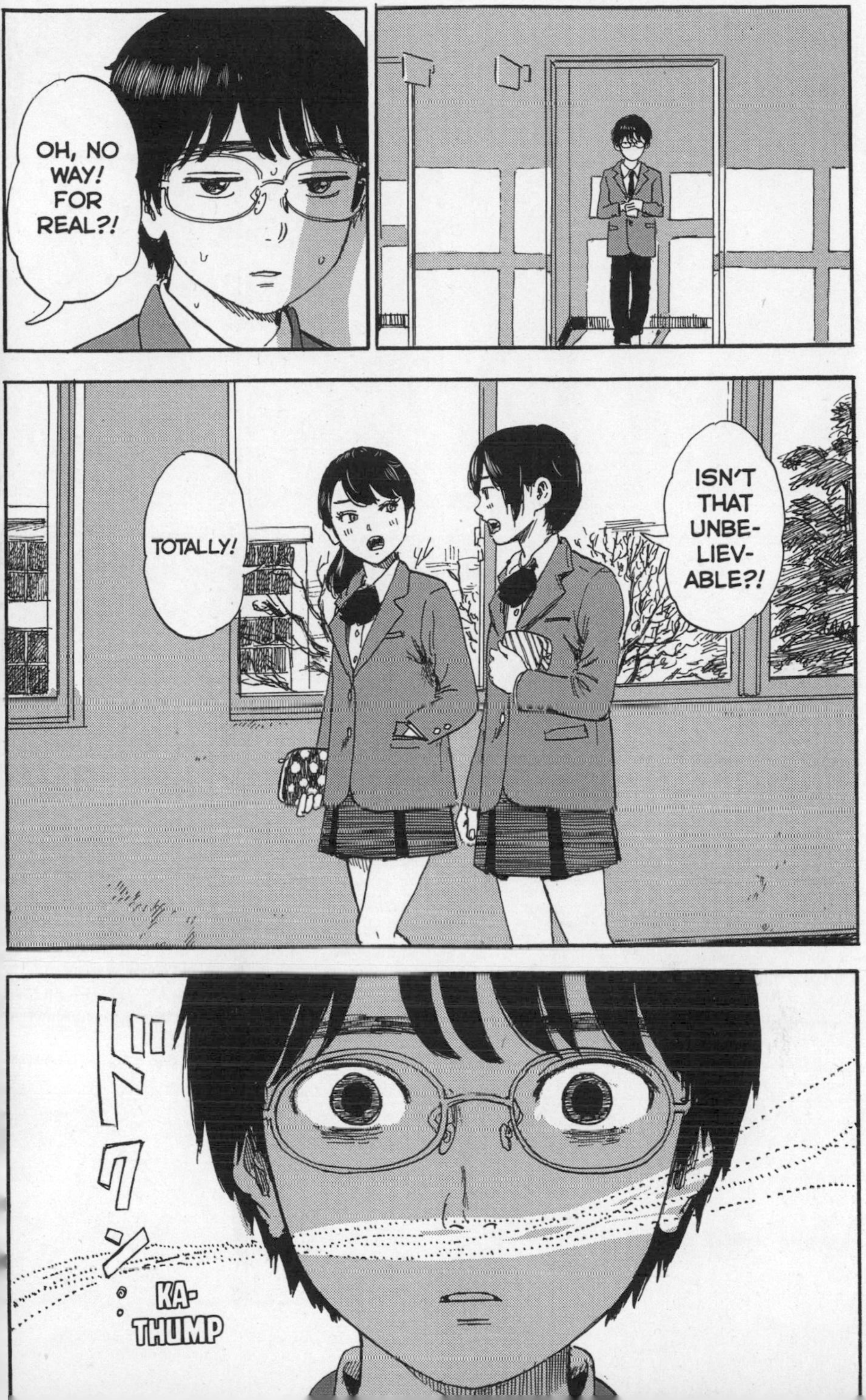
OH, NO WAY! FOR REAL?!
ISN'T THAT UNBE-LIEV-ABLE?!
TOTALLY!
KA-THUMP

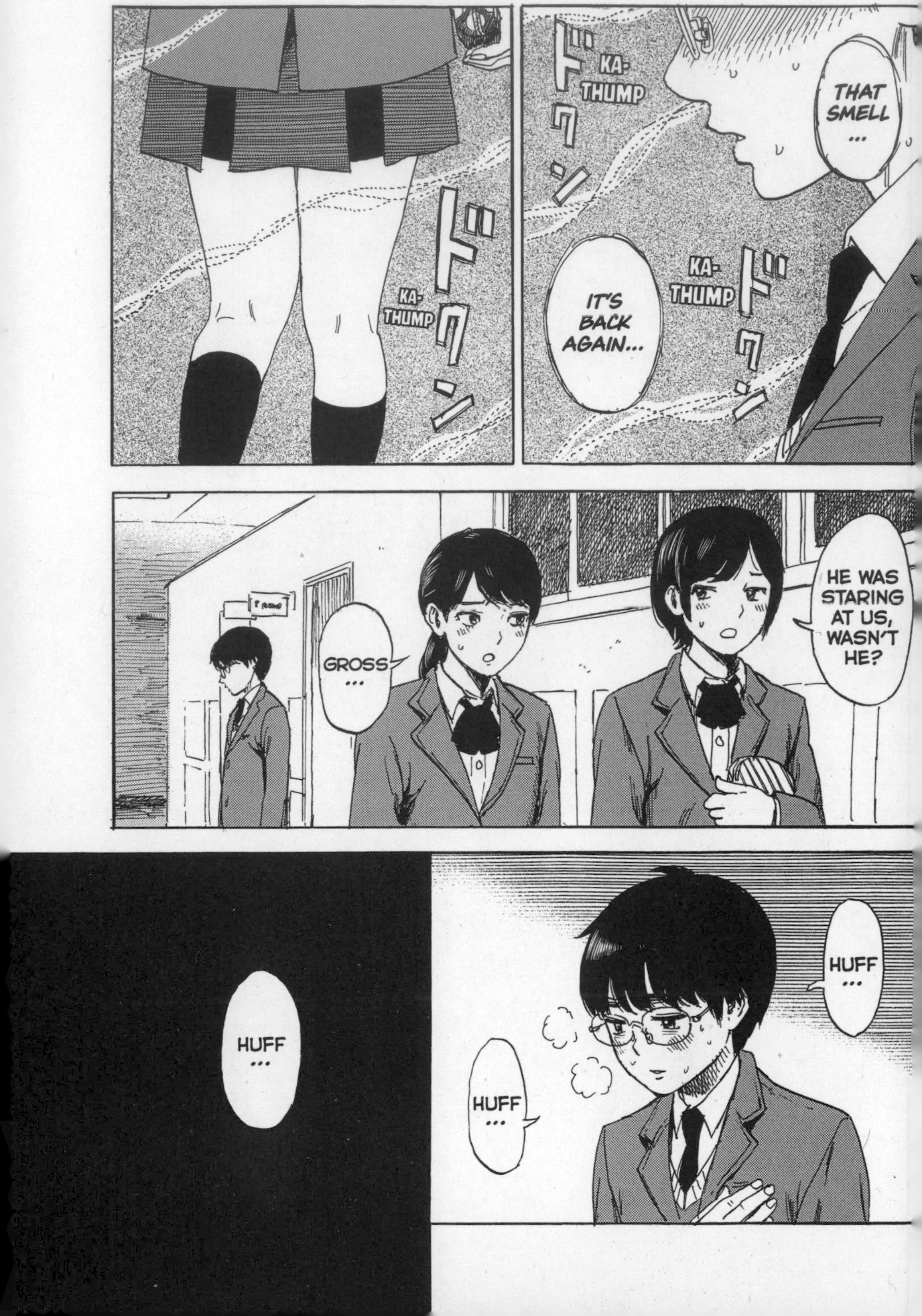
THAT SMELL ...
ドクン
KA-THUMP
ドクン
KA-THUMP
IT'S BACK AGAIN...
ドクン
KA-THUMP
HE WAS STARING AT US, WASN'T HE?
GROSS ...
HUFF ...
HUFF ...
HUFF ...

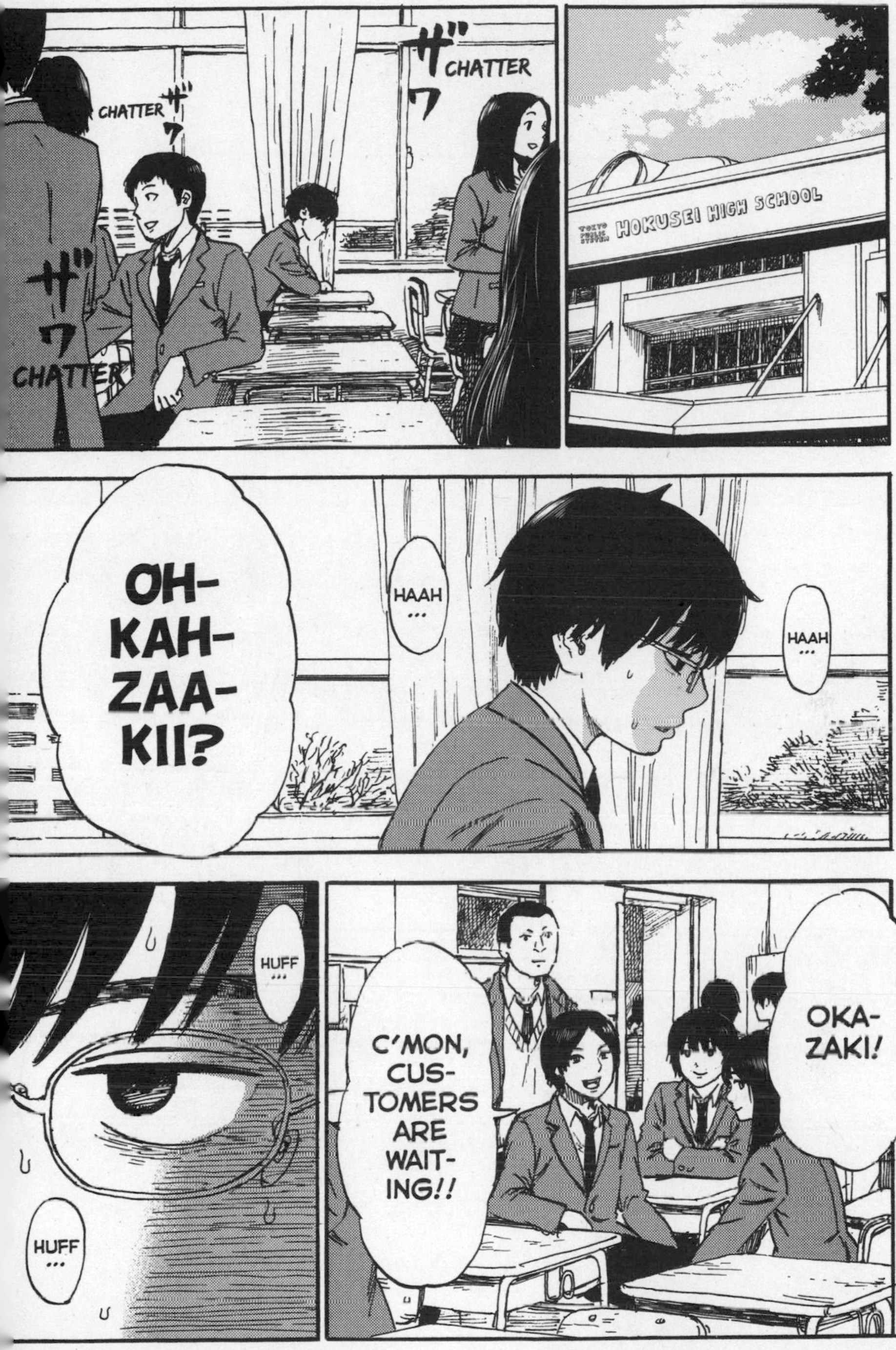
HOKUSEI HIGH SCHOOL
ザワ CHATTER
ザワ CHATTER
ザワ CHATTER
HAAH...
HAAH...
OH-KAH-ZAA-KII?
OKA-ZAKI!
C'MON, CUS-TOMERS ARE WAIT-ING!!
HUFF...
HUFF...

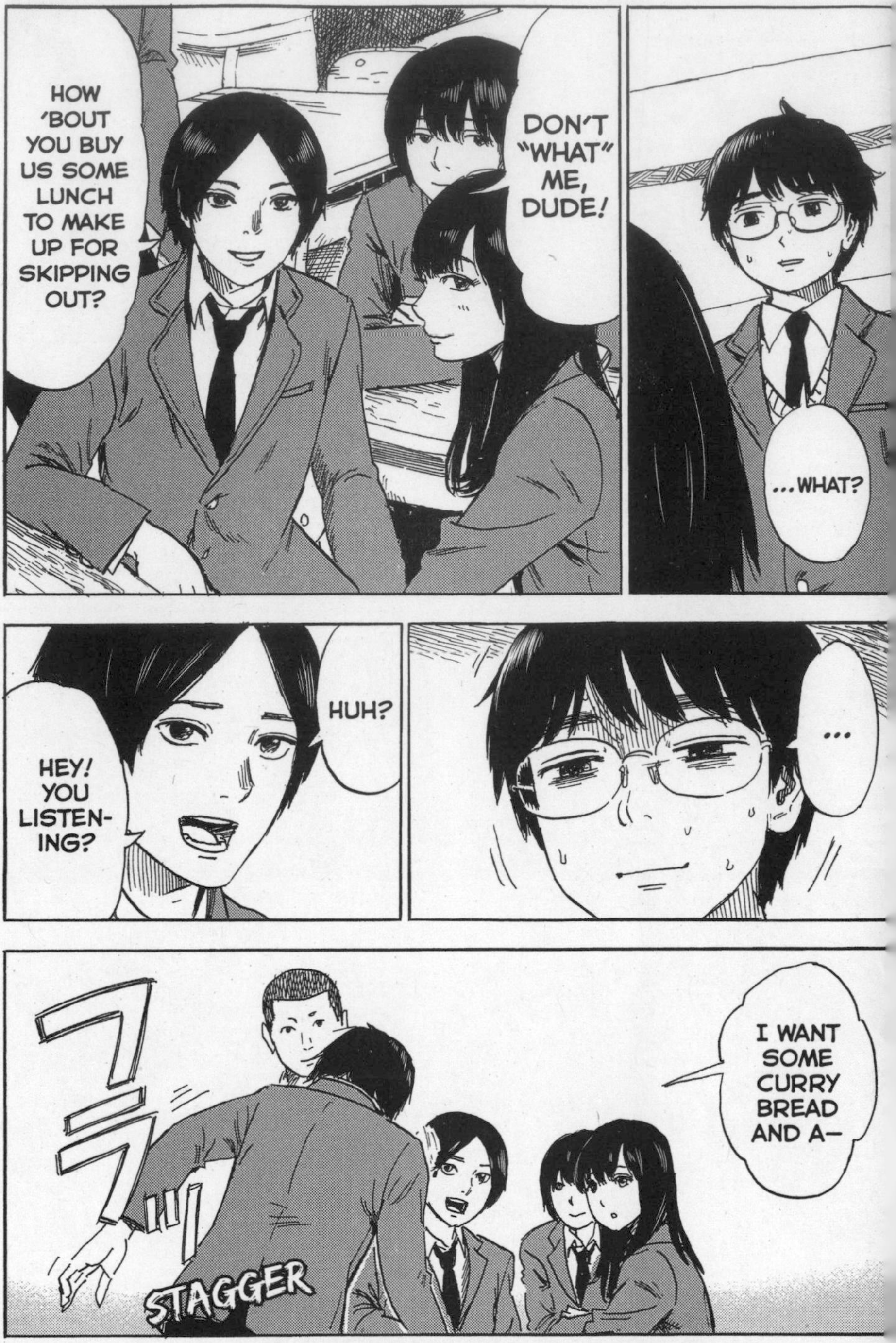
...WHAT?
DON'T "WHAT" ME, DUDE!
HOW 'BOUT YOU BUY US SOME LUNCH TO MAKE UP FOR SKIPPING OUT?
...
HUH?
HEY! YOU LISTEN-ING?
I WANT SOME CURRY BREAD AND A—
STAGGER

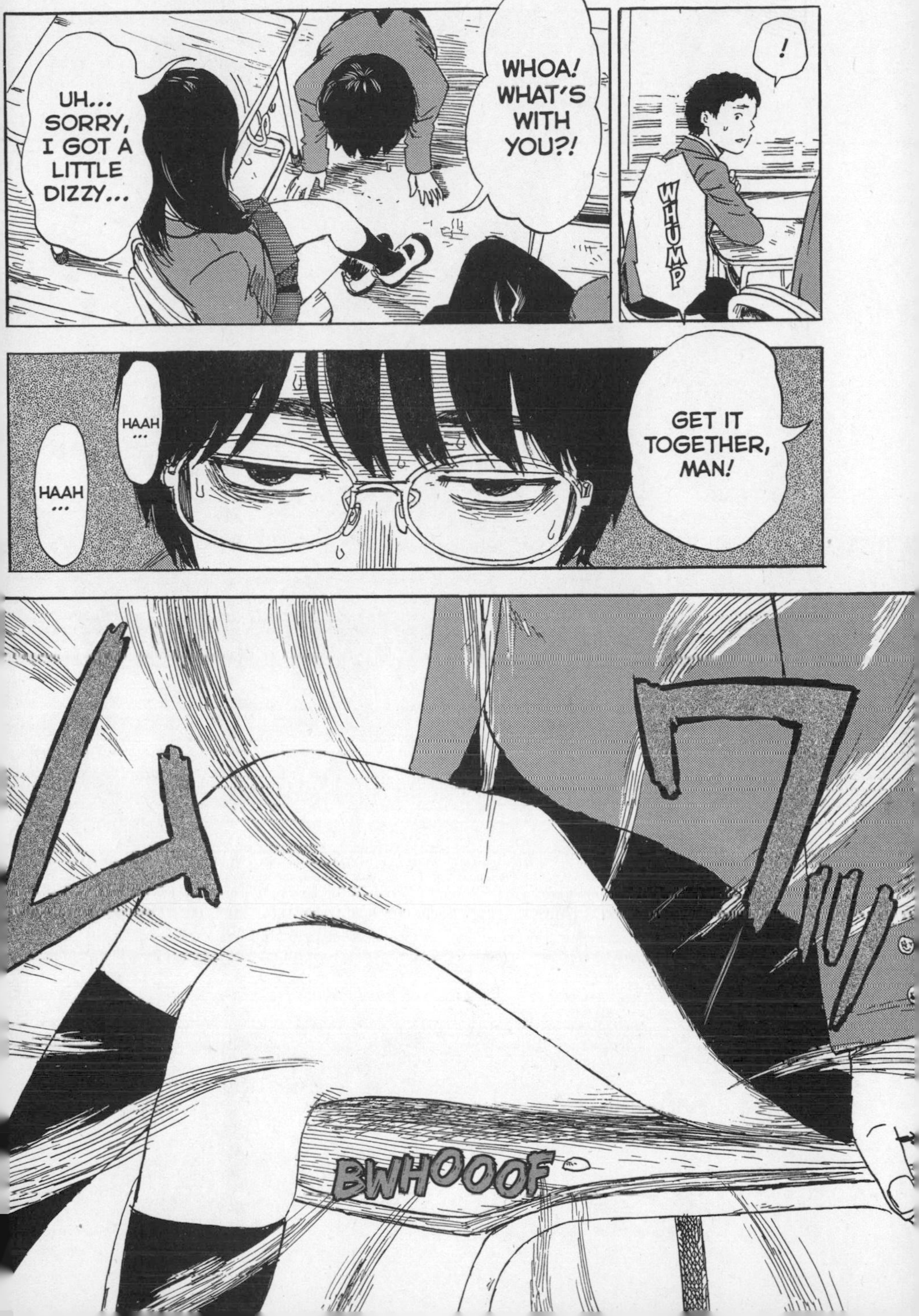
!
WHUMP
WHOA! WHAT'S WITH YOU?!
UH... SORRY, I GOT A LITTLE DIZZY...
GET IT TOGETHER, MAN!
HAAH...
HAAH...
BWHOOOF

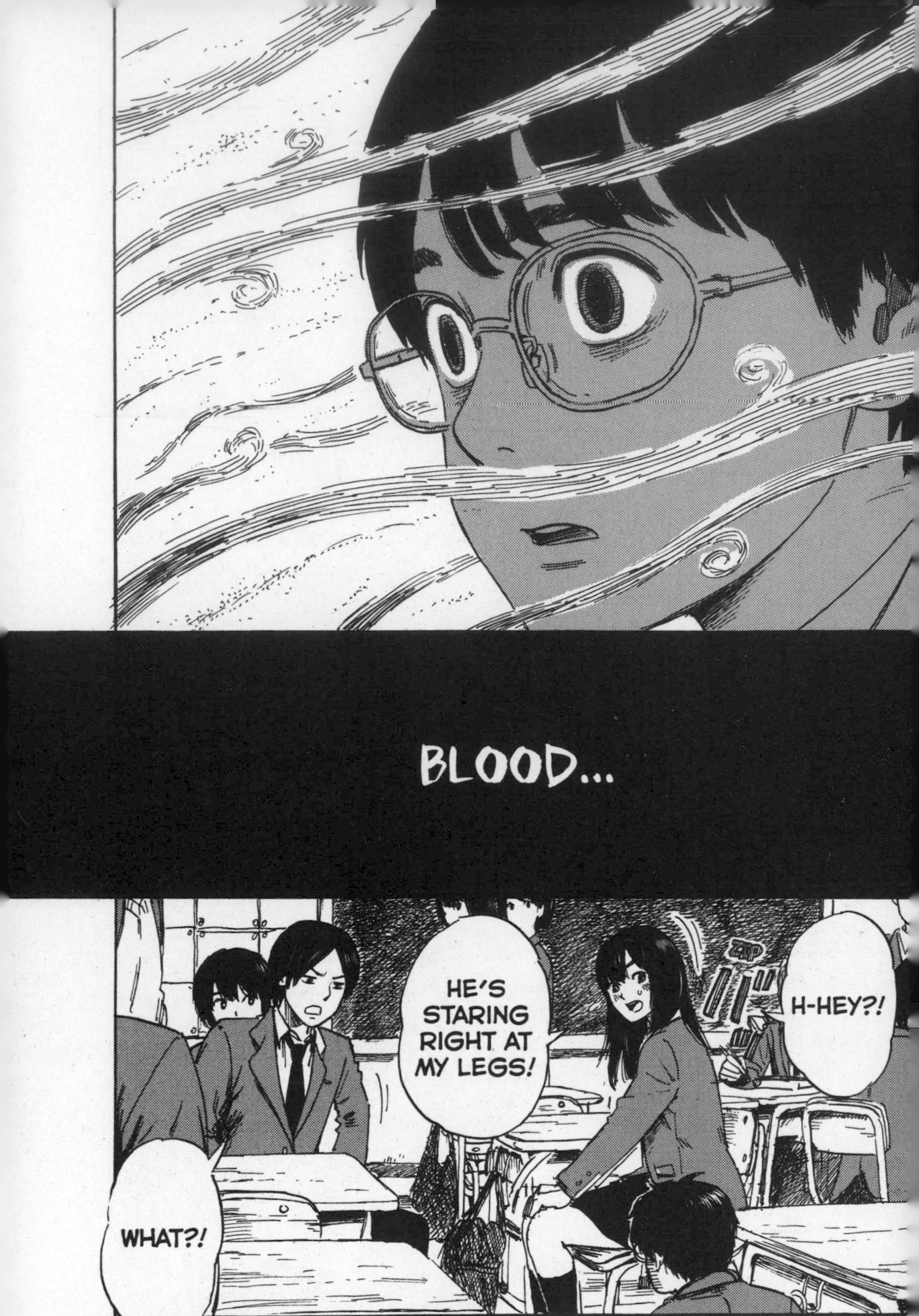
BLOOD...
H-HEY?!
HE'S STARING RIGHT AT MY LEGS!
WHAT?!

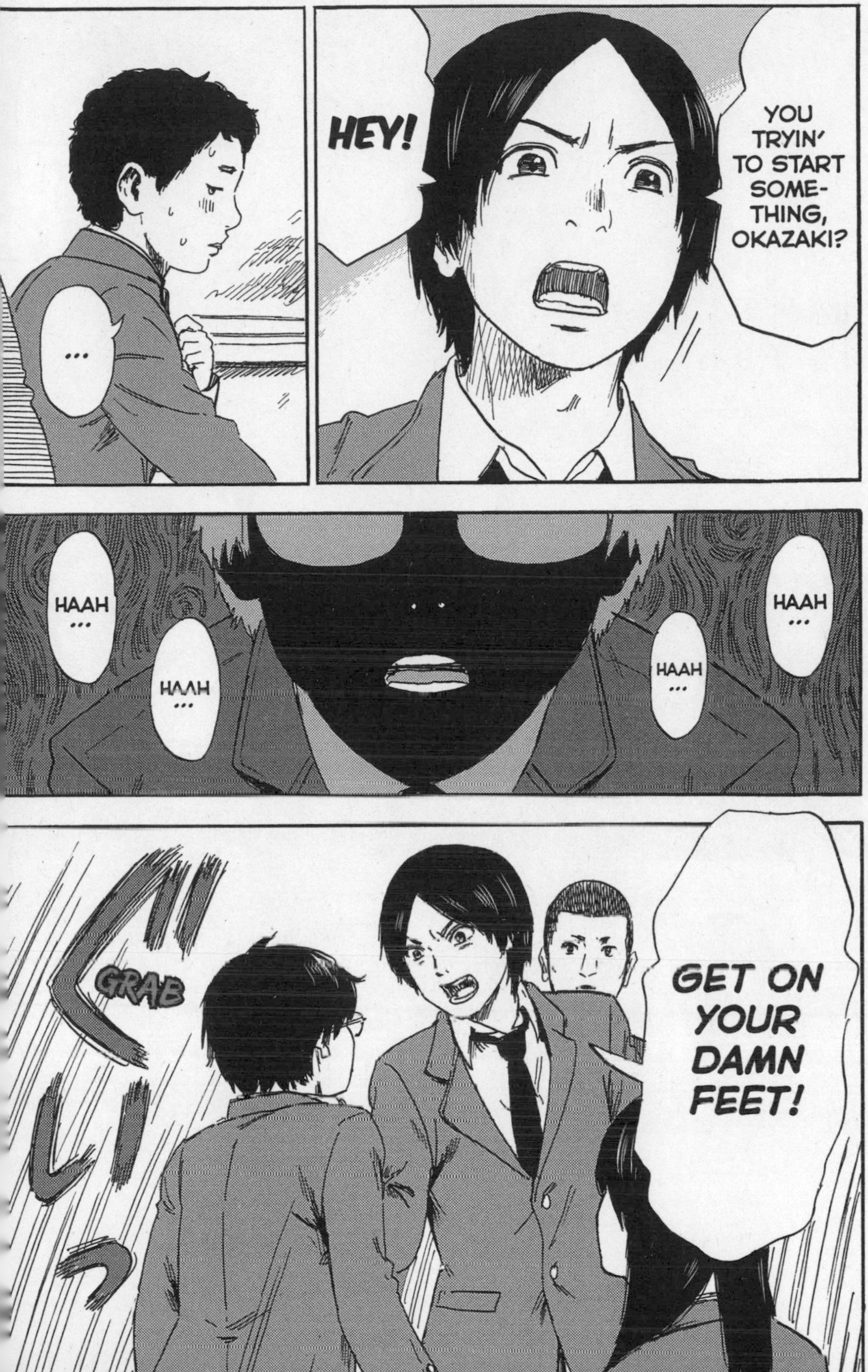
HEY!
YOU TRYIN' TO START SOME-THING, OKAZAKI?
...
HAAH ...
HAAH ...
HAAH ...
HAAH ...
GET ON YOUR DAMN FEET!
GRAB

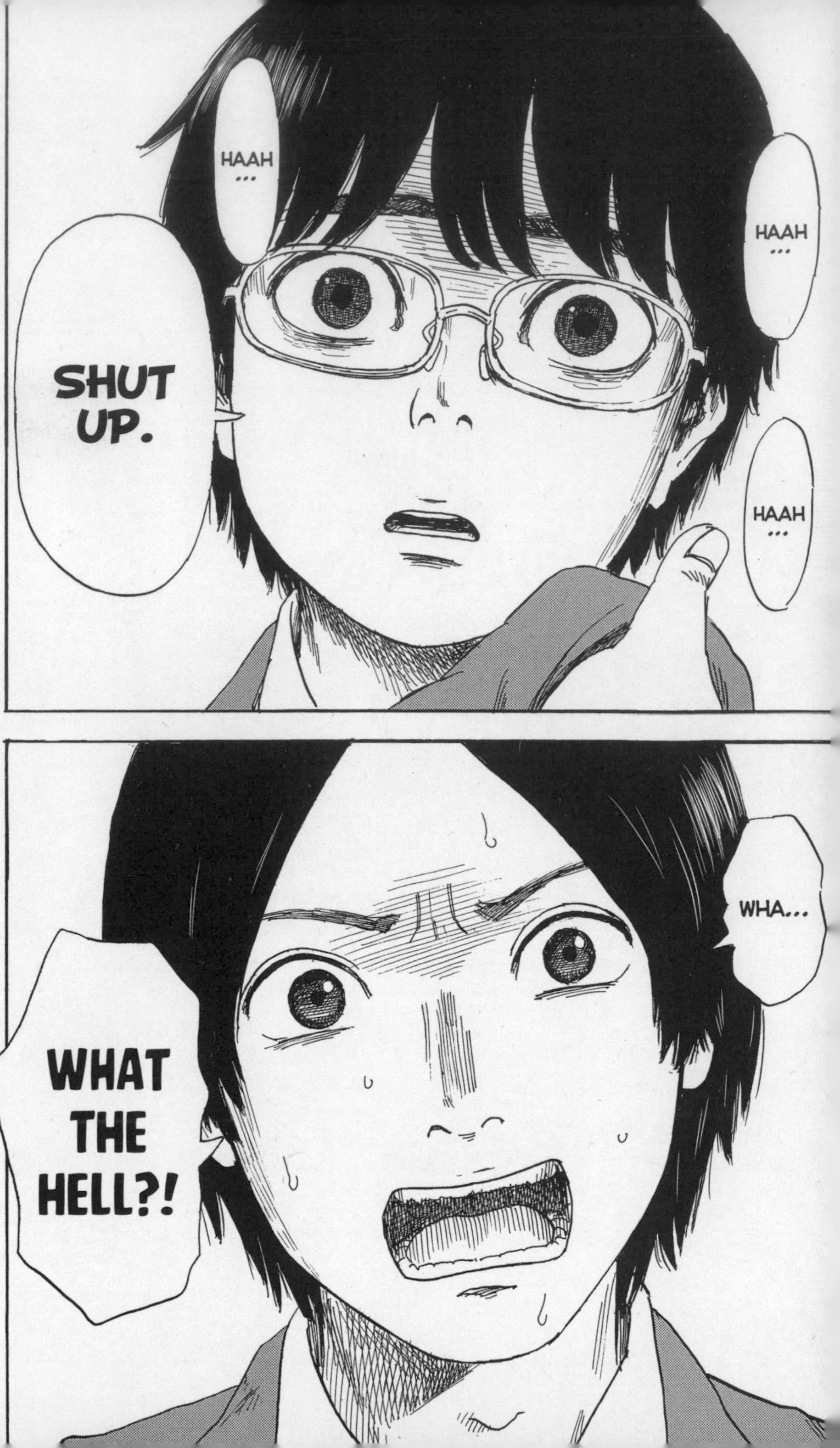
HAAH...
HAAH...
HAAH...
SHUT UP.
WHA...
WHAT THE HELL?!

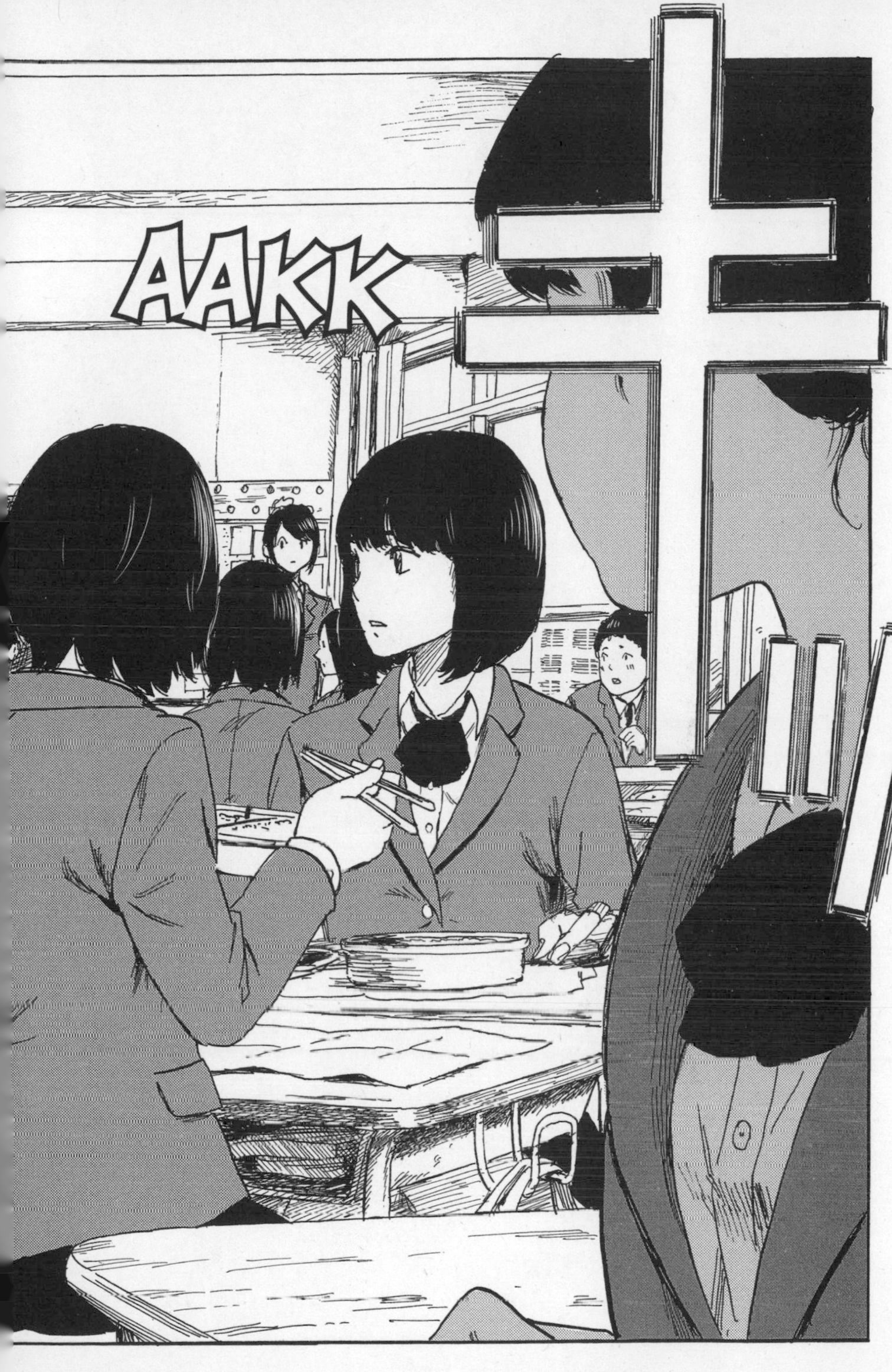
AAKK

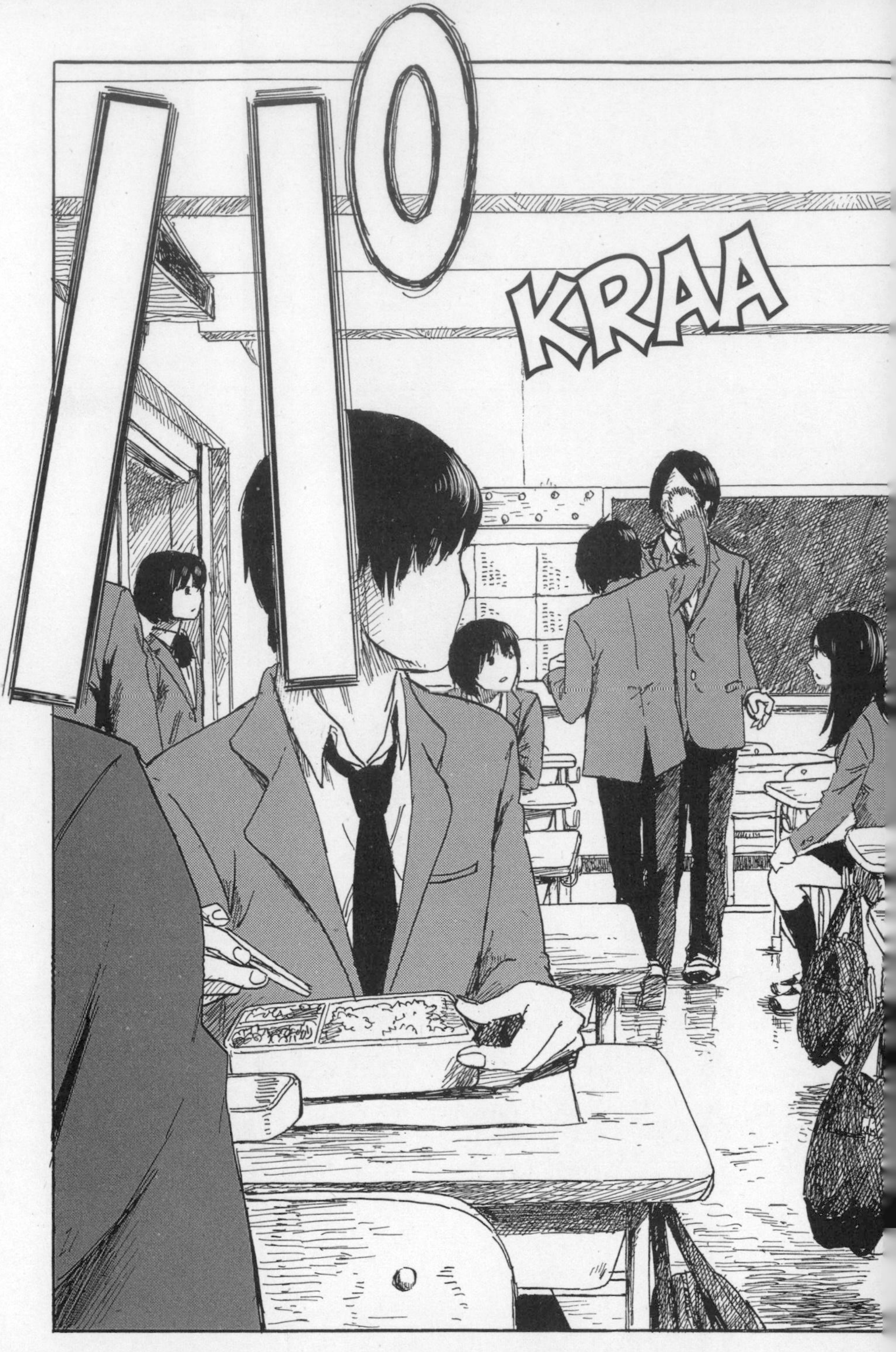
KRAA

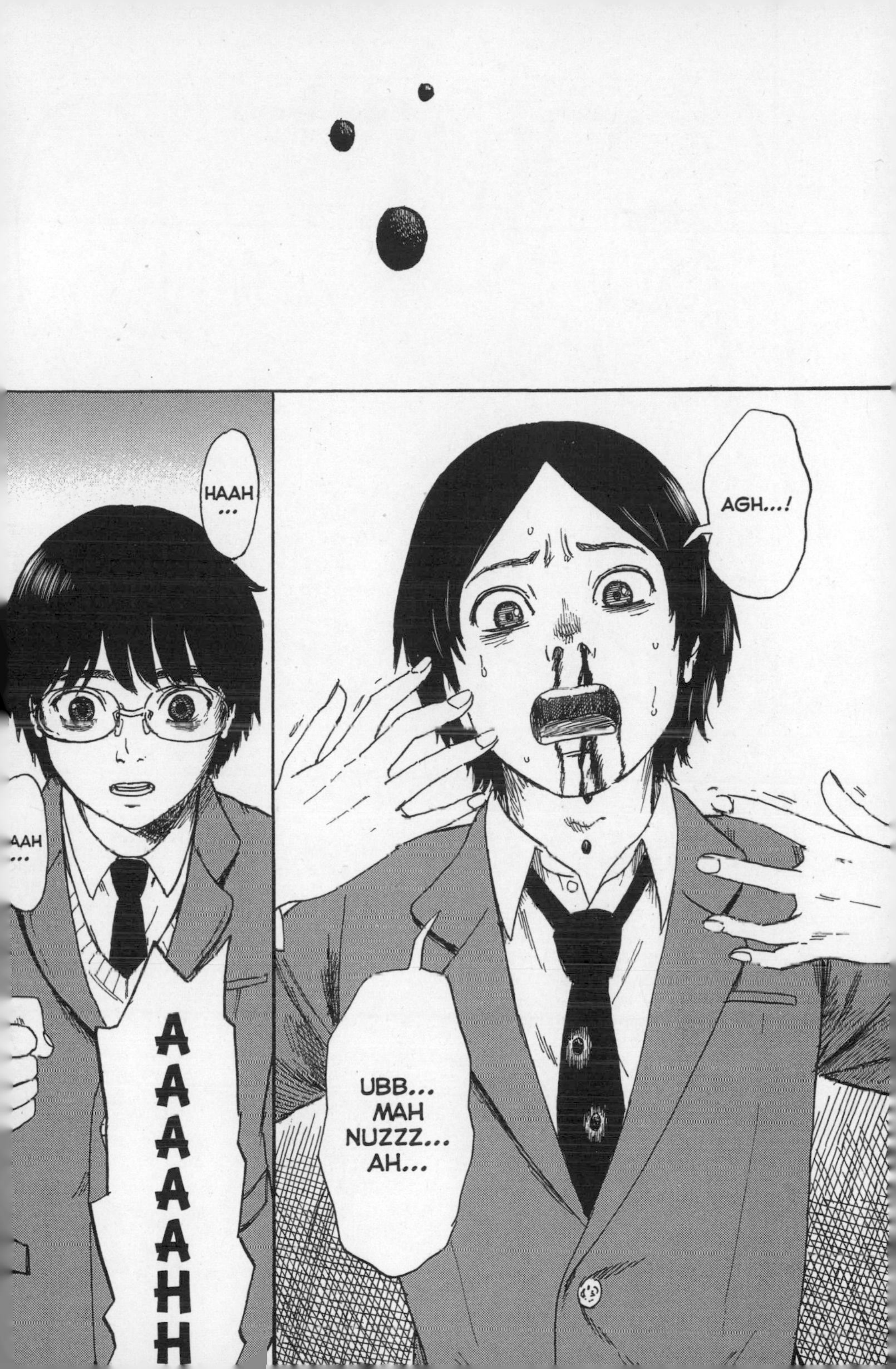
AGH...!
UBB... MAH NUZZZ... AH...
HAAH...
AAH...
AAAAAHH

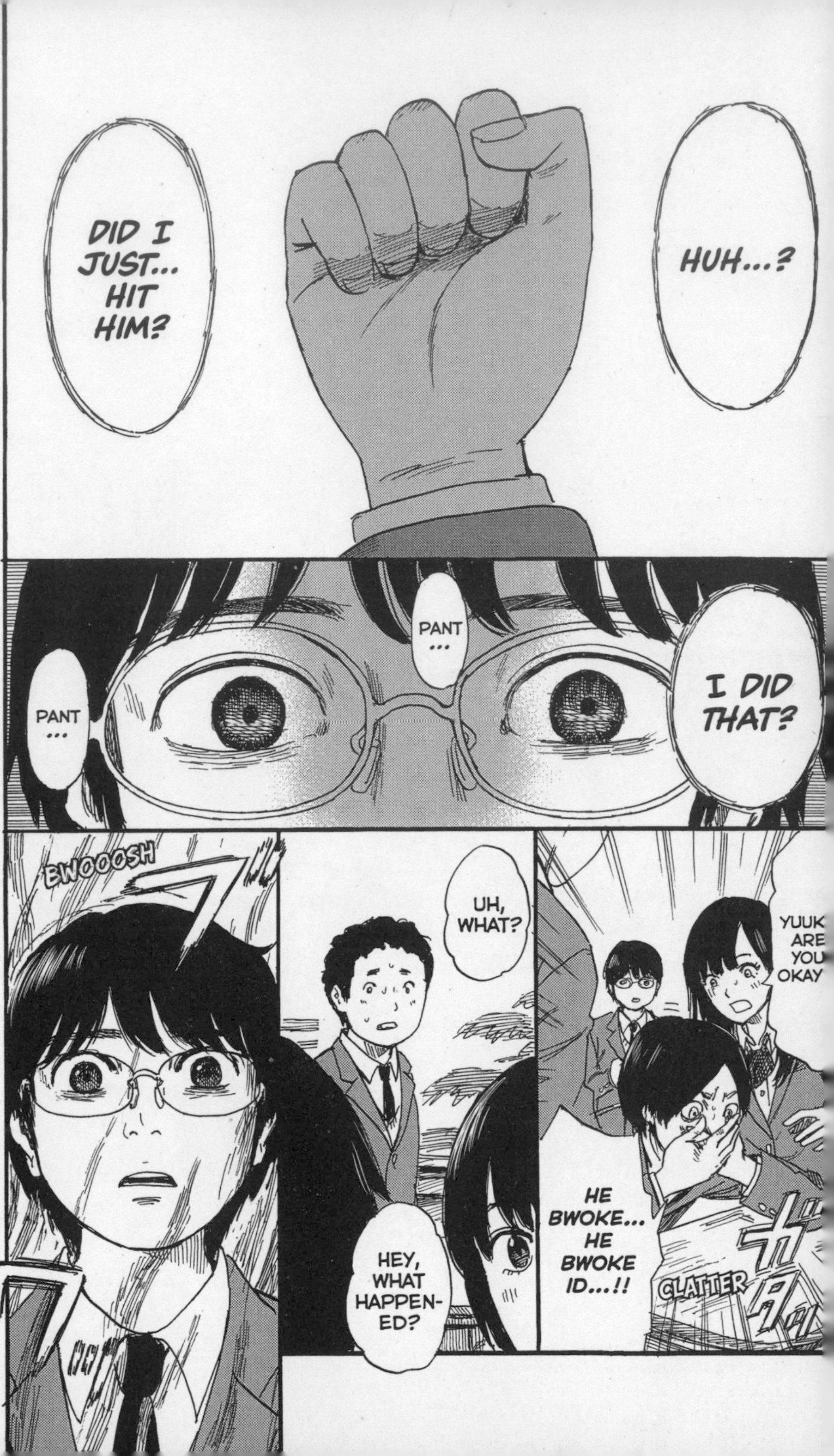
HUH...?
DID I JUST... HIT HIM?
I DID THAT?
PANT ...
PANT ...
YUUK ARE YOU OKAY
HE BWOKE... HE BWOKE ID...!!
CLATTER
UH, WHAT?
HEY, WHAT HAPPEN-ED?
BWOOOSH

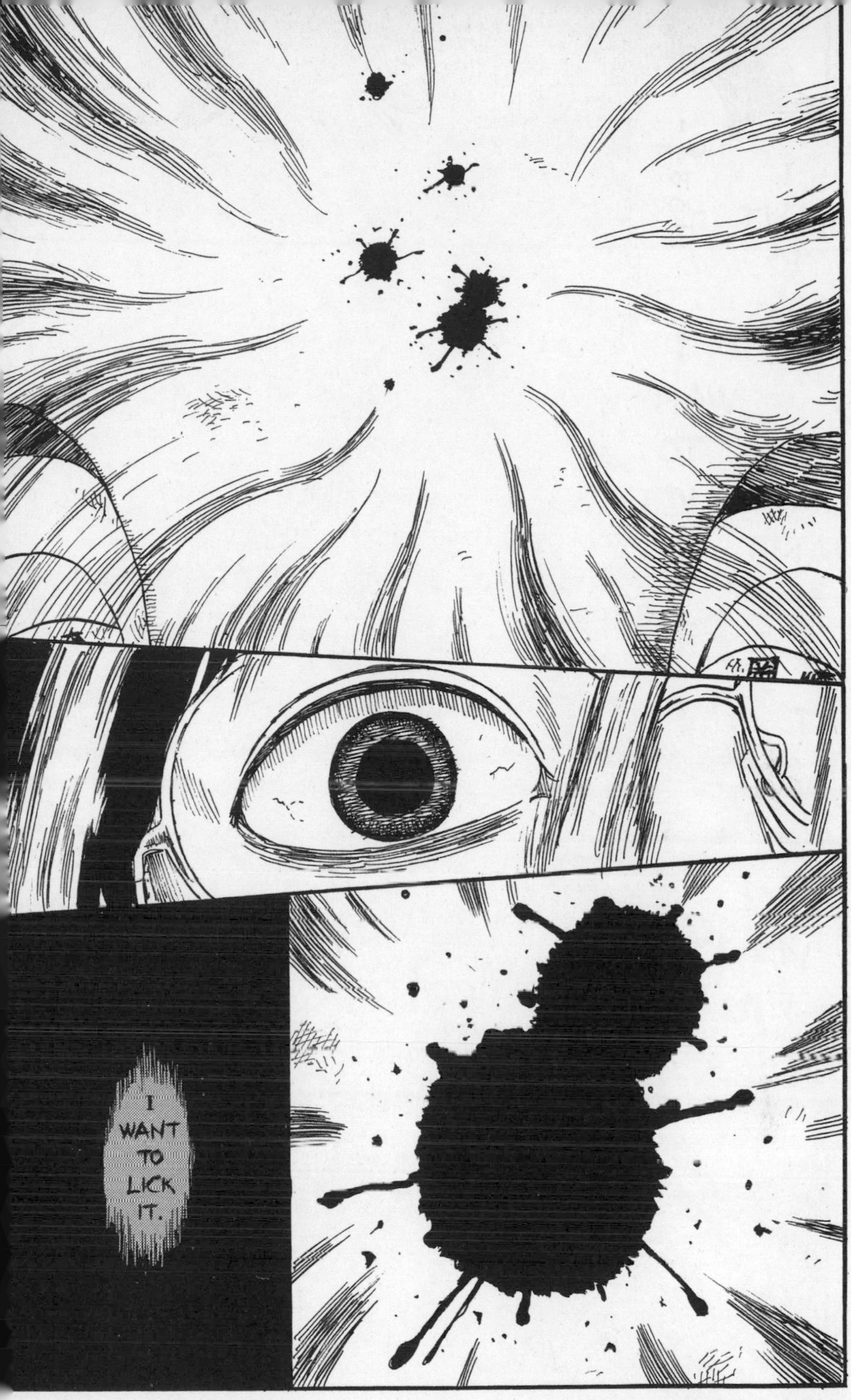
I WANT TO LICK IT.

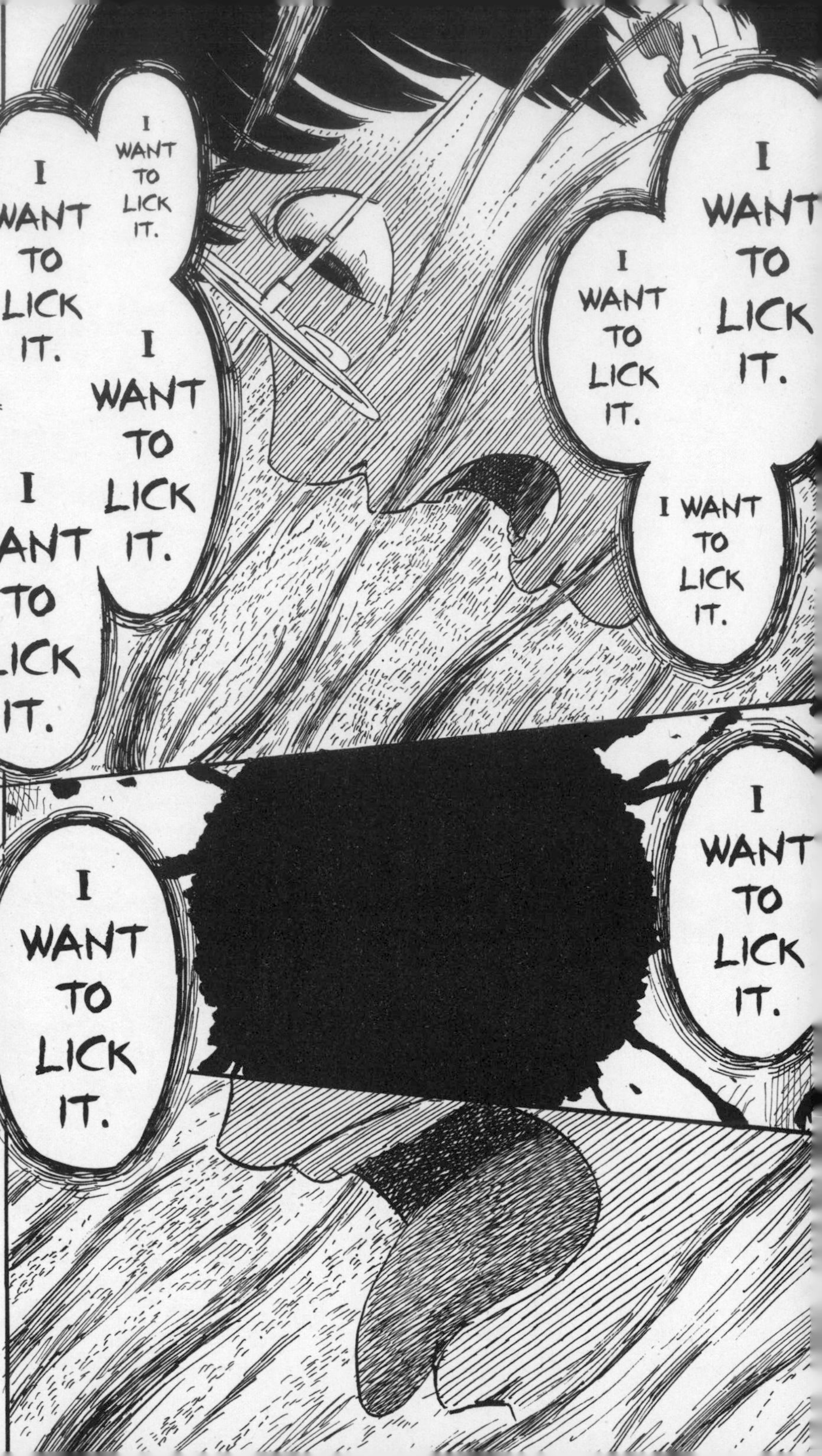
I WANT TO LICK IT.
I WANT TO LICK IT.
I WANT TO LICK IT.
I WANT TO LICK IT.
I WANT TO LICK IT.
I WANT TO LICK IT.
I WANT TO LICK IT.
I WANT TO LICK IT.
I WANT TO LICK IT.

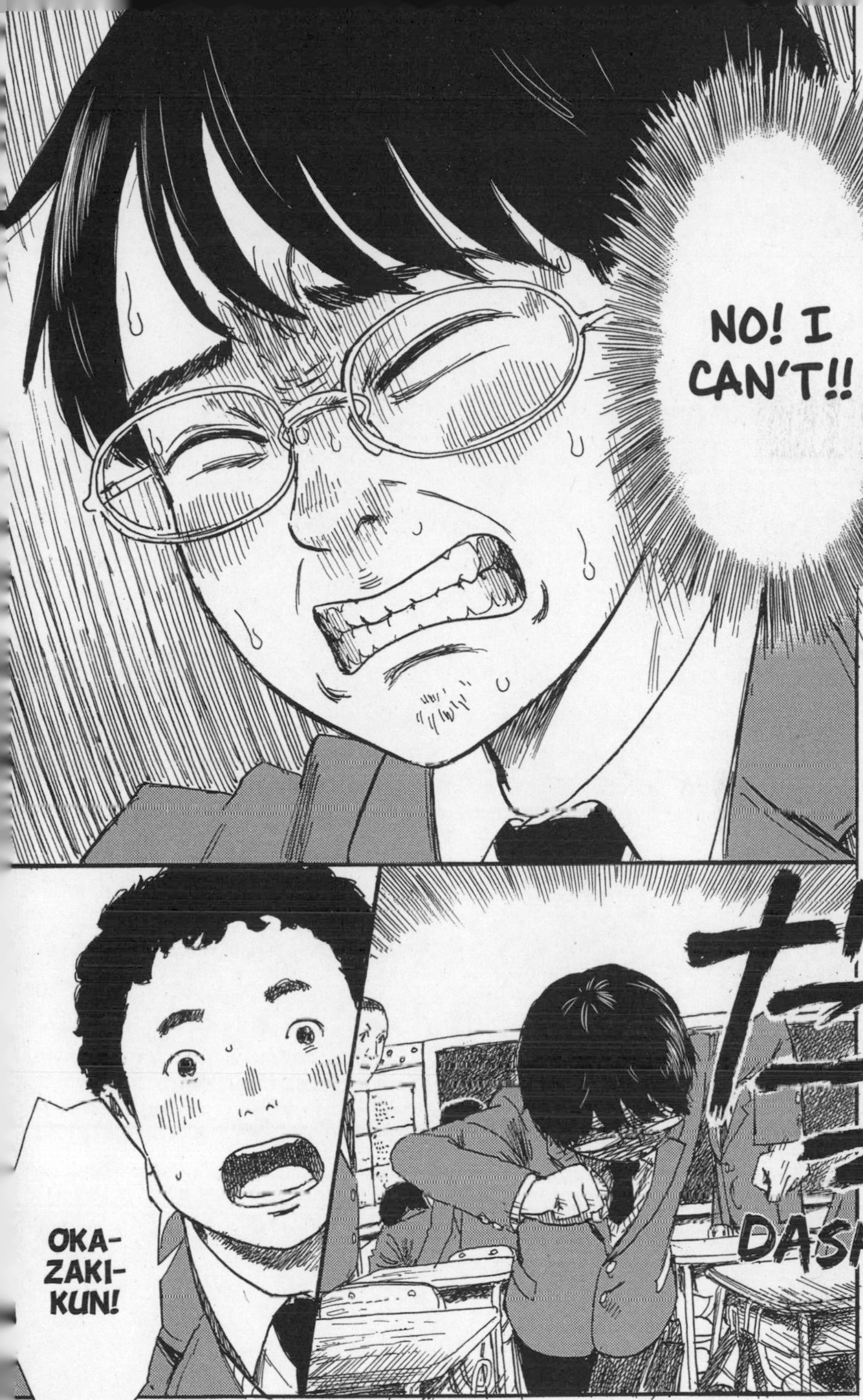
NO! I CAN'T!!
ダーッ
DASH
OKA-ZAKI-KUN!

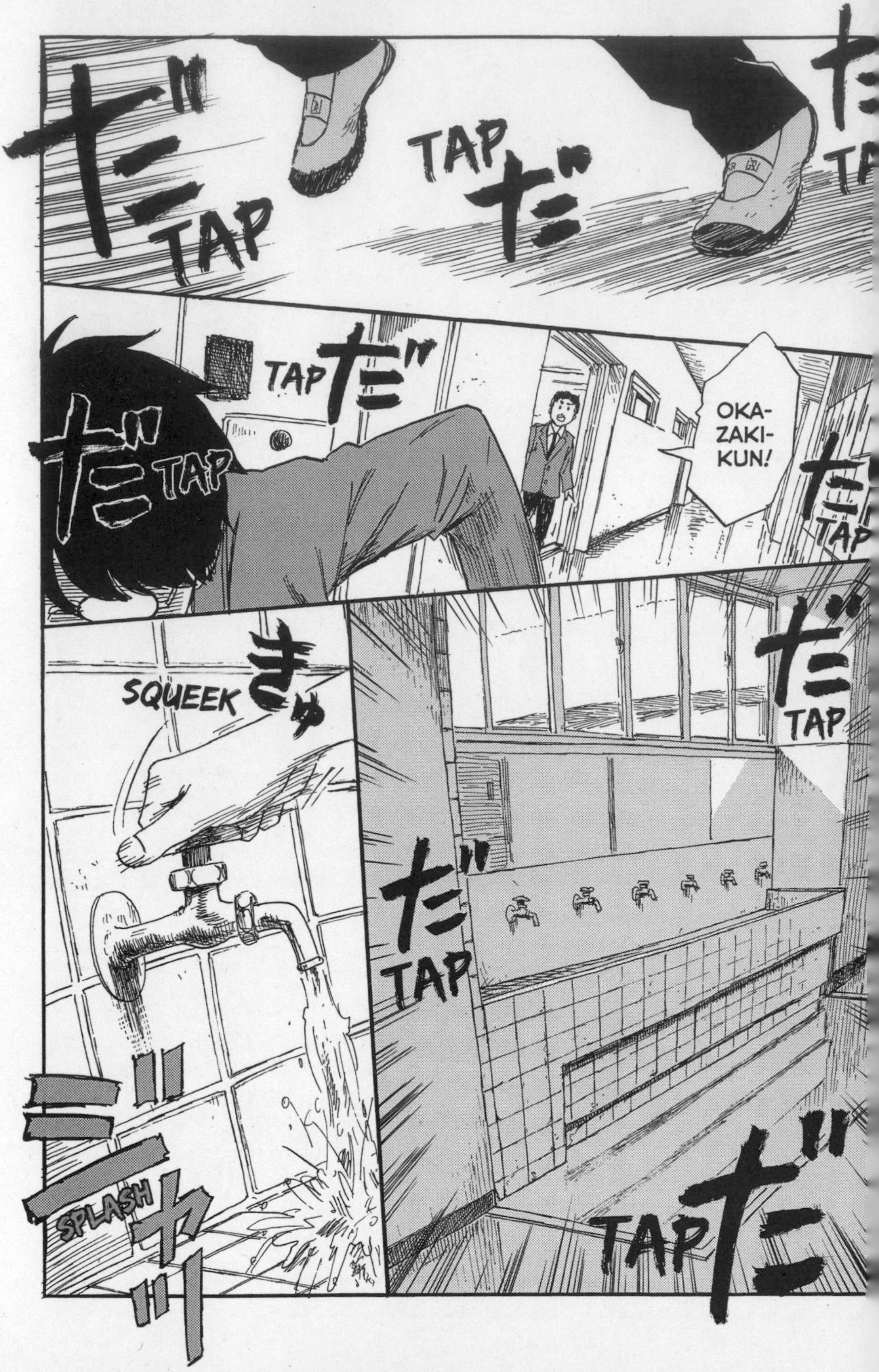

だ TAP
TAP だ
TAP
だ TAP
OKA-ZAKI-KUN!
だ TAP
TAP だ
だ TAP
だ TAP
だ TAP
TAP だ
SQUEEK きゅ
SPLASH

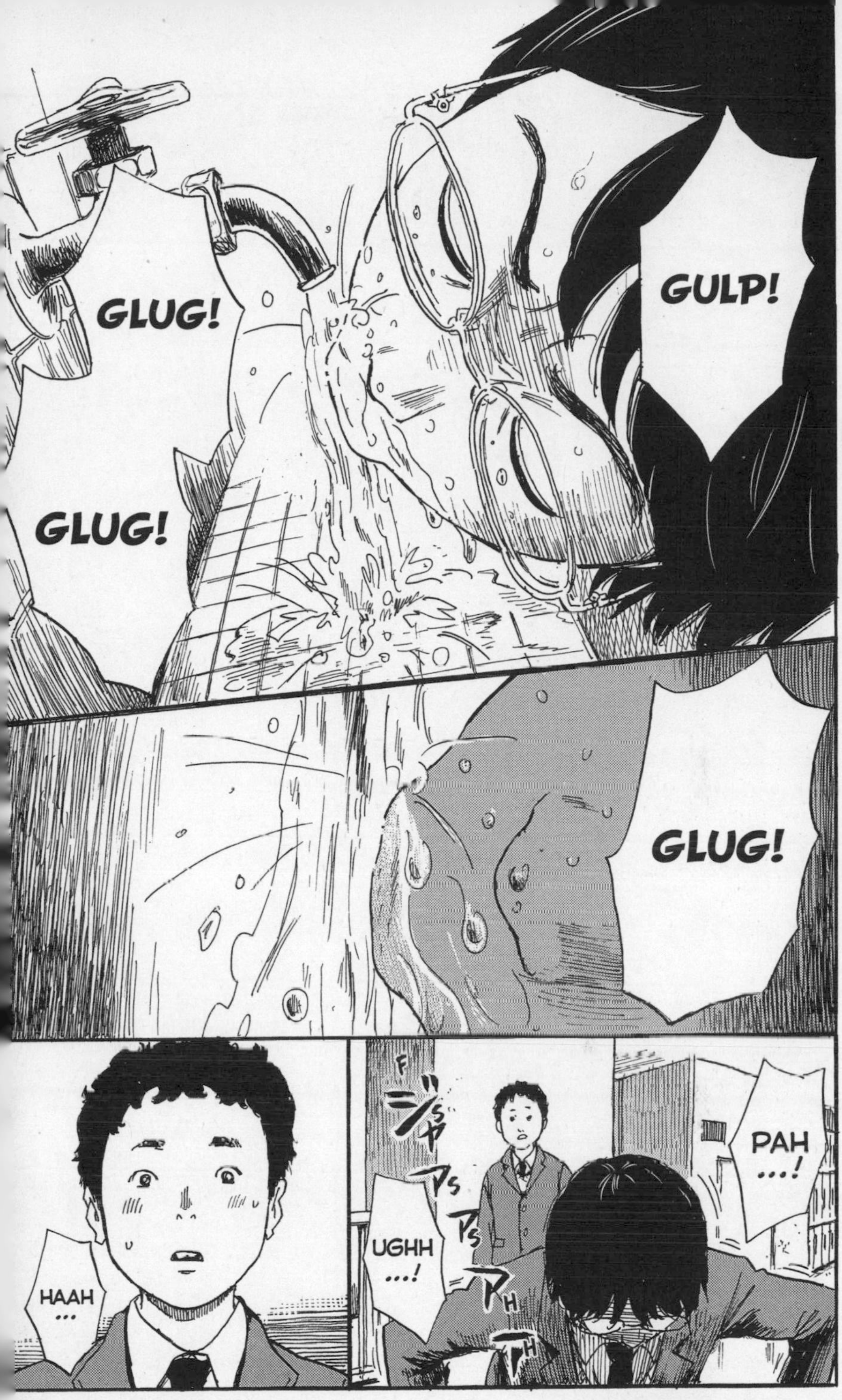
GULP!
GLUG!
GLUG!
GLUG!
PAH ...!
UGHH ...!
HAAH ...

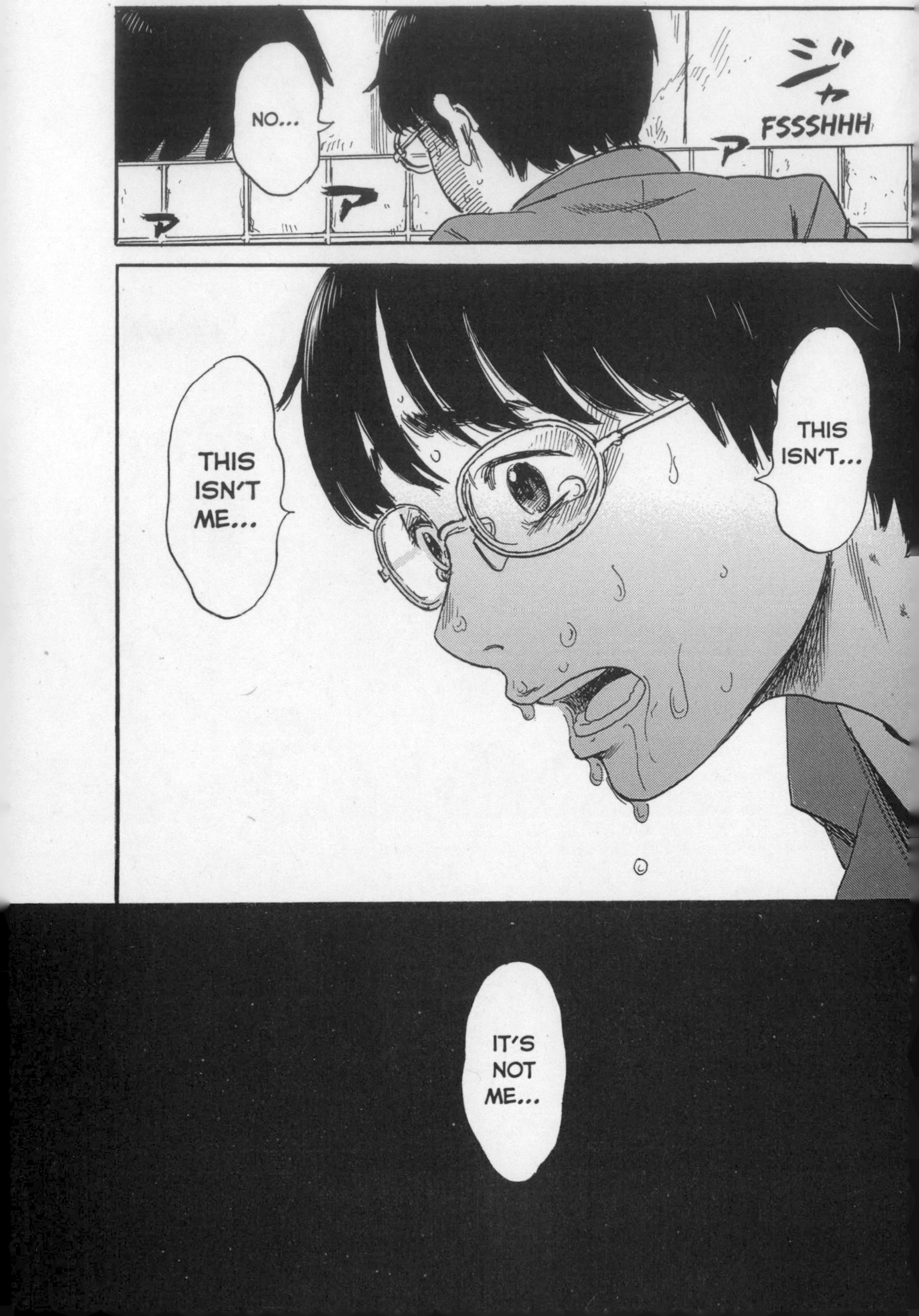

ジャ
FSSSHHH
ア
ア
ア
NO...
THIS ISN'T...
THIS ISN'T ME...
IT'S NOT ME...

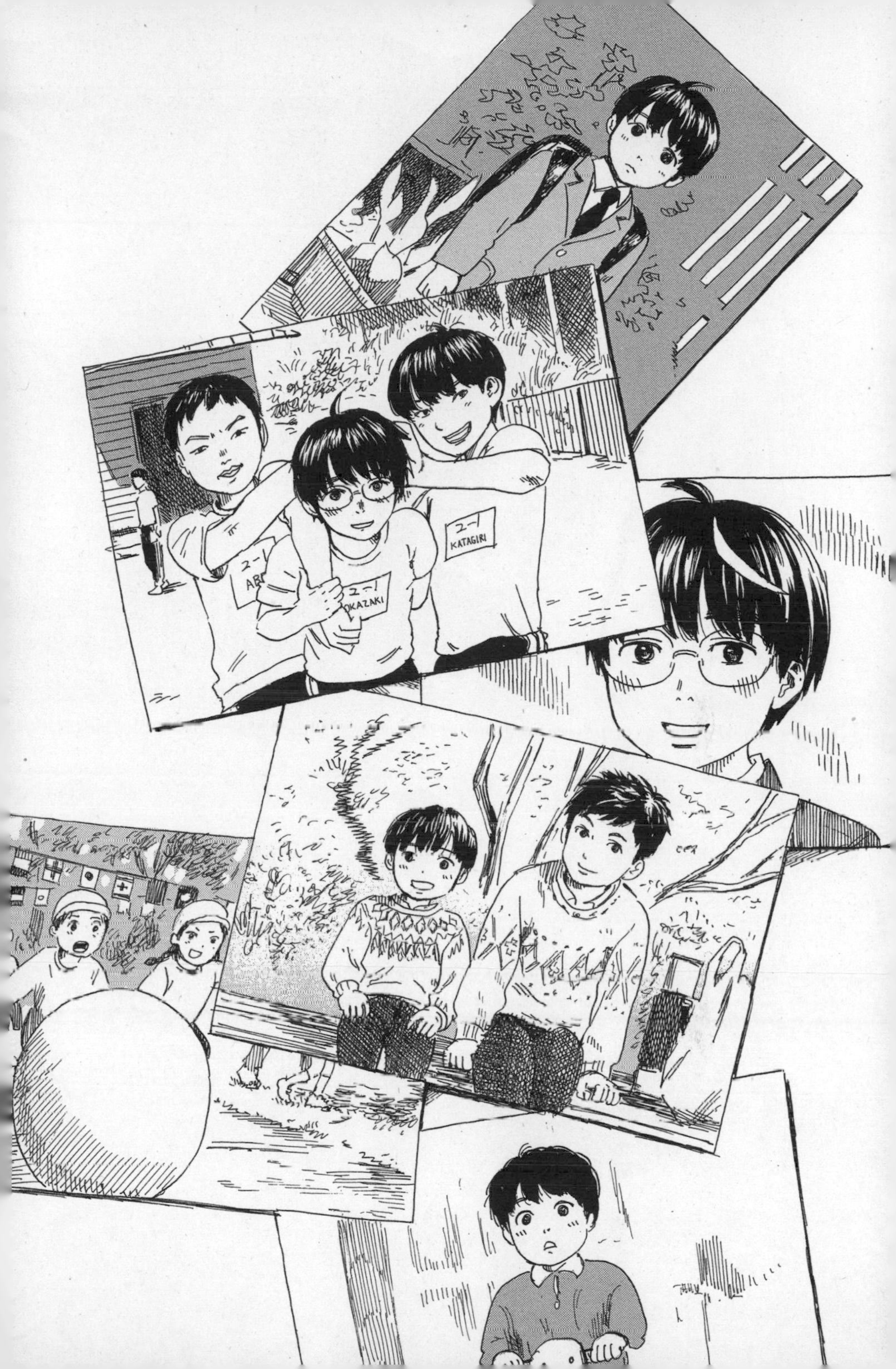
2-1 KATAGIRI
2-1 OKAZAKI
2-1 AB

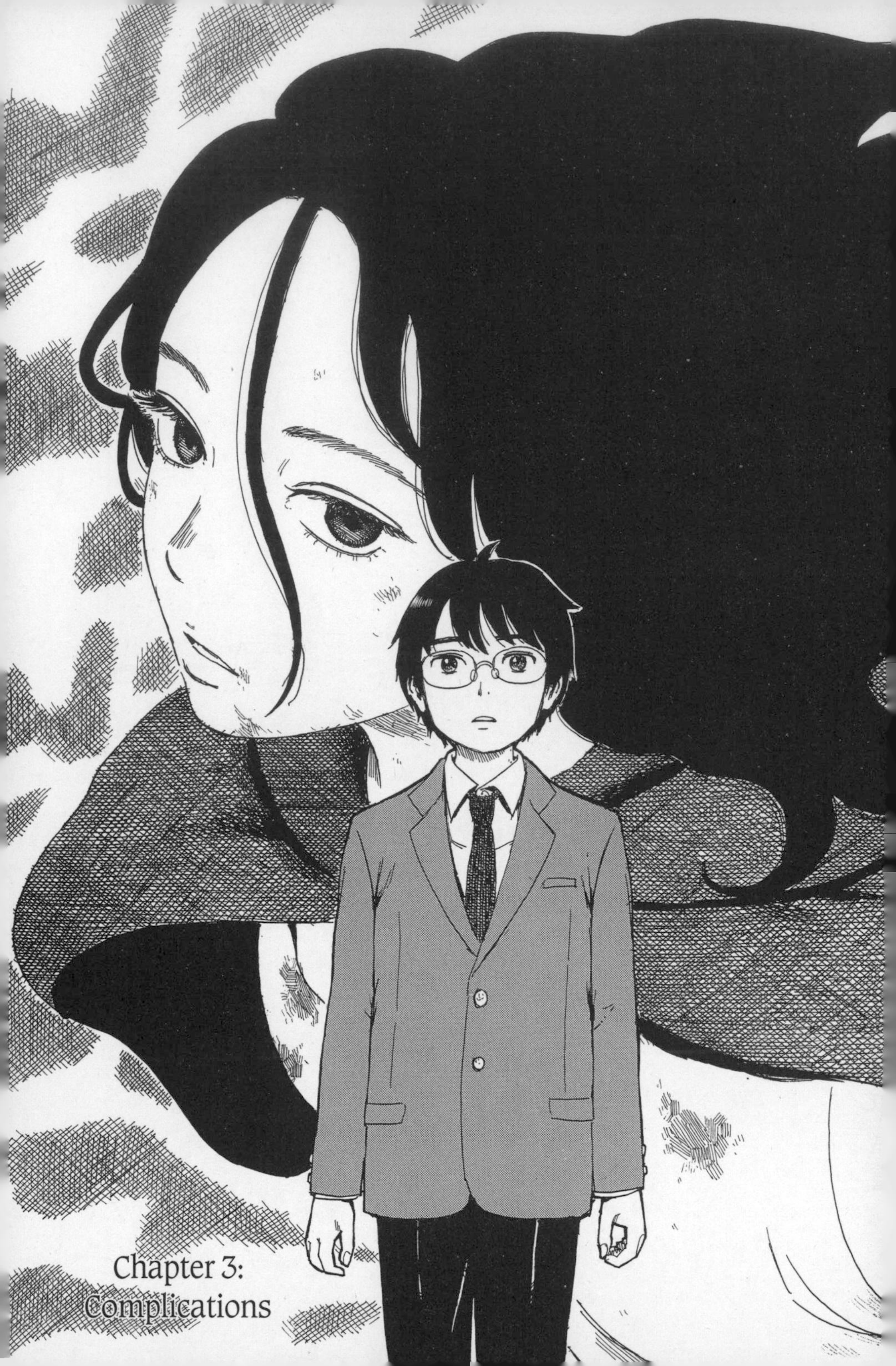

Chapter 3: Complications

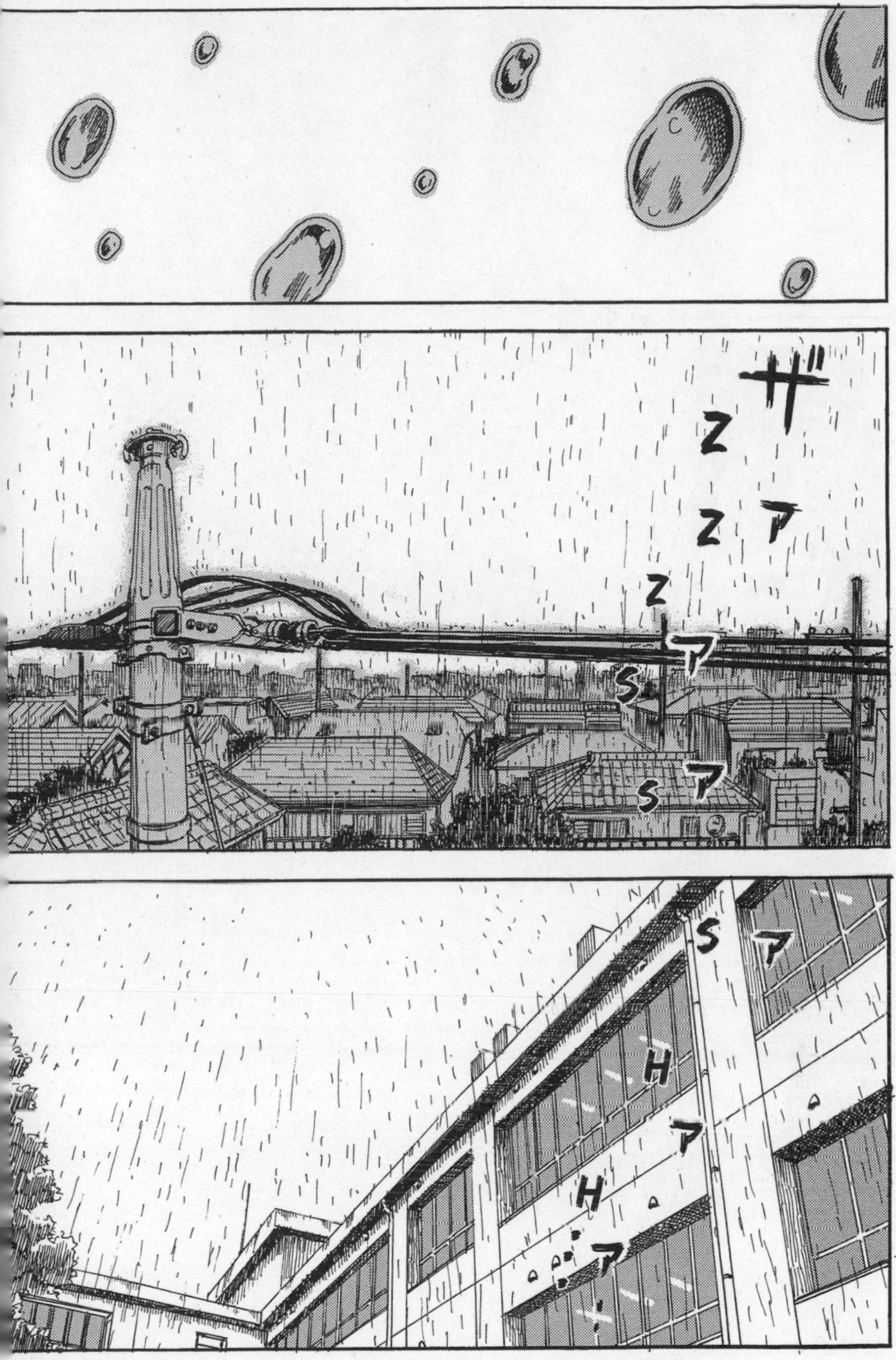
ザアアア
ZZZSS
アアア
SHH

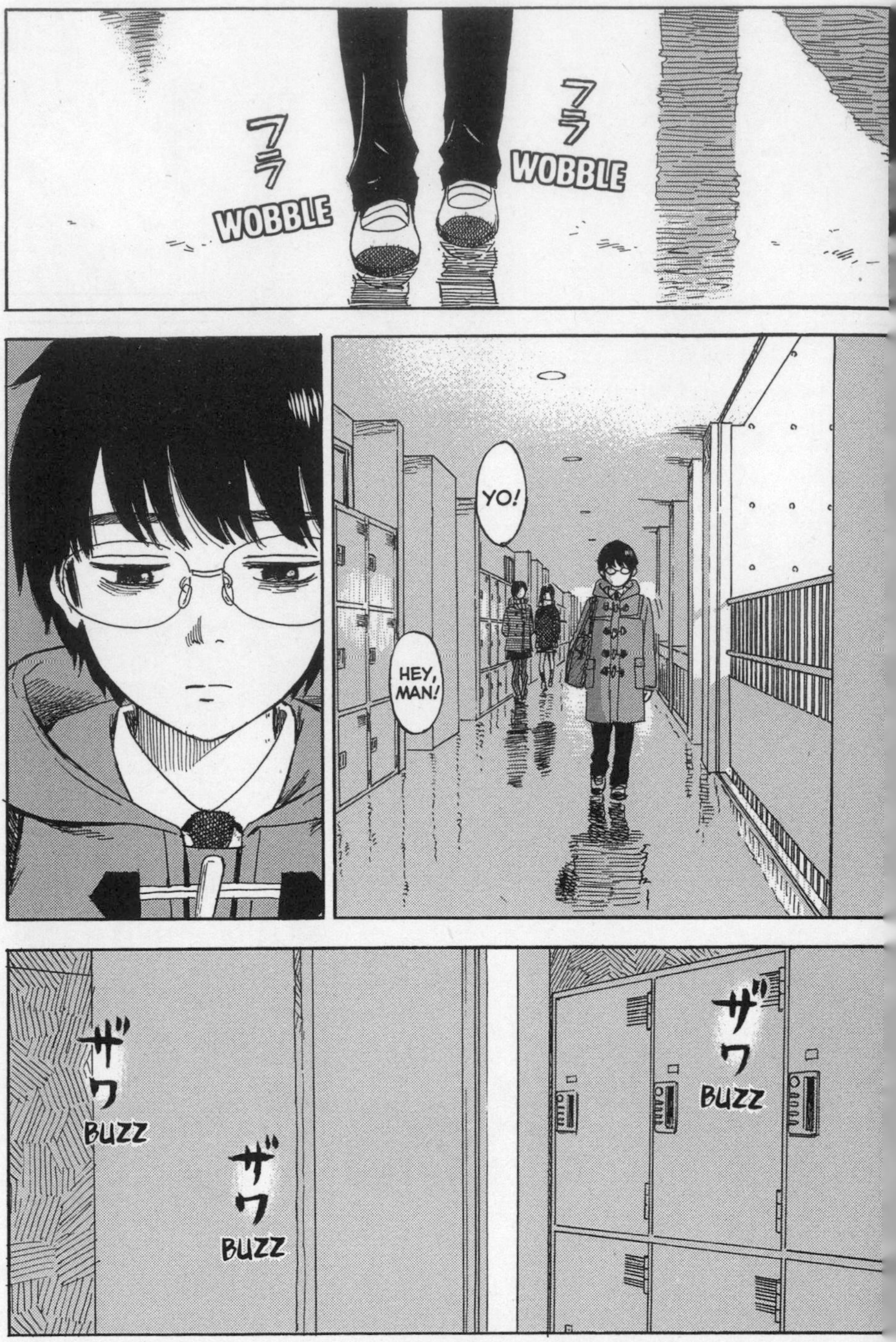

フラ
WOBBLE
フラ
WOBBLE
YO!
HEY, MAN!
ザワ
BUZZ
ザワ
BUZZ
ザワ
BUZZ

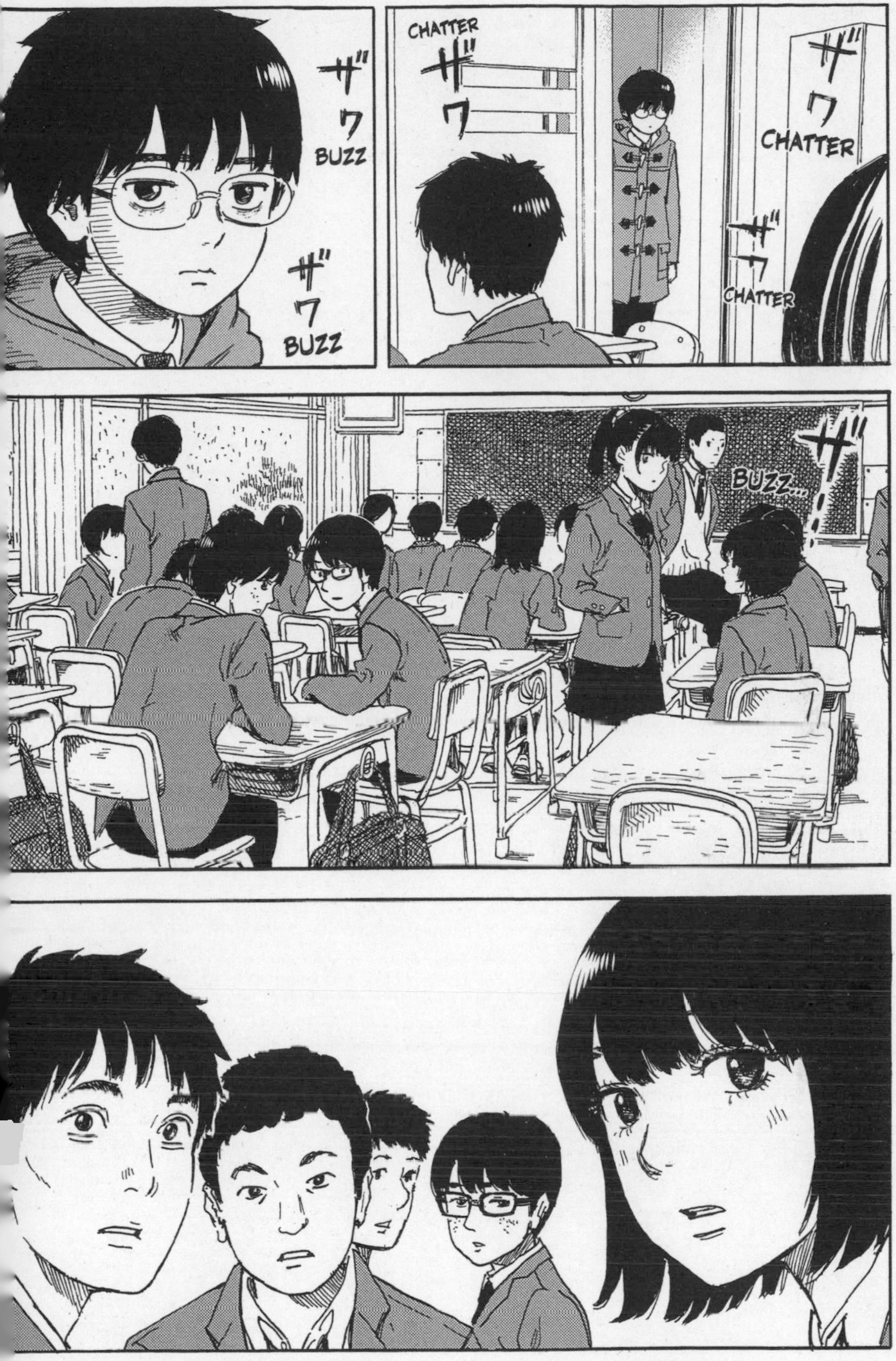
ザワ CHATTER
CHATTER ザワ
ザワ CHATTER
ザワ BUZZ
ザワ BUZZ
ザ BUZZ...

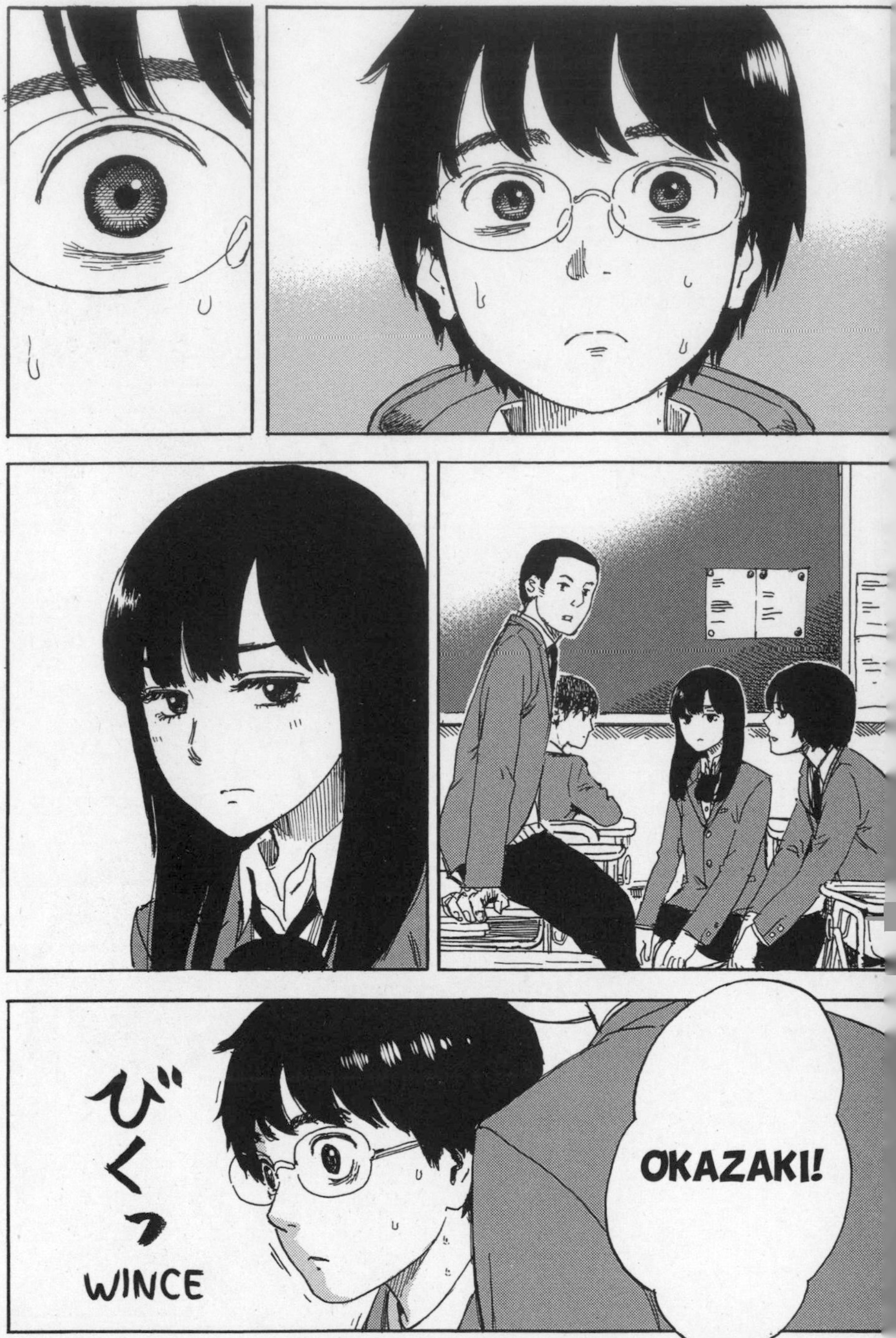
OKAZAKI!
びくっ
WINCE

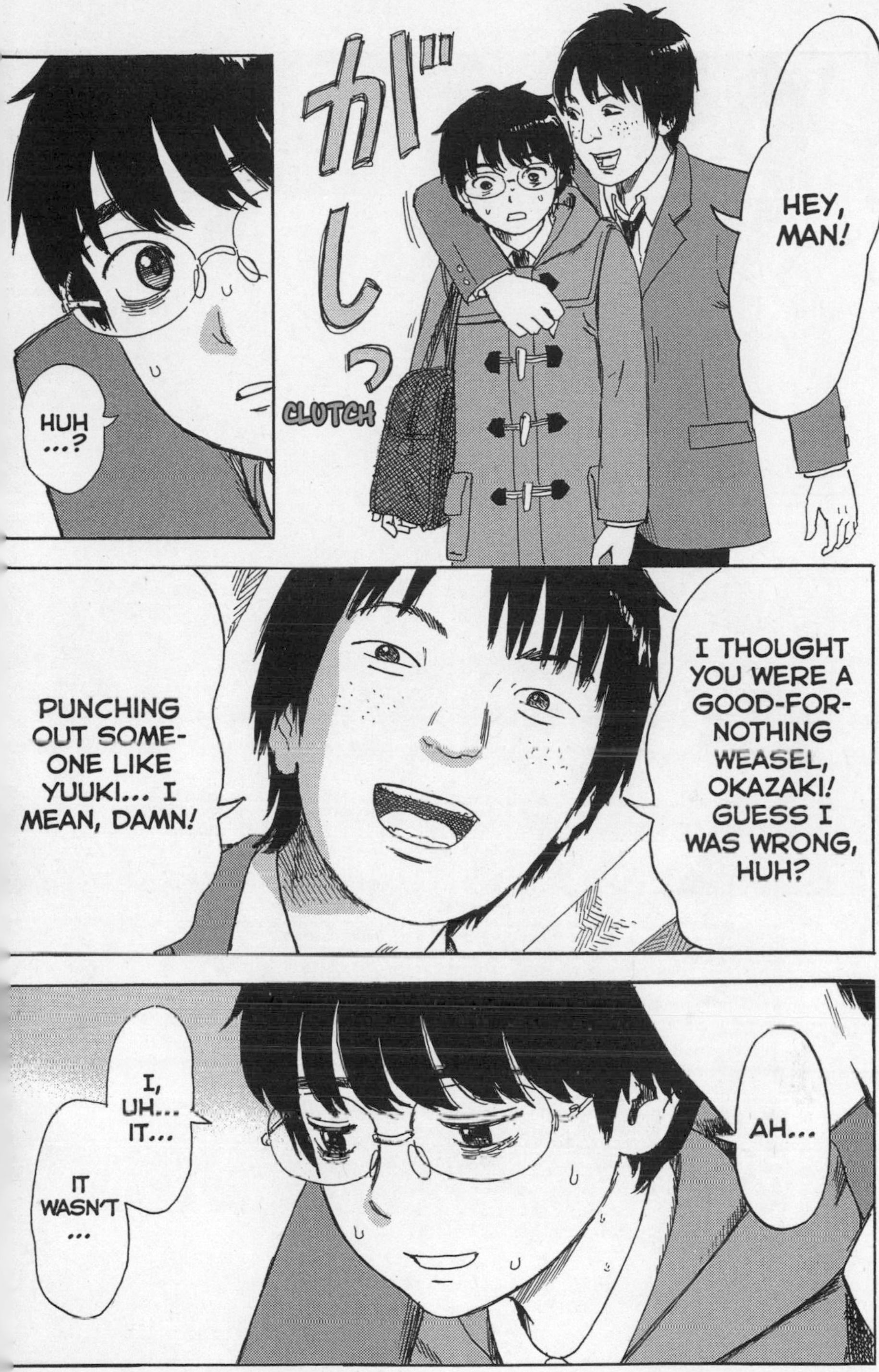
HEY, MAN!
がしっ
CLUTCH
HUH ...?
I THOUGHT YOU WERE A GOOD-FOR-NOTHING WEASEL, OKAZAKI! GUESS I WAS WRONG, HUH?
PUNCHING OUT SOME-ONE LIKE YUUKI... I MEAN, DAMN!
AH...
I, UH... IT...
IT WASN'T ...

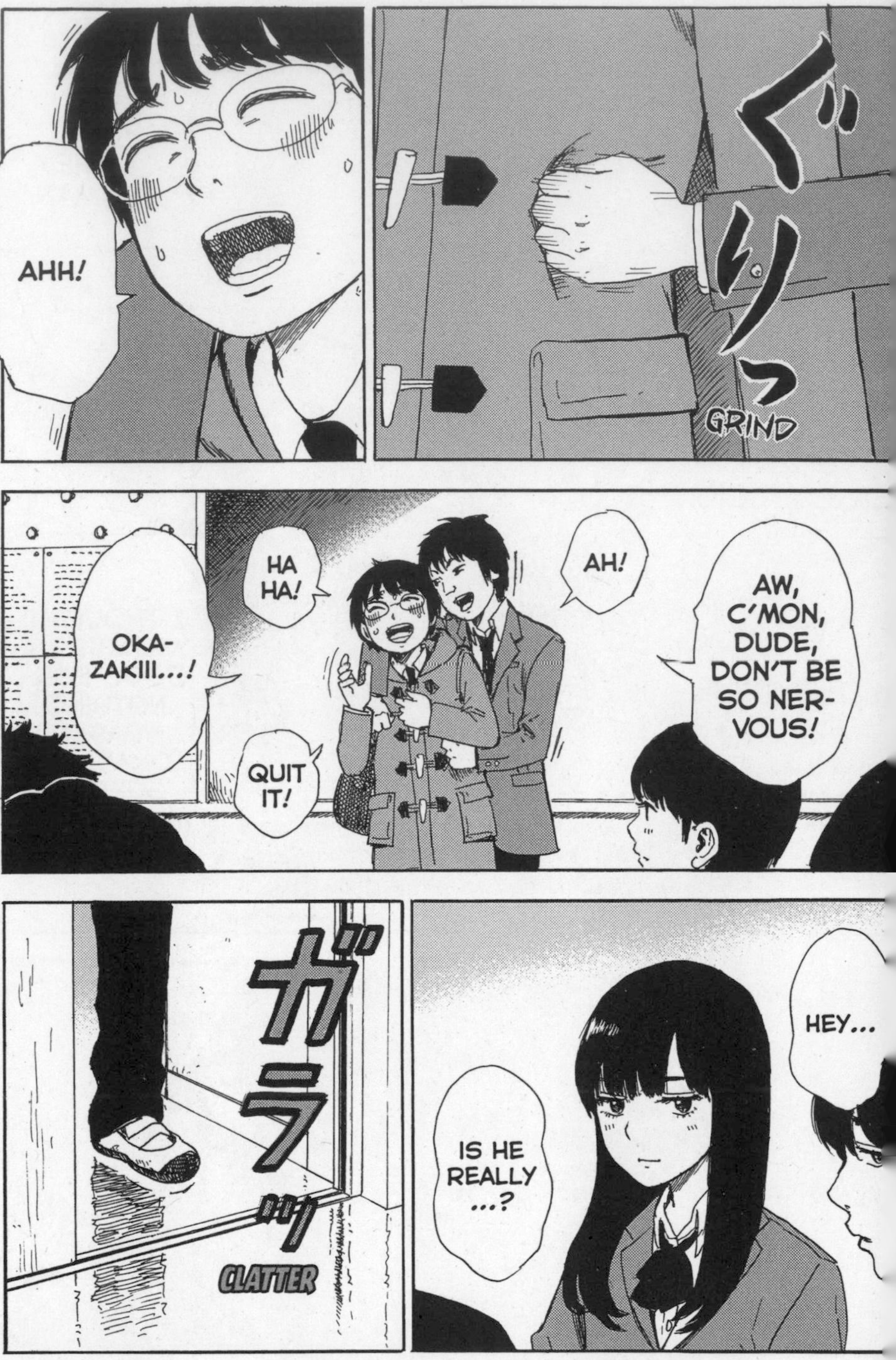
ぐりっ
GRIND
AHH!
AW, C'MON, DUDE, DON'T BE SO NER-VOUS!
AH!
HA HA!
OKA-ZAKIII...!
QUIT IT!
HEY...
IS HE REALLY ...?
ガラッ
CLATTER

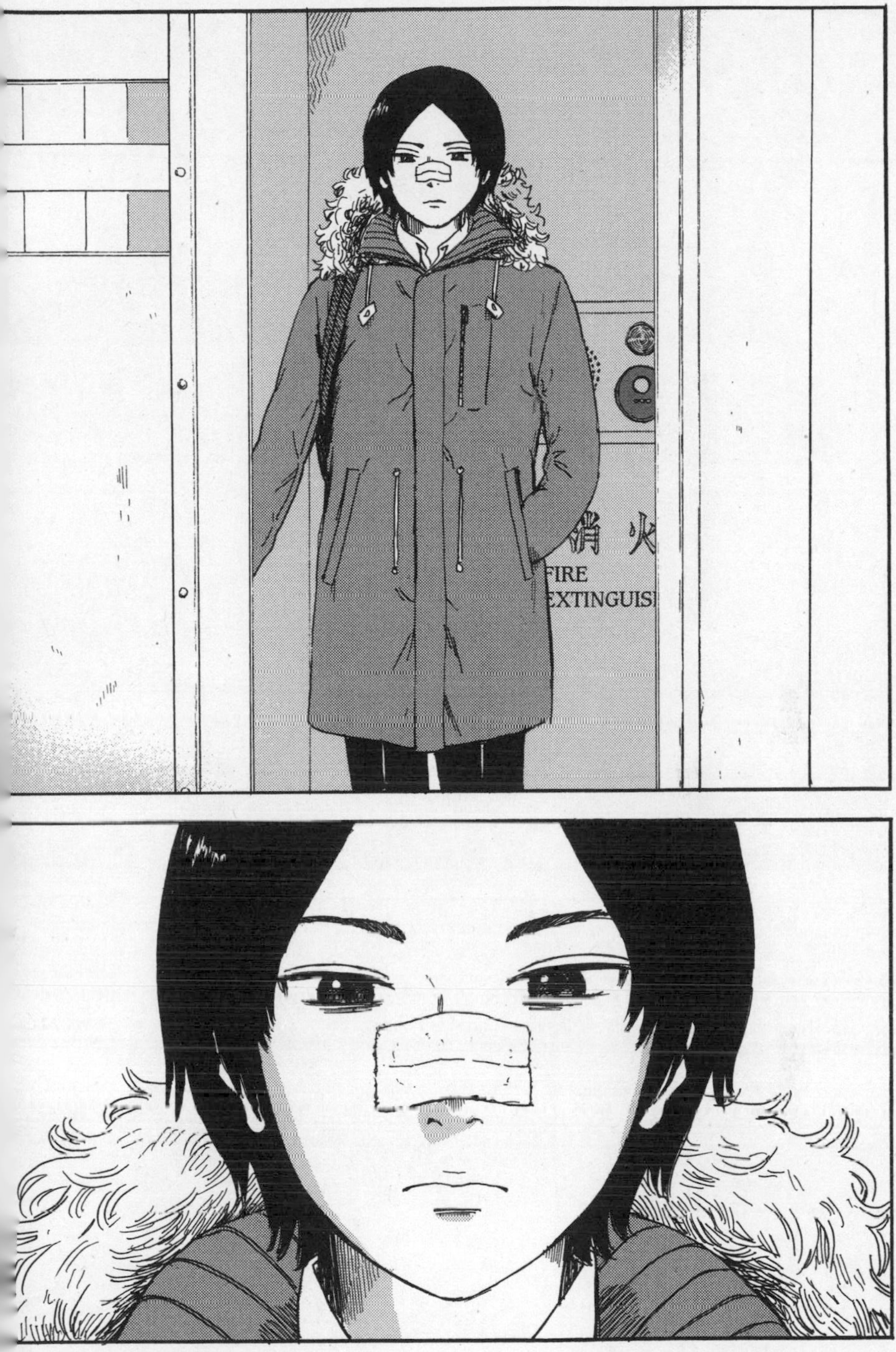
消 火
FIRE
EXTINGUIS

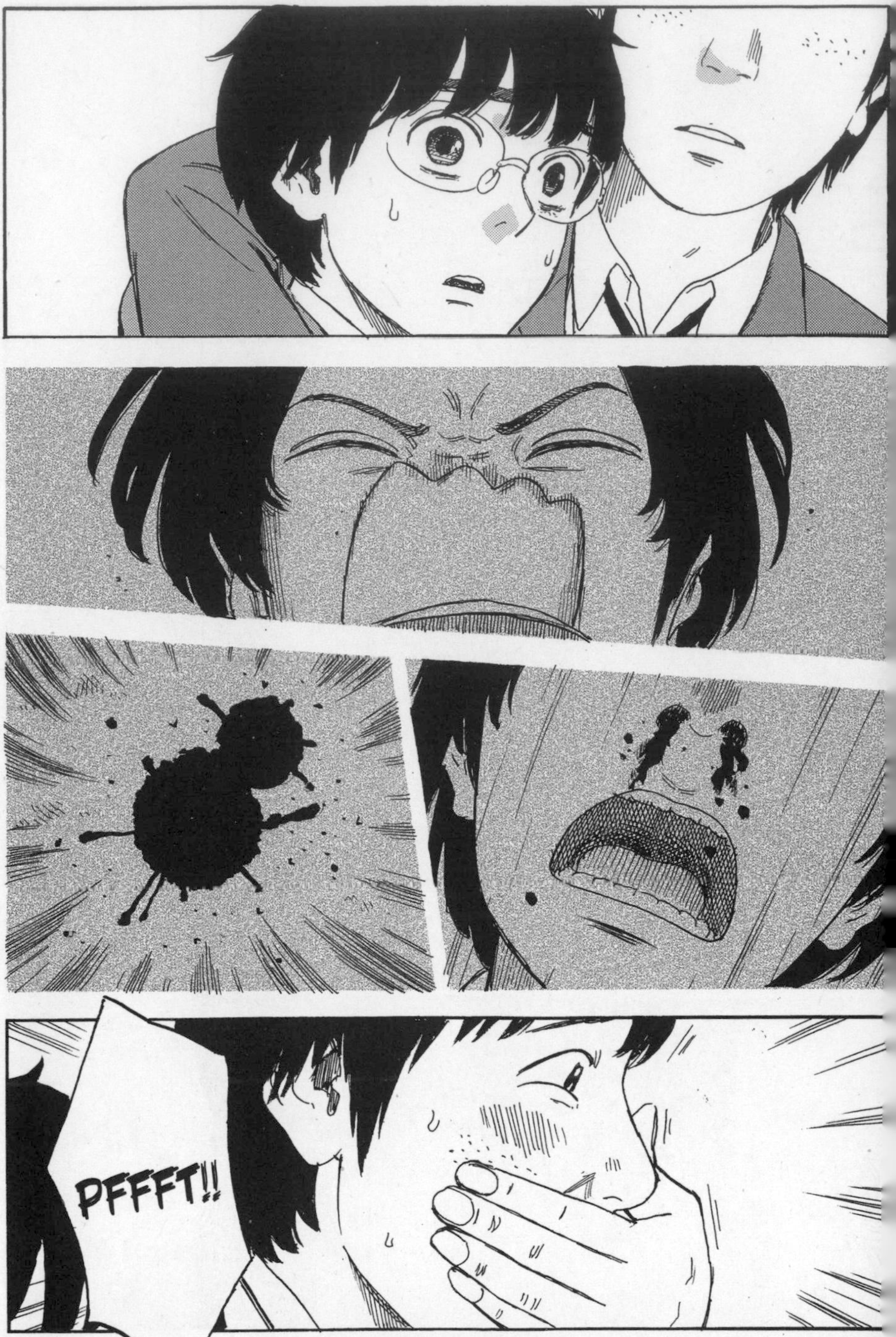
PFFFT!!

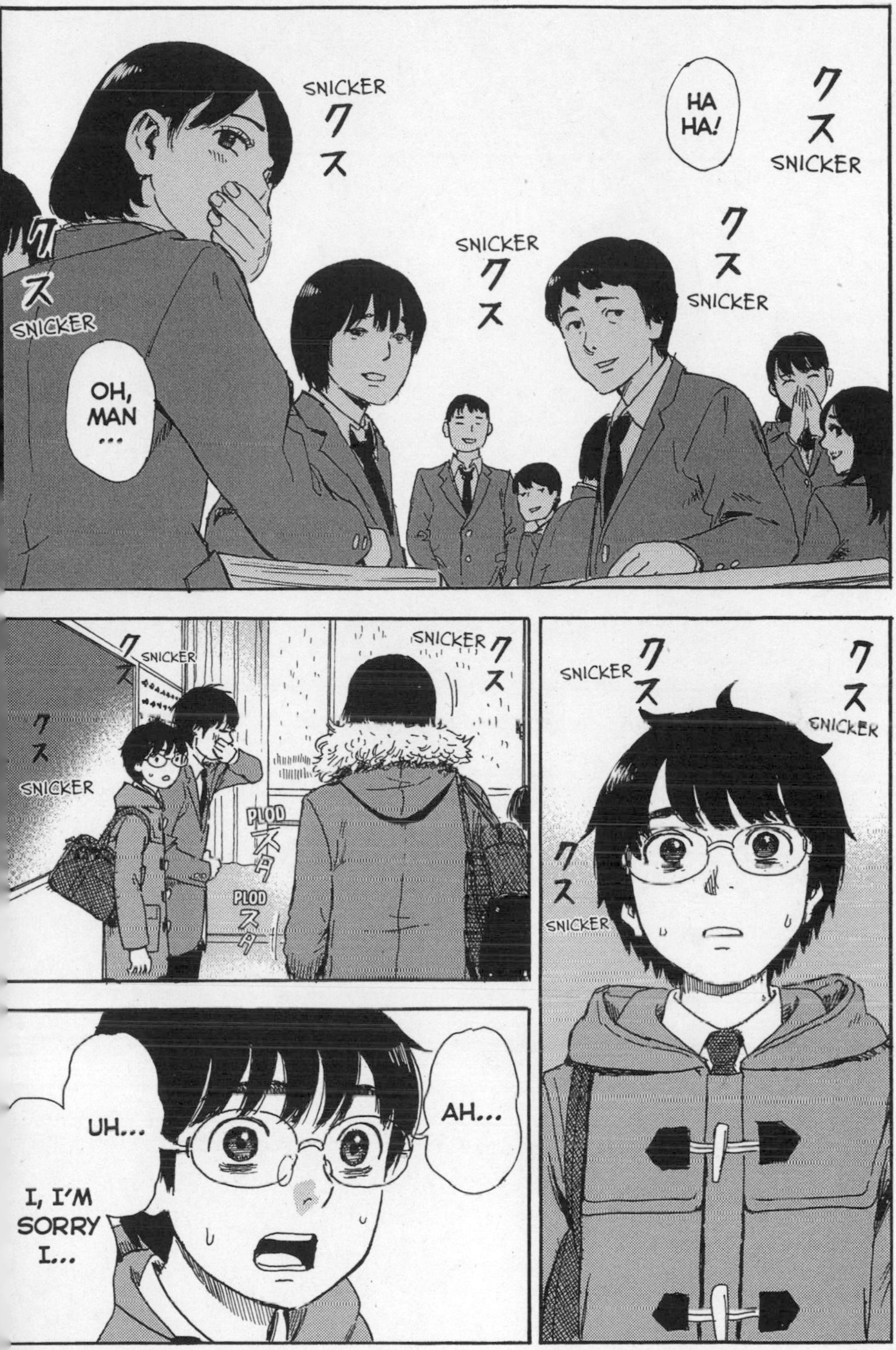
クス
SNICKER
HA HA!
クス
SNICKER
SNICKER
クス
SNICKER
クス
クス
SNICKER
OH, MAN...
クス
SNICKER
SNICKER
クス
クス
SNICKER
SNICKER
クス
PLOD
スタ
PLOD
スタ
クス
SNICKER
クス
SNICKER
AH...
UH...
I, I'M SORRY I...

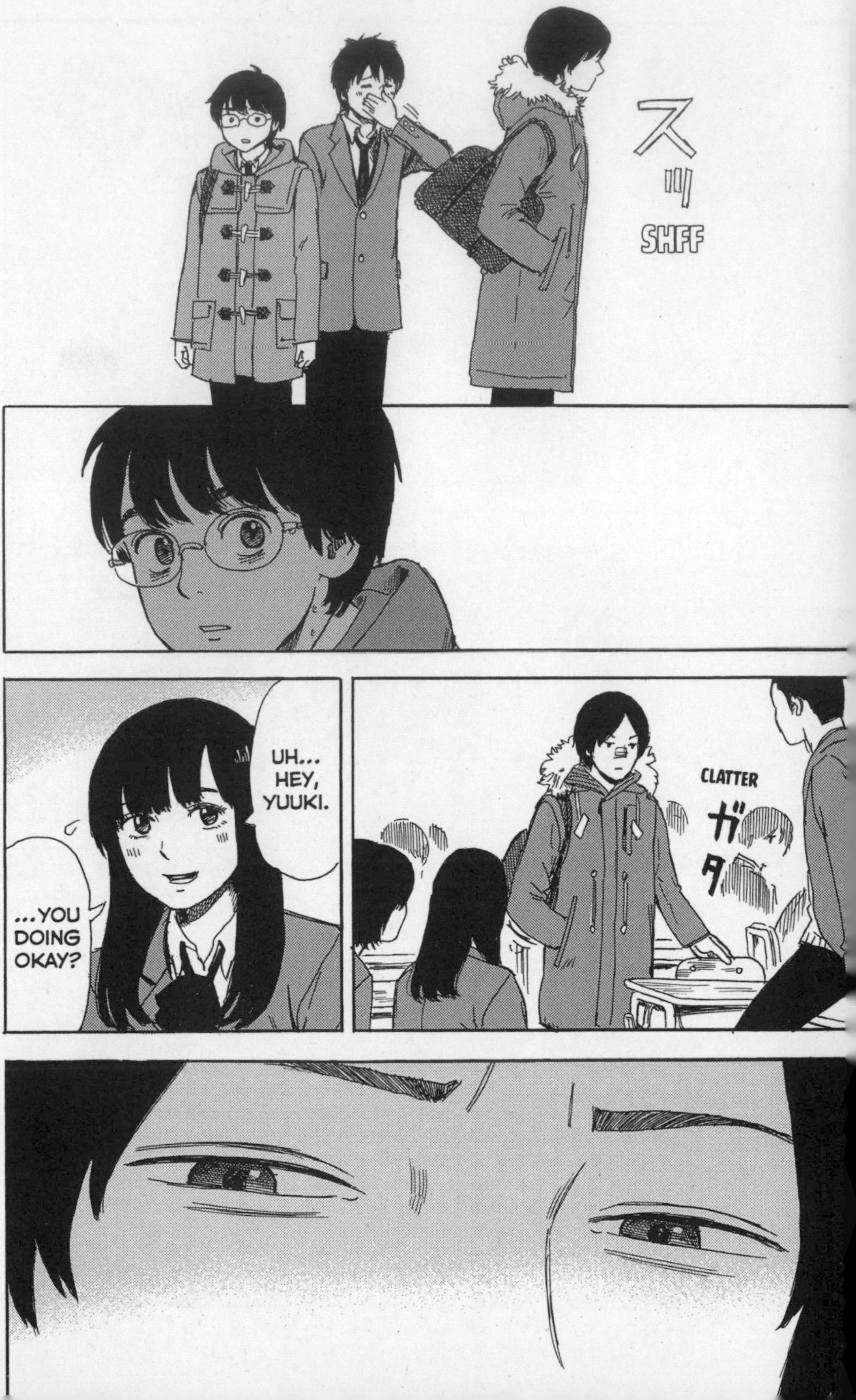
スッ
SHFF
CLATTER
ガタ
UH... HEY, YUUKI.
...YOU DOING OKAY?

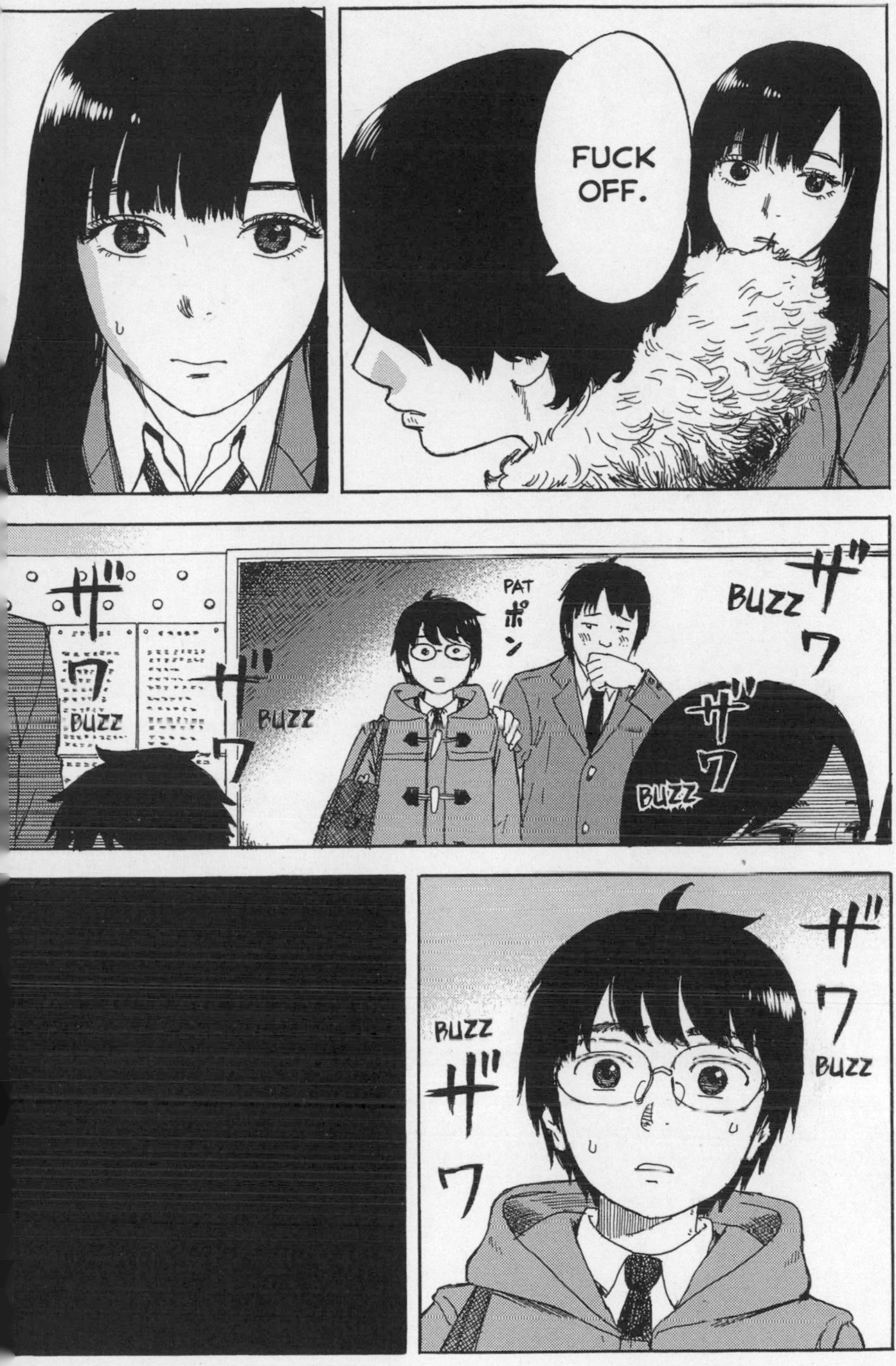
FUCK OFF.
ザワ
BUZZ
PAT
ポン
ザワ
BUZZ
ザワ
BUZZ
ザワ
BUZZ
ザワ
BUZZ
BUZZ
ザワ

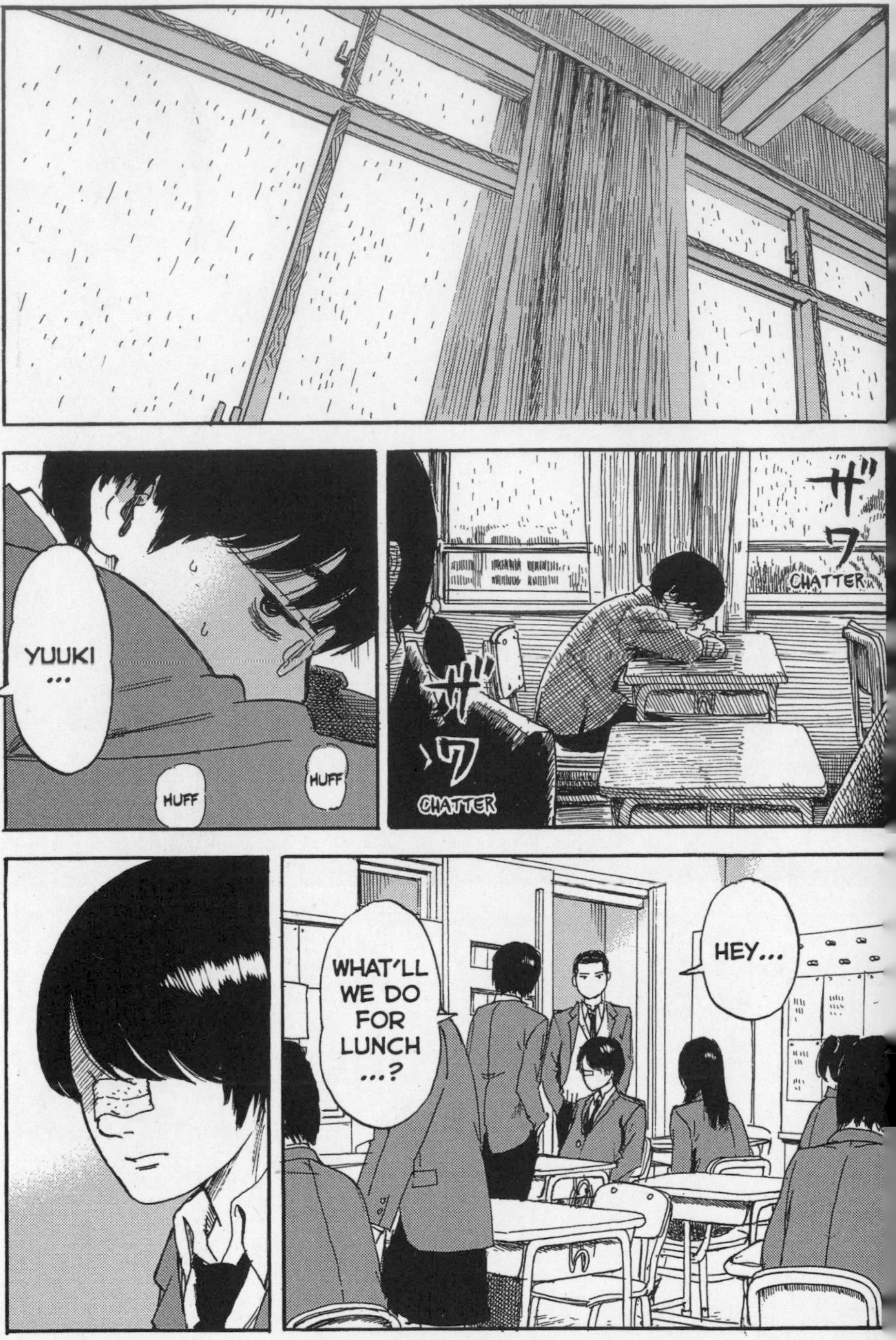
ザワ
CHATTER
ザワ
CHATTER
YUUKI ...
HUFF
HUFF
HEY...
WHAT'LL WE DO FOR LUNCH ...?

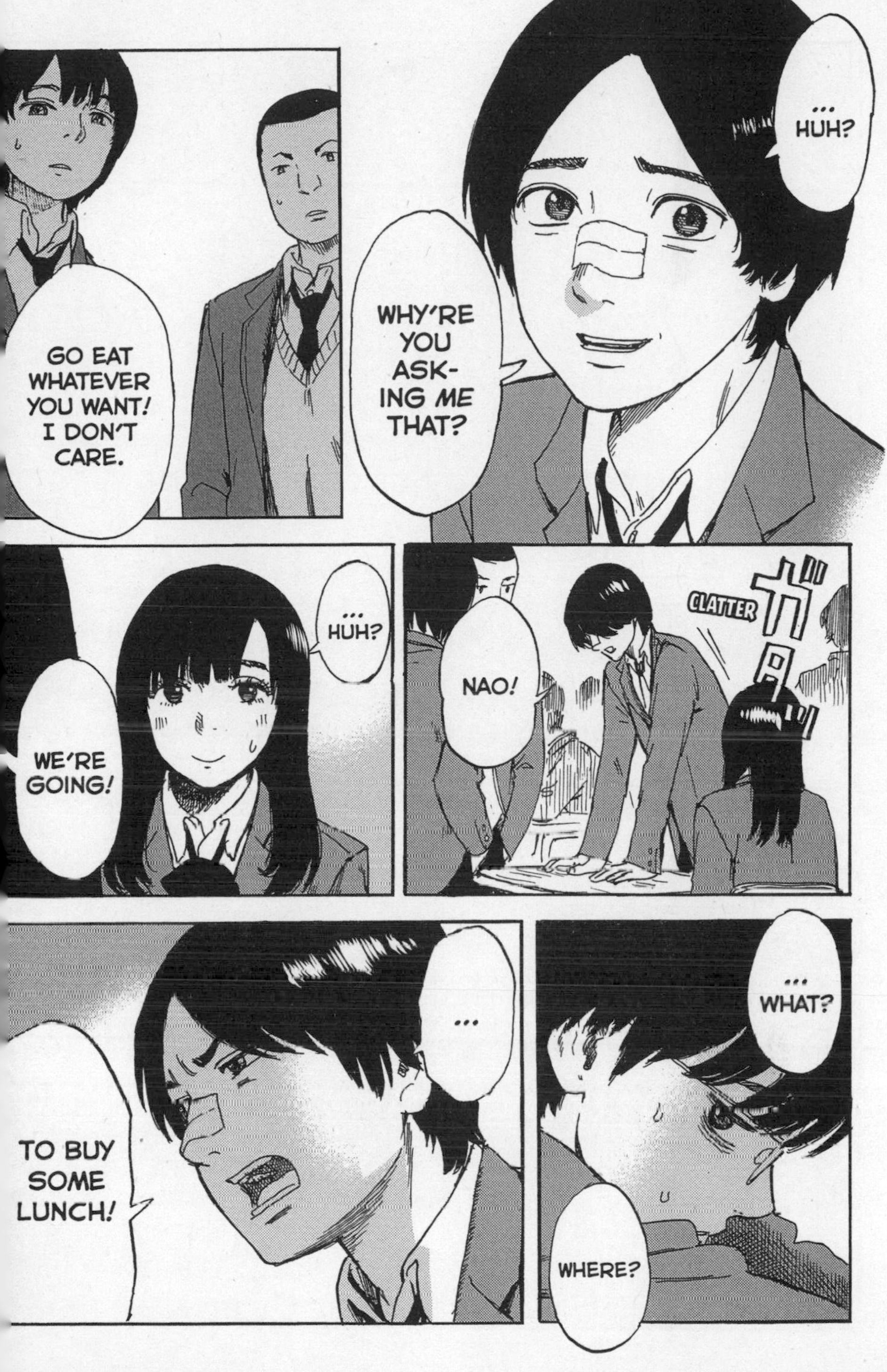
... HUH?
WHY'RE YOU ASK-ING *ME* THAT?
GO EAT WHATEVER YOU WANT! I DON'T CARE.
CLATTER
ガタッ
NAO!
... HUH?
WE'RE GOING!
... WHAT?
WHERE?
...
TO BUY SOME LUNCH!

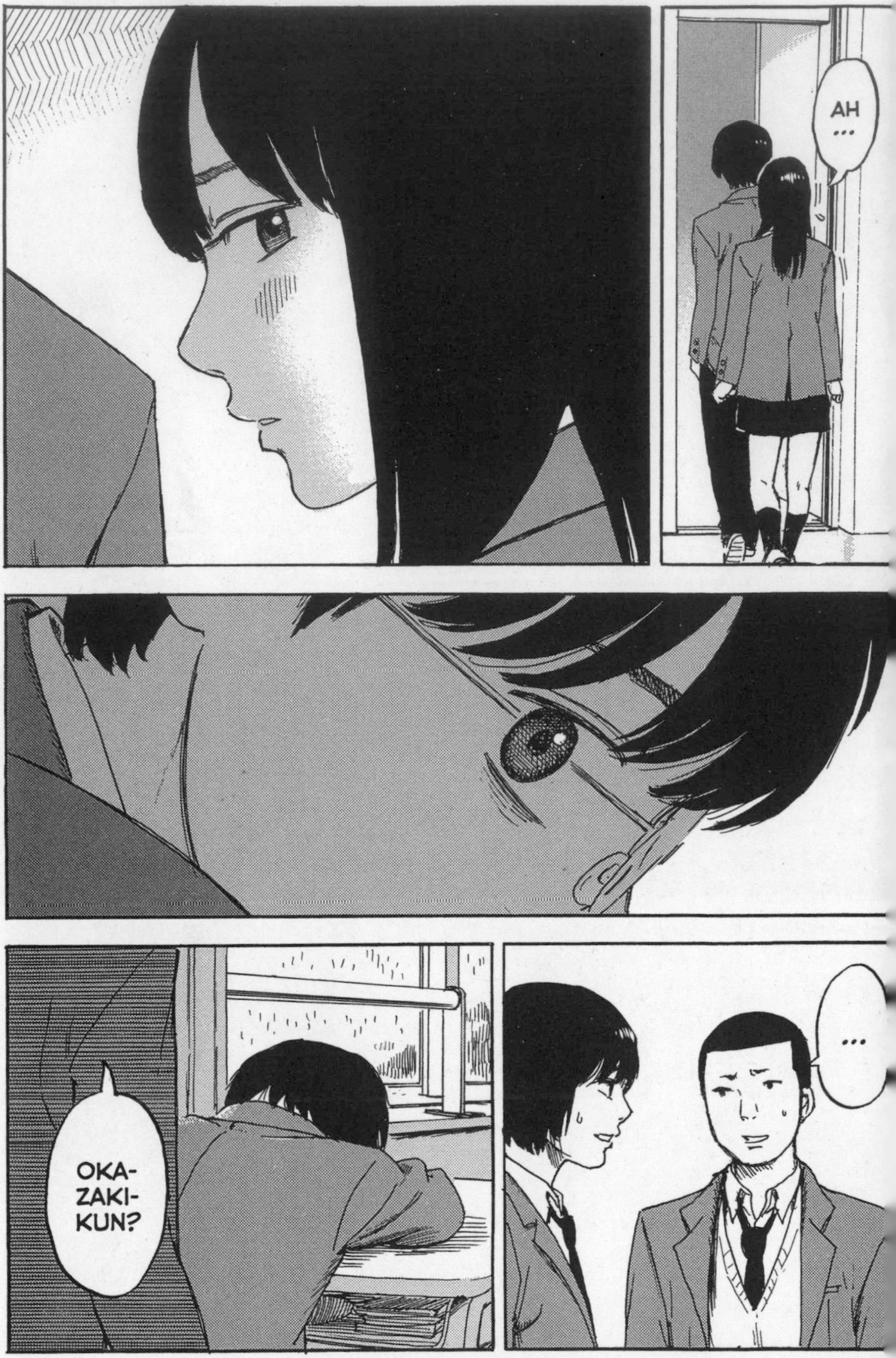
AH ...
...
OKA-ZAKI-KUN?

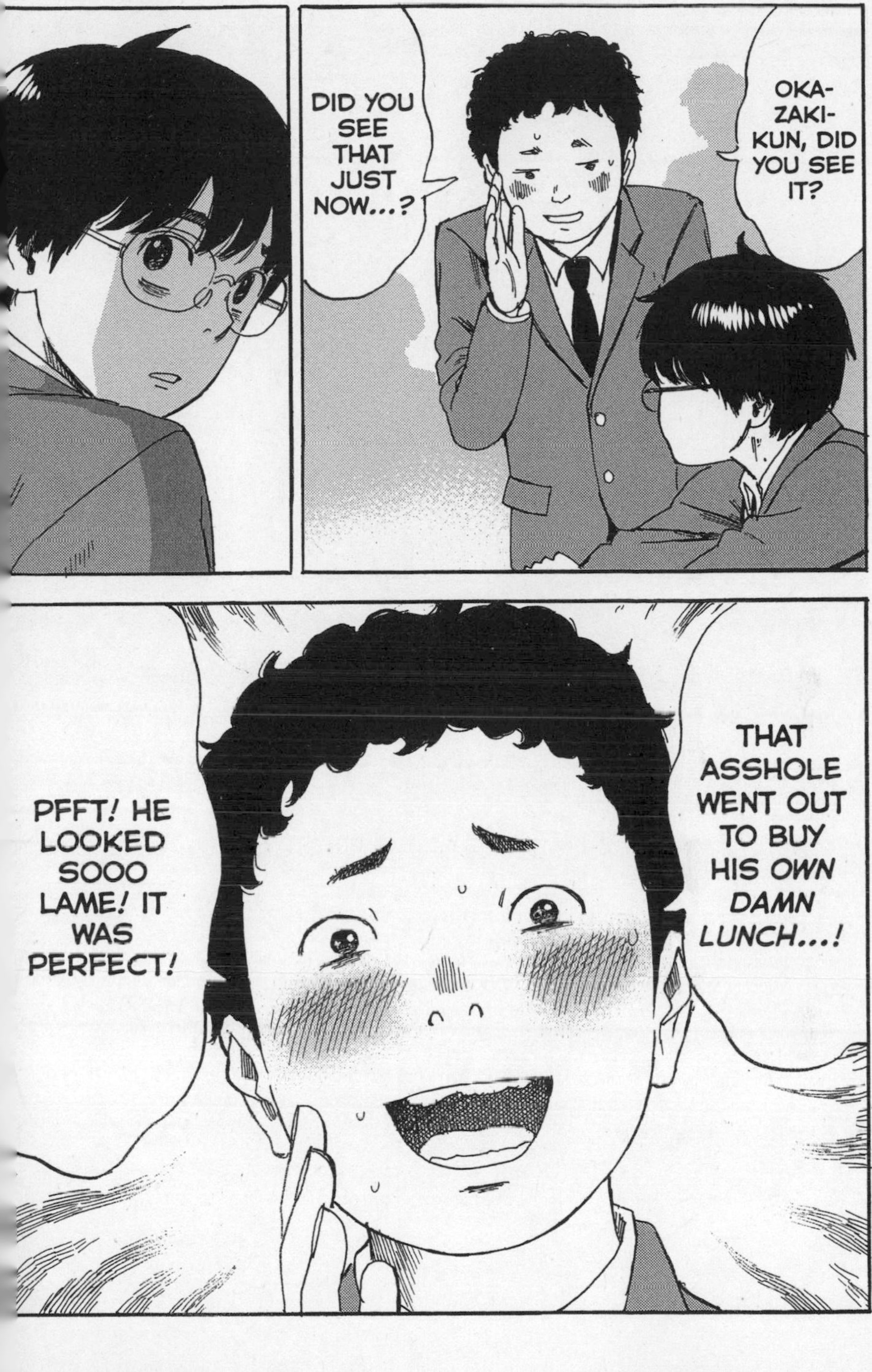
OKA-ZAKI-KUN, DID YOU SEE IT?
DID YOU SEE THAT JUST NOW...?
THAT ASSHOLE WENT OUT TO BUY HIS *OWN DAMN LUNCH*...!
PFFT! HE LOOKED SOOO LAME! IT WAS PERFECT!

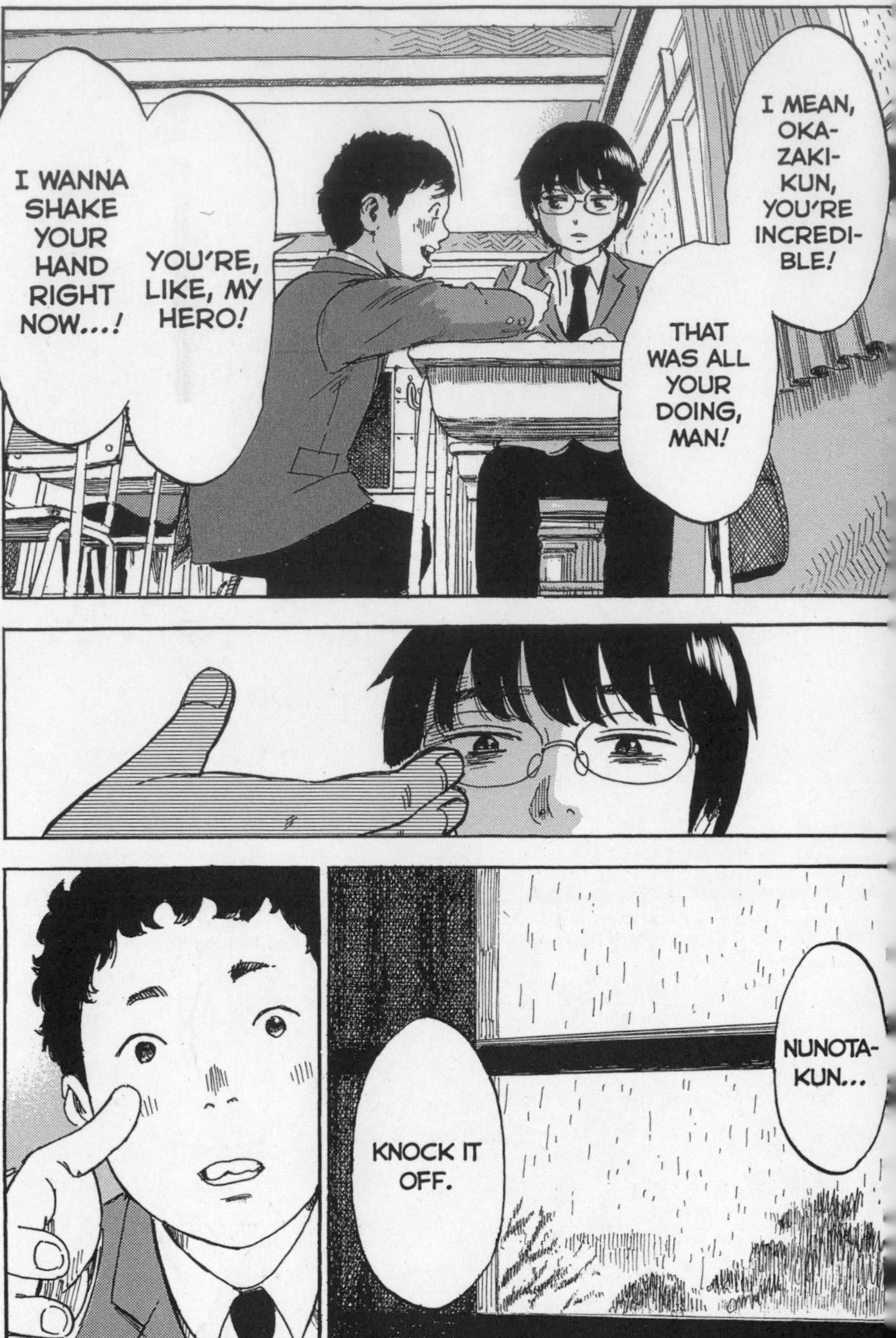
I MEAN, OKA-ZAKI-KUN, YOU'RE INCREDI-BLE!
THAT WAS ALL YOUR DOING, MAN!
YOU'RE, LIKE, MY HERO!
I WANNA SHAKE YOUR HAND RIGHT NOW...!
NUNOTA-KUN...
KNOCK IT OFF.

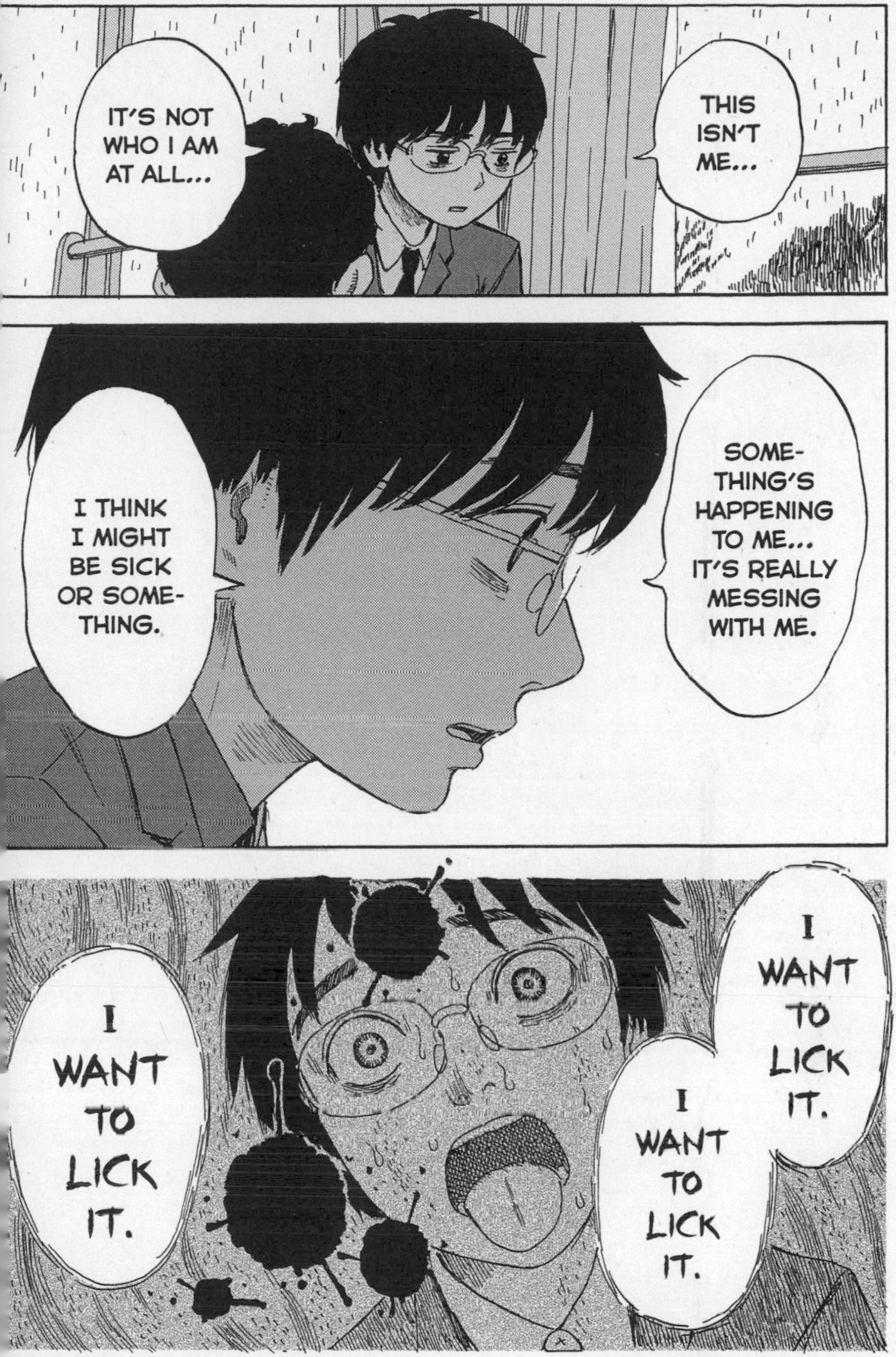
THIS ISN'T ME...
IT'S NOT WHO I AM AT ALL...
SOME-THING'S HAPPENING TO ME... IT'S REALLY MESSING WITH ME.
I THINK I MIGHT BE SICK OR SOME-THING.
I WANT TO LICK IT.
I WANT TO LICK IT.
I WANT TO LICK IT.

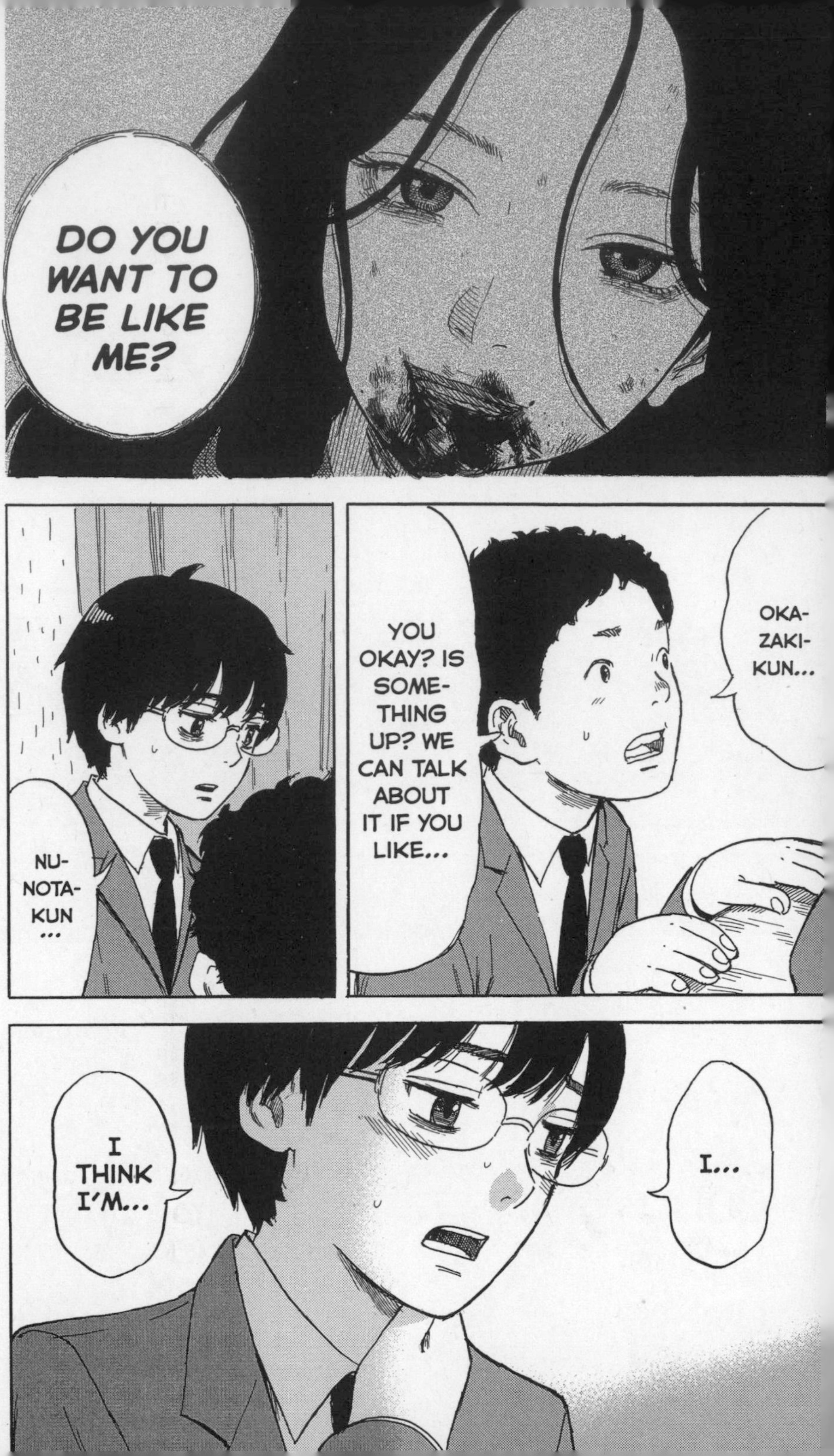
DO YOU WANT TO BE LIKE ME?
OKA-ZAKI-KUN...
YOU OKAY? IS SOME-THING UP? WE CAN TALK ABOUT IT IF YOU LIKE...
NU-NOTA-KUN ...
I...
I THINK I'M...

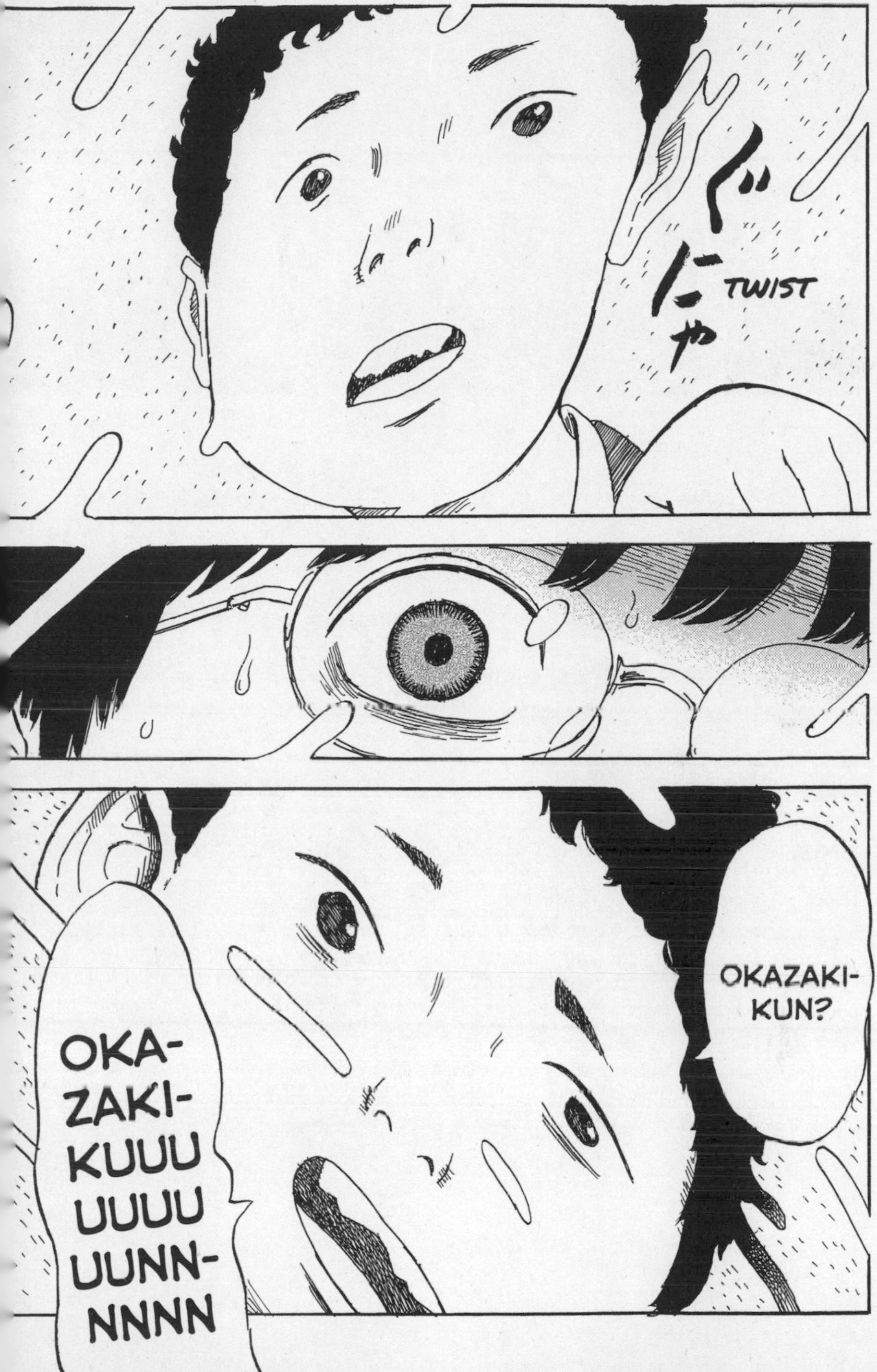
ぐにゃ
TWIST
OKAZAKI-KUN?
OKA-ZAKI-KUUUUUUUUUNN-NNNN

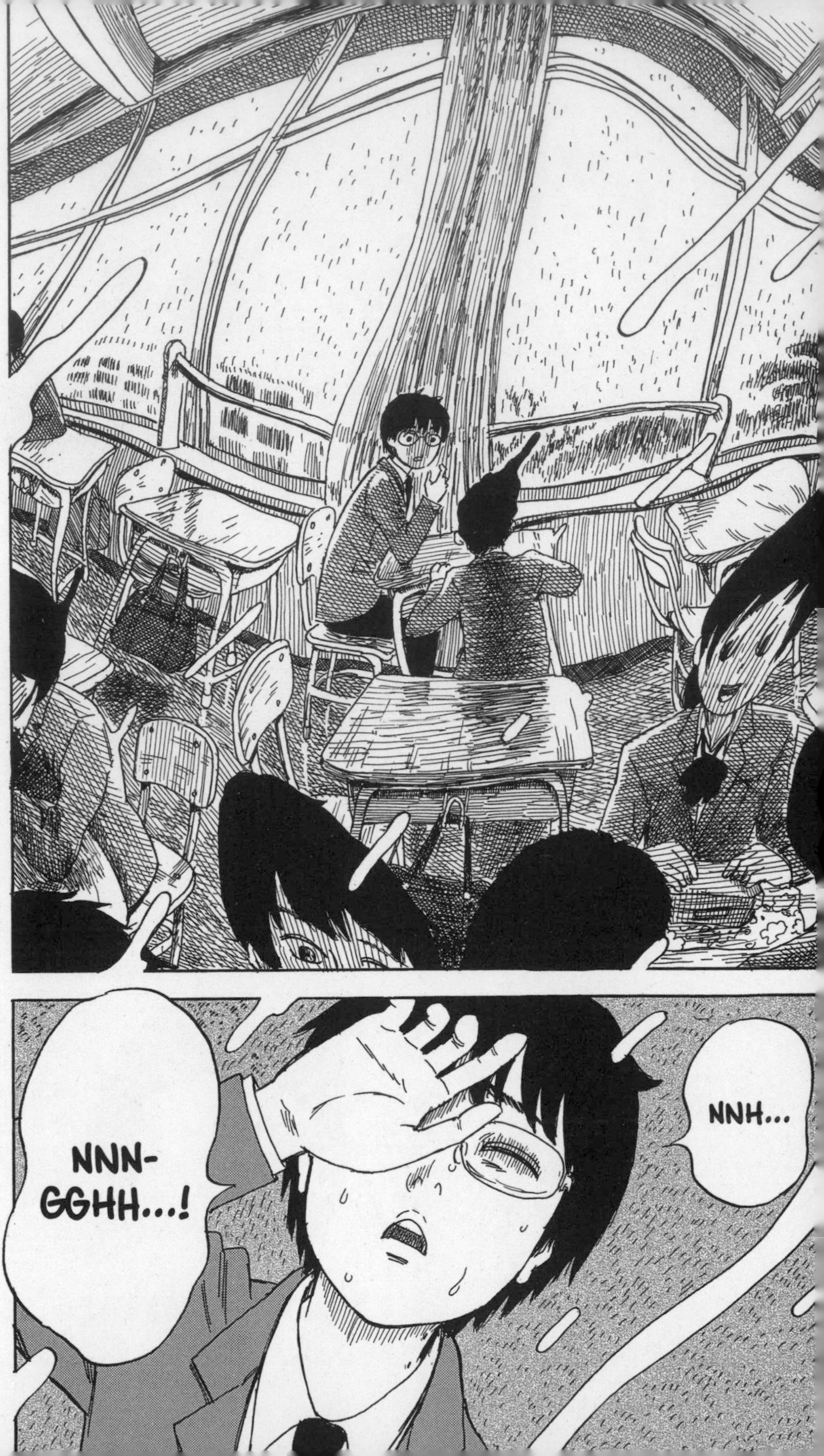
NNH...
NNN-GGHH...!

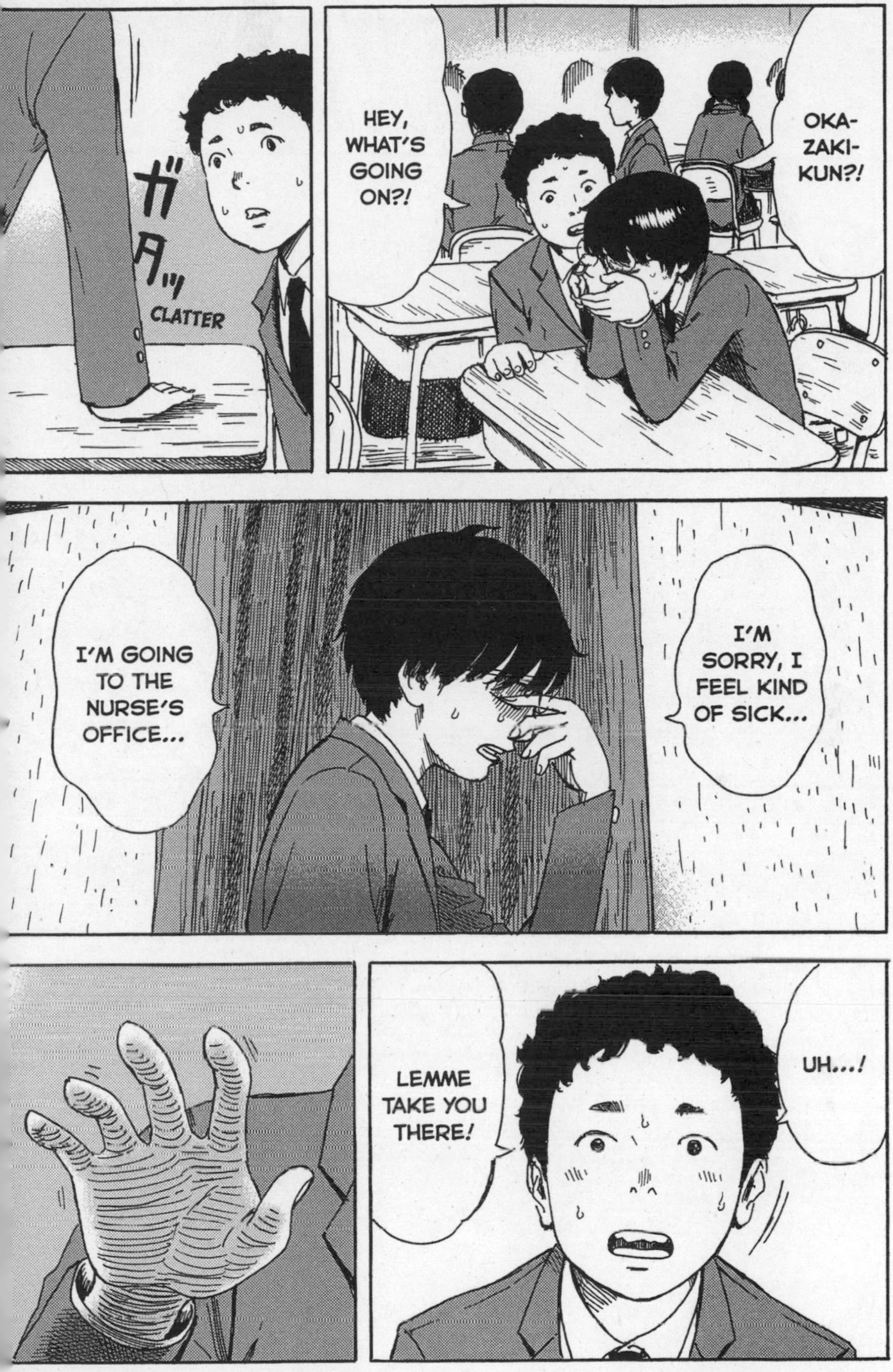
OKA-
ZAKI-
KUN?!
HEY, WHAT'S GOING ON?!
ガタッ
CLATTER
I'M SORRY, I FEEL KIND OF SICK...
I'M GOING TO THE NURSE'S OFFICE...
UH...!
LEMME TAKE YOU THERE!

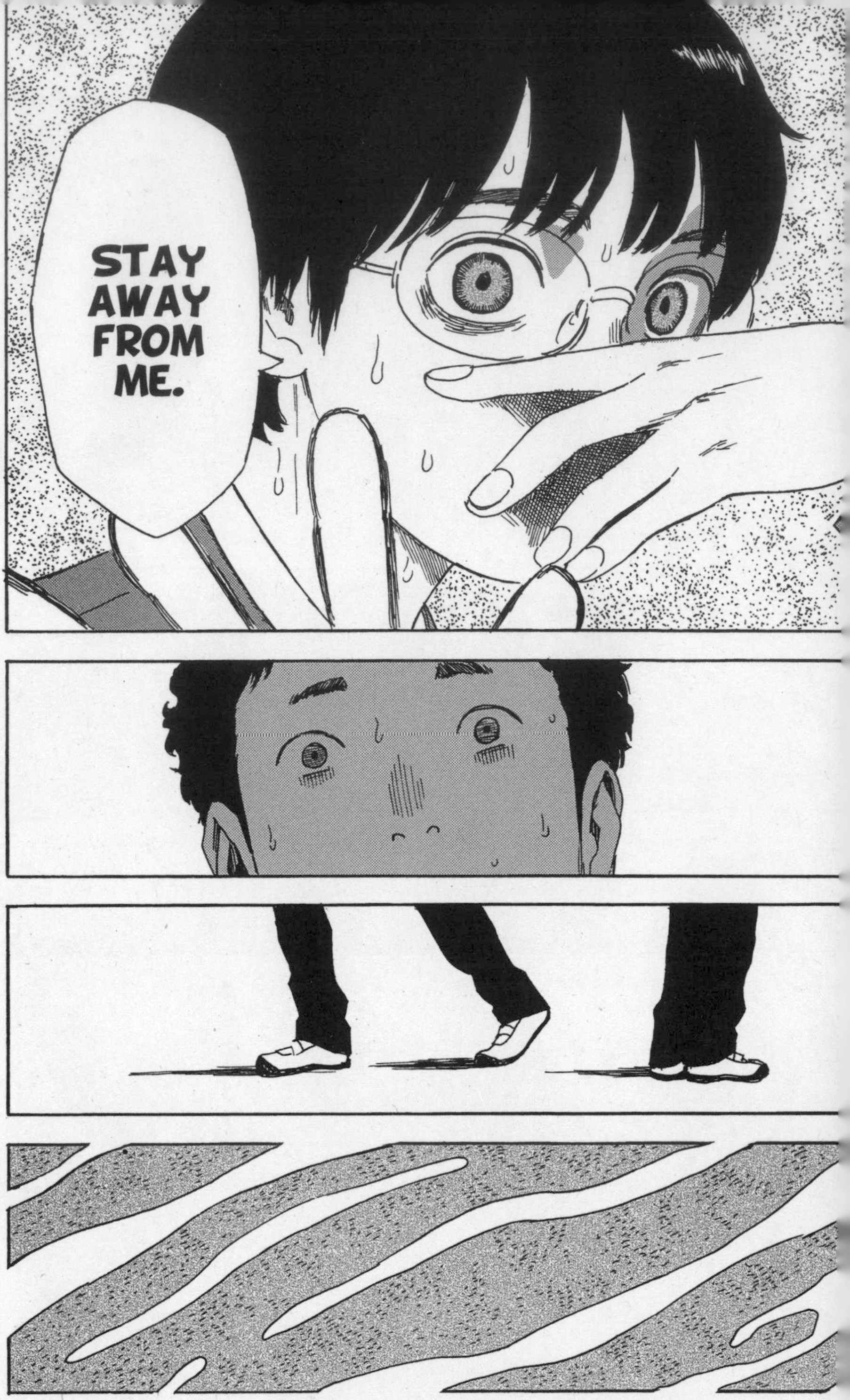
STAY AWAY FROM ME.

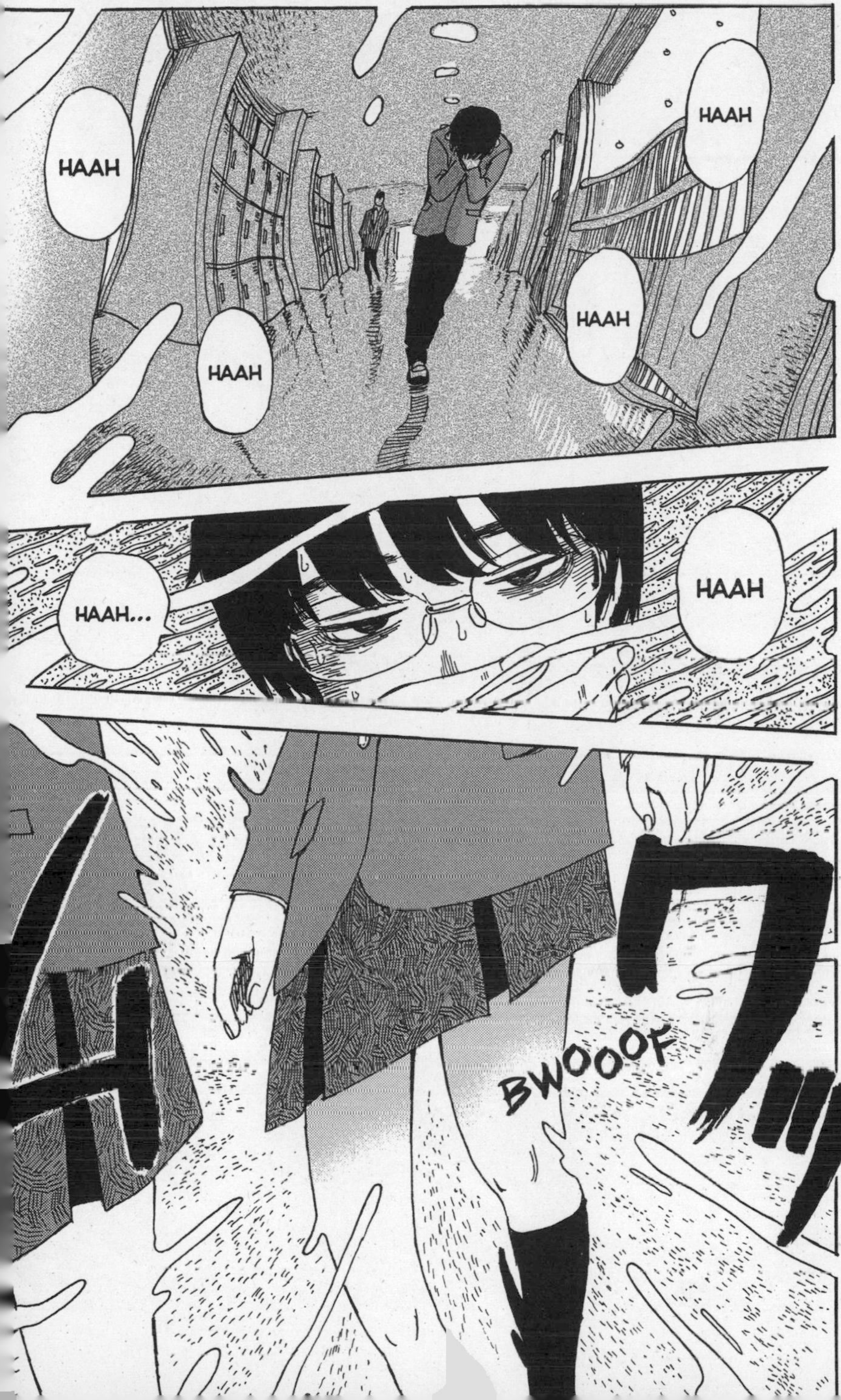
HAAH
HAAH
HAAH
HAAH
HAAH
HAAH...
BWOOOF

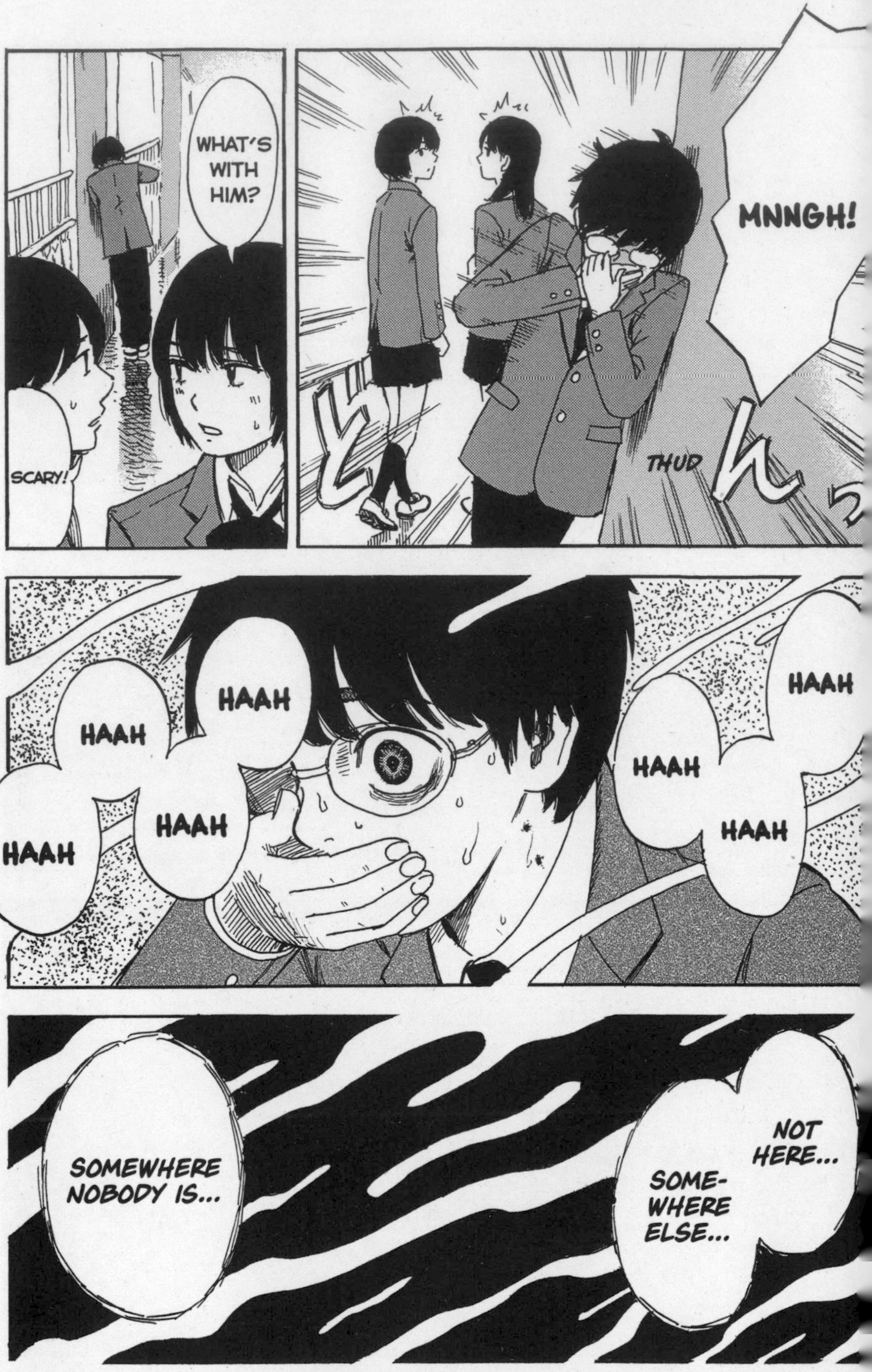
MNNGH!
THUD
WHAT'S WITH HIM?
SCARY!
HAAH
HAAH
HAAH
HAAH
HAAH
HAAH
NOT HERE...
SOME-WHERE ELSE...
SOMEWHERE NOBODY IS...

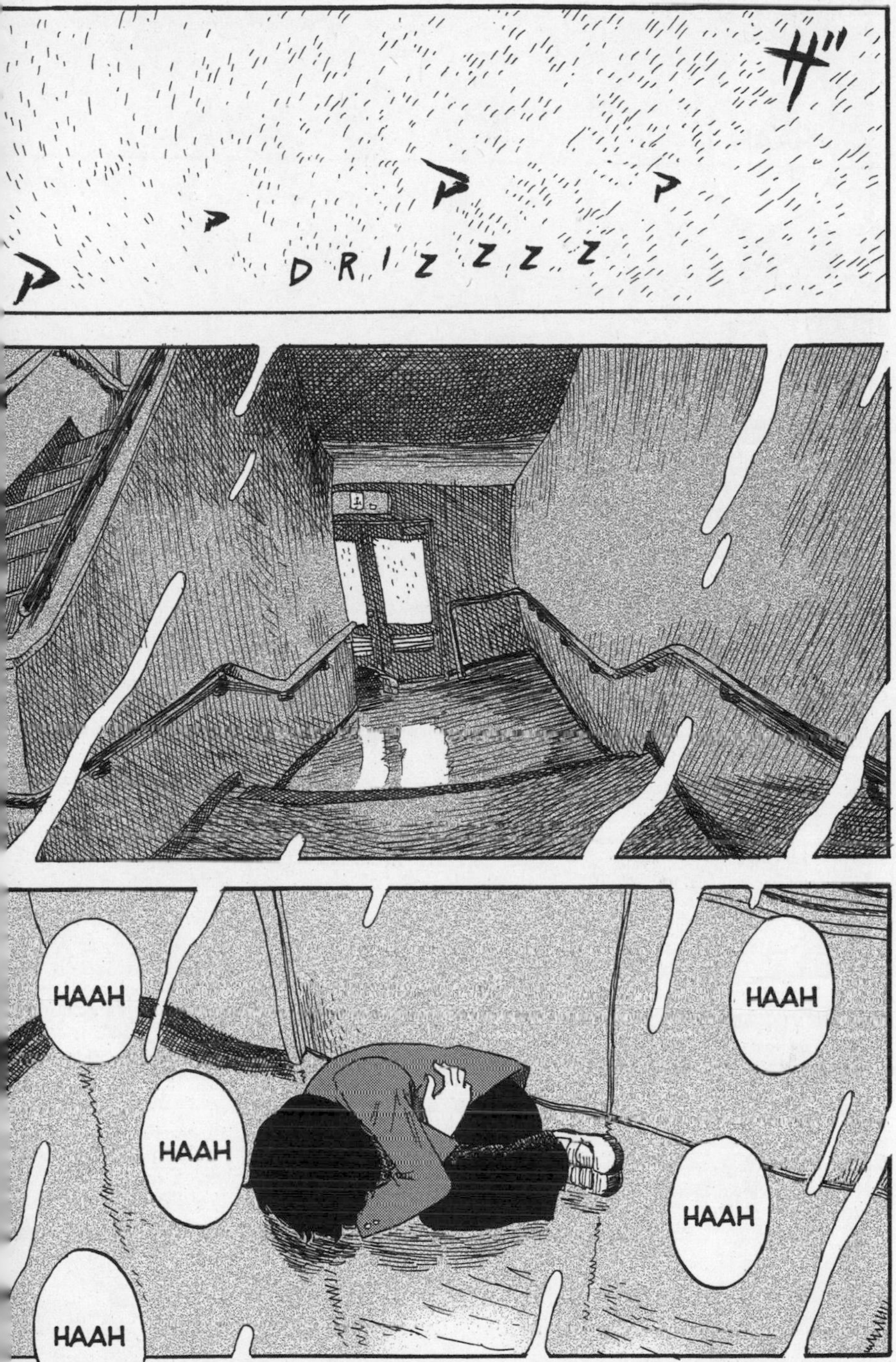
ザァァァァ
DRIZZZZ
HAAH
HAAH
HAAH
HAAH
HAAH

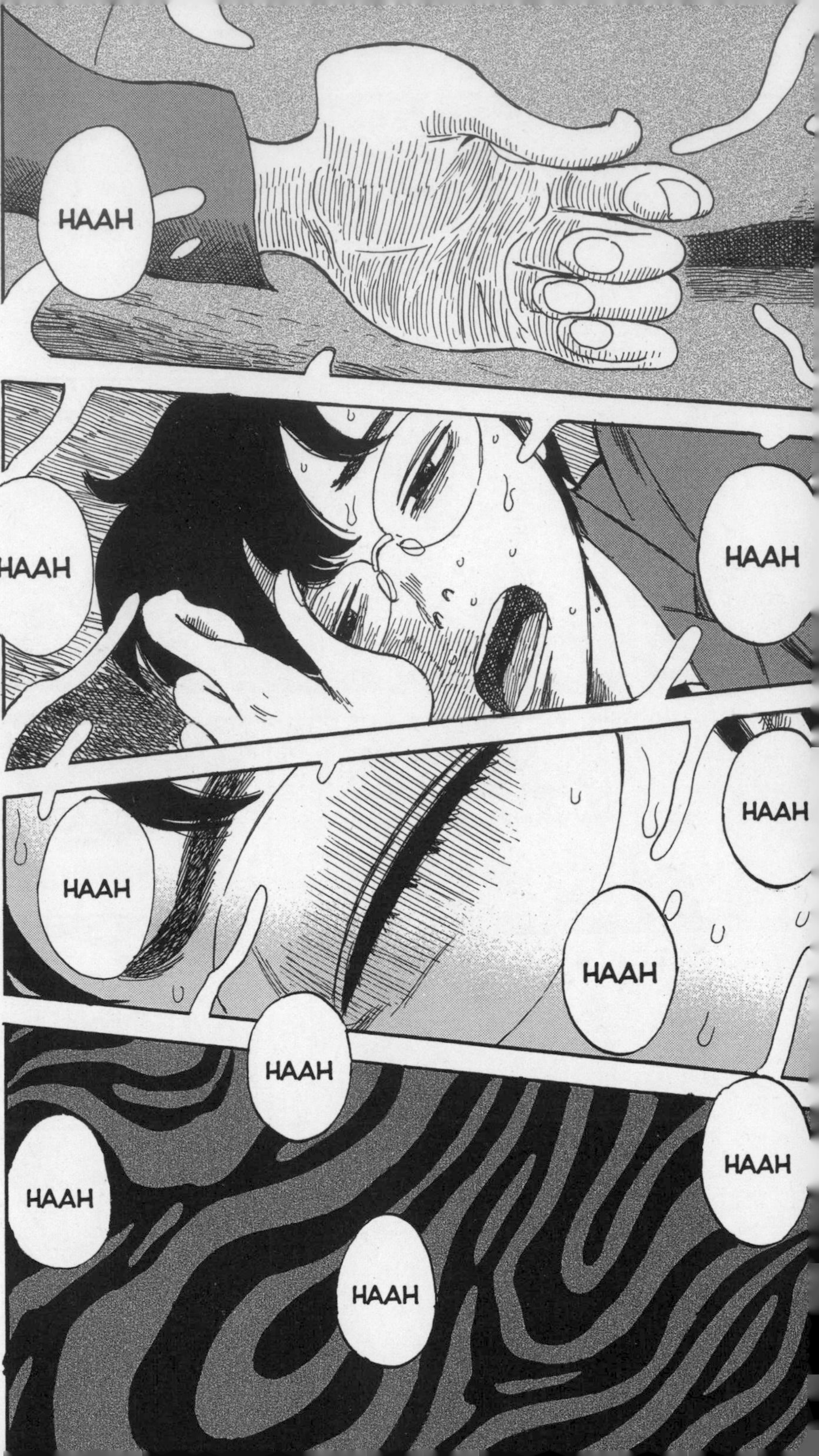
HAAH
HAAH
HAAH
HAAH
HAAH
HAAH
HAAH
HAAH
HAAH
HAAH

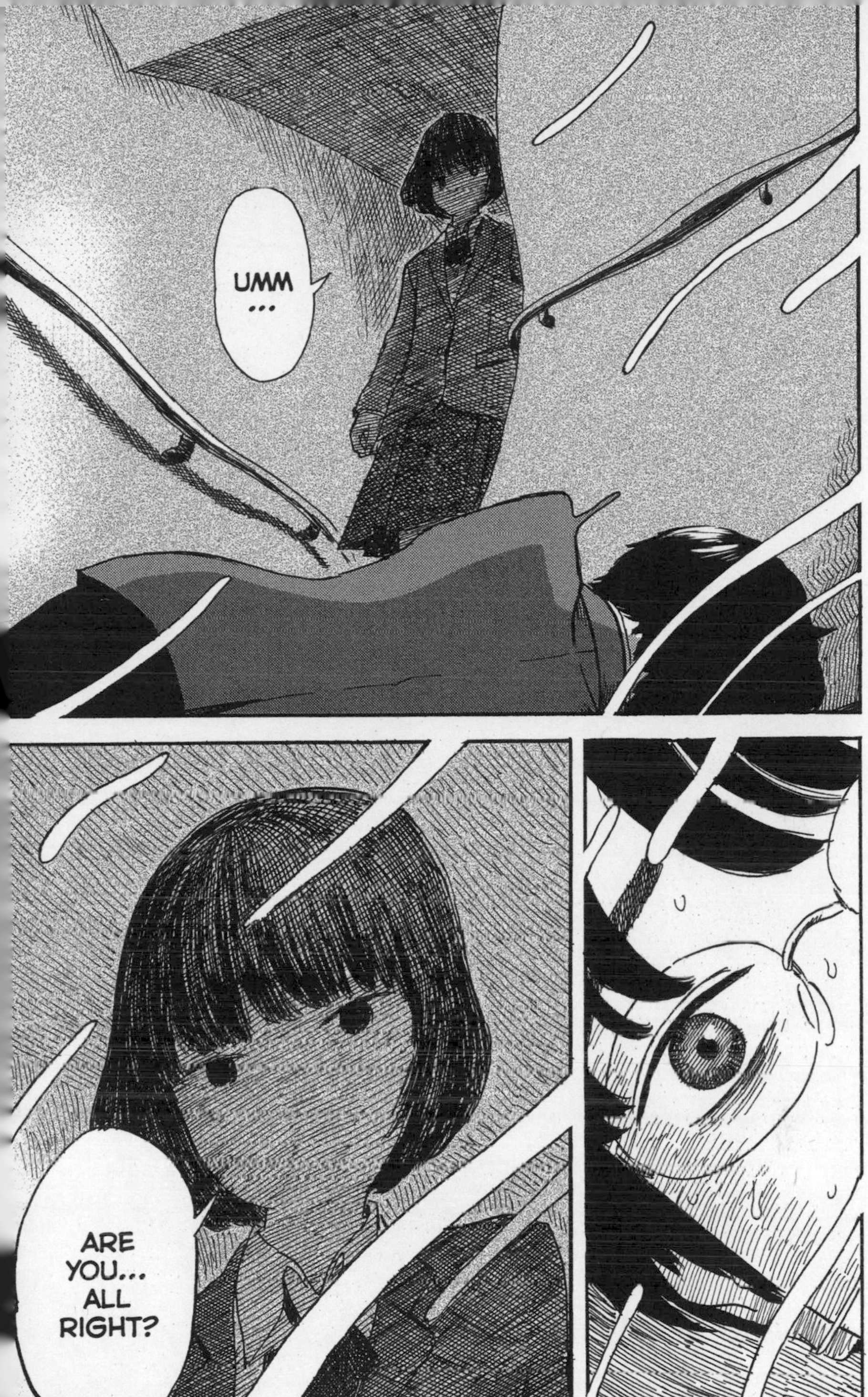
UMM ...
ARE YOU... ALL RIGHT?

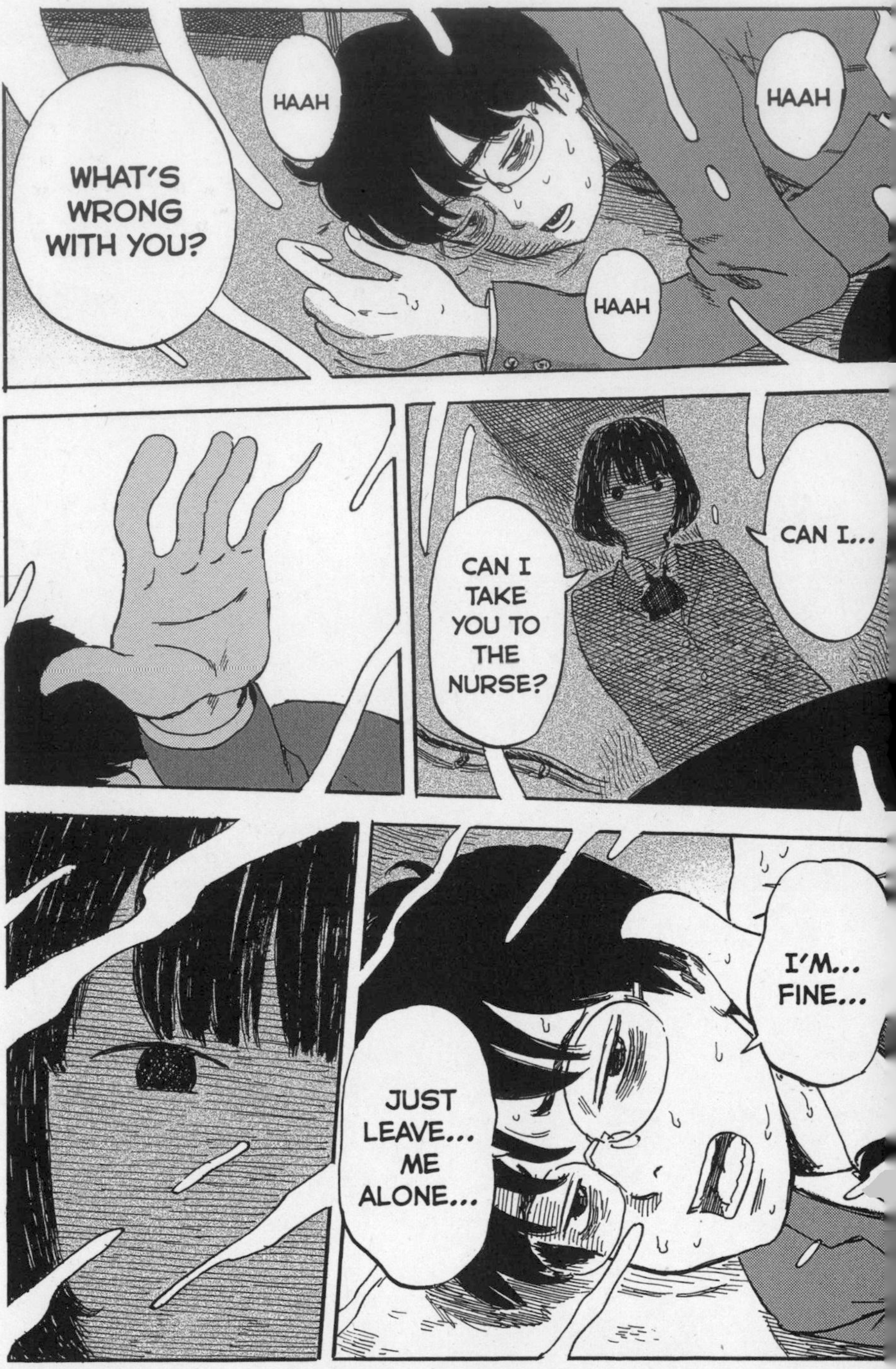
HAAH
HAAH
HAAH
WHAT'S WRONG WITH YOU?
CAN I...
CAN I TAKE YOU TO THE NURSE?
I'M... FINE...
JUST LEAVE... ME ALONE...

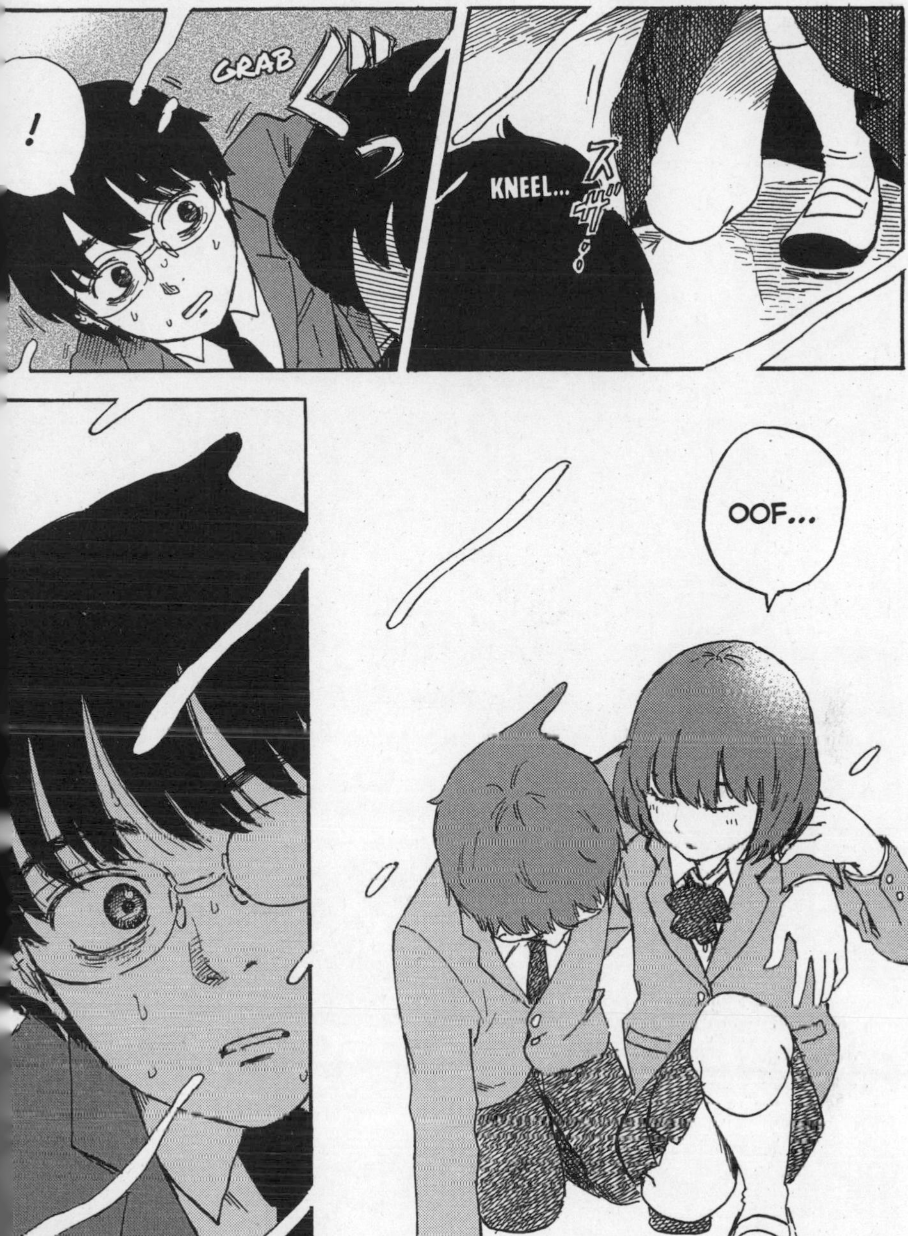
KNEEL...
GRAB
!
OOF...

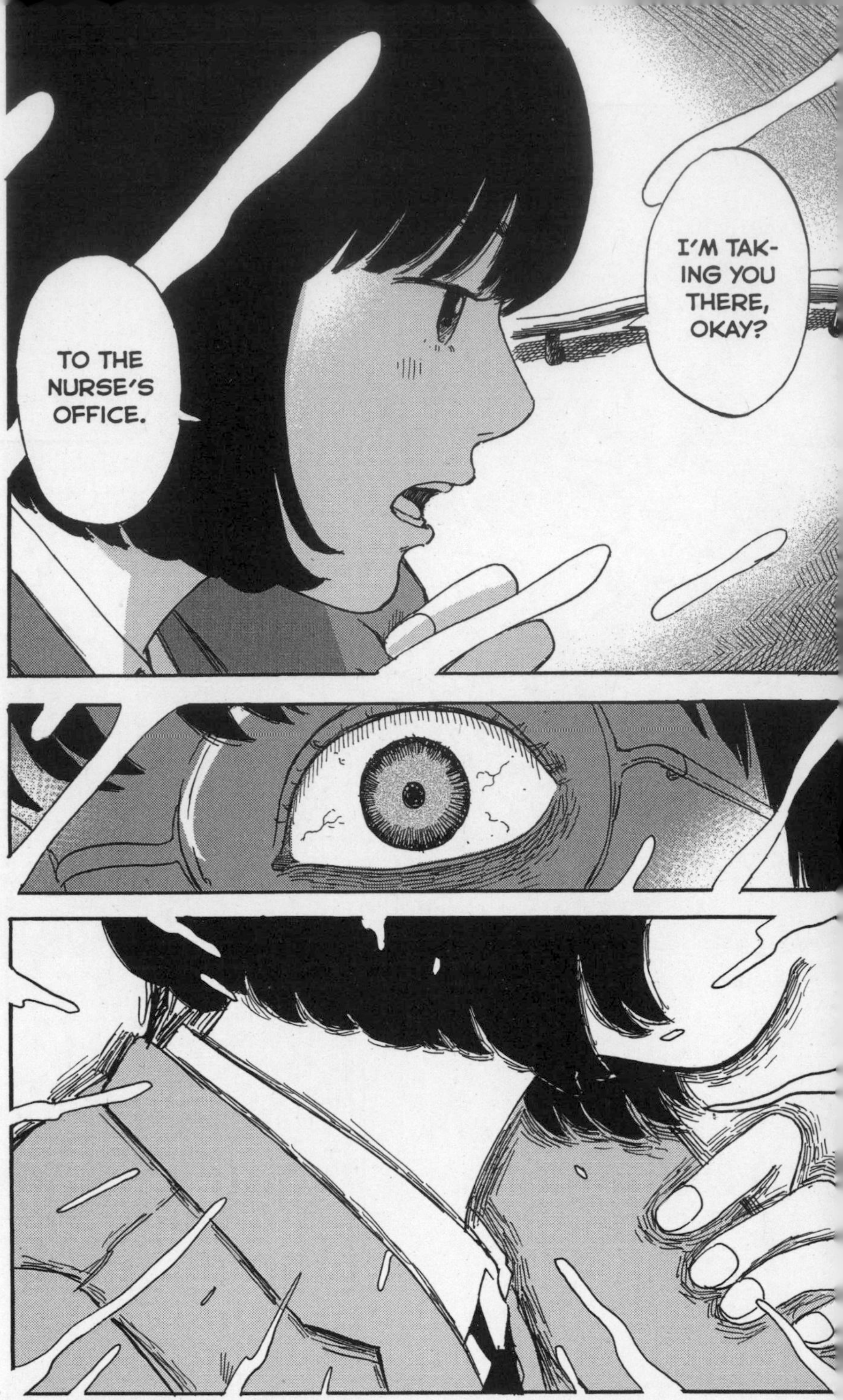
I'M TAKING YOU THERE, OKAY?
TO THE NURSE'S OFFICE.

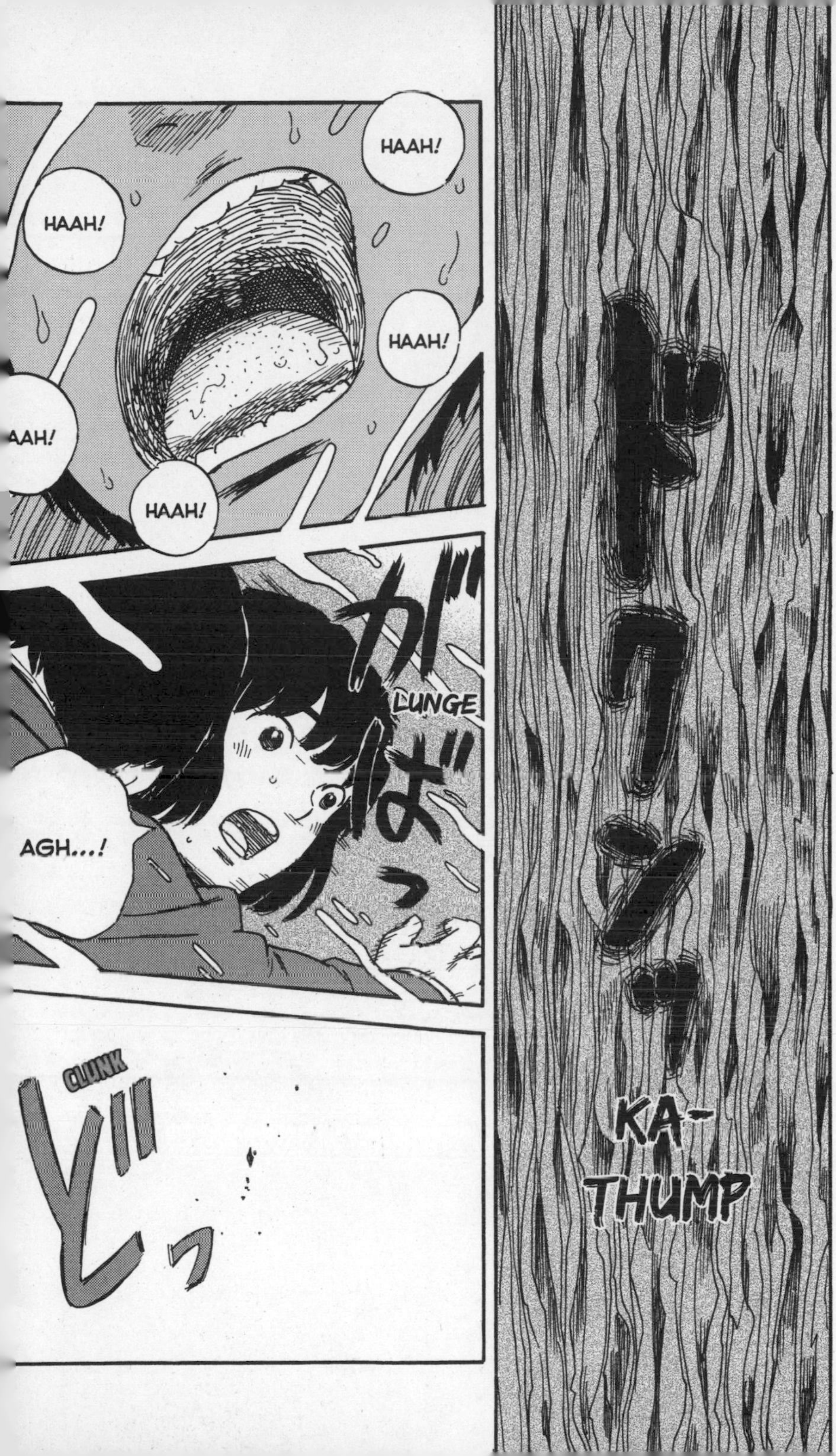
KA-THUMP
HAAH!
HAAH!
HAAH!
HAAH!
AAH!
LUNGE
AGH...!
CLUNK

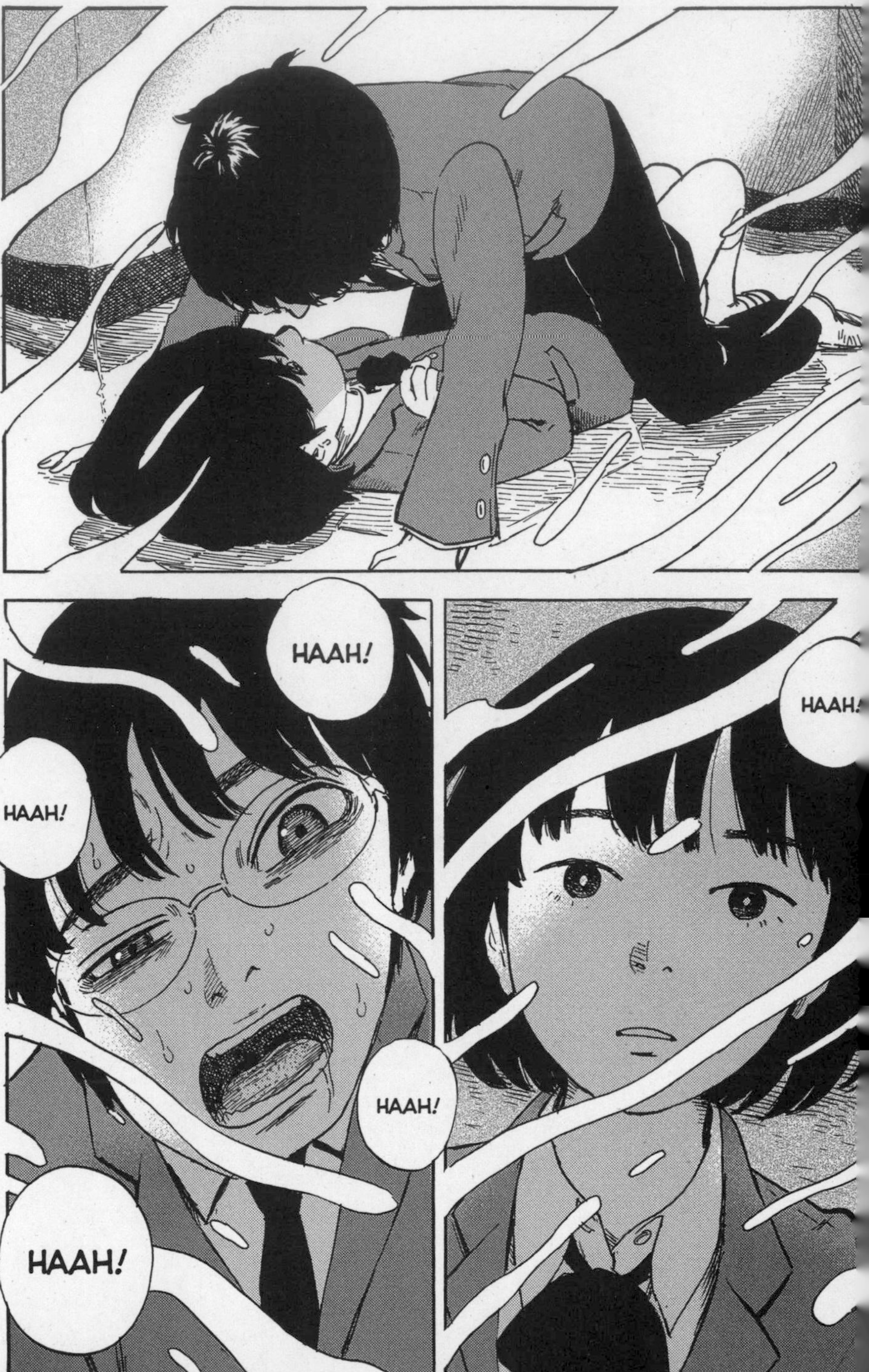
HAAH!
HAAH!
HAAH!
HAAH!
HAAH!

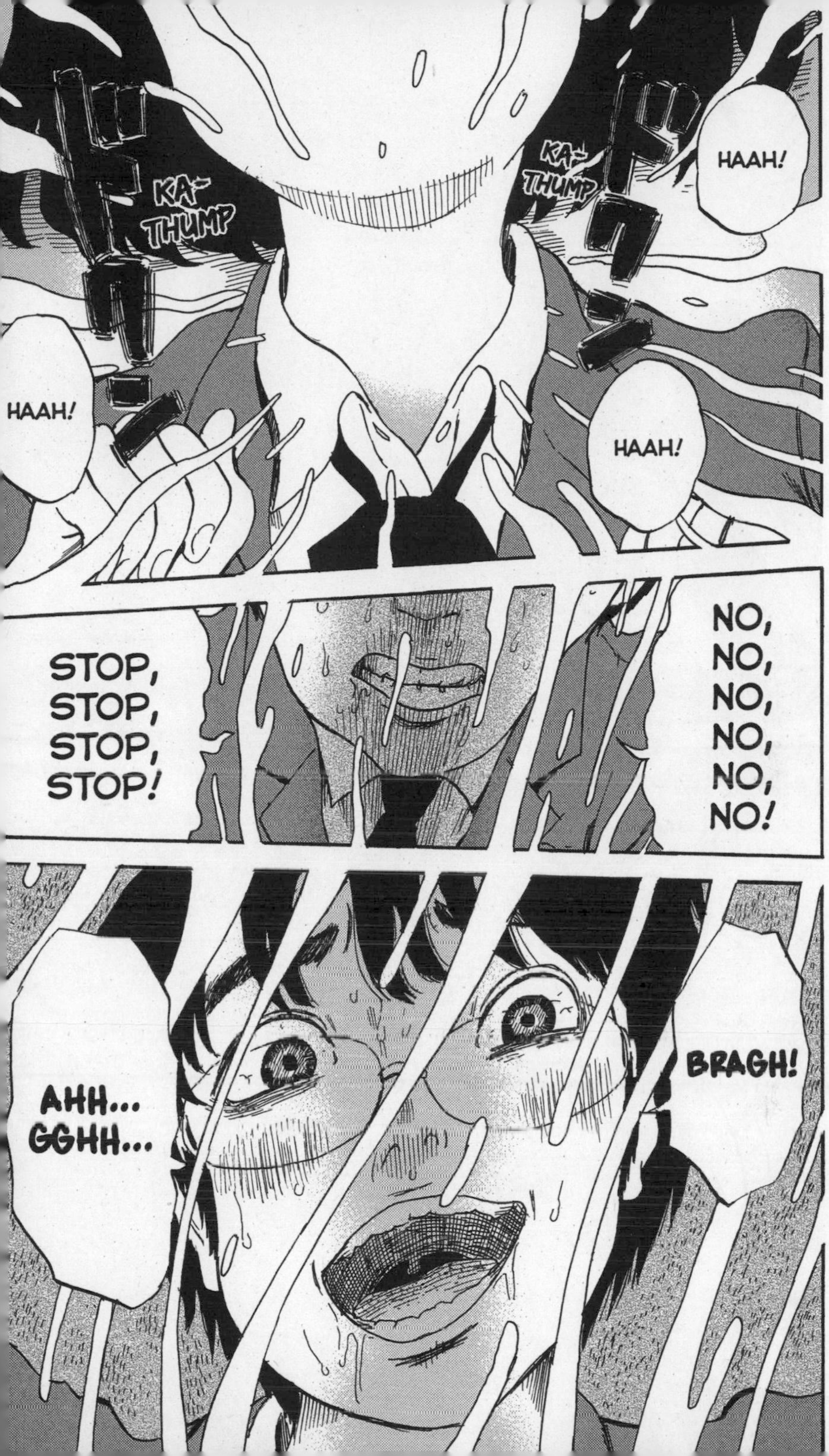
HAAH!
KA-THUMP
HAAH!
KA-THUMP
HAAH!
NO, NO, NO, NO, NO, NO!
STOP, STOP, STOP, STOP!
BRAGH!
AHH... GGHH...

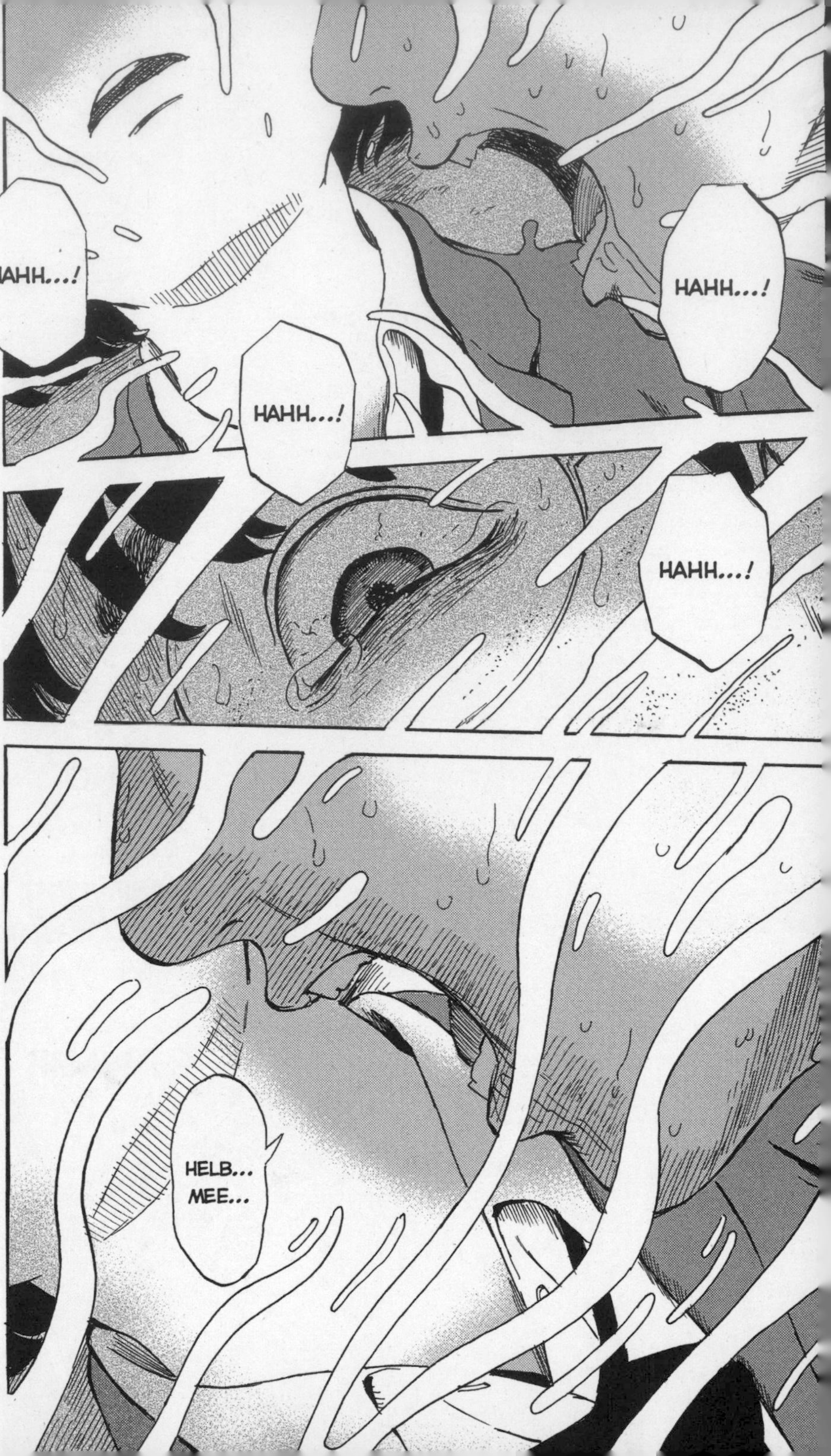
HAHH...!
HAHH...!
HAHH...!
HAHH...!
HELB... MEE...

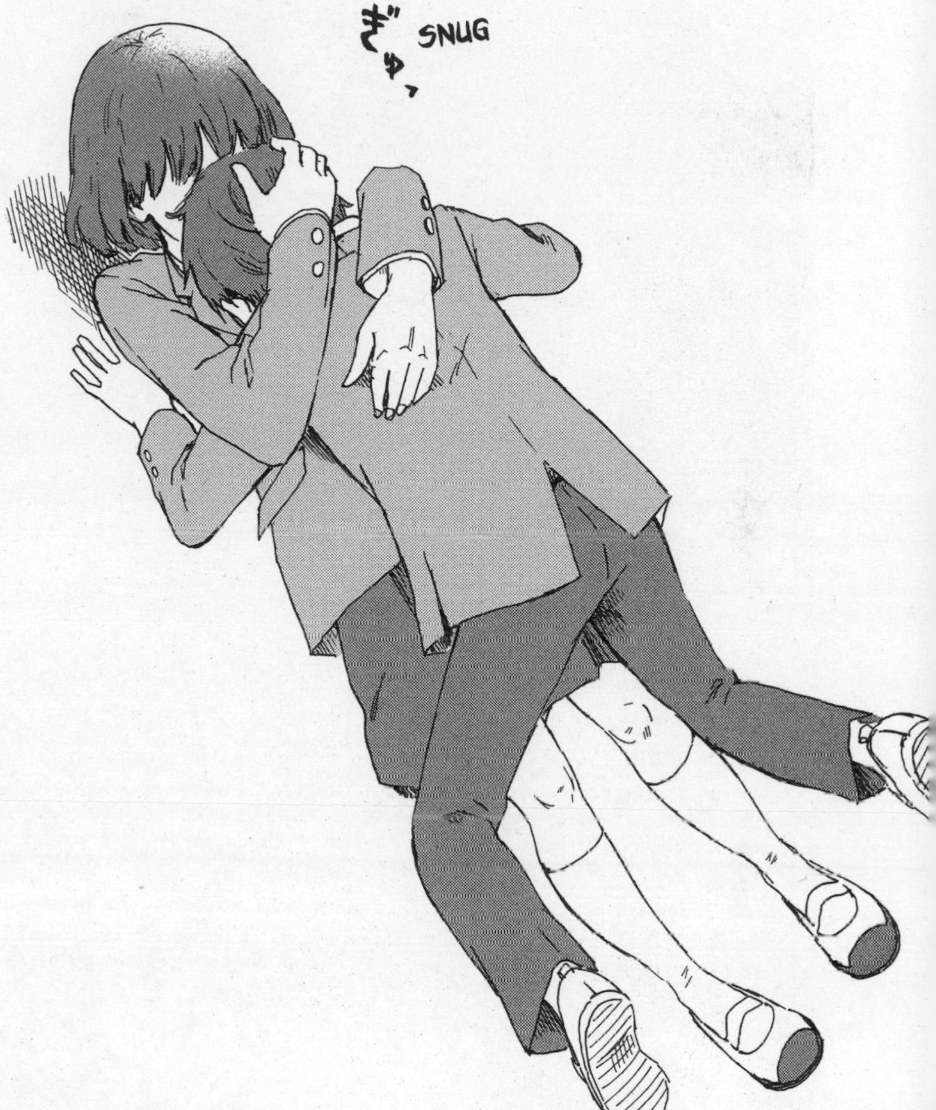
ぎゅっ
SNUG

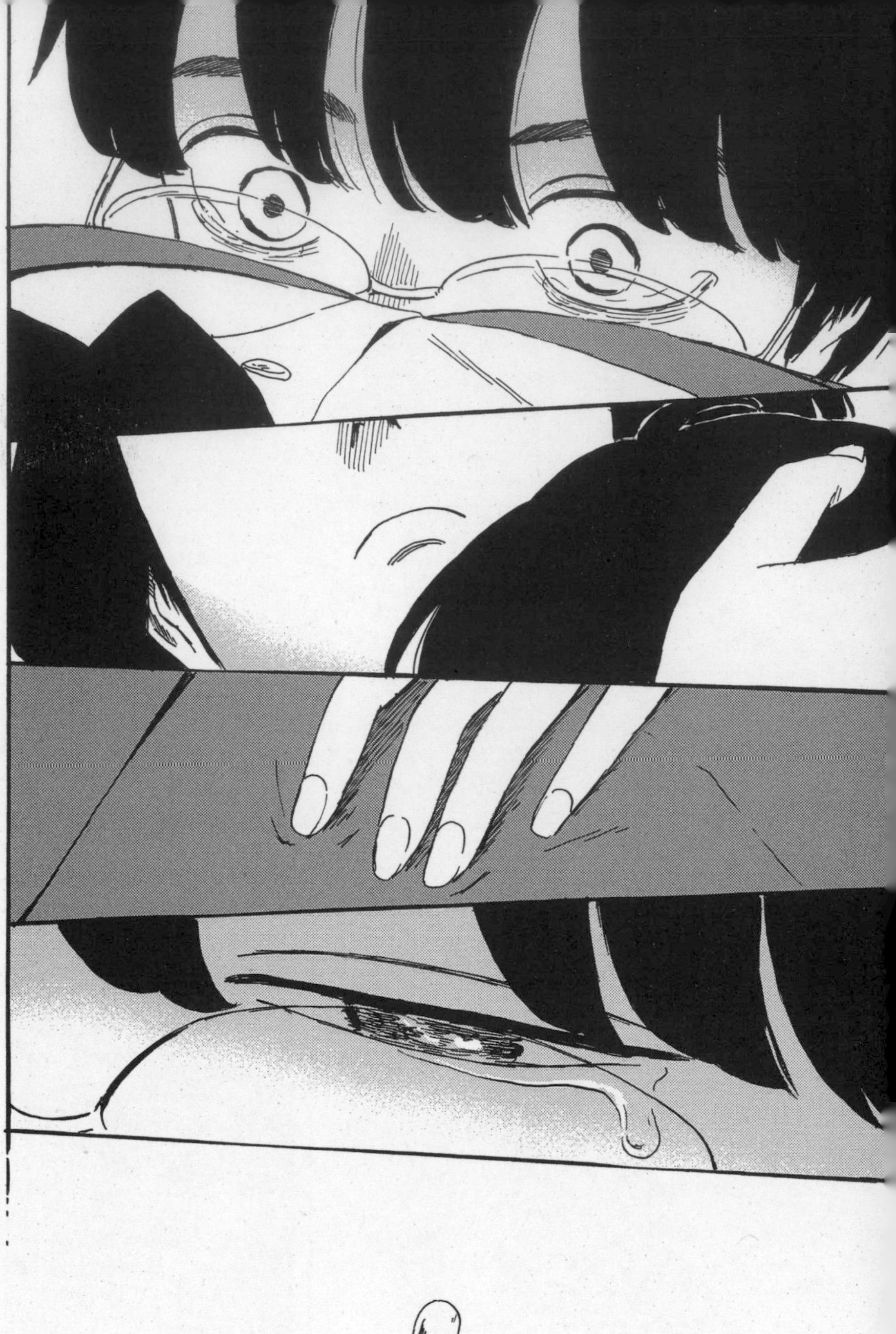

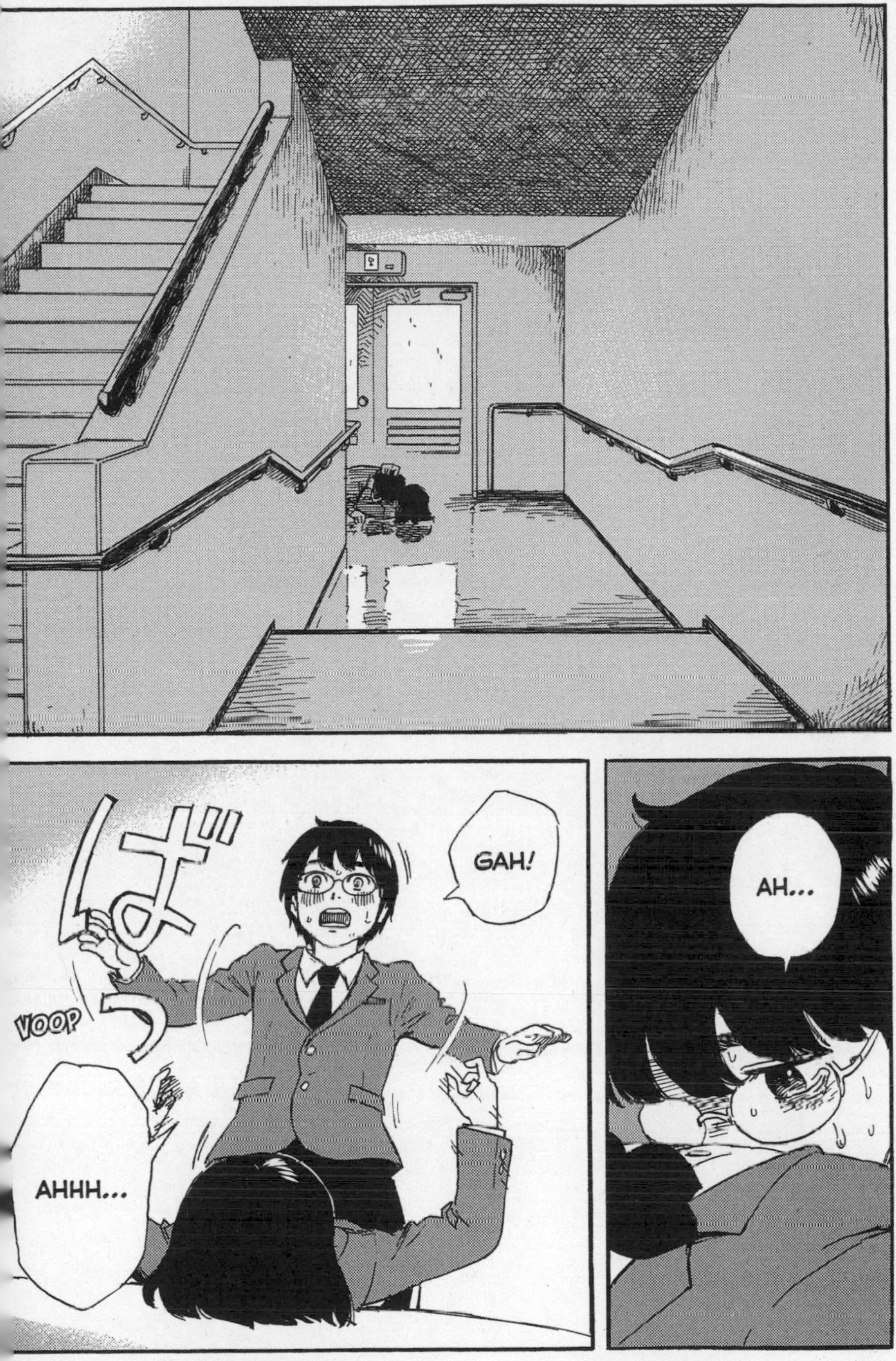
AH...
GAH!
ばっ
VOOP
AHHH...

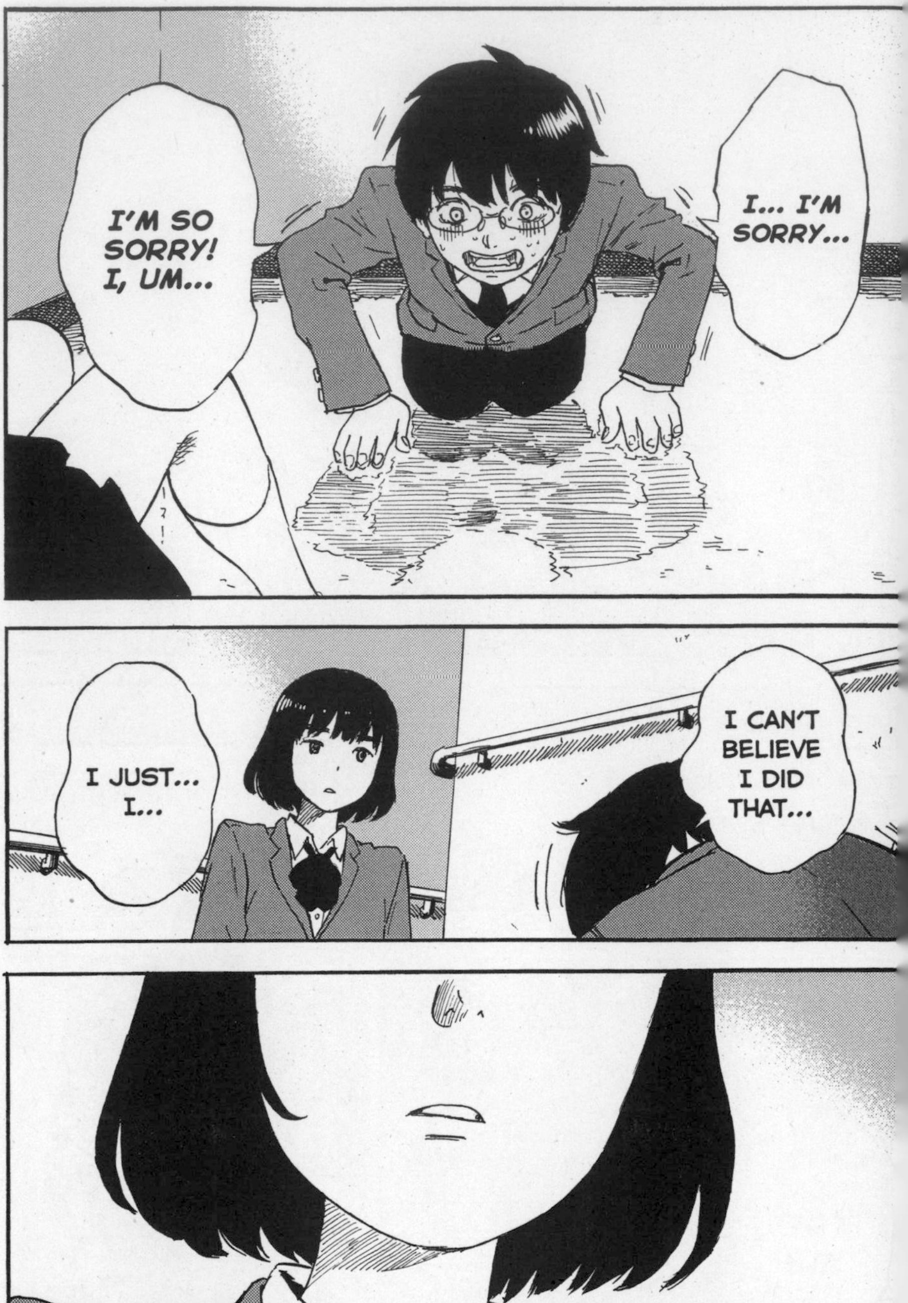
I... I'M SORRY...
I'M SO SORRY! I, UM...
I CAN'T BELIEVE I DID THAT...
I JUST... I...

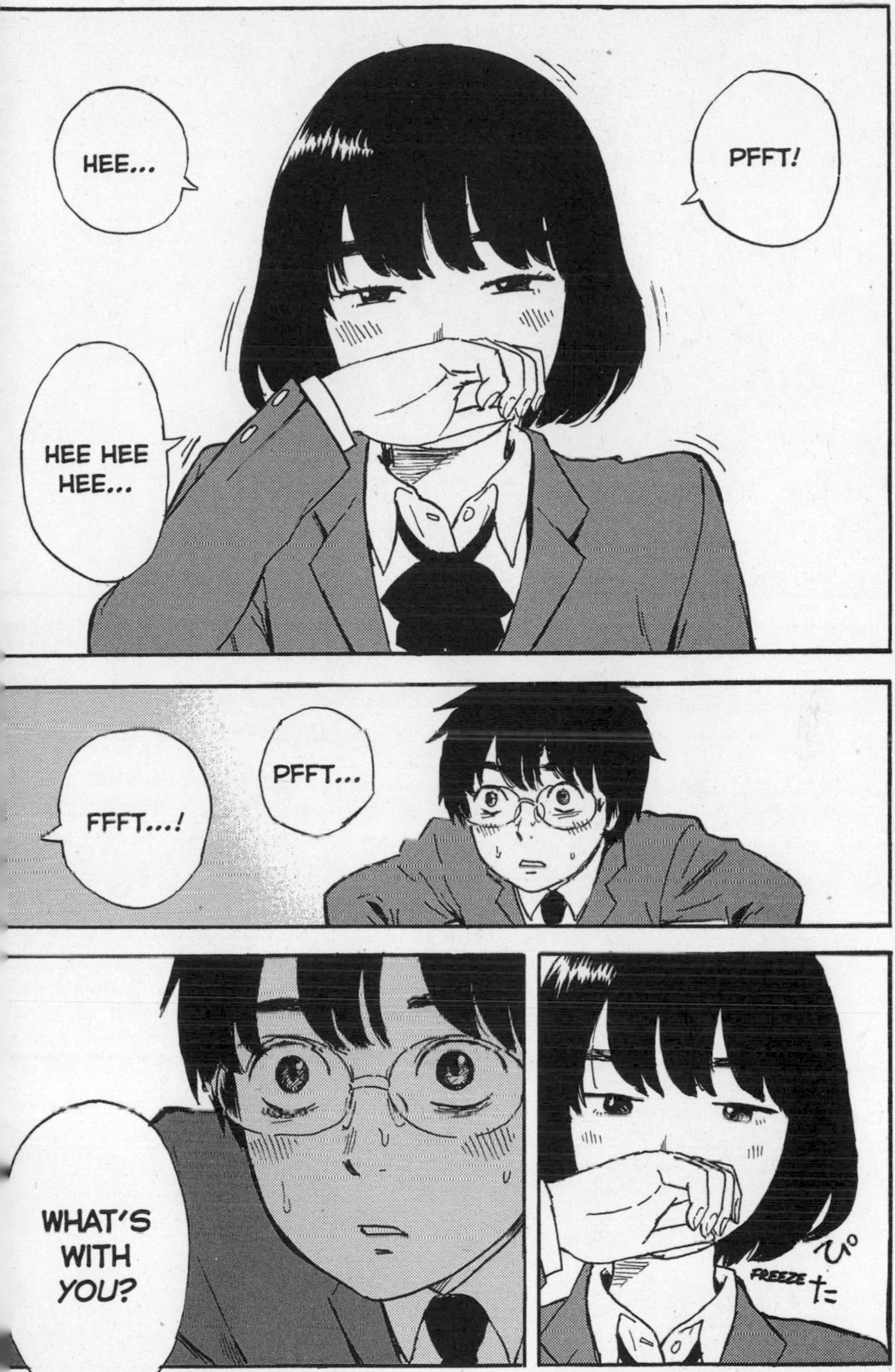
PFFT!
HEE...
HEE HEE HEE...
PFFT...
FFFT...!
FREEZE
ぴた
WHAT'S WITH YOU?

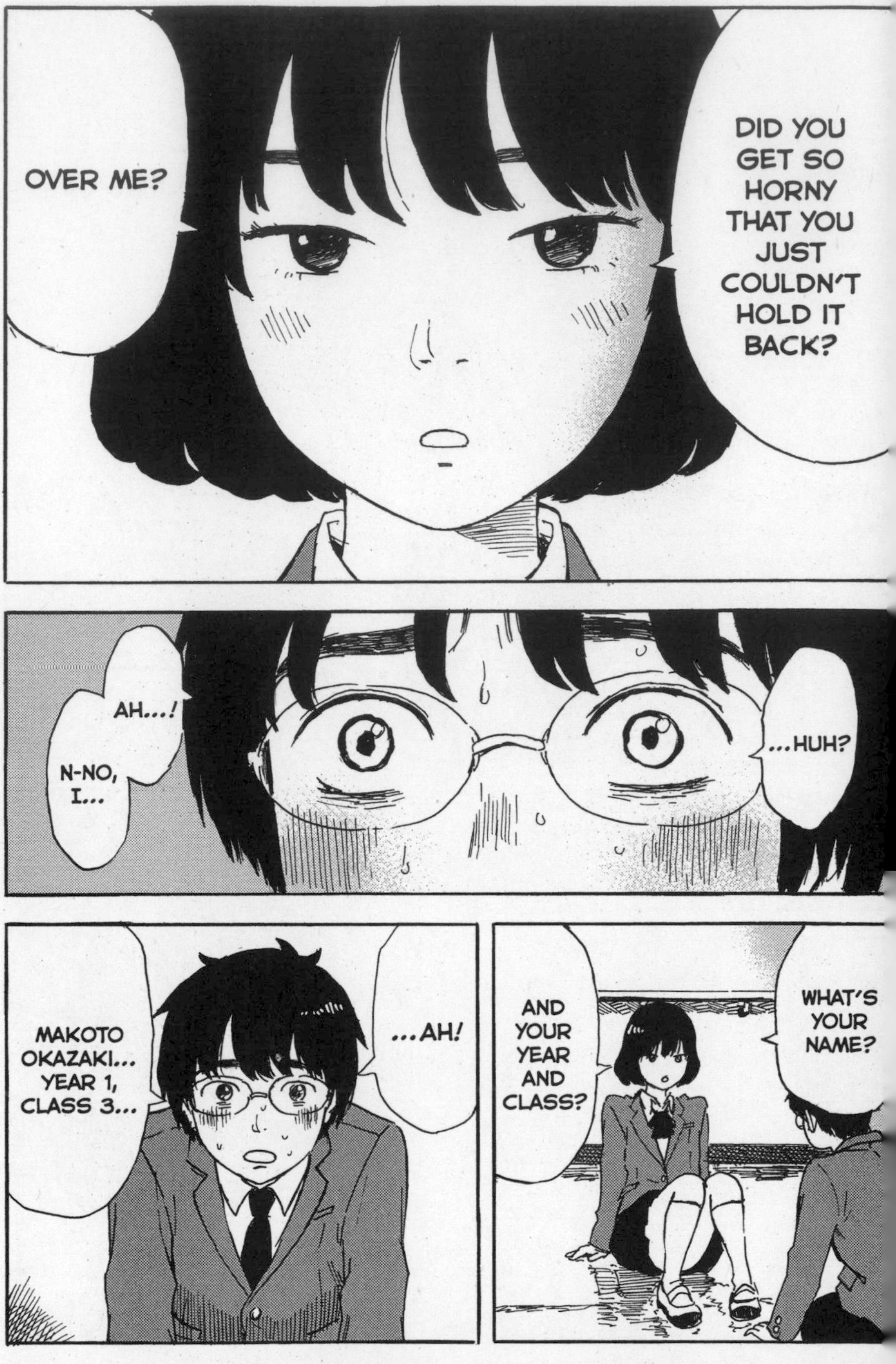
DID YOU GET SO HORNY THAT YOU JUST COULDN'T HOLD IT BACK?
OVER ME?
...HUH?
AH...!
N-NO, I...
WHAT'S YOUR NAME?
AND YOUR YEAR AND CLASS?
...AH!
MAKOTO OKAZAKI... YEAR 1, CLASS 3...

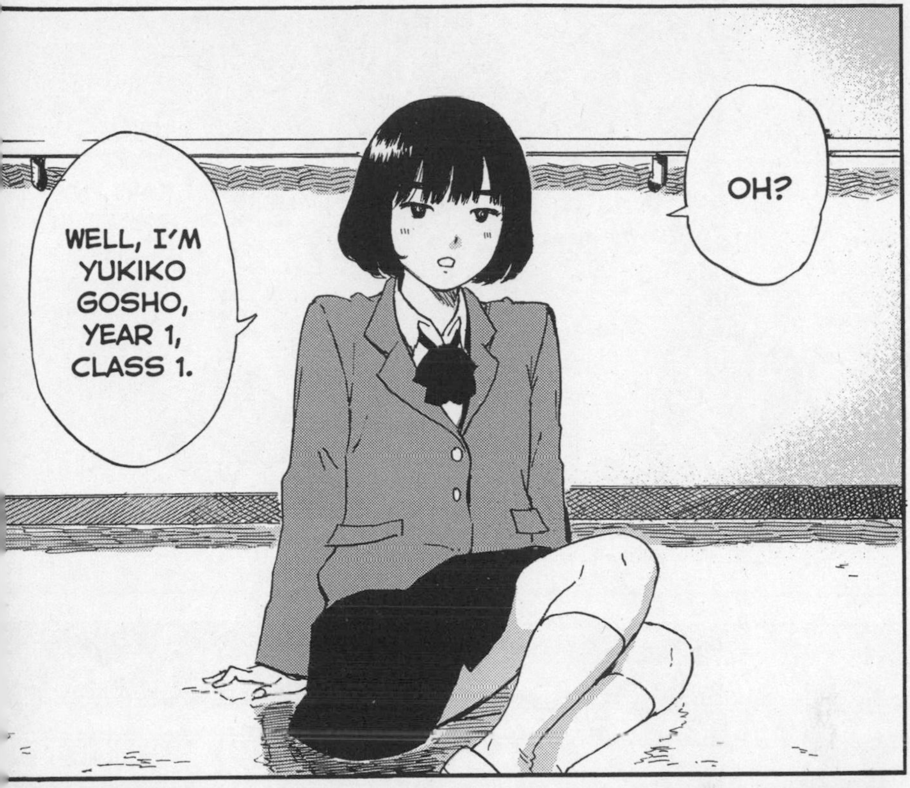
OH?
WELL, I'M YUKIKO GOSHO, YEAR 1, CLASS 1.
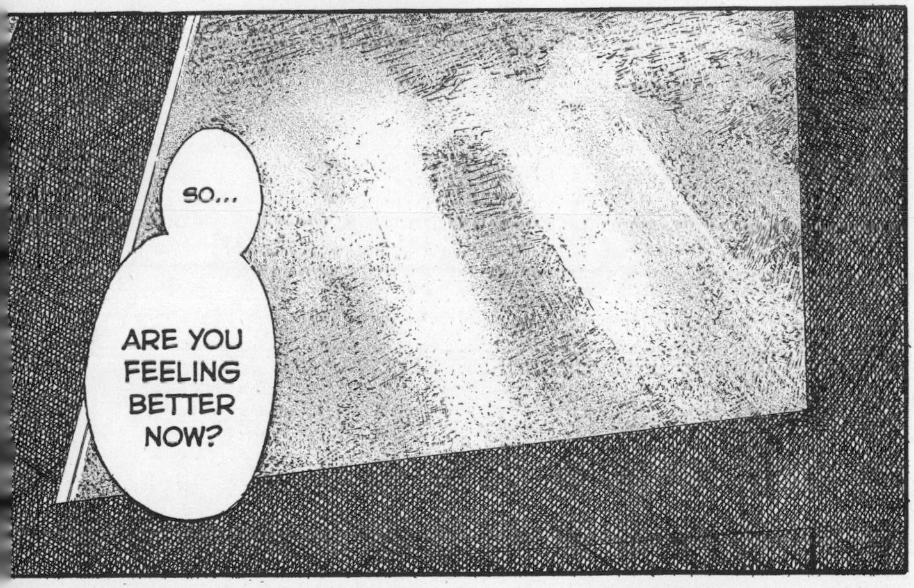
SO...
ARE YOU FEELING BETTER NOW?

Chapter 4: Nightwalking

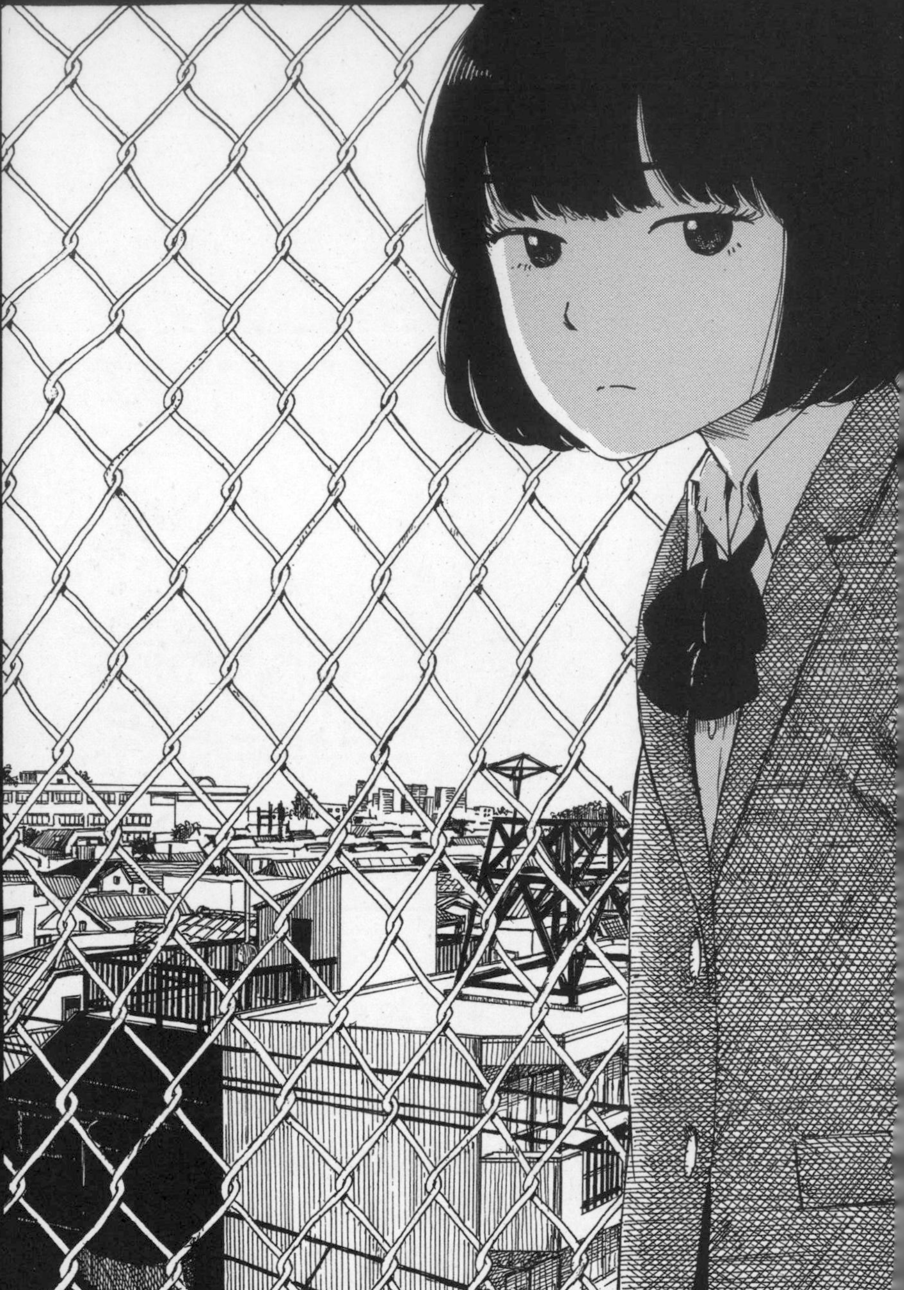

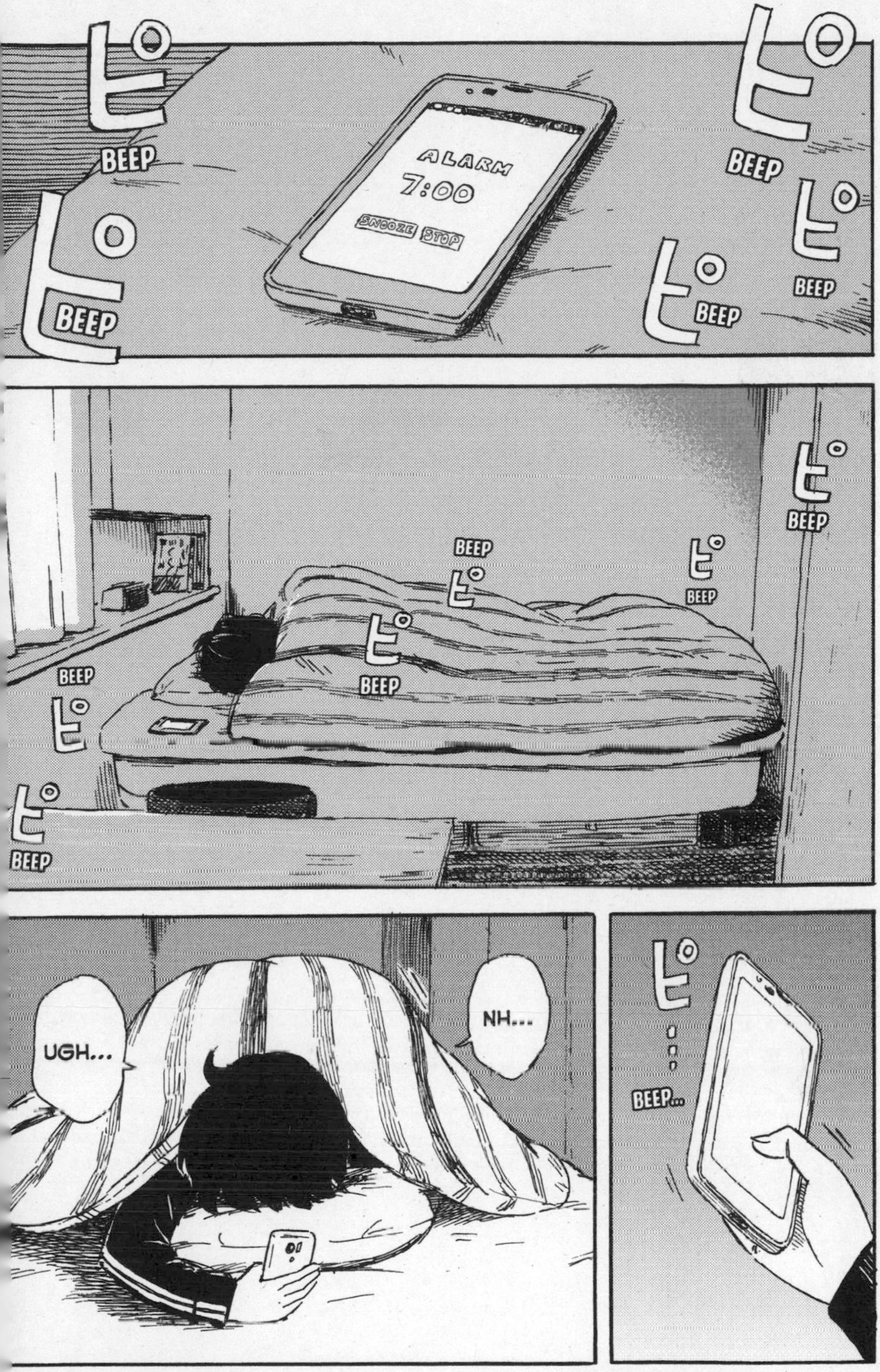
ピ
BEEP
ピ
BEEP
ピ
BEEP
ALARM
7:00
SNOOZE
STOP
ピ
BEEP
ピ
BEEP
ピ
BEEP
ピ
BEEP
BEEP
ピ
ピ
BEEP
BEEP
ピ
ピ
BEEP
ピ...
BEEP...
NH...
UGH...

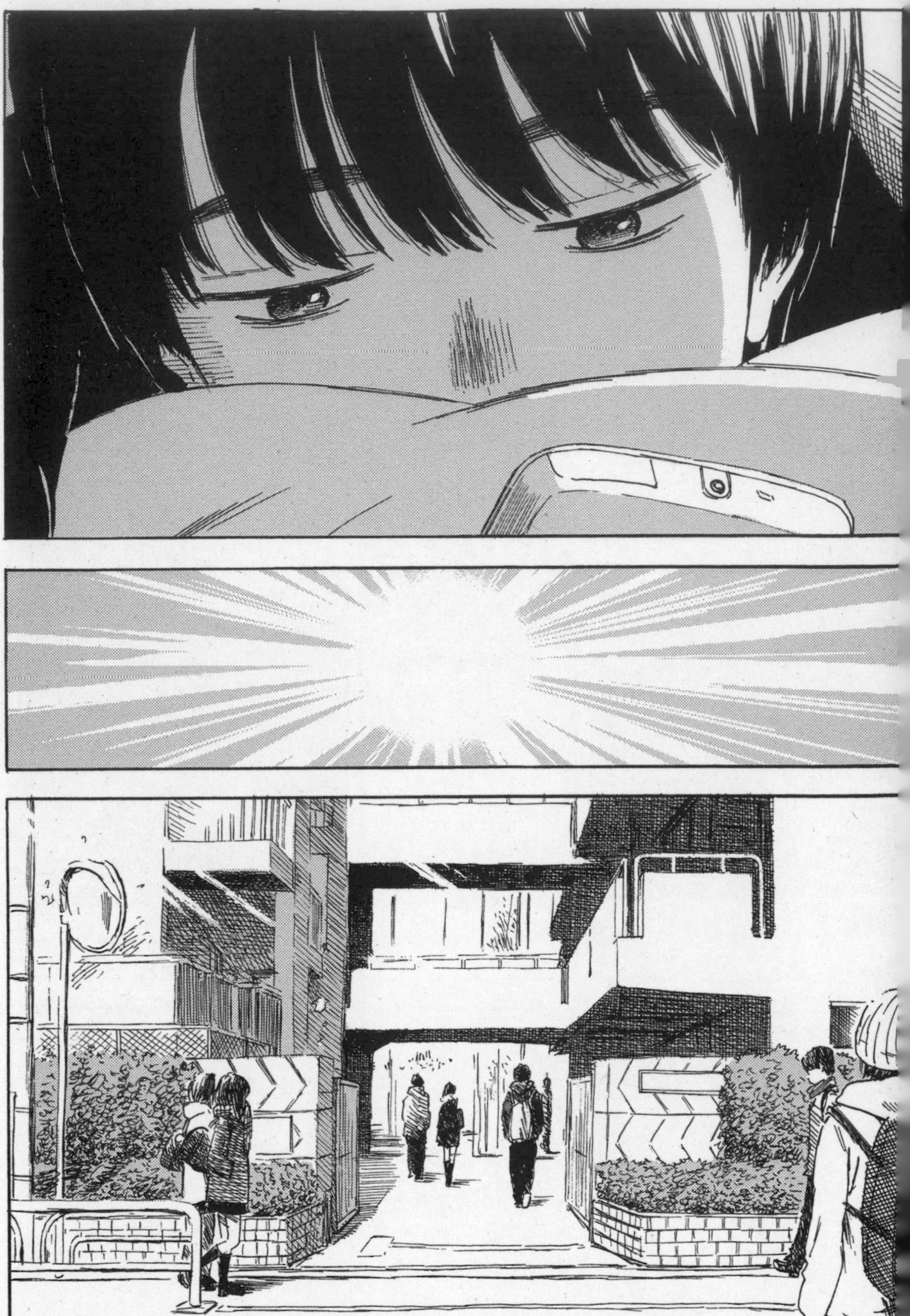

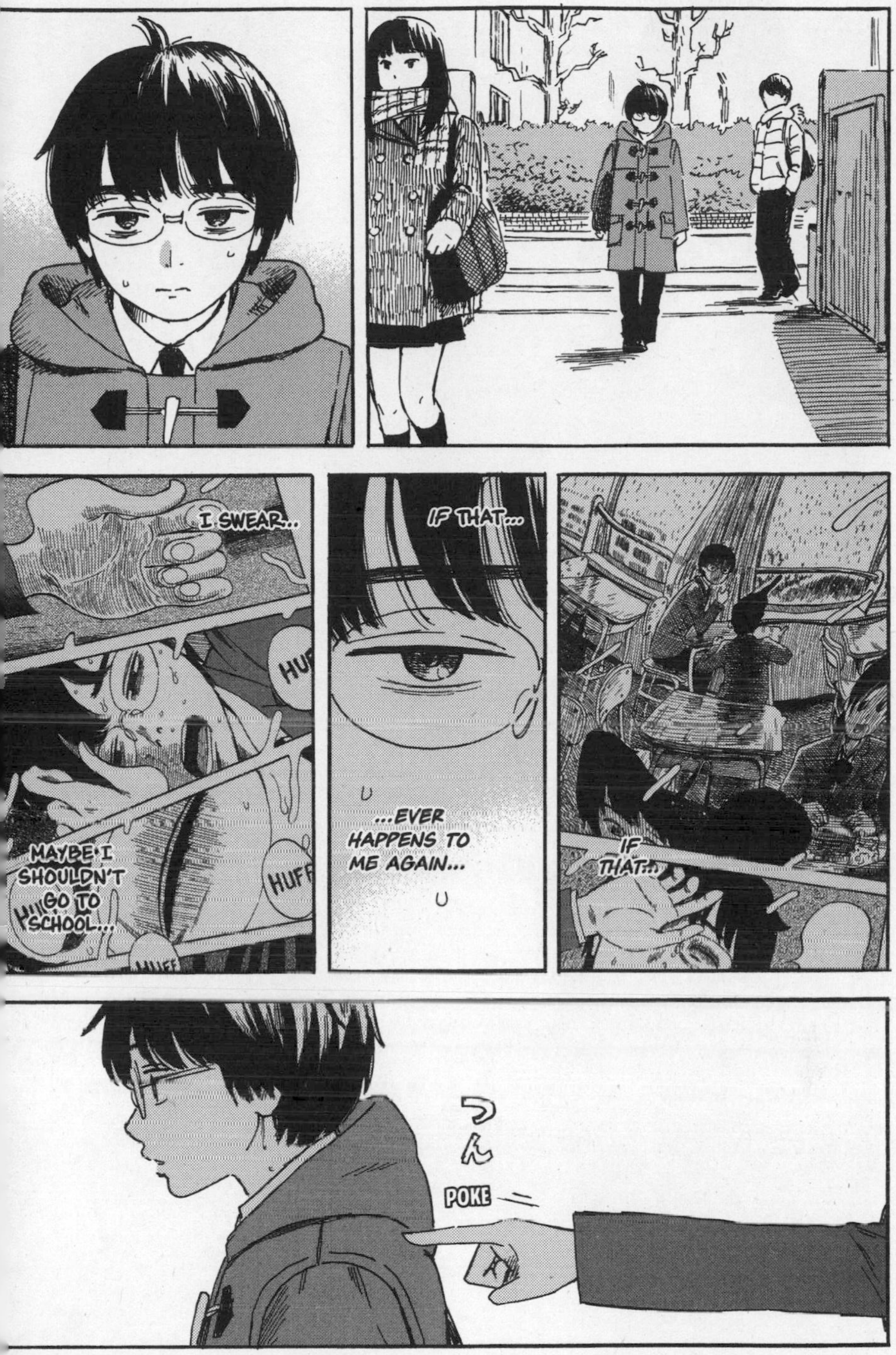
IF THAT...
IF THAT...
...EVER HAPPENS TO ME AGAIN...
I SWEAR...
HUFF
MAYBE I SHOULDN'T GO TO SCHOOL...
HUFF
つん
POKE

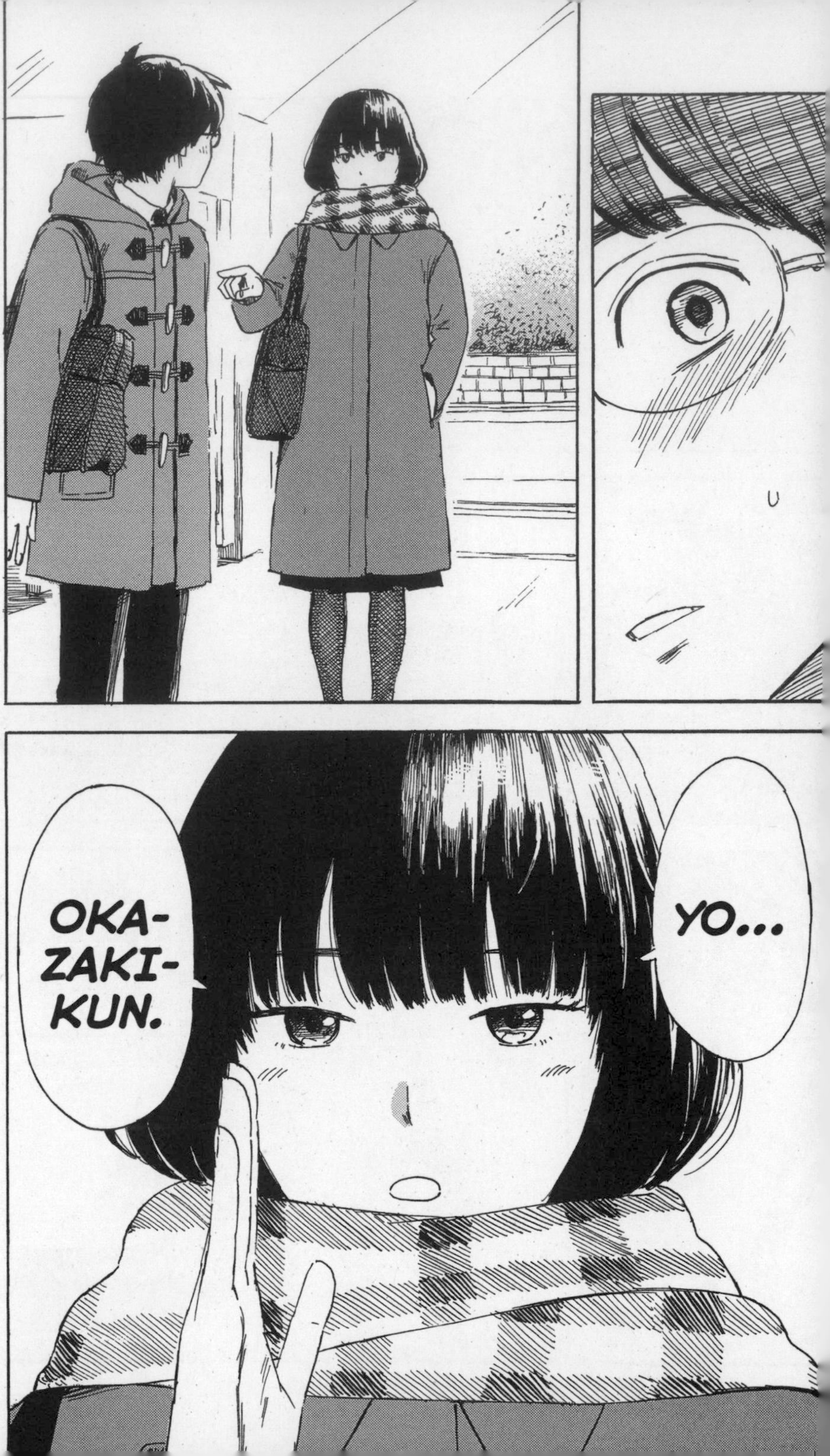
YO...
OKA-ZAKI-KUN.

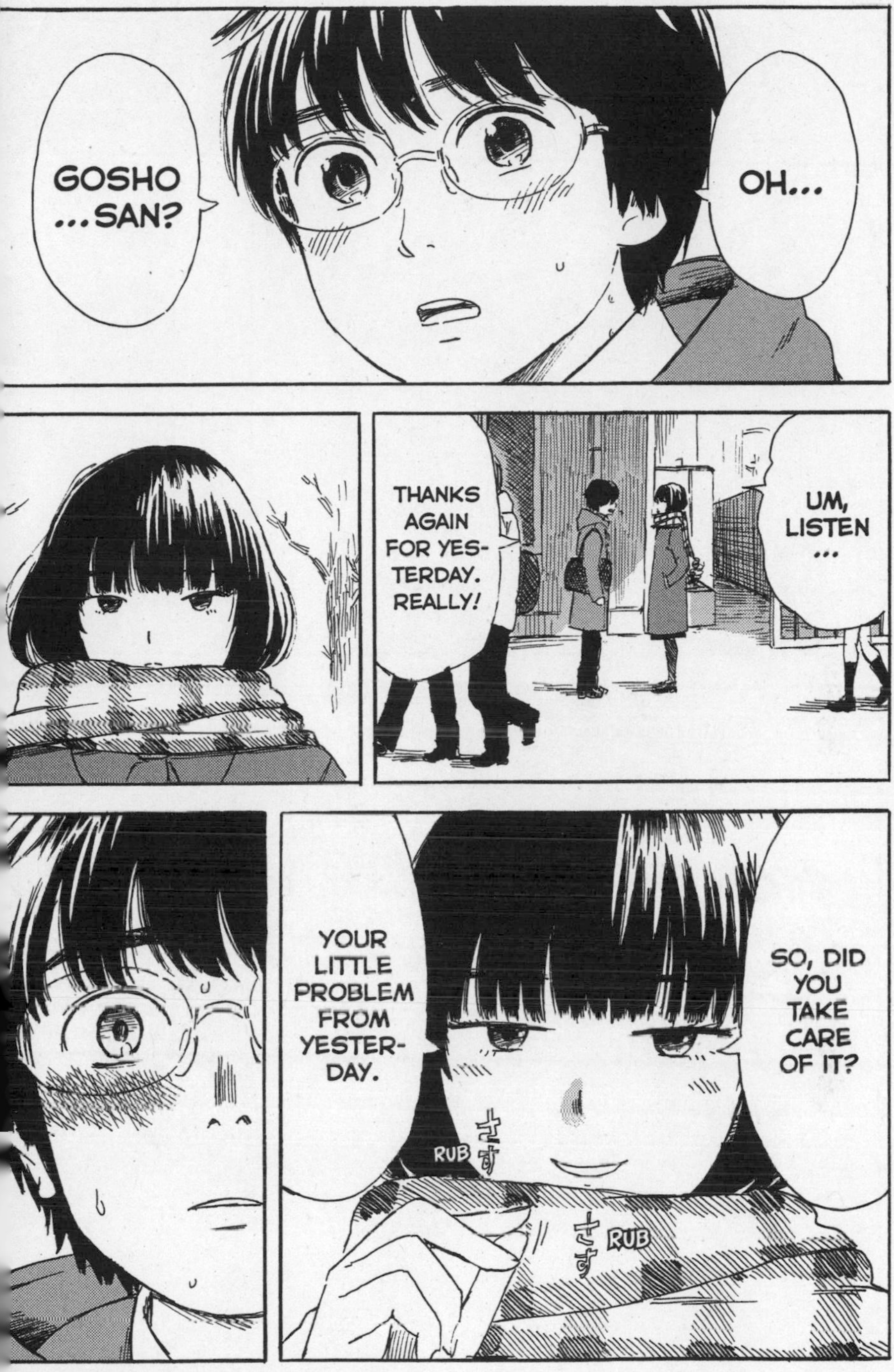
OH...
GOSHO ...SAN?
UM, LISTEN ...
THANKS AGAIN FOR YES-TERDAY. REALLY!
SO, DID YOU TAKE CARE OF IT?
YOUR LITTLE PROBLEM FROM YESTER-DAY.
さす
RUB
さす
RUB

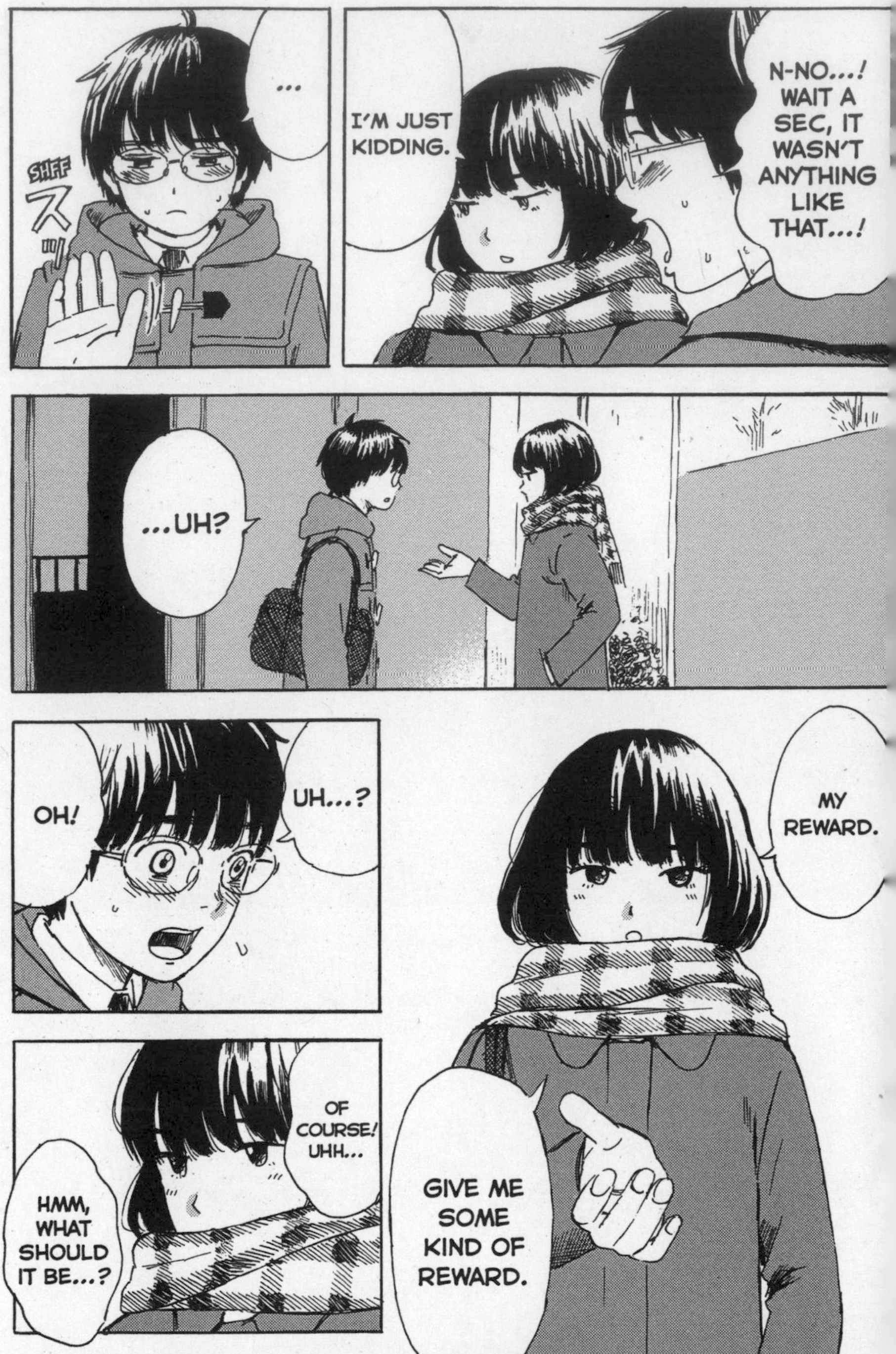
N-NO...! WAIT A SEC, IT WASN'T ANYTHING LIKE THAT...!
I'M JUST KIDDING.
...
SHFF
ス
ッ
...UH?
MY REWARD.
GIVE ME SOME KIND OF REWARD.
UH...?
OH!
OF COURSE! UHH...
HMM, WHAT SHOULD IT BE...?

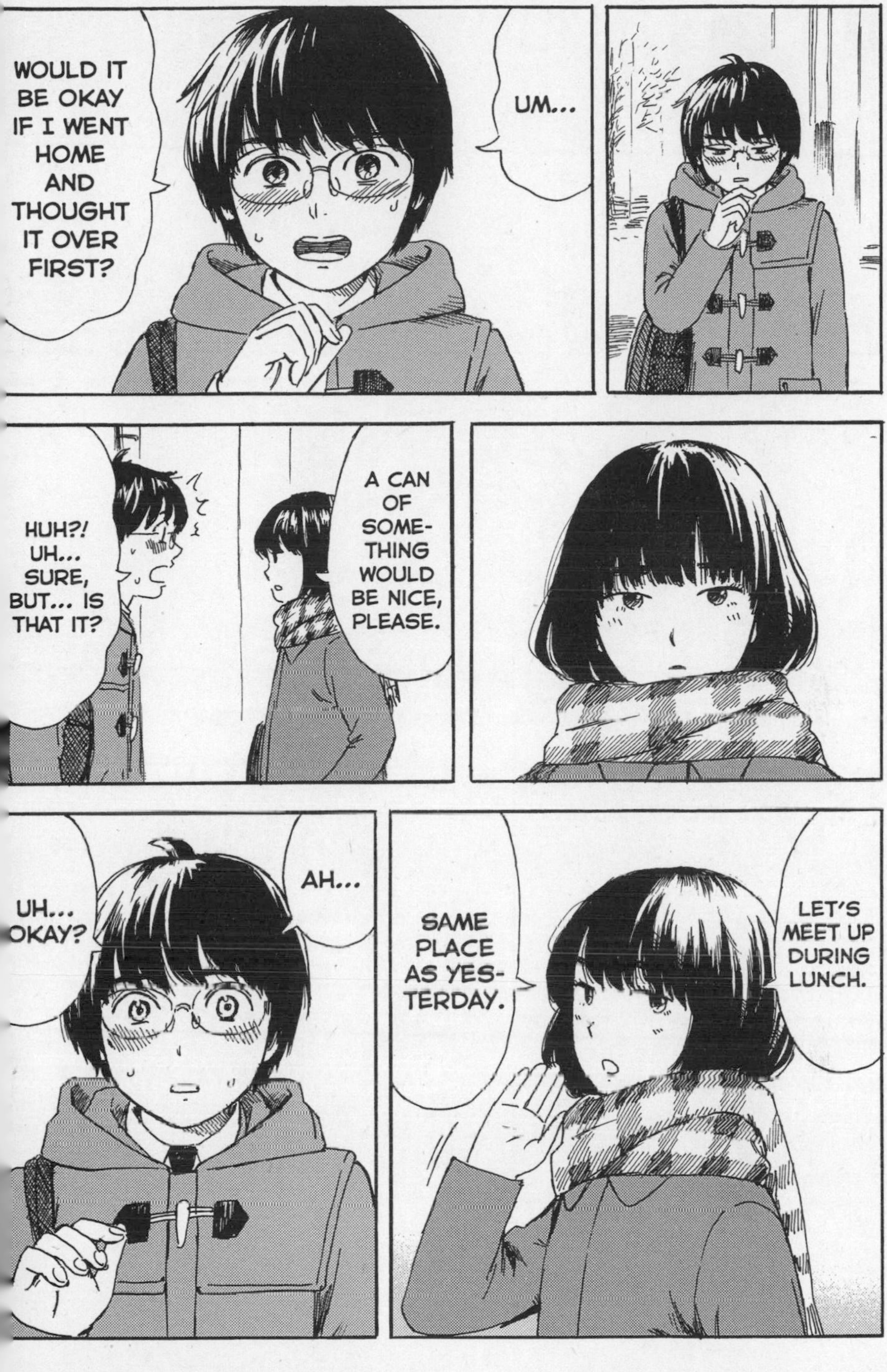
UM...
WOULD IT BE OKAY IF I WENT HOME AND THOUGHT IT OVER FIRST?
A CAN OF SOME-THING WOULD BE NICE, PLEASE.
HUH?! UH... SURE, BUT... IS THAT IT?
LET'S MEET UP DURING LUNCH.
SAME PLACE AS YES-TERDAY.
AH...
UH... OKAY?

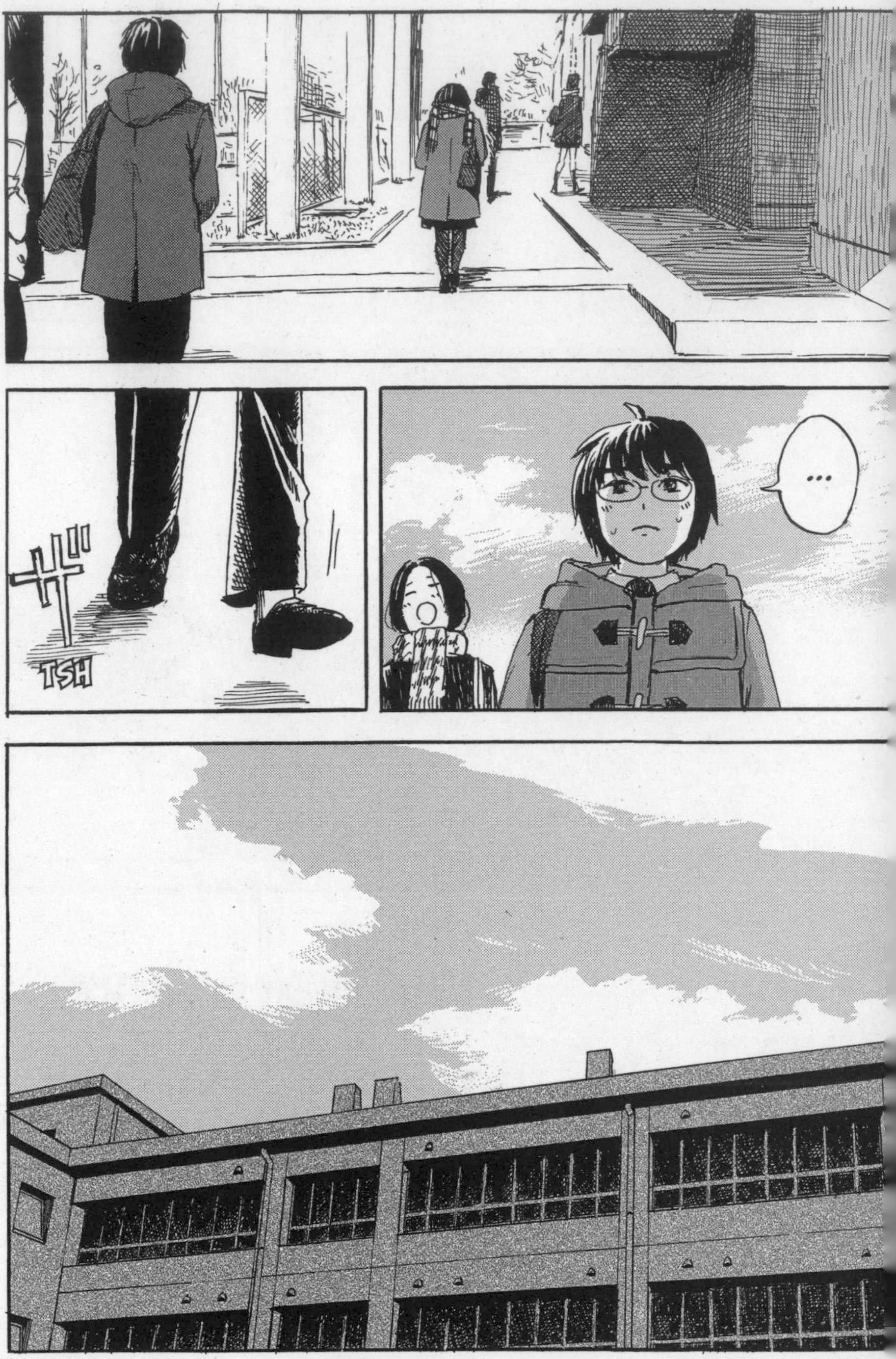
...
TSH

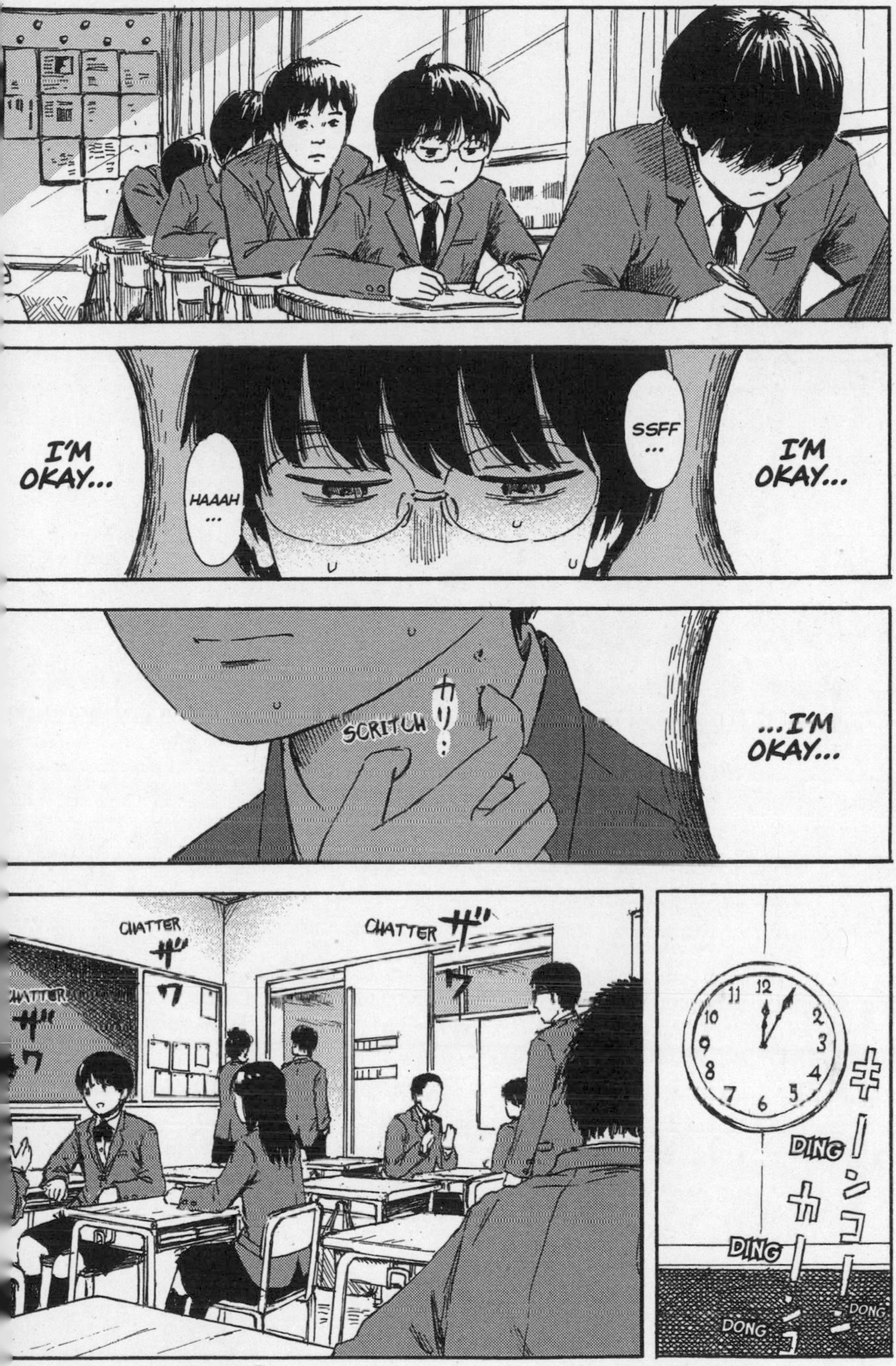
I'M OKAY...
SSFF ...
HAAAH ...
I'M OKAY...
...I'M OKAY...
SCRITCH
DING
DING
DONG
DONG
CHATTER
CHATTER
CHATTER

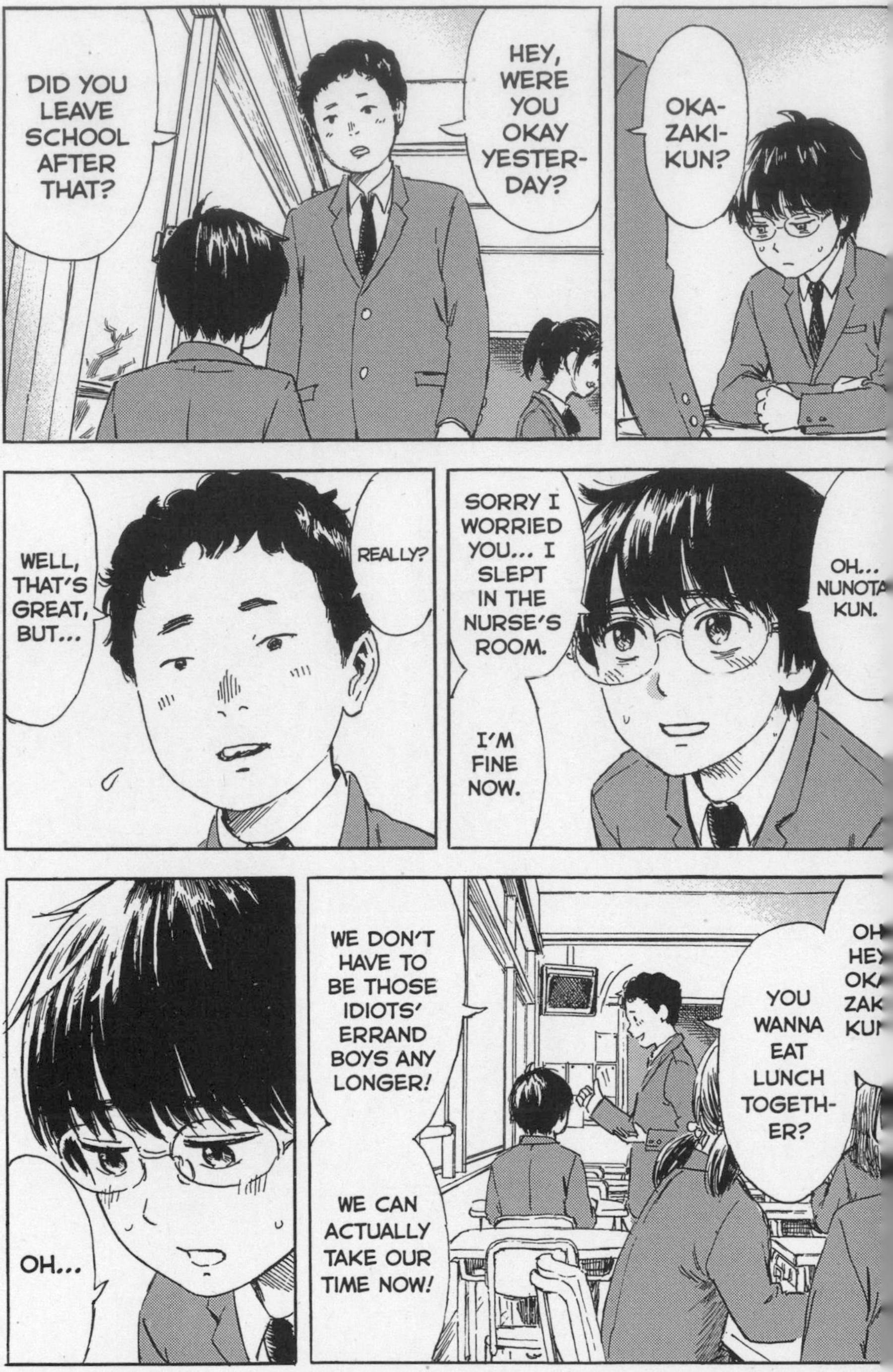
OKA-ZAKI-KUN?
HEY, WERE YOU OKAY YESTER-DAY?
DID YOU LEAVE SCHOOL AFTER THAT?
OH... NUNOTA KUN.
SORRY I WORRIED YOU... I SLEPT IN THE NURSE'S ROOM.
I'M FINE NOW.
REALLY?
WELL, THAT'S GREAT, BUT...
YOU WANNA EAT LUNCH TOGETH-ER?
WE DON'T HAVE TO BE THOSE IDIOTS' ERRAND BOYS ANY LONGER!
WE CAN ACTUALLY TAKE OUR TIME NOW!
OH...

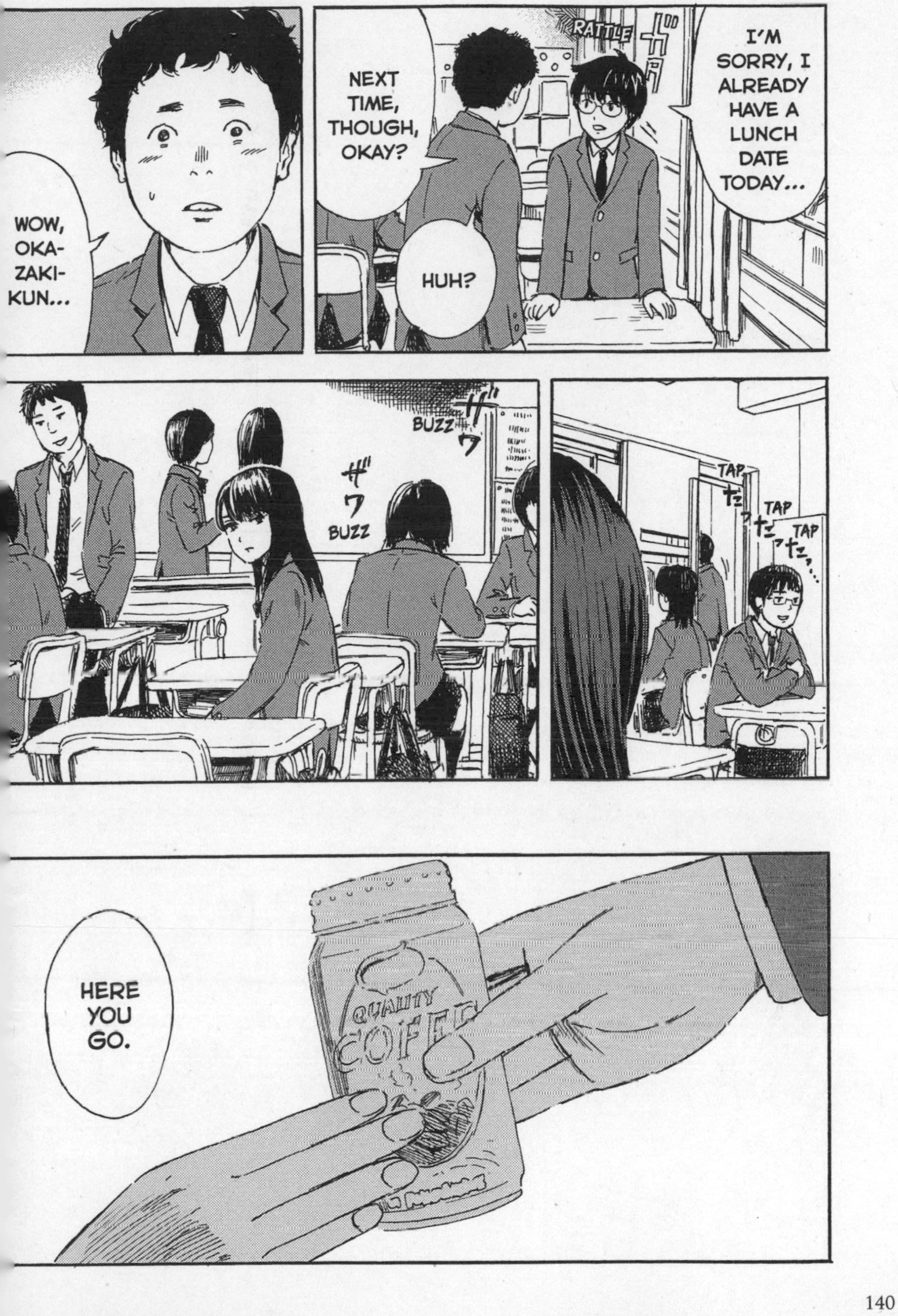
RATTLE
I'M SORRY, I ALREADY HAVE A LUNCH DATE TODAY...
NEXT TIME, THOUGH, OKAY?
HUH?
WOW, OKA-ZAKI-KUN...
TAP
TAP
TAP
BUZZ
BUZZ
HERE YOU GO.
QUALITY

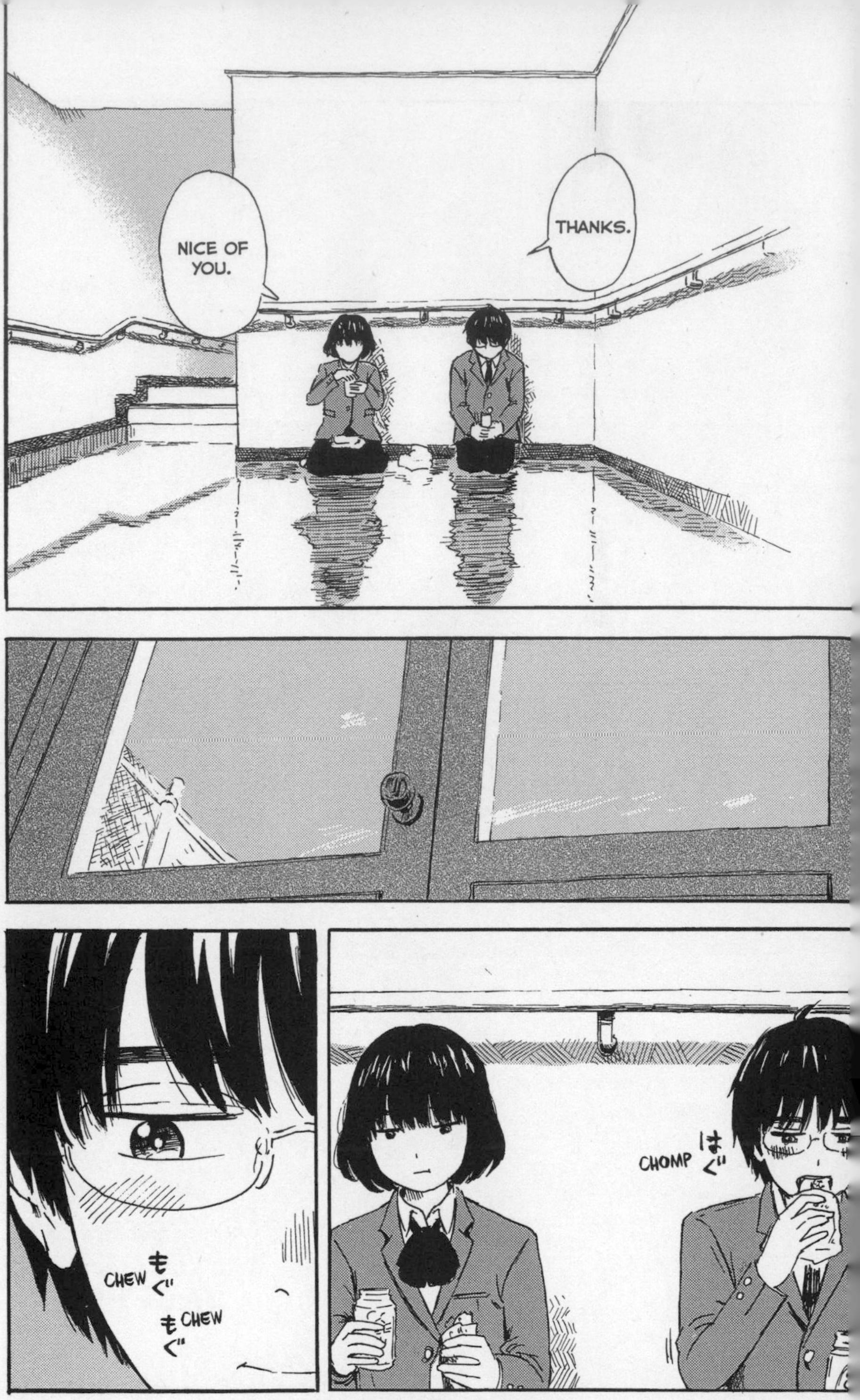
THANKS.
NICE OF YOU.
CHOMP はぐ
CHEW もぐ
もぐ CHEW

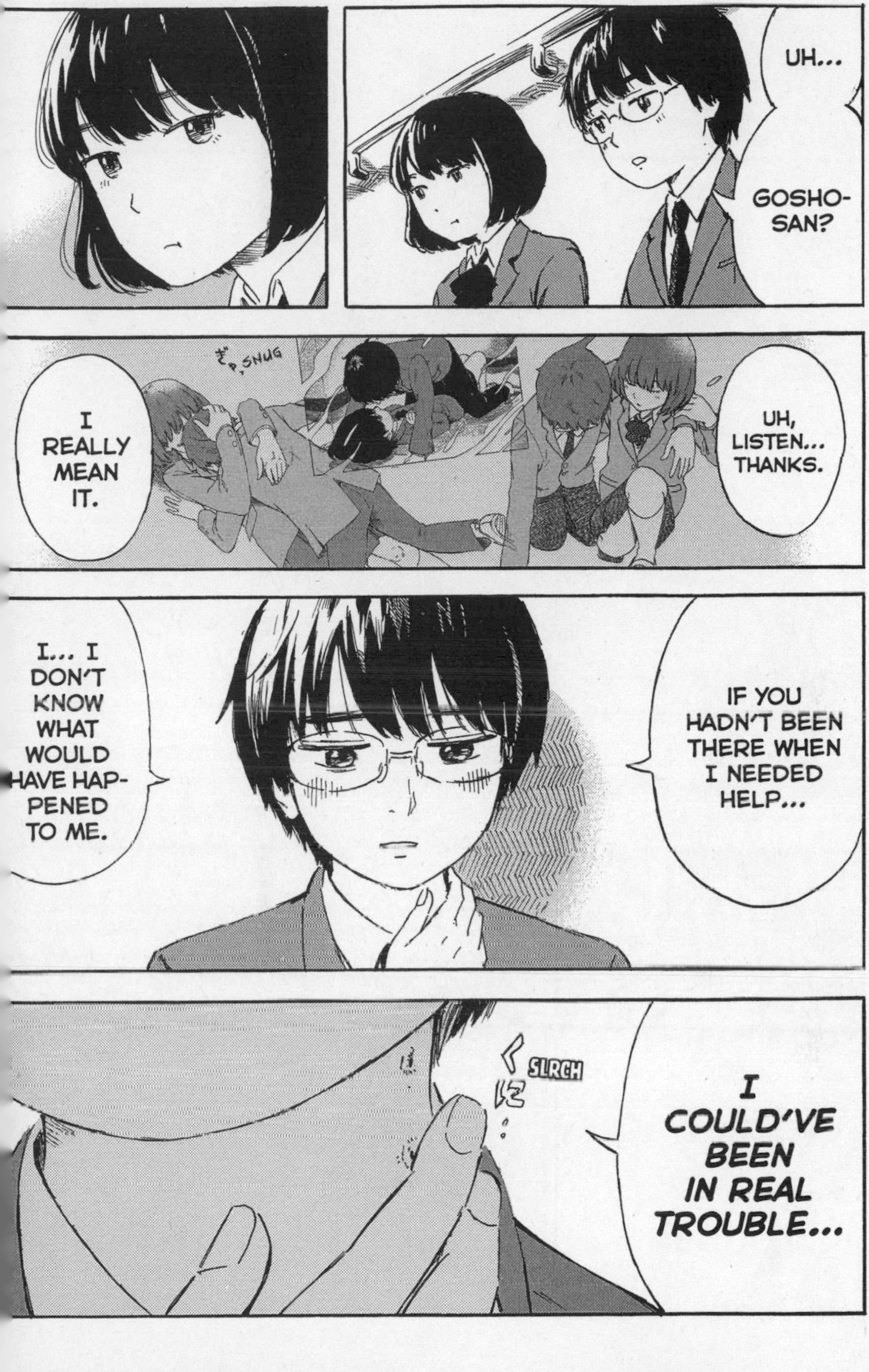
UH...
GOSHO-SAN?
UH, LISTEN... THANKS.
SNUG
I REALLY MEAN IT.
IF YOU HADN'T BEEN THERE WHEN I NEEDED HELP...
I... I DON'T KNOW WHAT WOULD HAVE HAP-PENED TO ME.
I COULD'VE BEEN IN REAL TROUBLE...
SLRCH

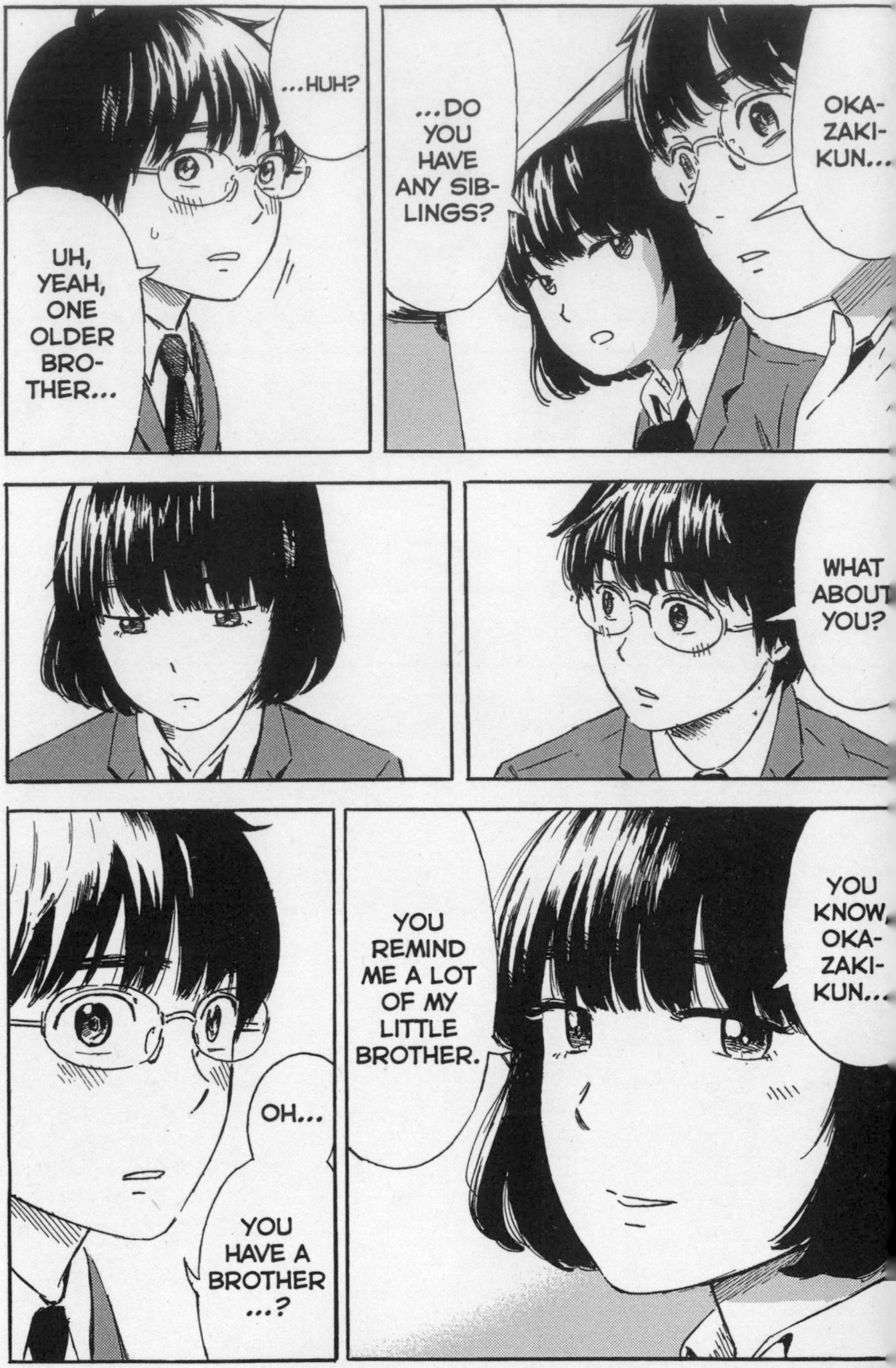
OKA-ZAKI-KUN...
...DO YOU HAVE ANY SIB-LINGS?
...HUH?
UH, YEAH, ONE OLDER BRO-THER...
WHAT ABOUT YOU?
YOU KNOW, OKA-ZAKI-KUN...
YOU REMIND ME A LOT OF MY LITTLE BROTHER.
OH...
YOU HAVE A BROTHER ...?

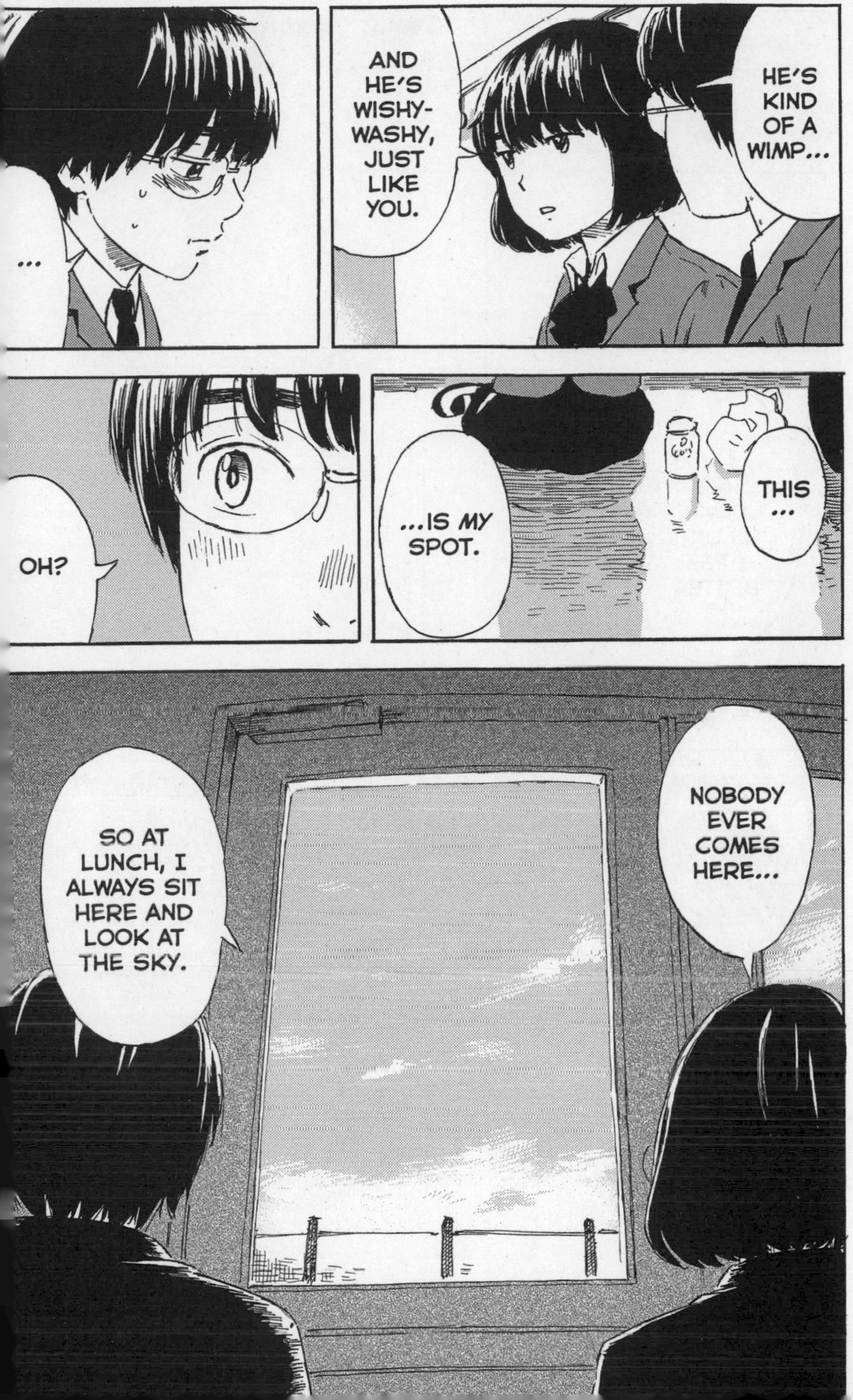
HE'S KIND OF A WIMP...
AND HE'S WISHY-WASHY, JUST LIKE YOU.
...
THIS...
...IS *MY* SPOT.
OH?
NOBODY EVER COMES HERE...
SO AT LUNCH, I ALWAYS SIT HERE AND LOOK AT THE SKY.

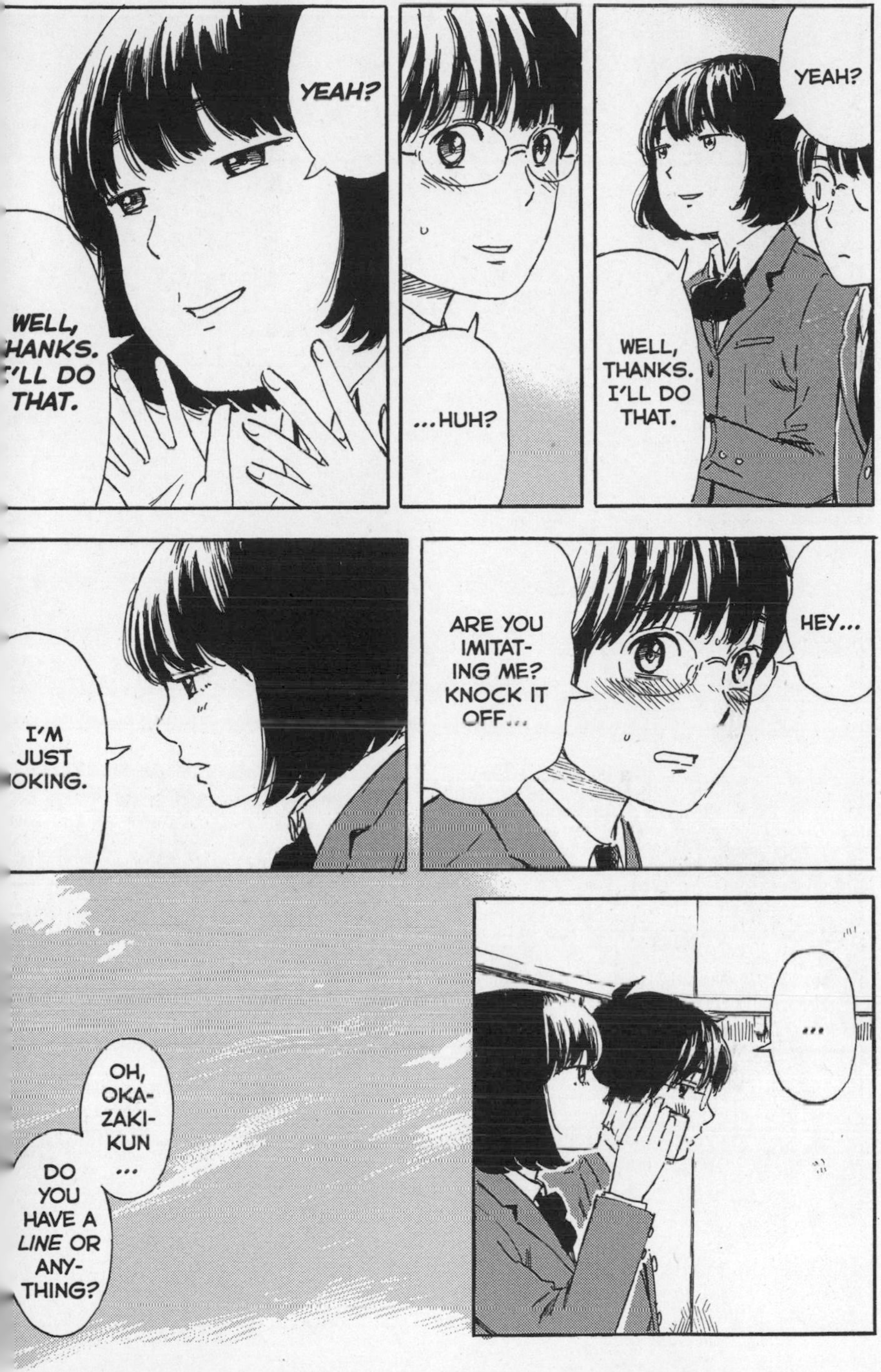
YEAH?
WELL, THANKS. I'LL DO THAT.
...HUH?
YEAH?
WELL, HANKS. 'LL DO THAT.
HEY...
ARE YOU IMITATING ME? KNOCK IT OFF...
I'M JUST OKING.
...
OH, OKAZAKI-KUN...
DO YOU HAVE A *LINE* OR ANYTHING?

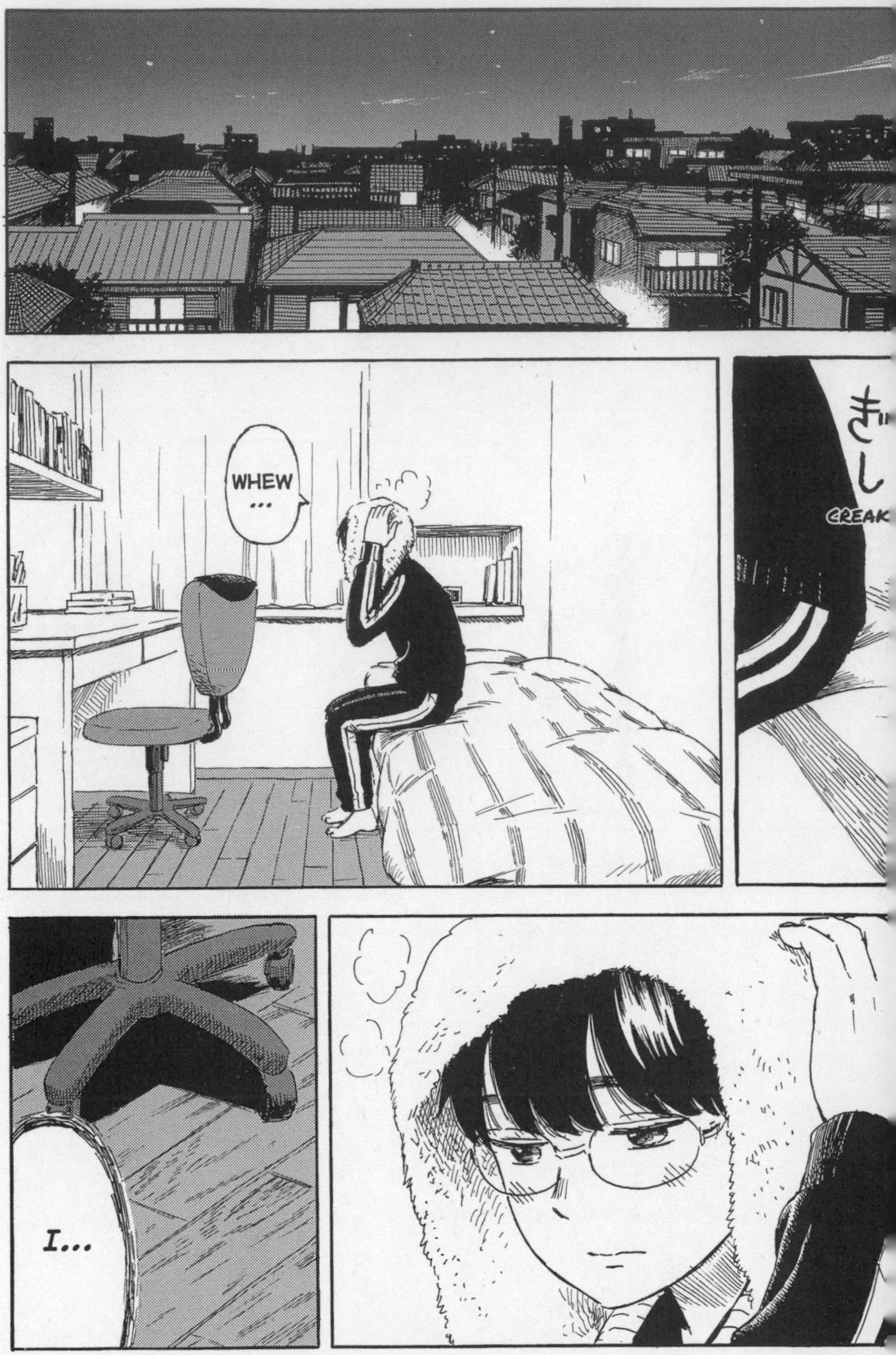
ぎし
CREAK
WHEW ...
I...

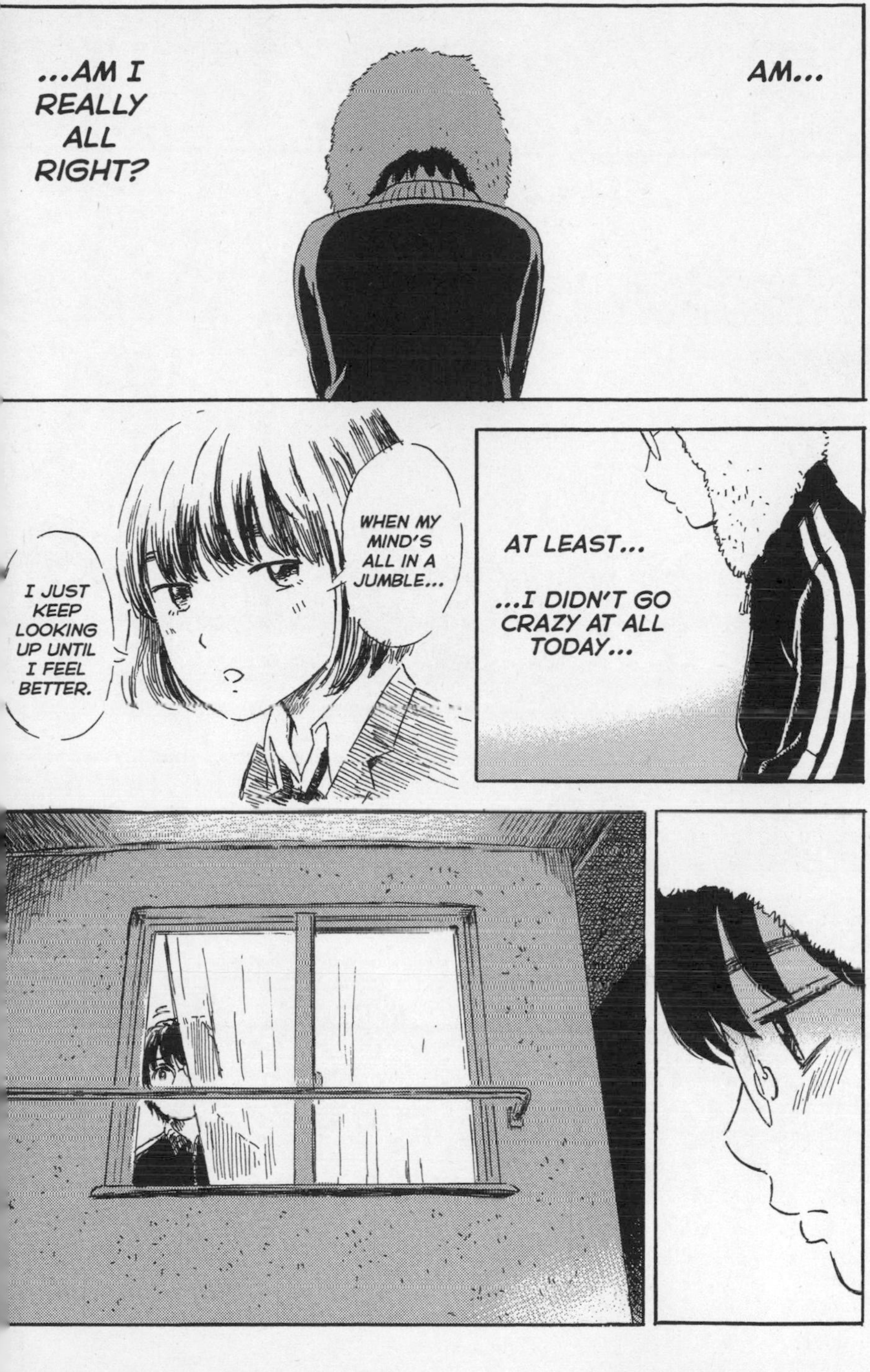
AM...
...AM I REALLY ALL RIGHT?
AT LEAST...
...I DIDN'T GO CRAZY AT ALL TODAY...
WHEN MY MIND'S ALL IN A JUMBLE...
I JUST KEEP LOOKING UP UNTIL I FEEL BETTER.

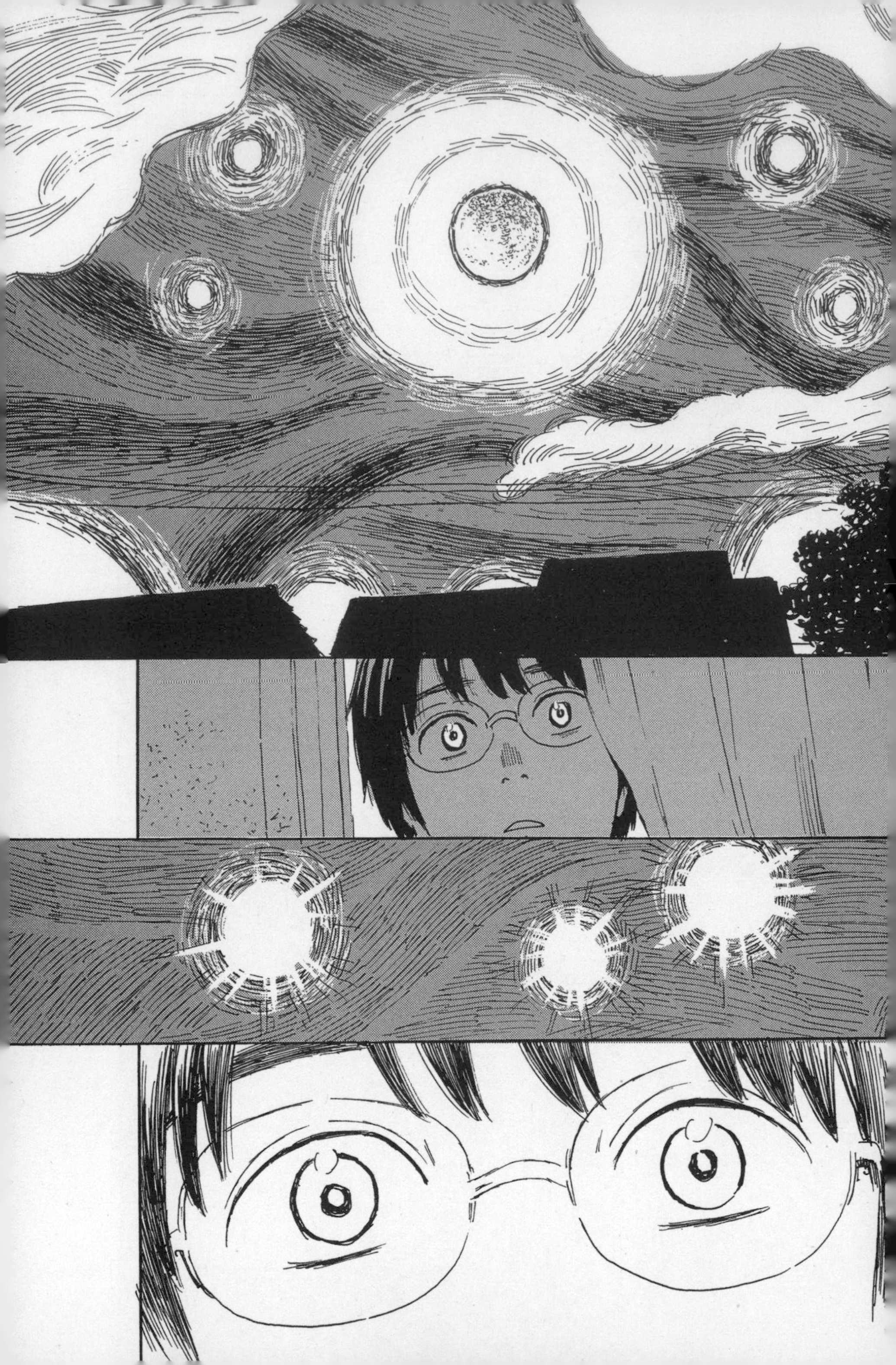

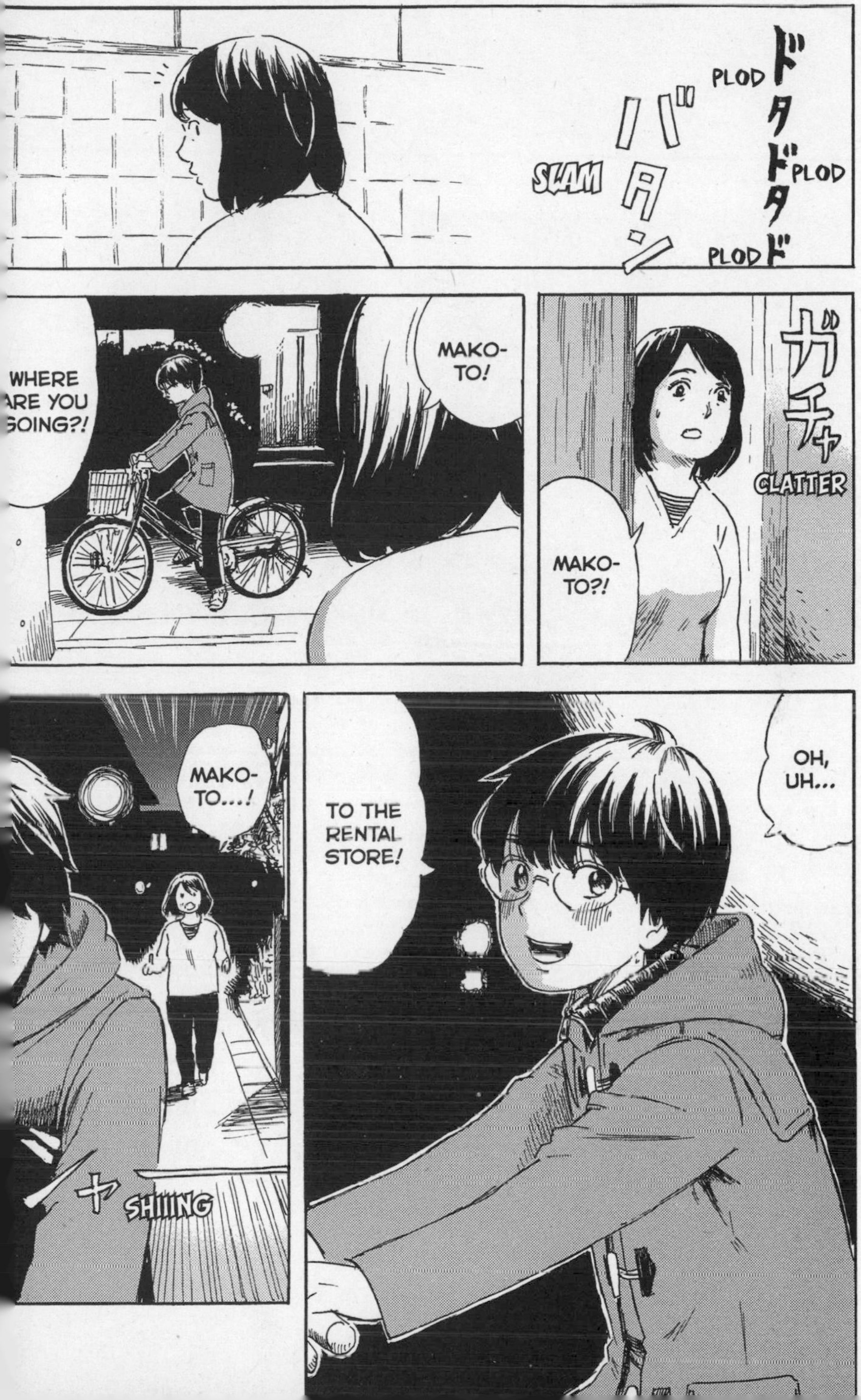
ドタドタド
PLOD
PLOD
PLOD
バタン
SLAM
ガチャ
CLATTER
MAKO-TO?!
MAKO-TO!
WHERE ARE YOU GOING?!
OH, UH...
TO THE RENTAL STORE!
MAKO-TO...!
SHIIING

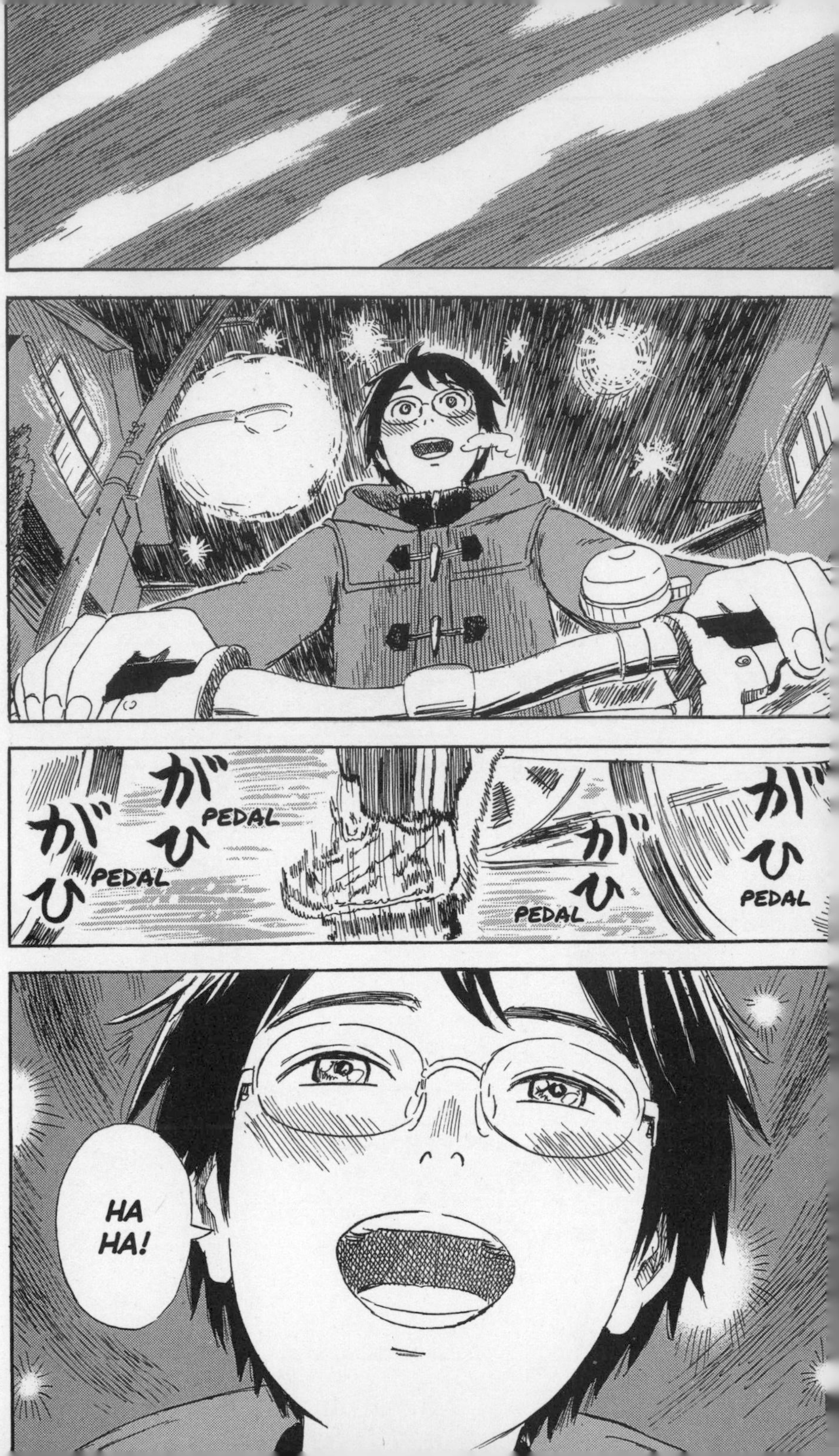
がひ
PEDAL
がひ
PEDAL
がひ
PEDAL
がひ
PEDAL
HA HA!

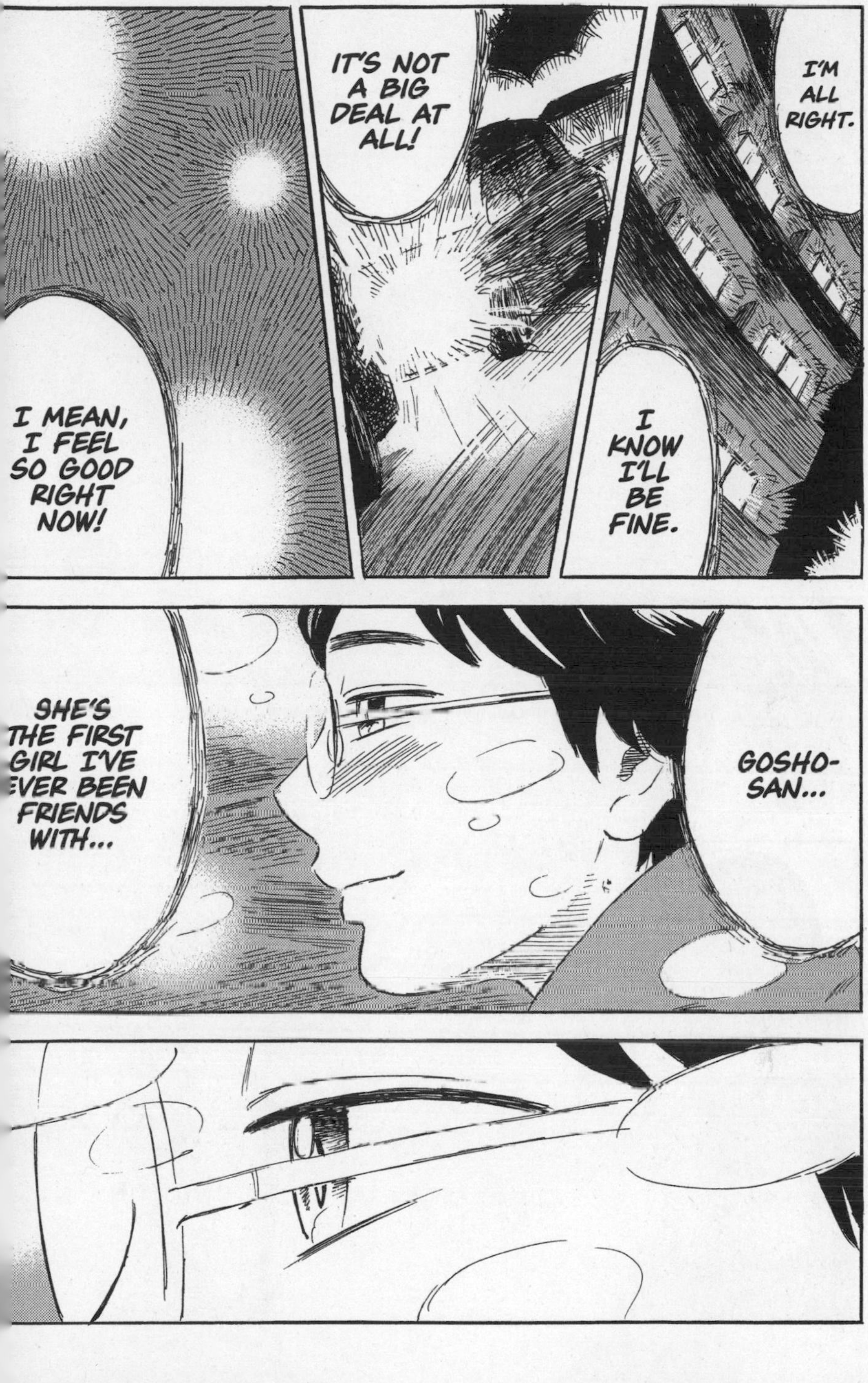
I'M ALL RIGHT.
I KNOW I'LL BE FINE.
IT'S NOT A BIG DEAL AT ALL!
I MEAN, I FEEL SO GOOD RIGHT NOW!
GOSHO-SAN...
SHE'S THE FIRST GIRL I'VE EVER BEEN FRIENDS WITH...

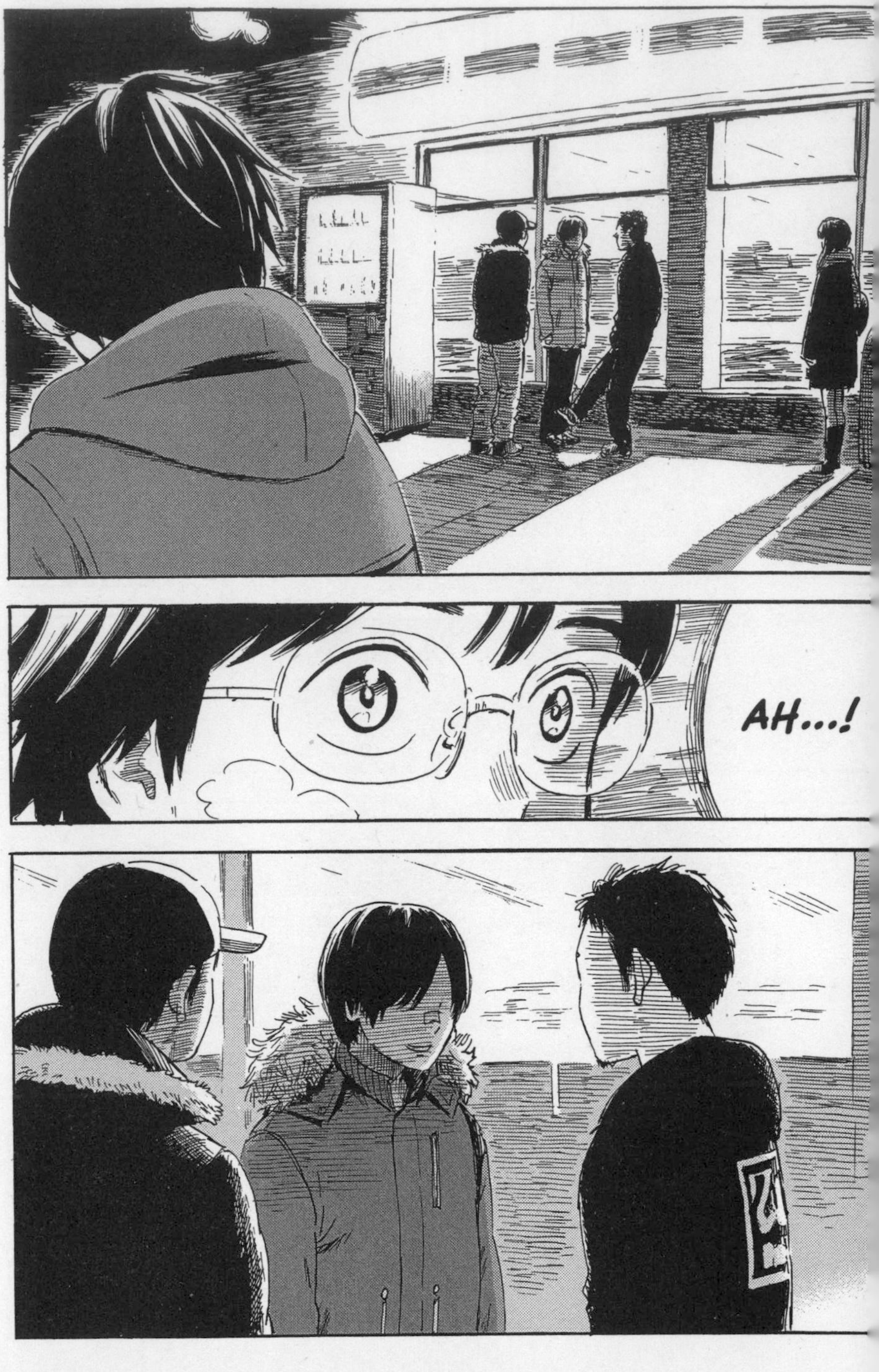
AH...!

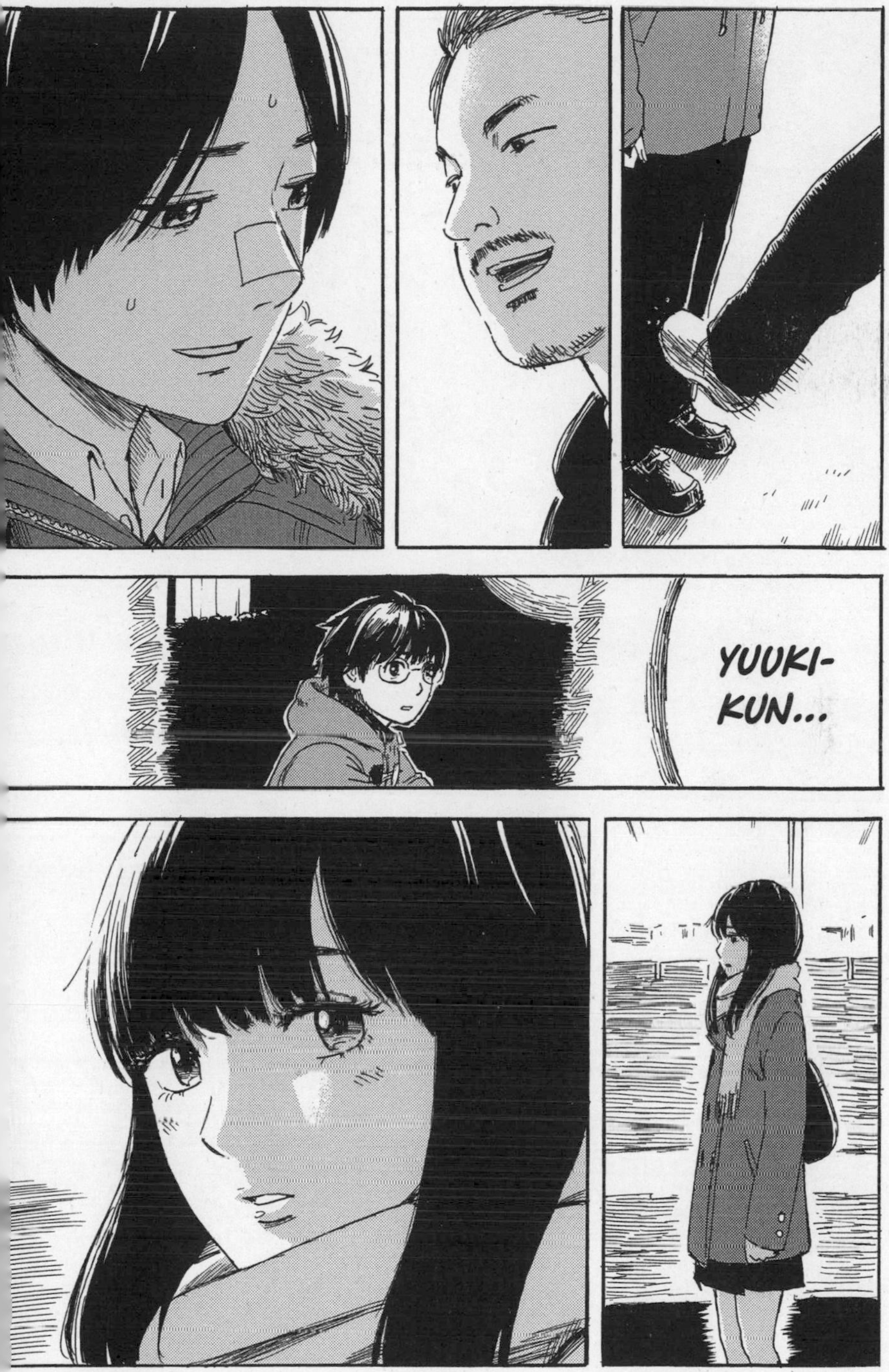
YUUKI-
KUN...

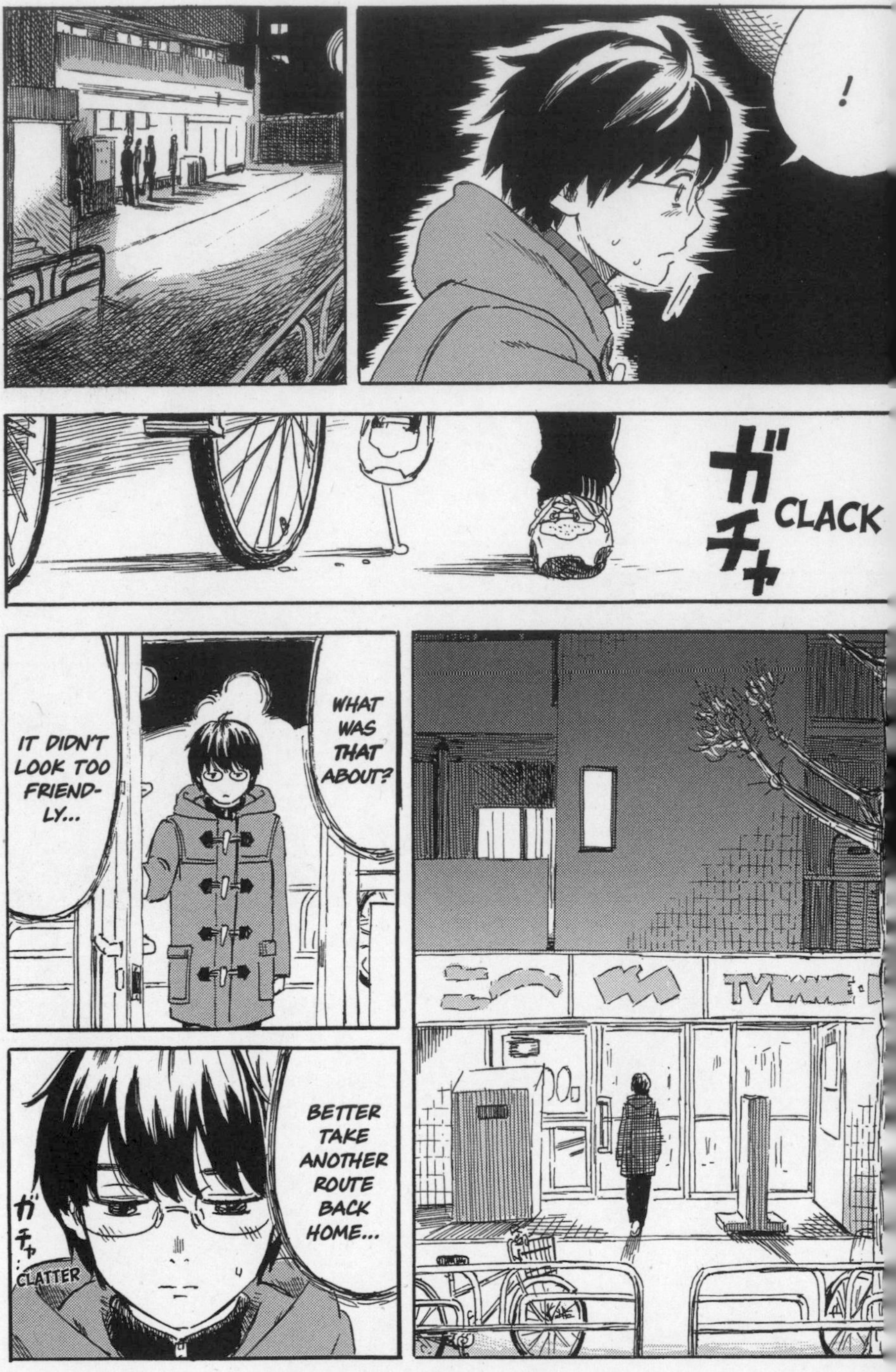
!
ガチャ
CLACK
WHAT WAS THAT ABOUT?
IT DIDN'T LOOK TOO FRIEND-LY...
BETTER TAKE ANOTHER ROUTE BACK HOME...
ガチャ
CLATTER

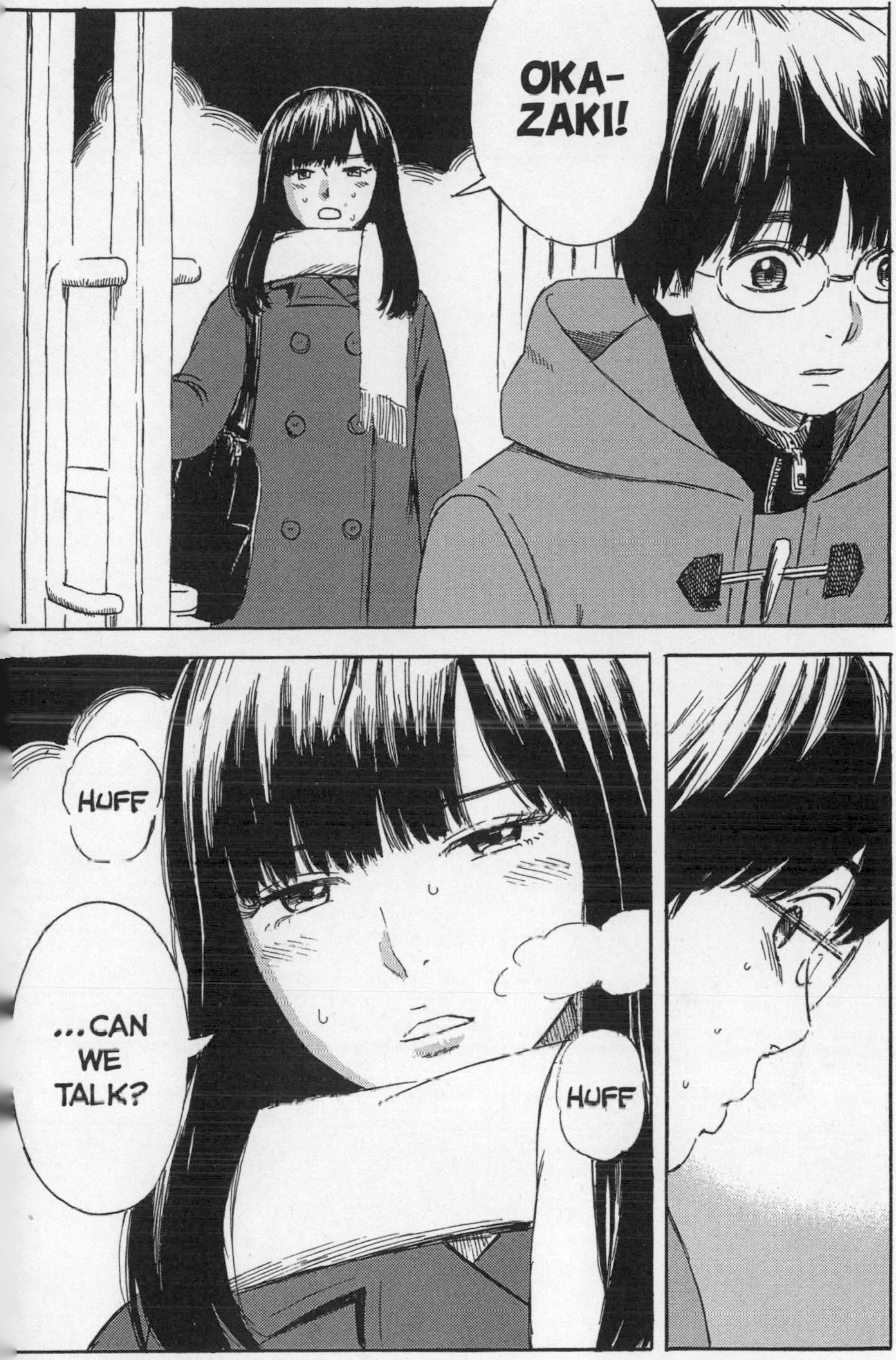
OKA-ZAKI!
HUFF
HUFF
...CAN WE TALK?

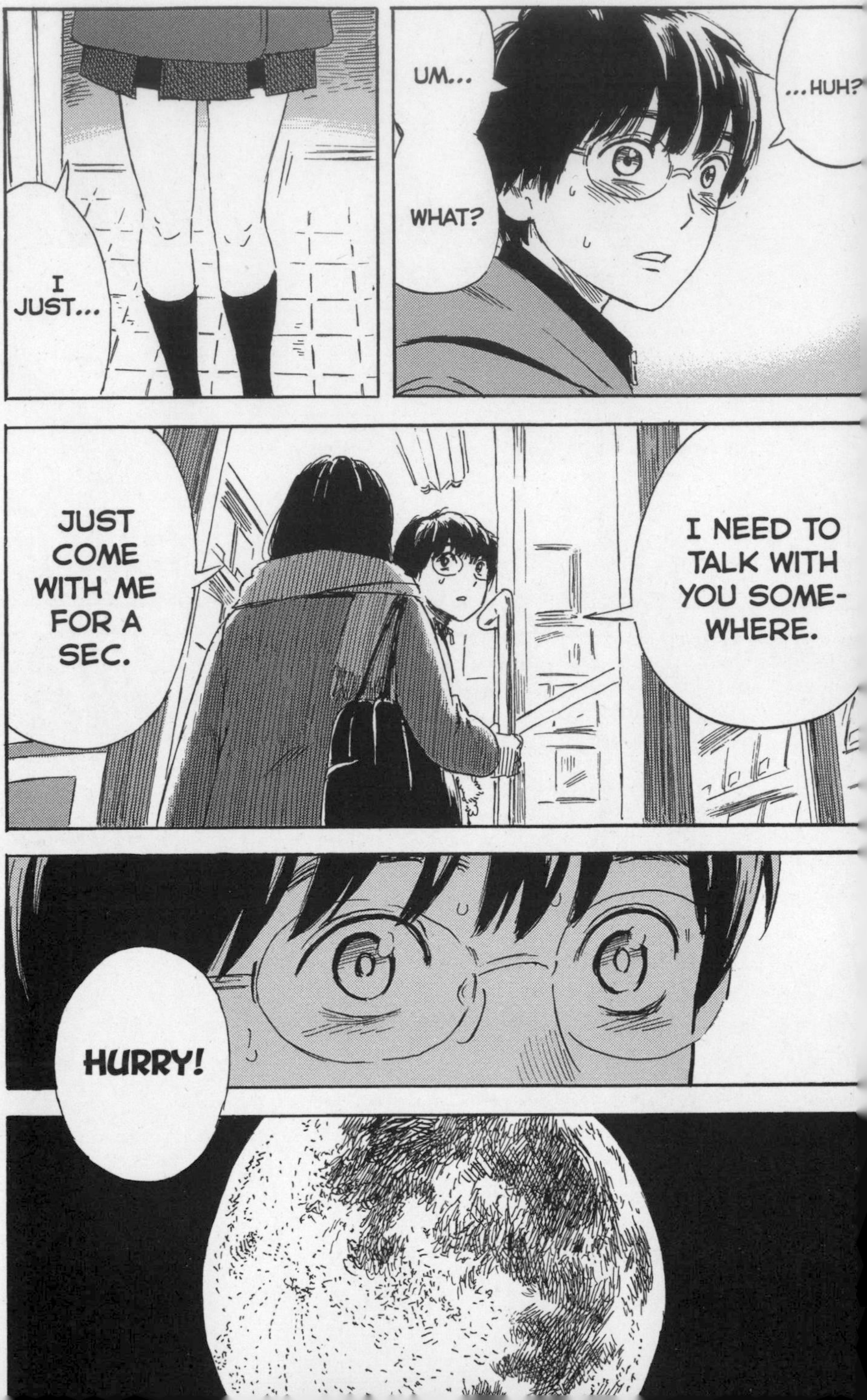
...HUH?
UM...
WHAT?
I JUST...
I NEED TO TALK WITH YOU SOME-WHERE.
JUST COME WITH ME FOR A SEC.
HURRY!

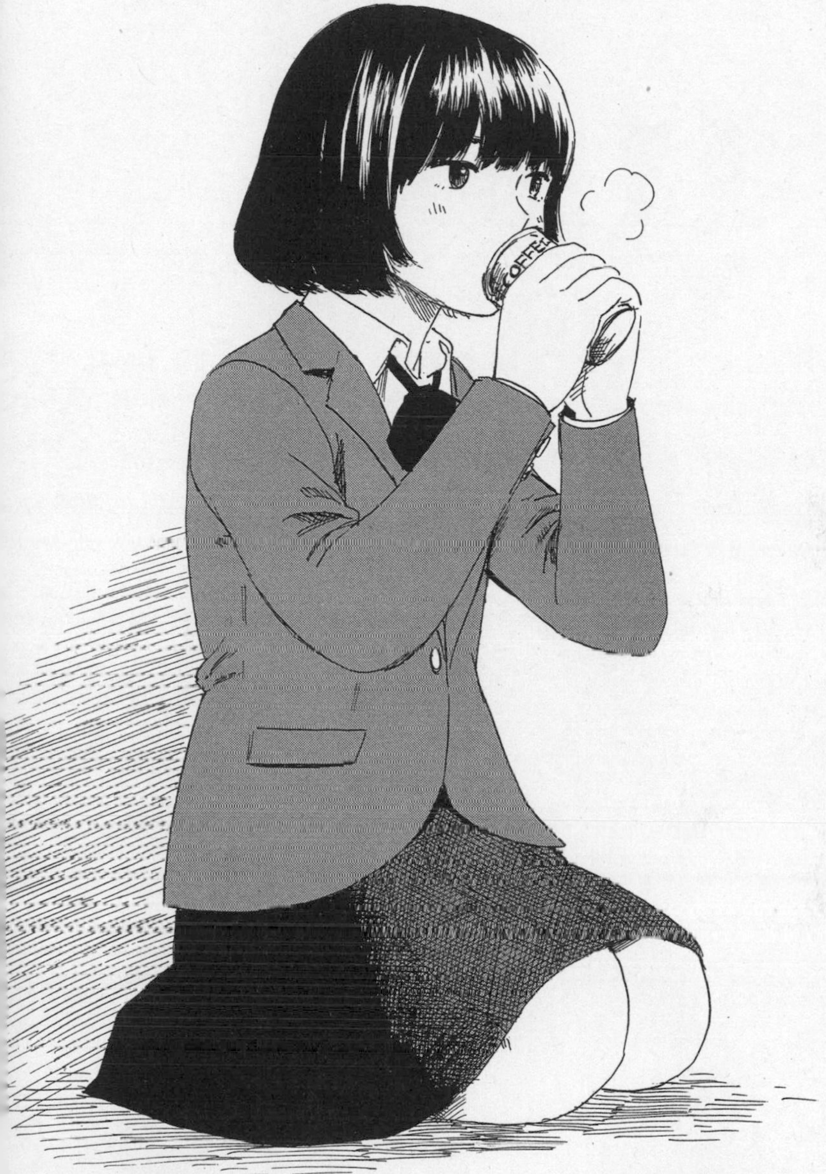

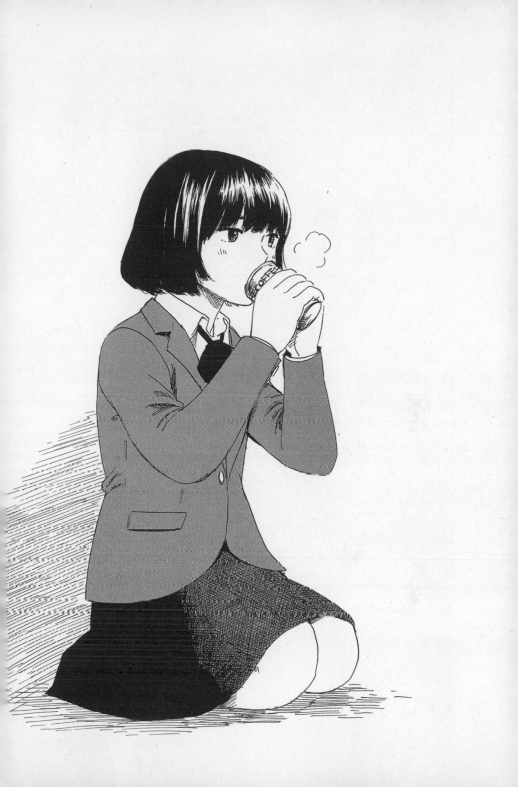

Chapter 5: Payback

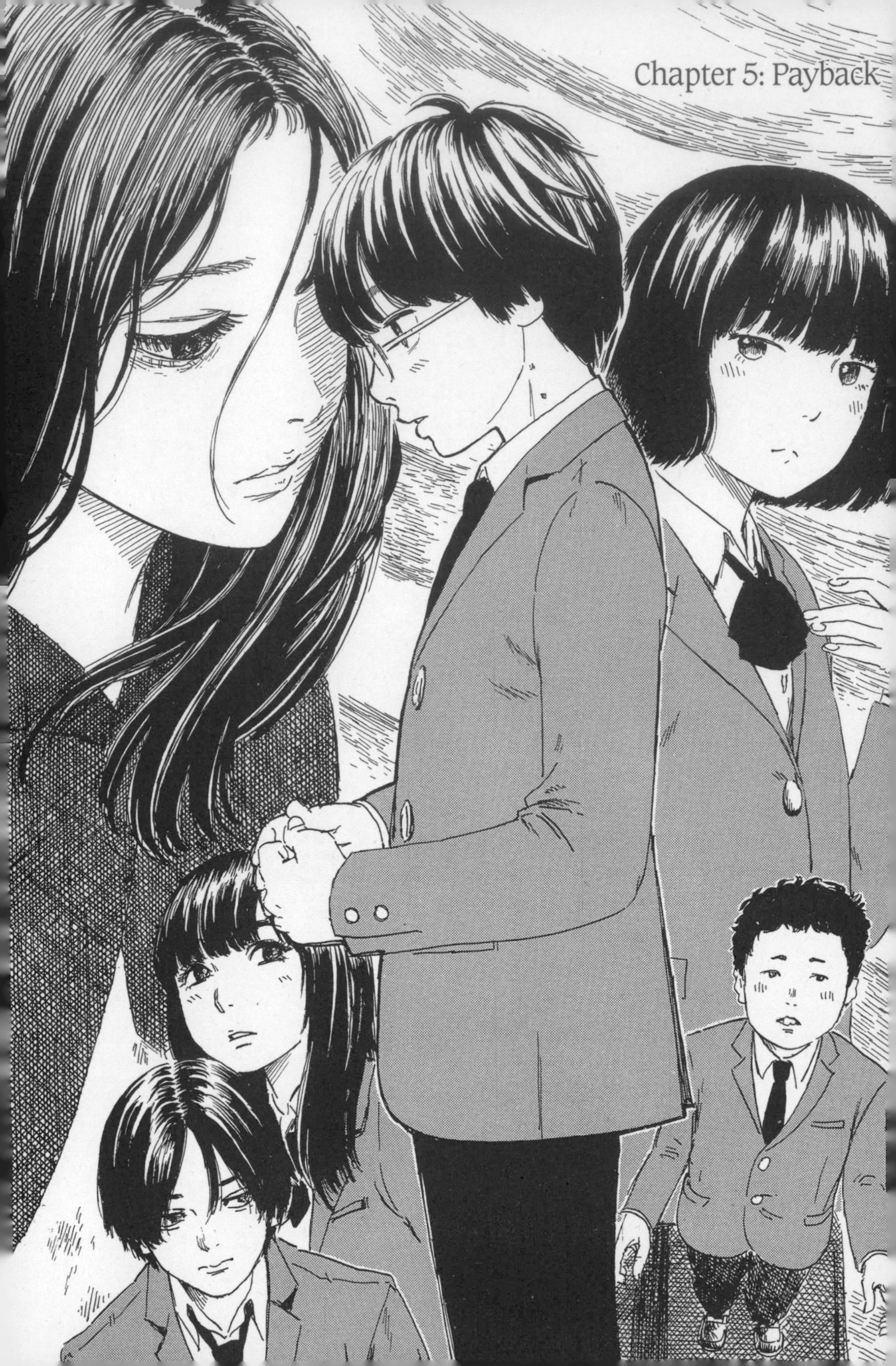

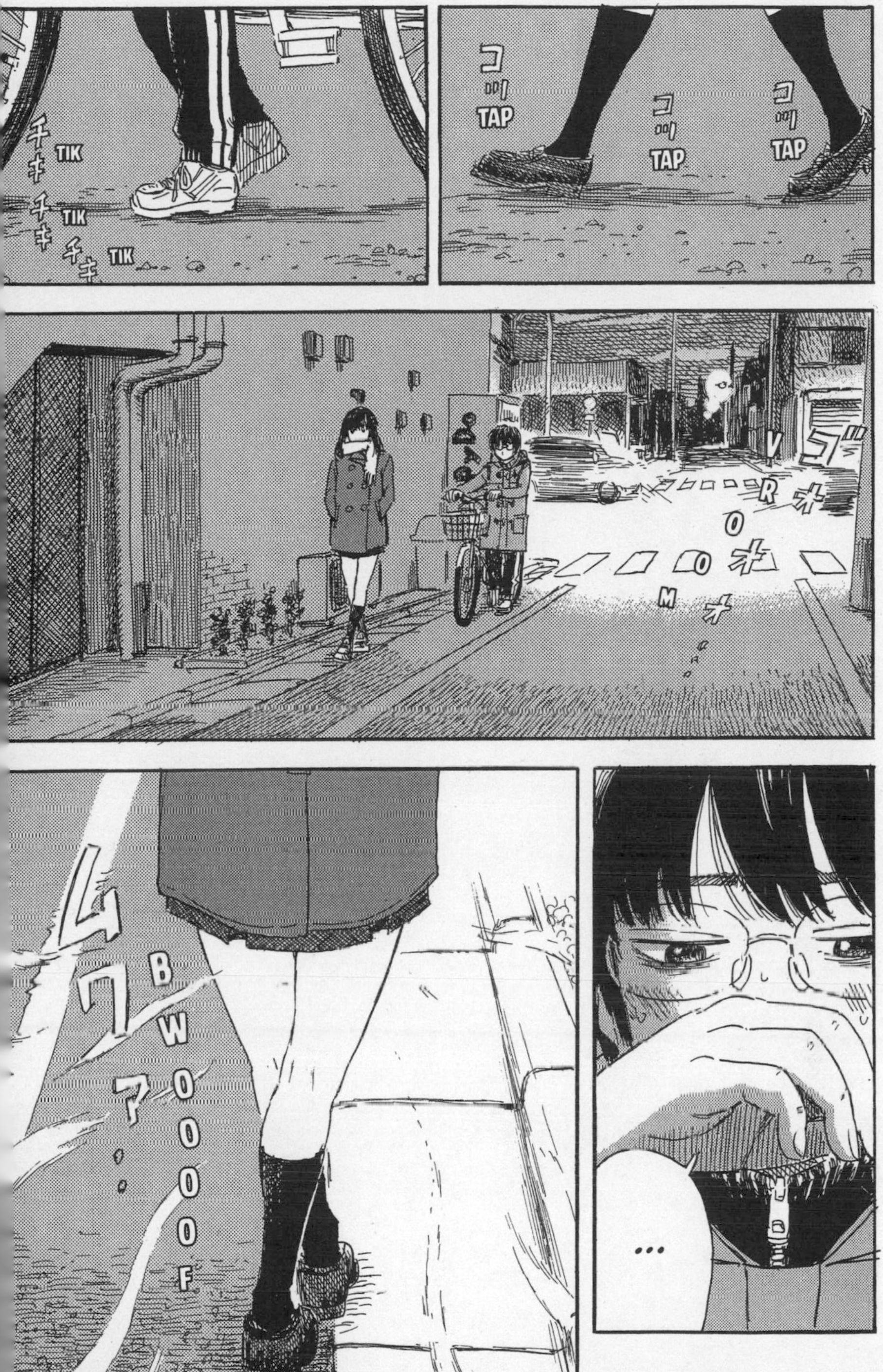
コッ
TAP
コッ
TAP
コッ
TAP
チキ
TIK
チキ
TIK
チキ
TIK
ブォオオオ
VROOOM
...
ムワァ
BWOOOOF

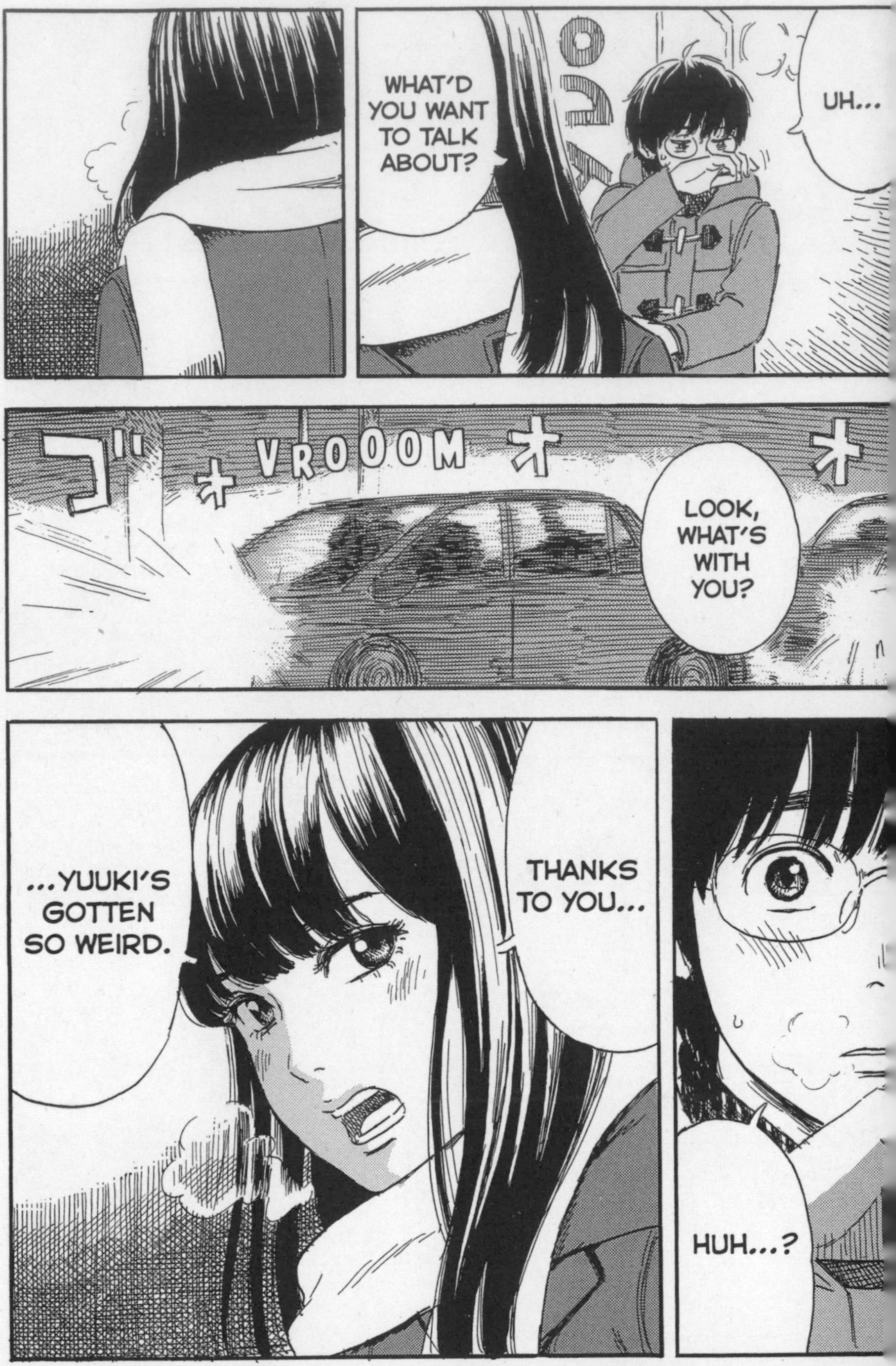
UH...
WHAT'D YOU WANT TO TALK ABOUT?
LOOK, WHAT'S WITH YOU?
VROOOM
HUH...?
THANKS TO YOU...
...YUUKI'S GOTTEN SO WEIRD.

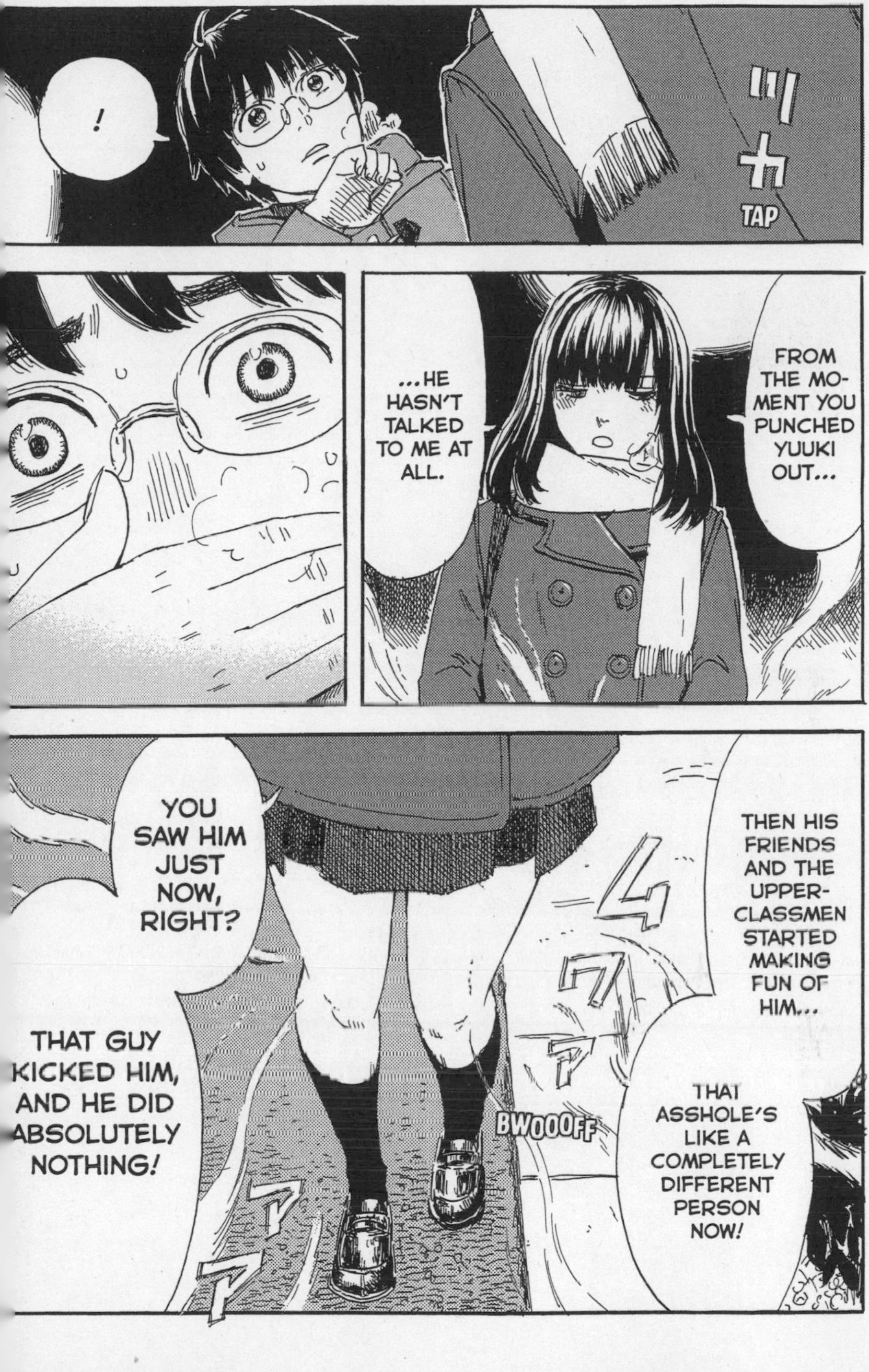
TAP
!
FROM THE MOMENT YOU PUNCHED YUUKI OUT...
...HE HASN'T TALKED TO ME AT ALL.
THEN HIS FRIENDS AND THE UPPERCLASSMEN STARTED MAKING FUN OF HIM...
THAT ASSHOLE'S LIKE A COMPLETELY DIFFERENT PERSON NOW!
BWOOOFF
YOU SAW HIM JUST NOW, RIGHT?
THAT GUY KICKED HIM, AND HE DID ABSOLUTELY NOTHING!

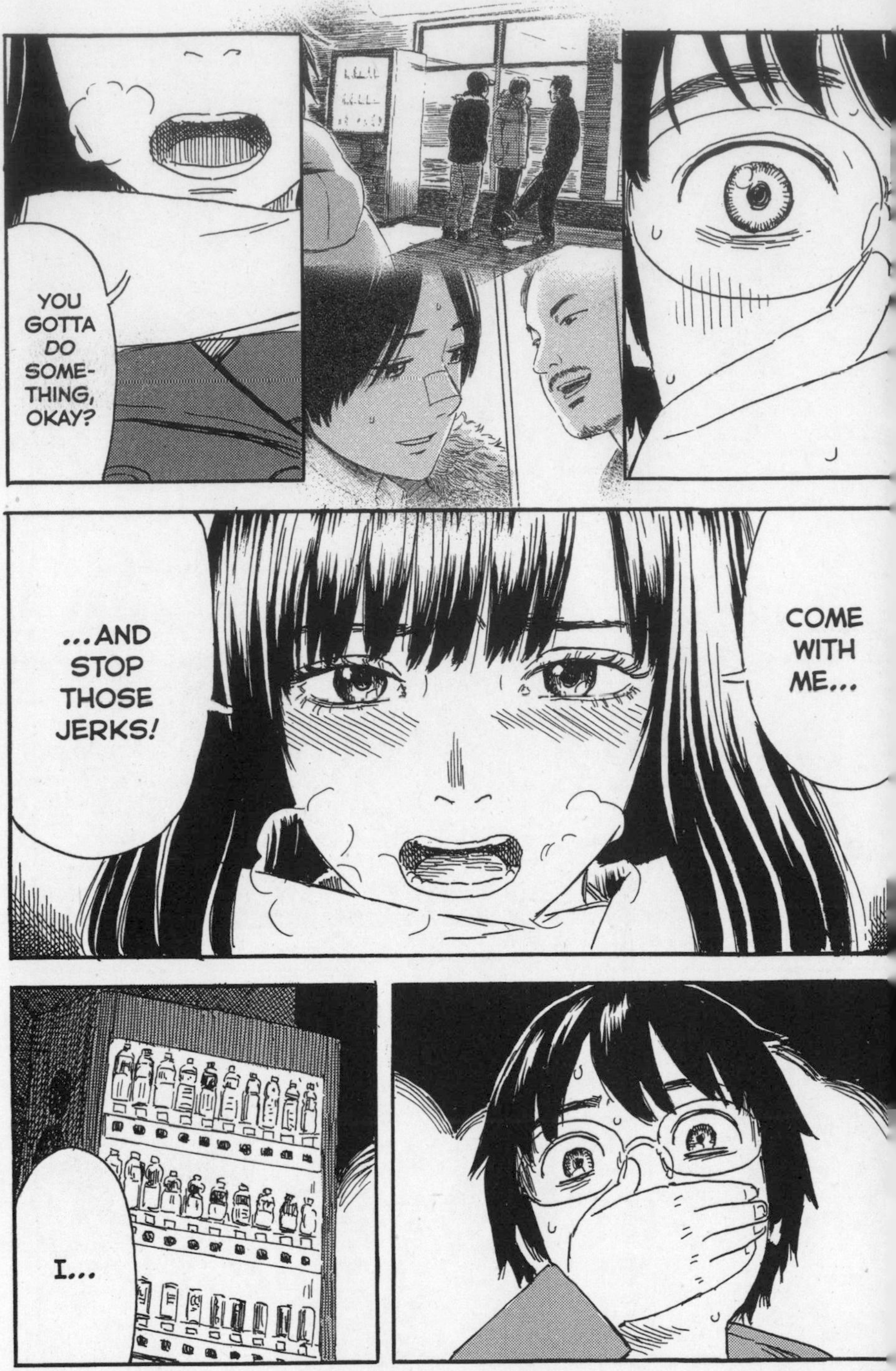
YOU GOTTA DO SOMETHING, OKAY?
COME WITH ME...
...AND STOP THOSE JERKS!
I...

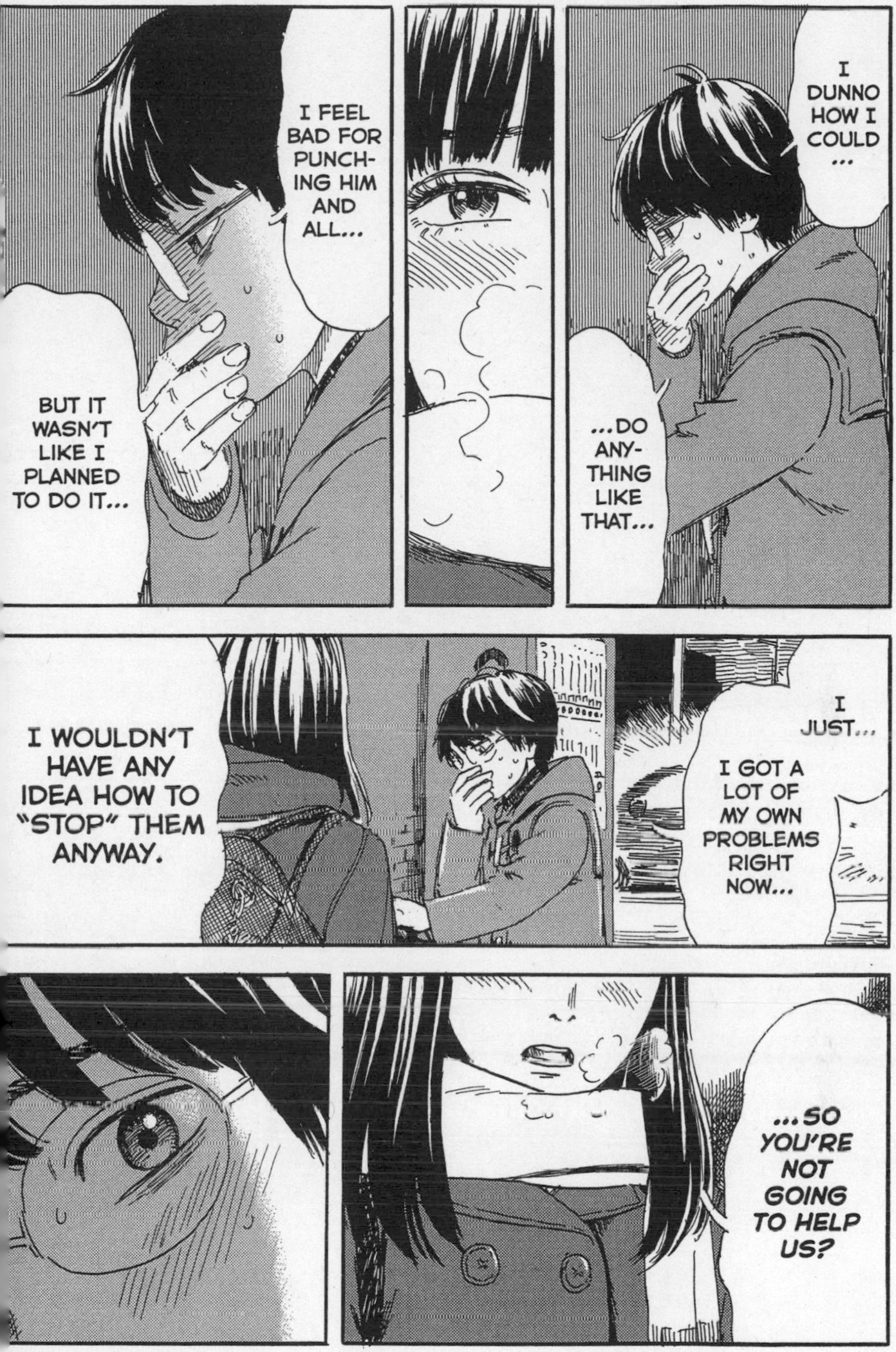
I DUNNO HOW I COULD ...
...DO ANY-THING LIKE THAT...
I FEEL BAD FOR PUNCH-ING HIM AND ALL...
BUT IT WASN'T LIKE I PLANNED TO DO IT...
I JUST...
I GOT A LOT OF MY OWN PROBLEMS RIGHT NOW...
I WOULDN'T HAVE ANY IDEA HOW TO "STOP" THEM ANYWAY.
...SO YOU'RE NOT GOING TO HELP US?

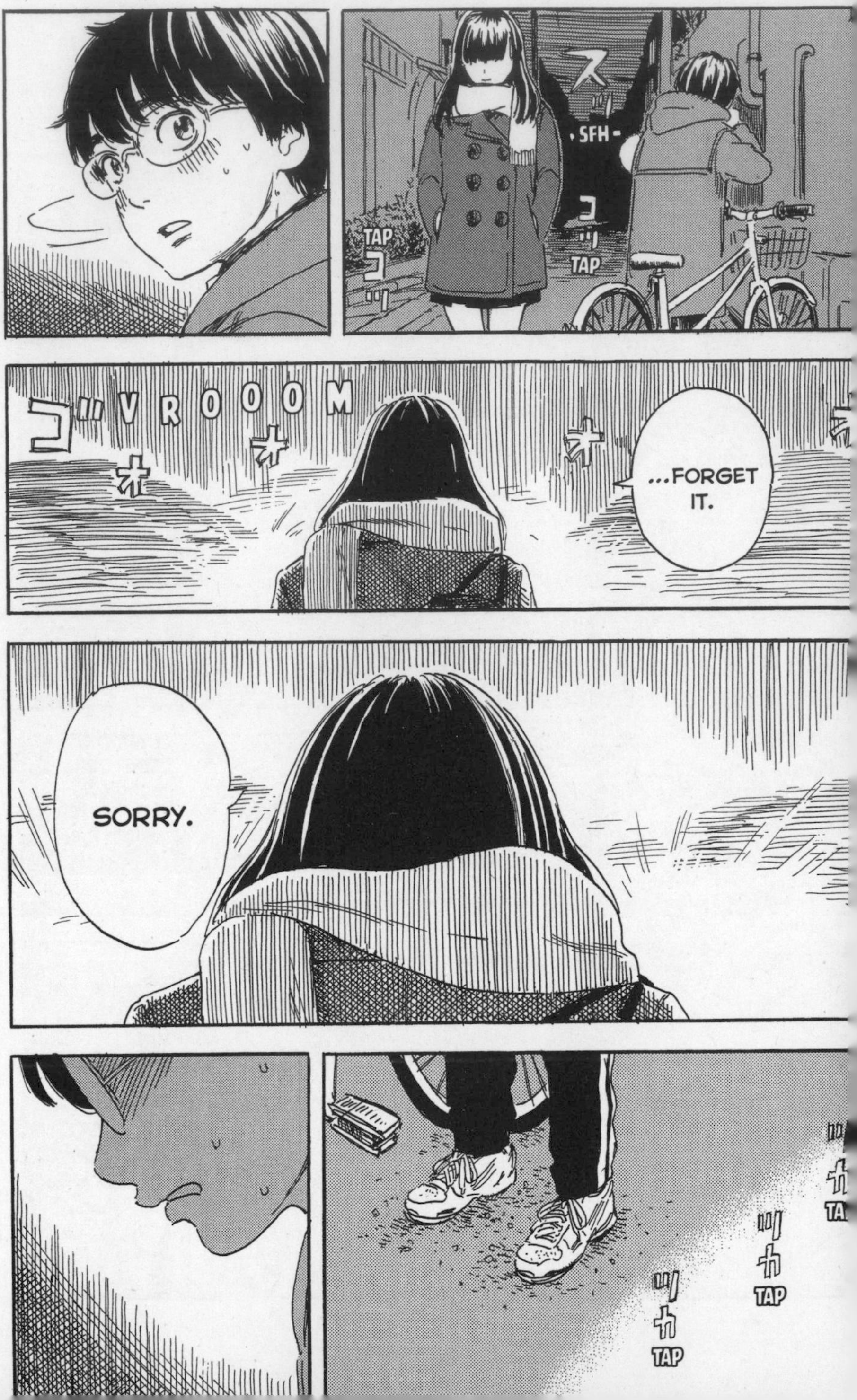

SFH
TAP
TAP
VROOOM
...FORGET IT.
SORRY.
TAP
TAP
TAP

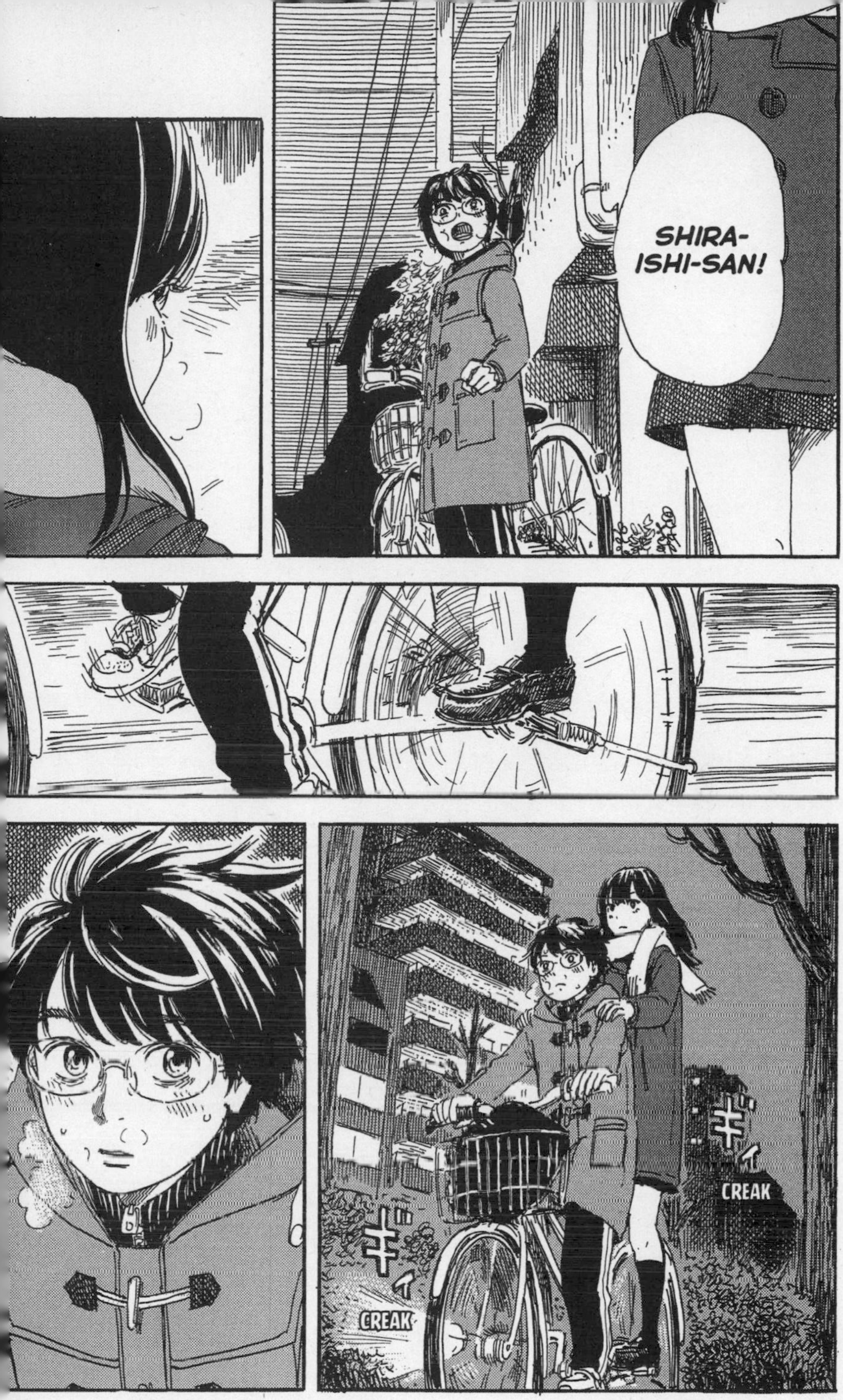
SHIRA-ISHI-SAN!
CREAK
CREAK

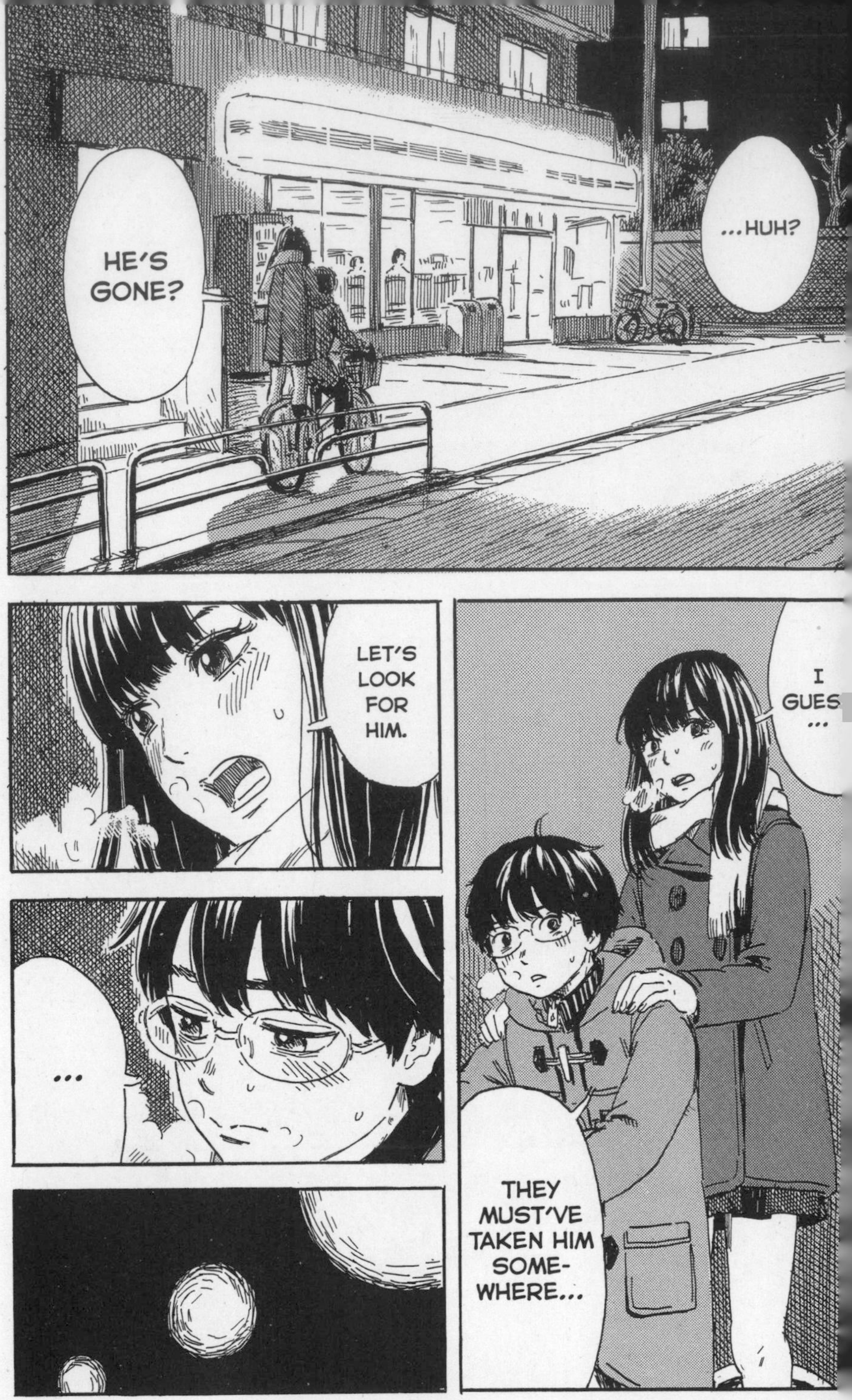
...HUH?
HE'S GONE?
I GUES...
THEY MUST'VE TAKEN HIM SOME-WHERE...
LET'S LOOK FOR HIM.
...

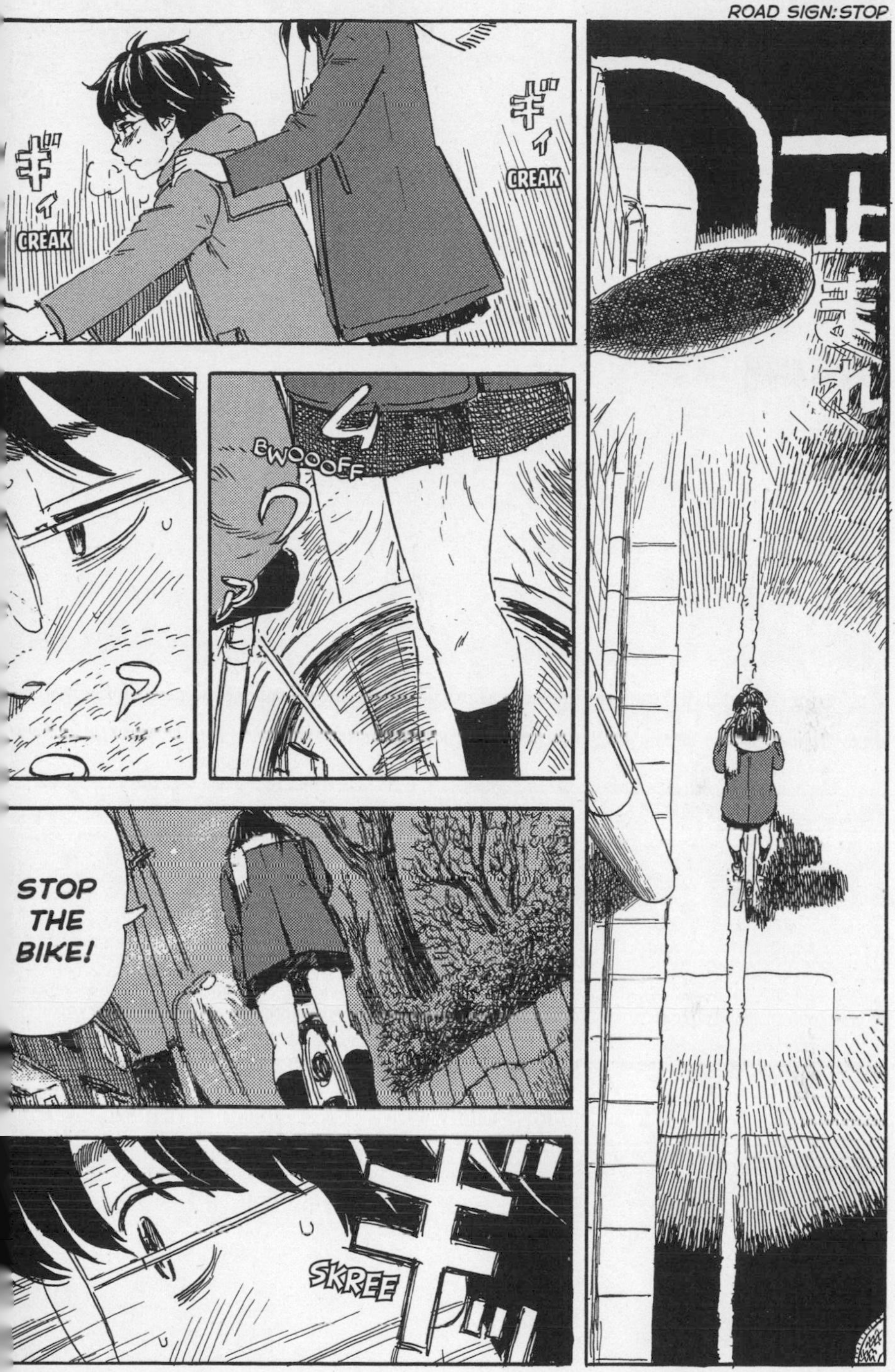
ROAD SIGN: STOP
止まれ
ギィ
CREAK
ギィ
CREAK
BWOOOFF
STOP THE BIKE!
SKREE

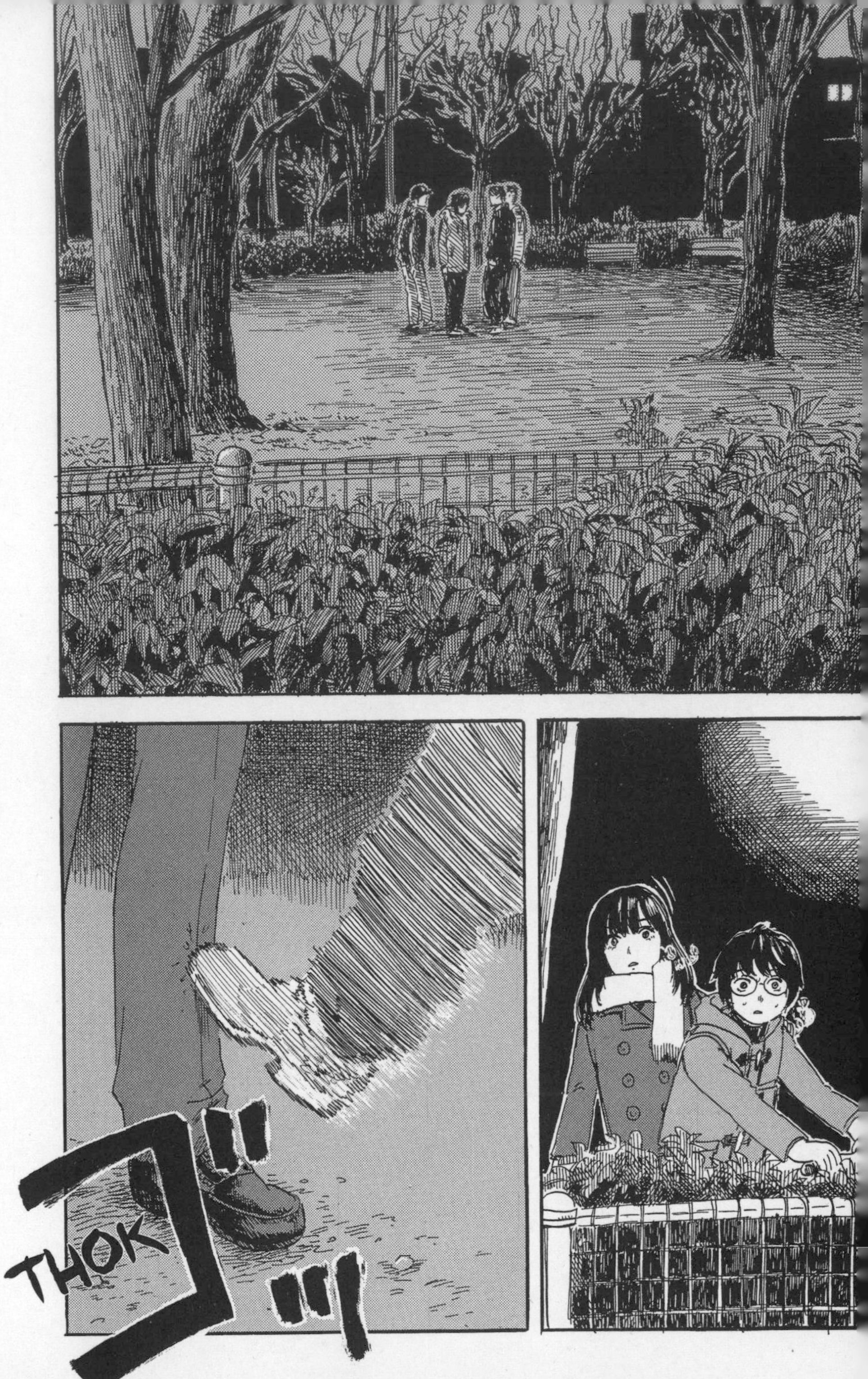
THOK

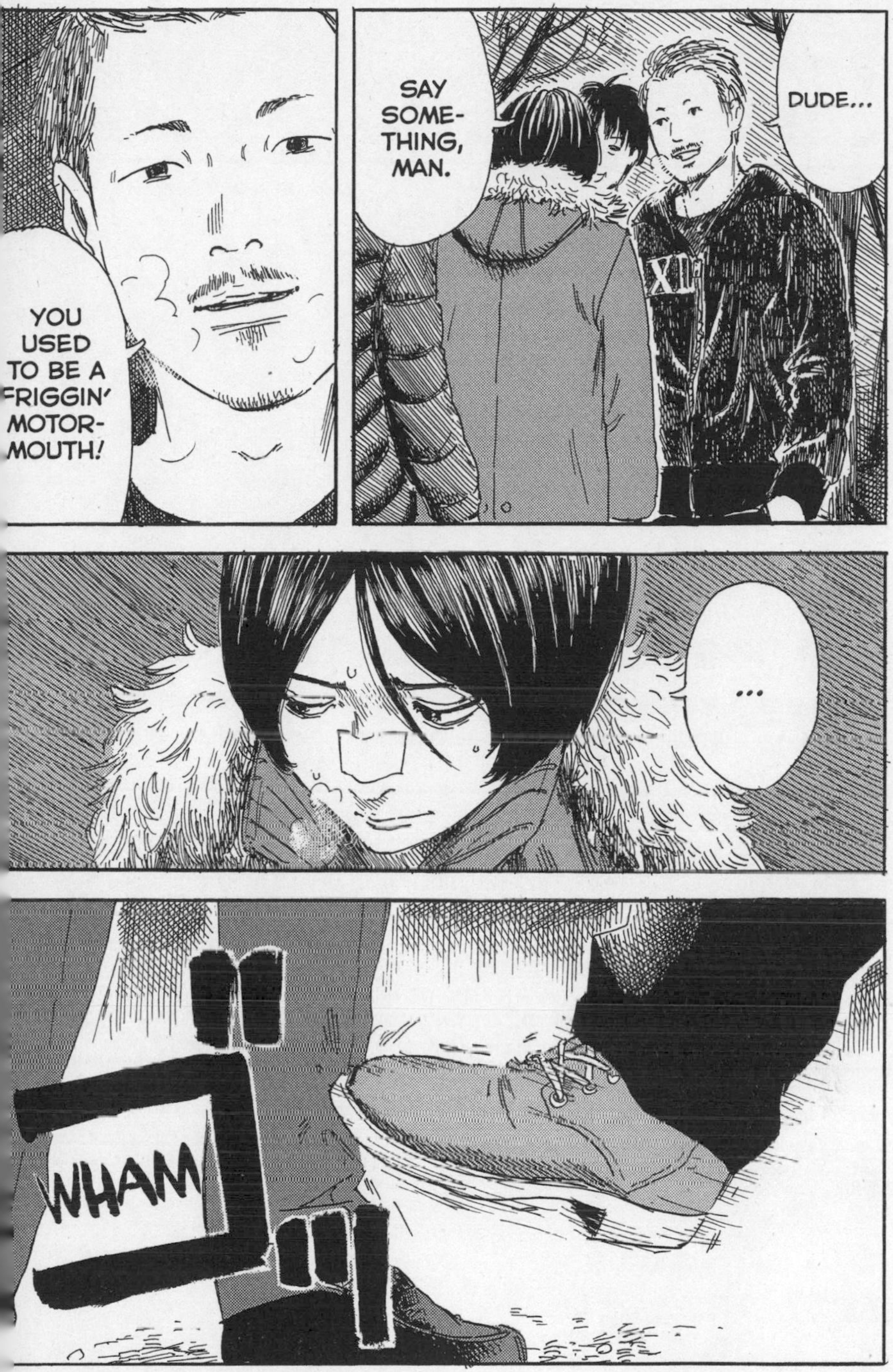
DUDE...
SAY SOME-THING, MAN.
YOU USED TO BE A FRIGGIN' MOTOR-MOUTH!
...
WHAM

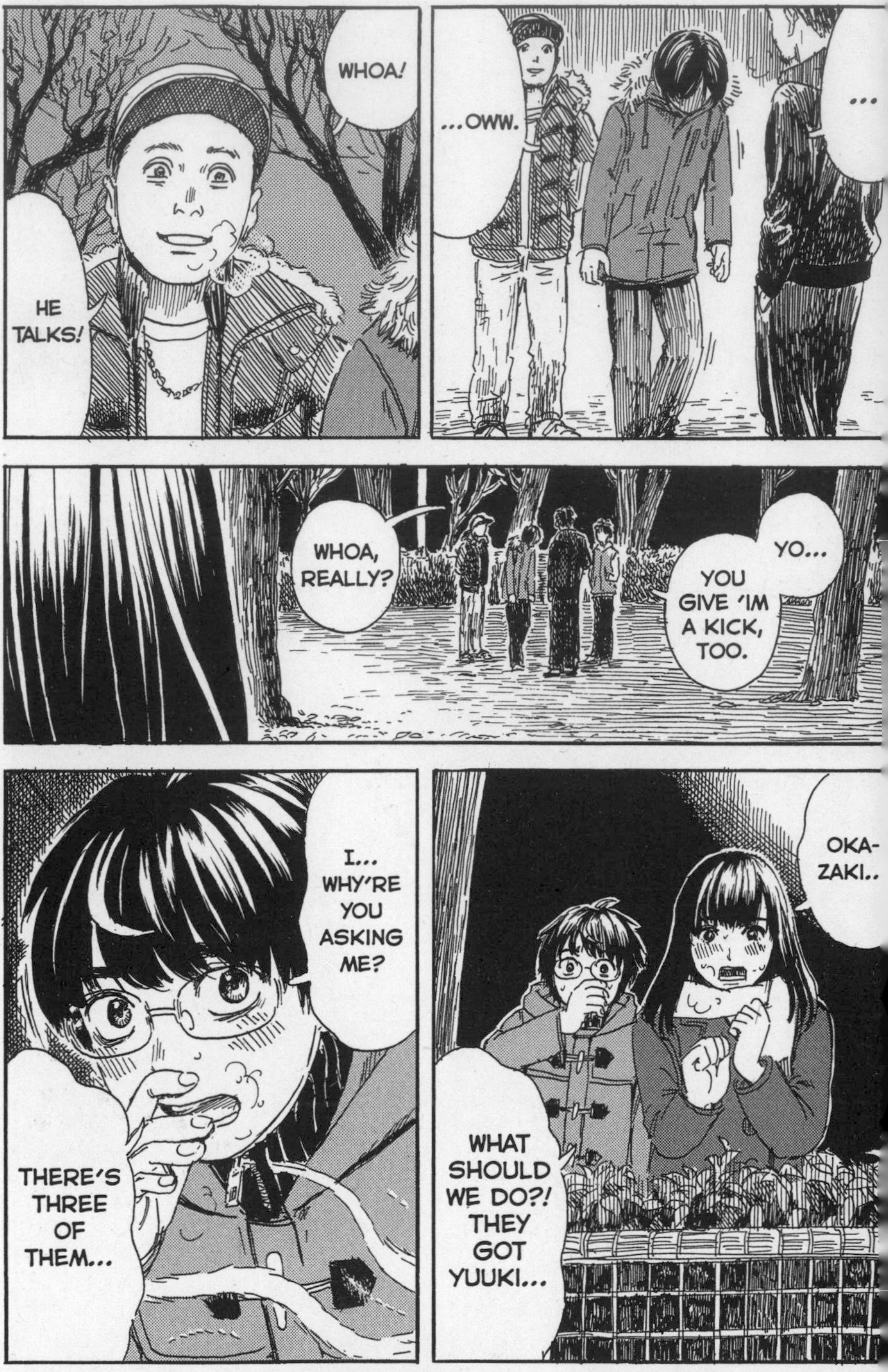
...
...OWW.
WHOA!
HE TALKS!
YO...
YOU GIVE 'IM A KICK, TOO.
WHOA, REALLY?
OKA-ZAKI..
WHAT SHOULD WE DO?! THEY GOT YUUKI...
I... WHY'RE YOU ASKING ME?
THERE'S THREE OF THEM...

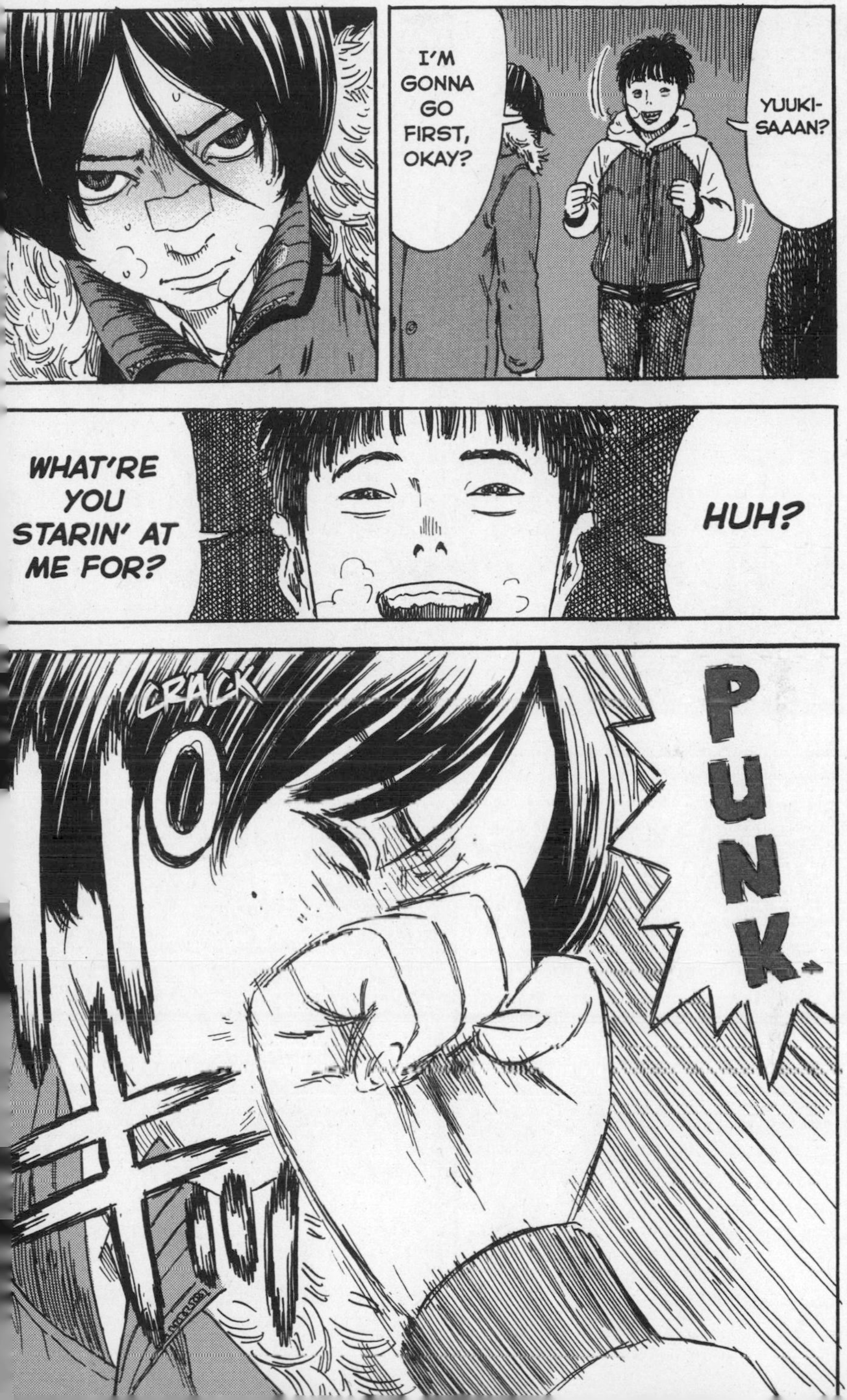
YUUKI-SAAAN?
I'M GONNA GO FIRST, OKAY?
HUH?
WHAT'RE YOU STARIN' AT ME FOR?
PUNK
CRACK

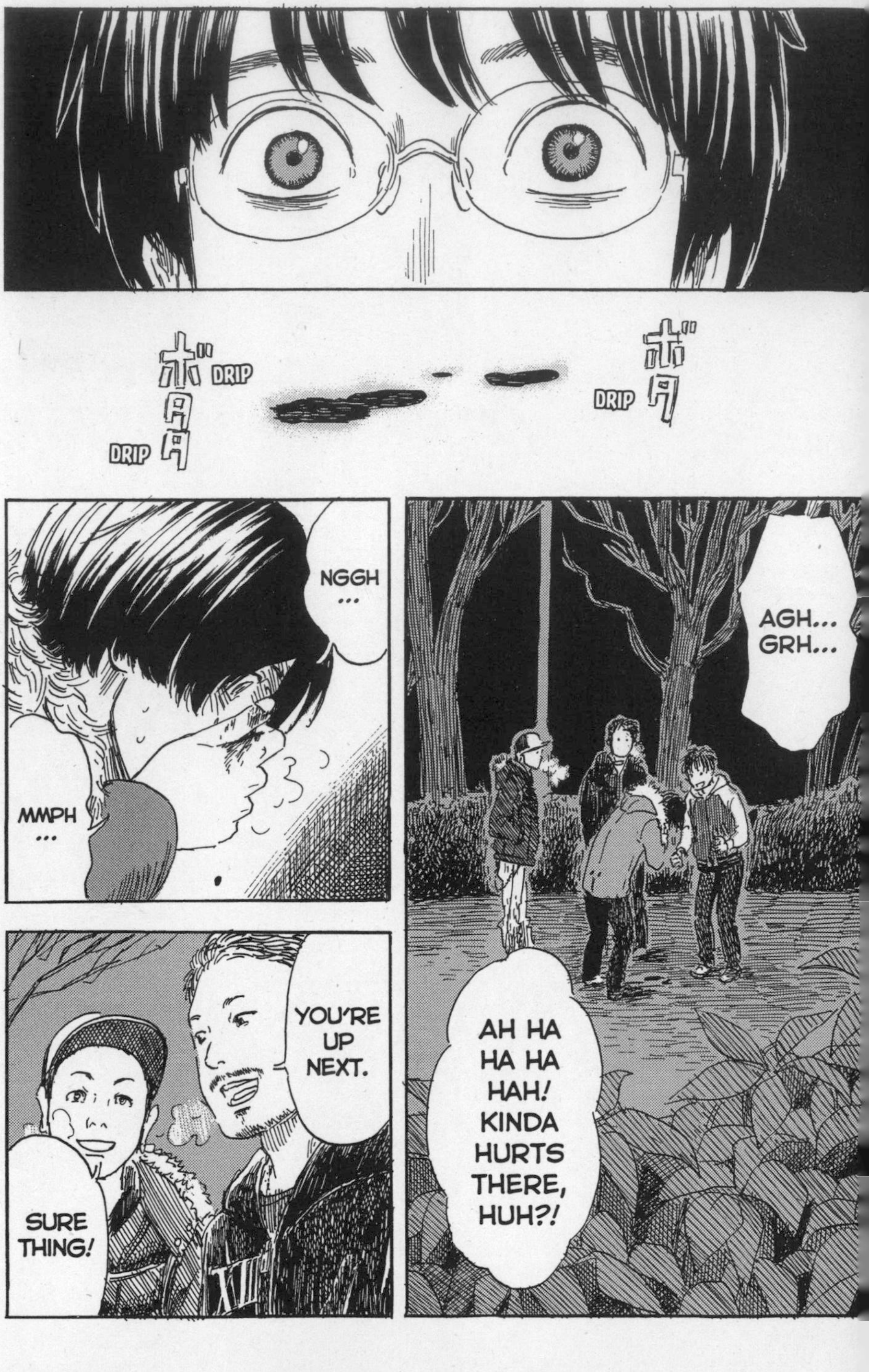

ボタ
DRIP
ボタボタ
DRIP
DRIP
AGH... GRH...
AH HA HA HA HAH! KINDA HURTS THERE, HUH?!
NGGH ...
MMPH ...
YOU'RE UP NEXT.
SURE THING!

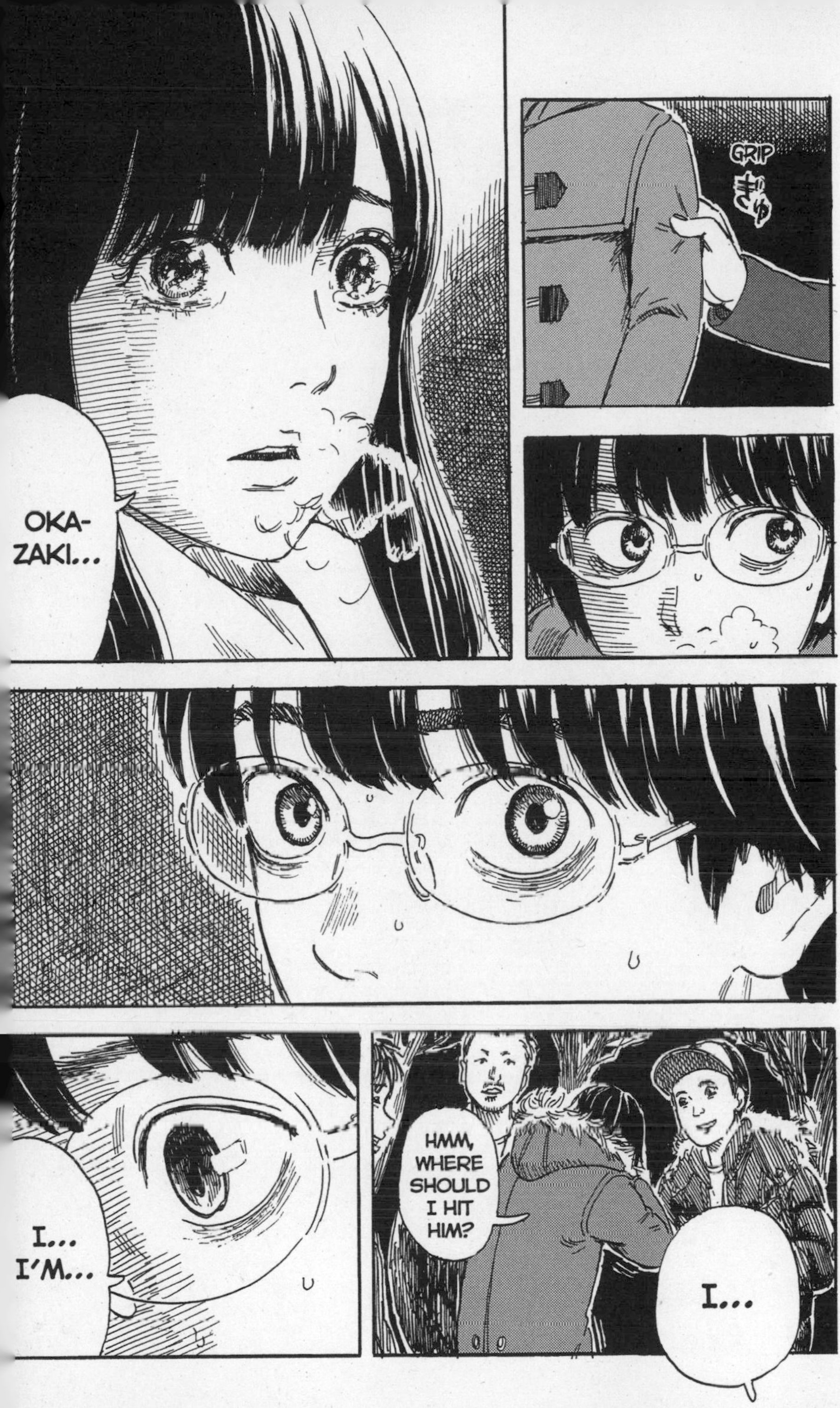
GRIP
ぎゅ
OKA-ZAKI...
HMM, WHERE SHOULD I HIT HIM?
I...
I... I'M...

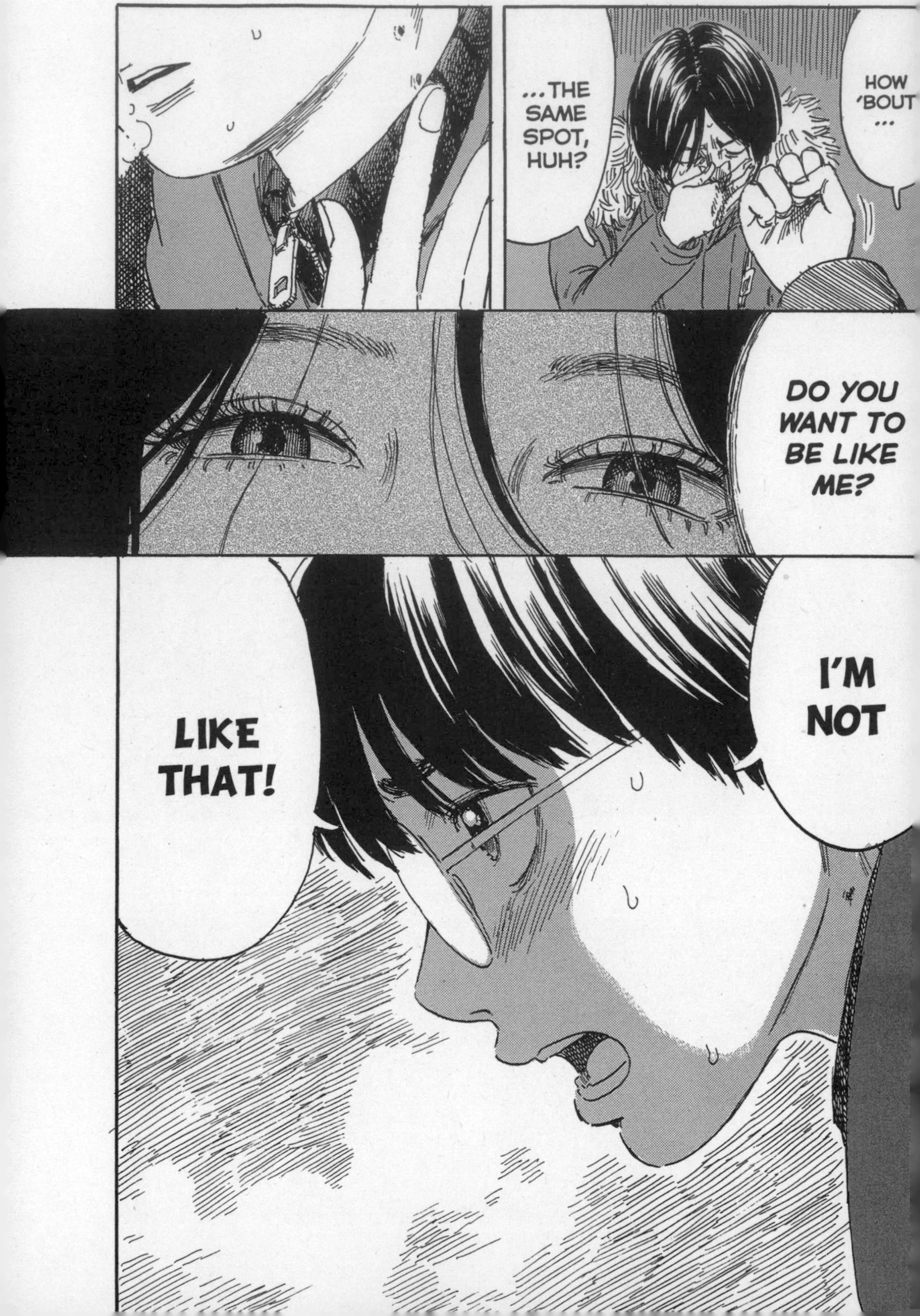
HOW 'BOUT ...
...THE SAME SPOT, HUH?
DO YOU WANT TO BE LIKE ME?
I'M NOT
LIKE THAT!

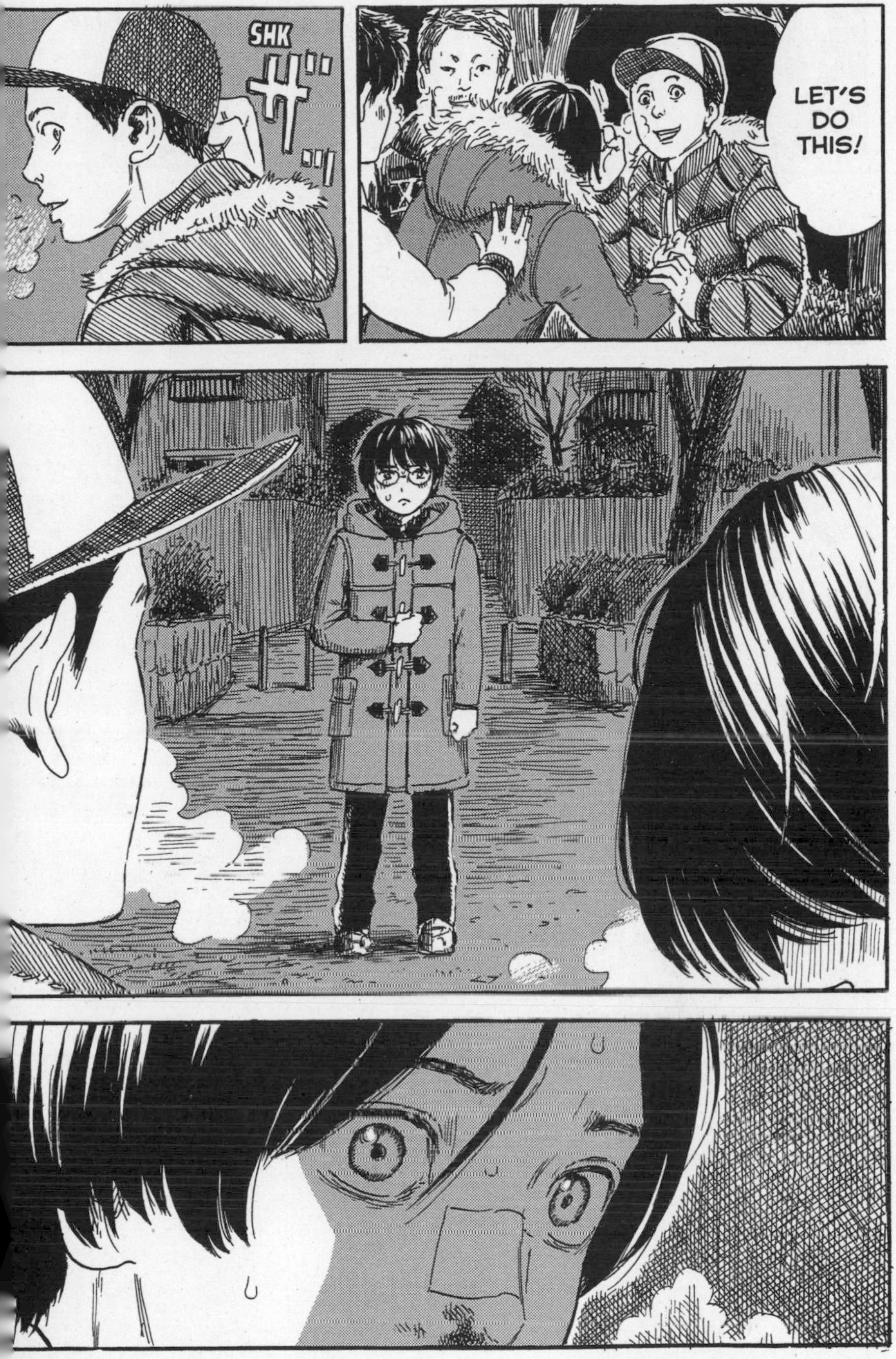
LET'S DO THIS!
SHK
ザッ

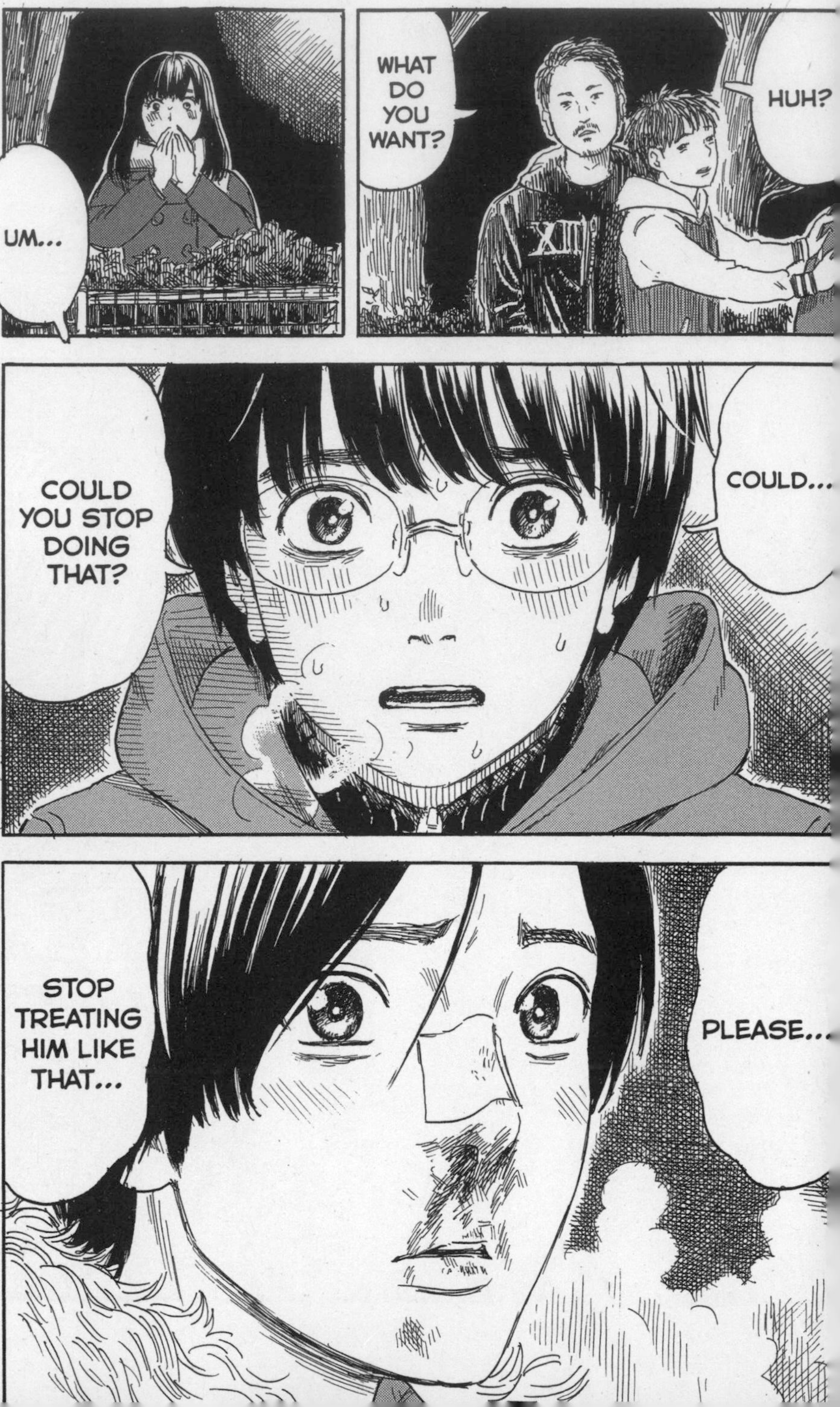
HUH?
WHAT DO YOU WANT?
UM...
COULD...
COULD YOU STOP DOING THAT?
PLEASE...
STOP TREATING HIM LIKE THAT...

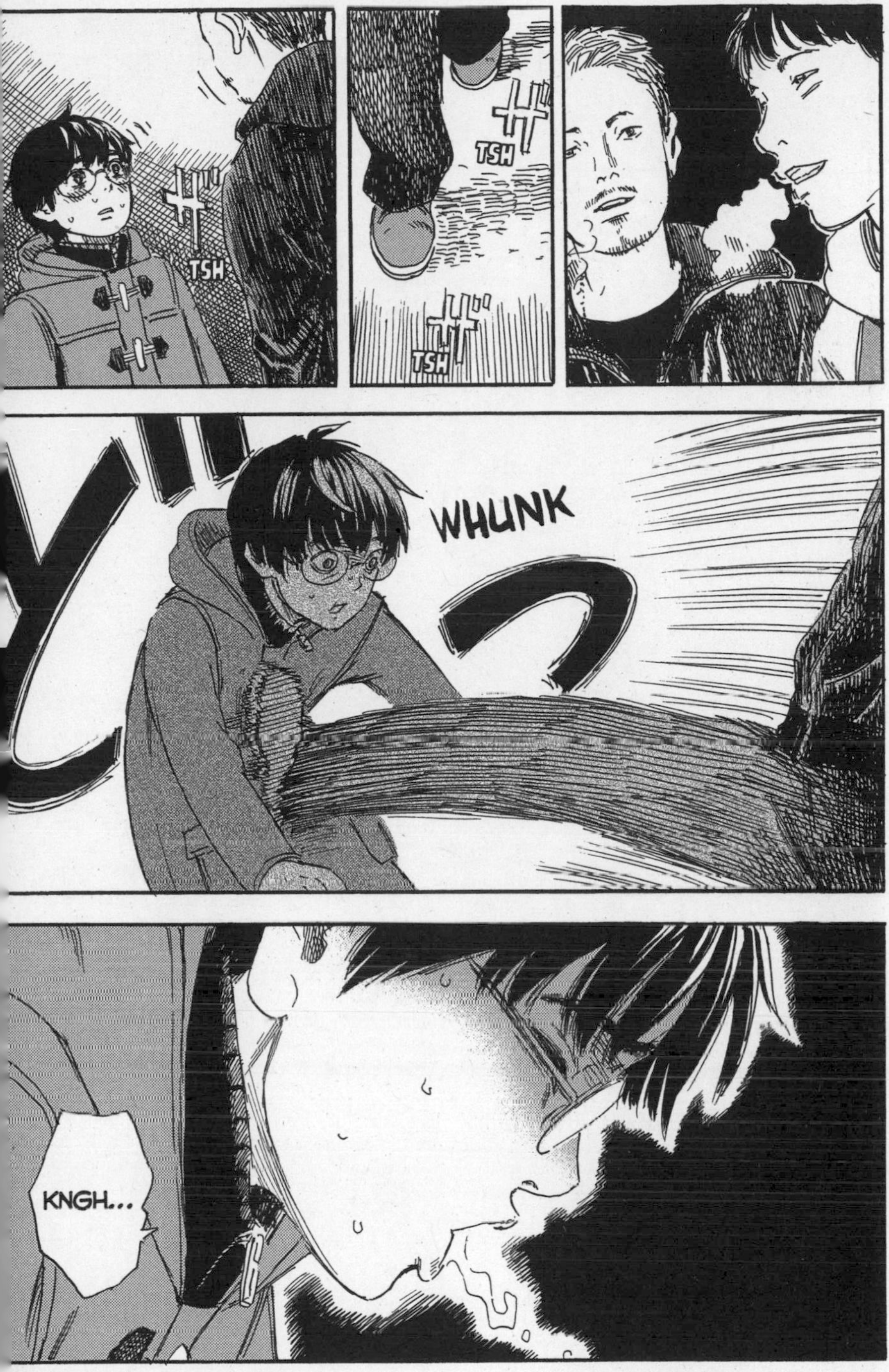
TSH
TSH
TSH
WHUNK
KNGH...

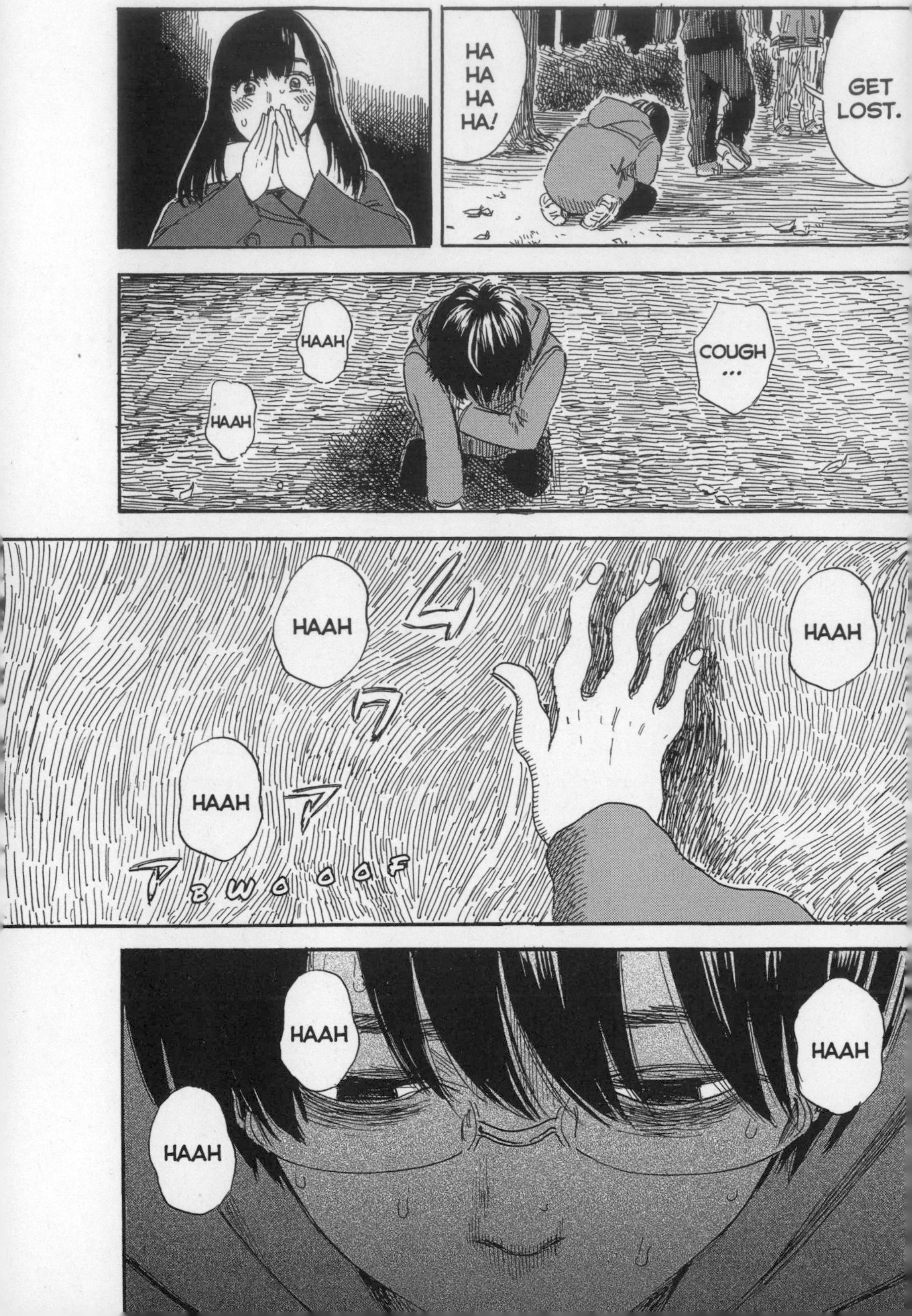
GET LOST.
HA HA HA HA!
COUGH ...
HAAH
HAAH
HAAH
HAAH
HAAH
BWOOOF
HAAH
HAAH
HAAH

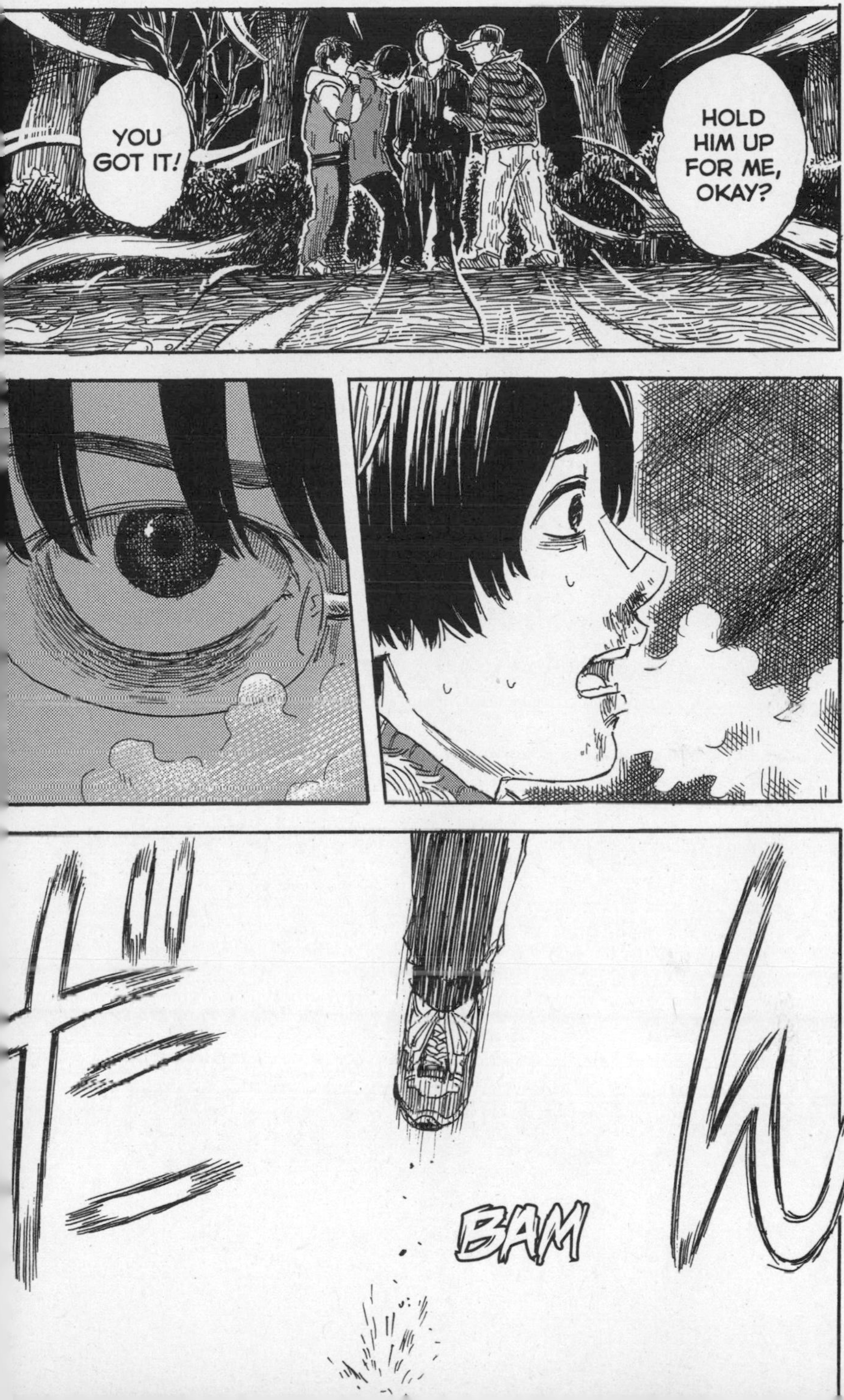
HOLD HIM UP FOR ME, OKAY?
YOU GOT IT!
BAM

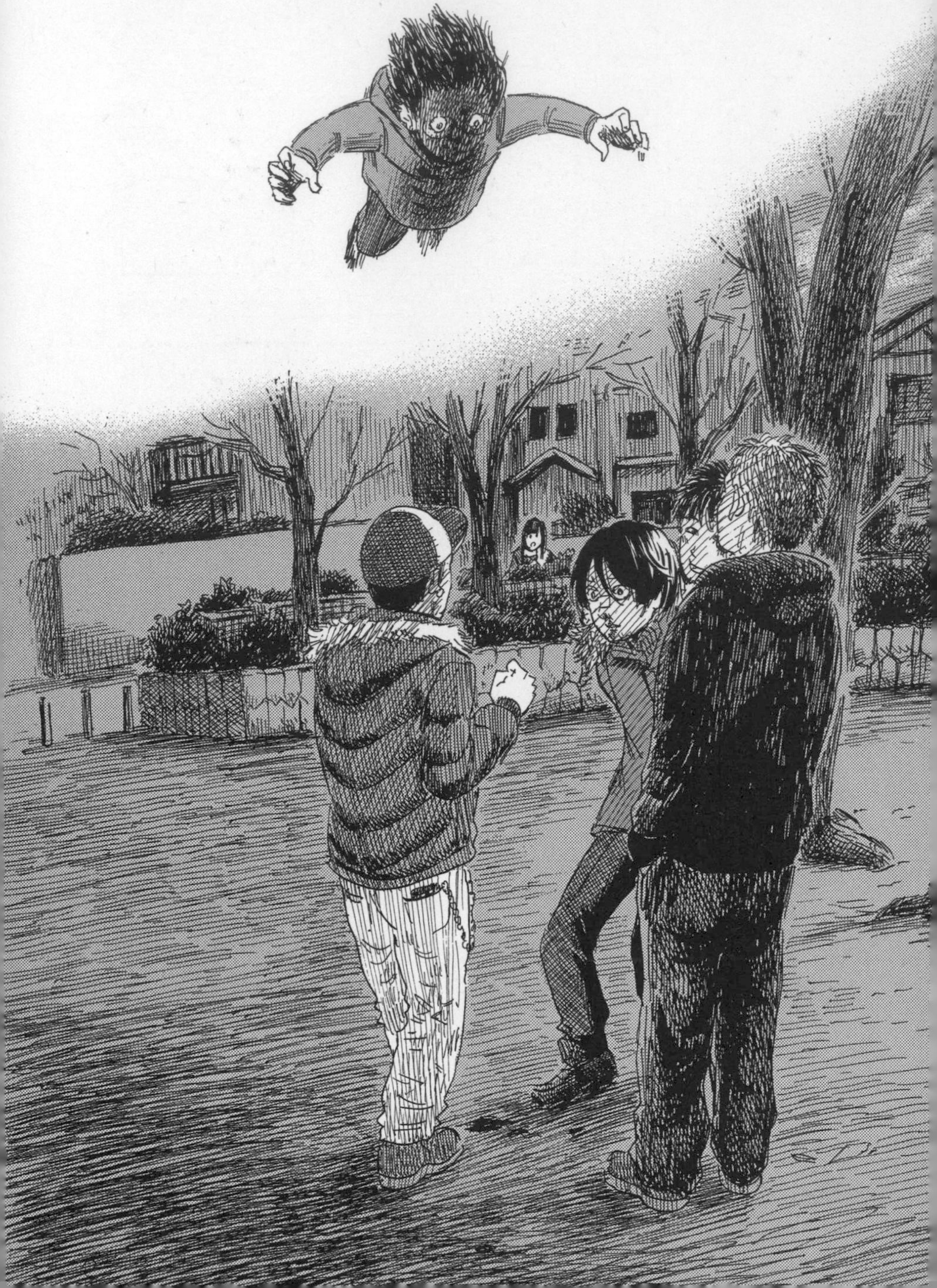

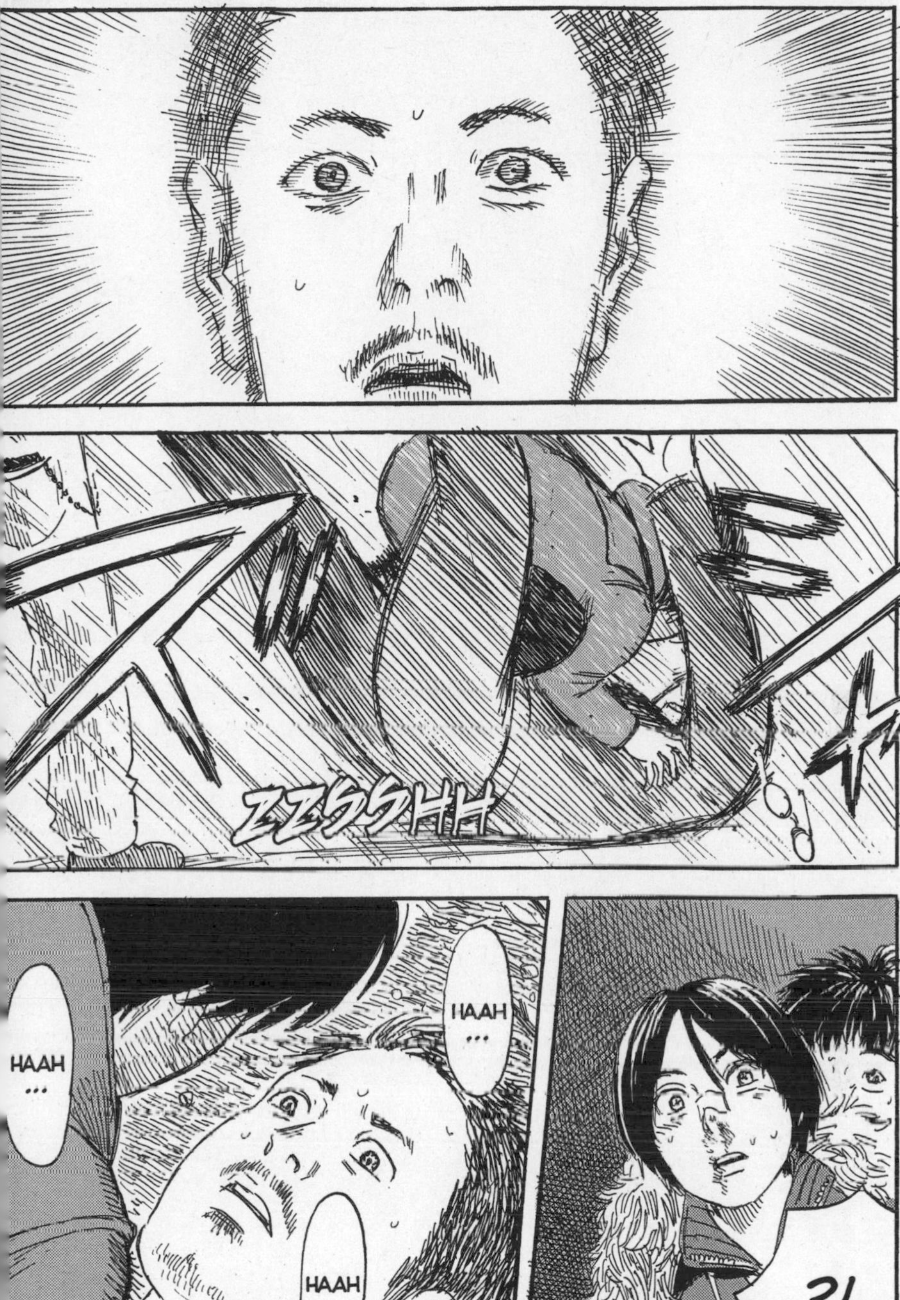
ZZSSHH
?!
HAAH...
HAAH...
HAAH...

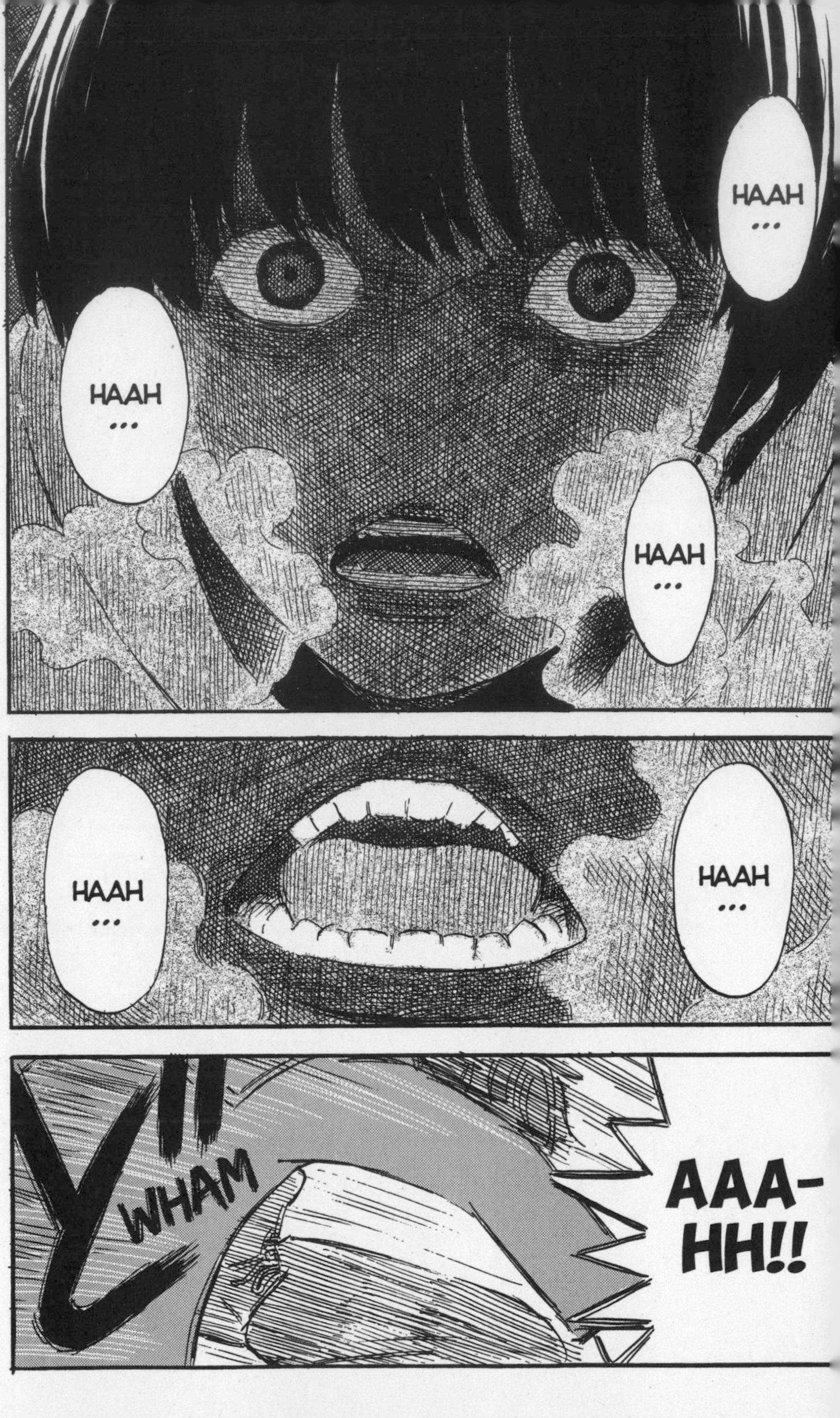
HAAH ...
HAAH ...
HAAH ...
HAAH ...
HAAH ...
AAA-HH!!
WHAM

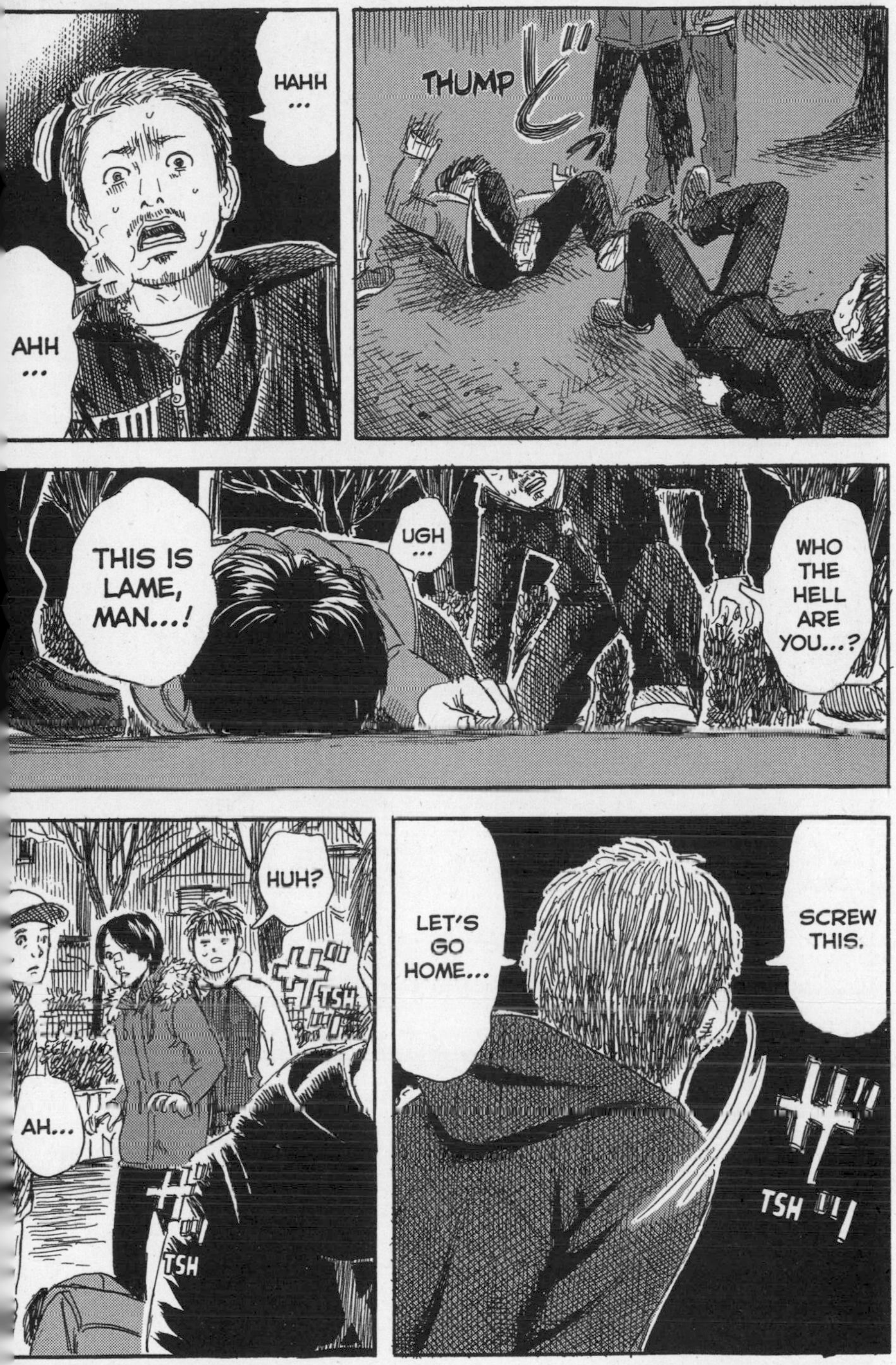
THUMP
HAHH...
AHH...
WHO THE HELL ARE YOU...?
UGH...
THIS IS LAME, MAN...!
SCREW THIS.
LET'S GO HOME...
TSH
HUH?
TSH
AH...
TSH

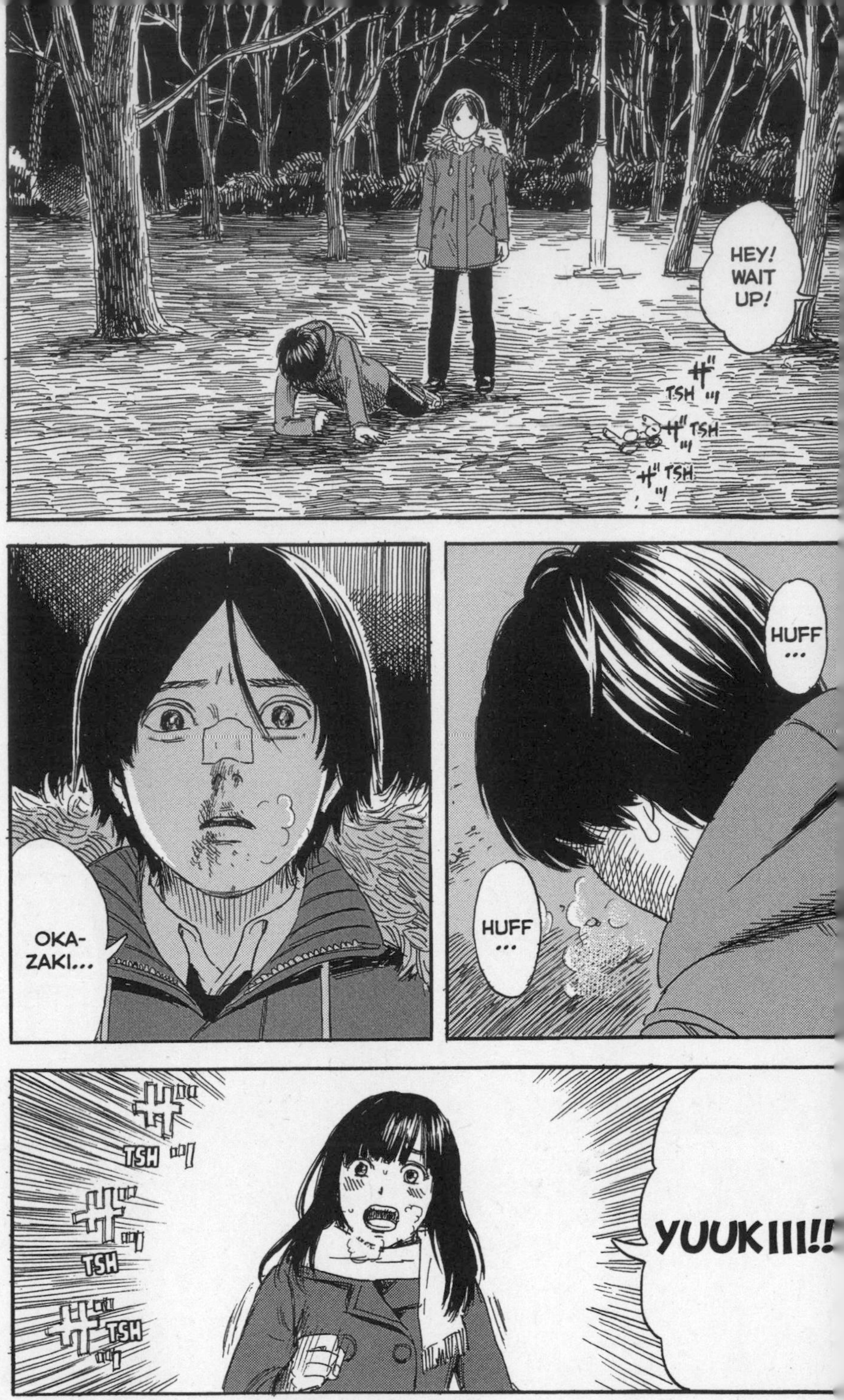
HEY! WAIT UP!
TSH
TSH
TSH
HUFF...
HUFF...
OKA-ZAKI...
YUUKIII!!
TSH
TSH
TSH

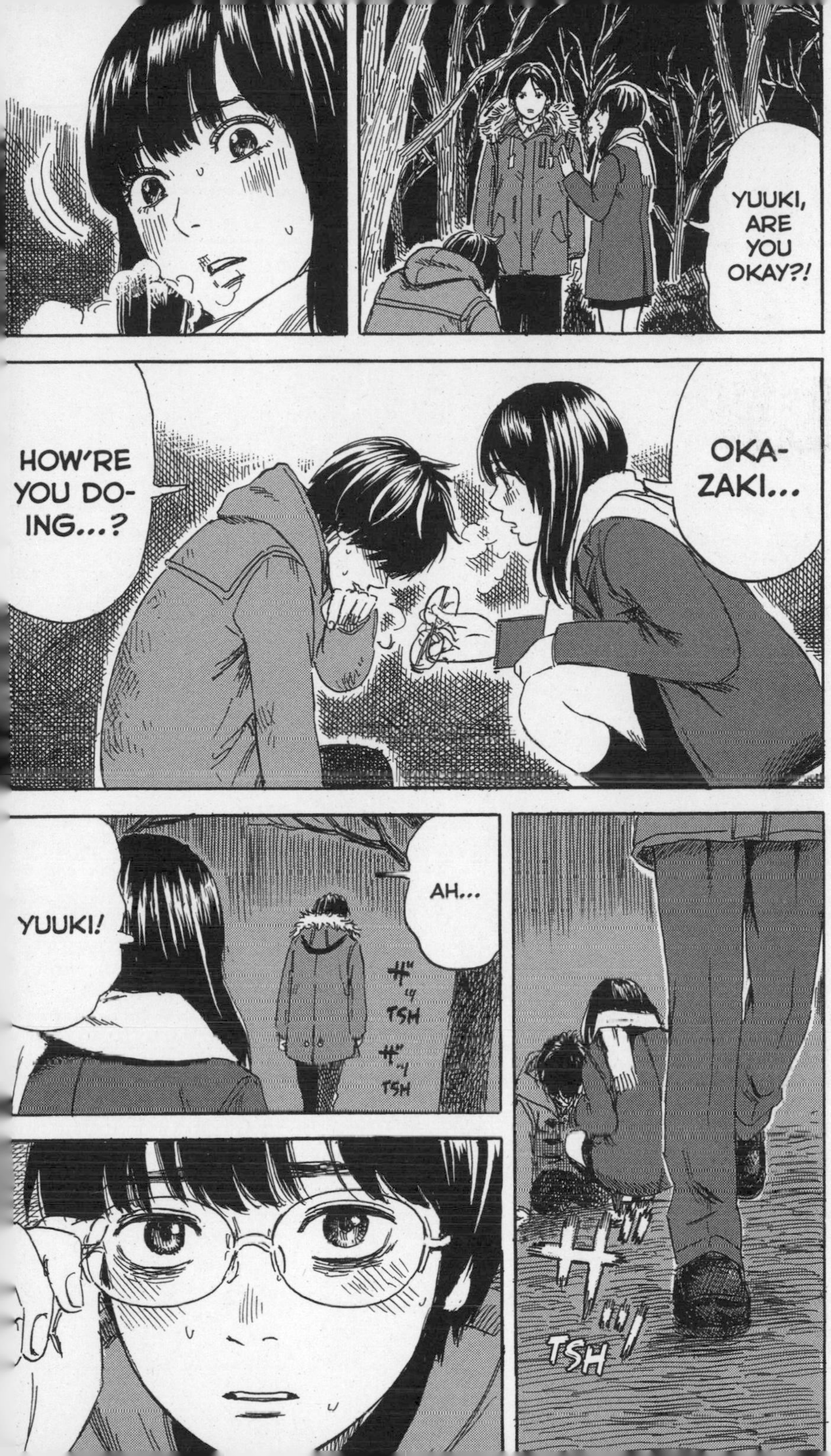

YUUKI, ARE YOU OKAY?!
OKA-ZAKI...
HOW'RE YOU DO-ING...?
ザッ
TSH
AH...
YUUKI!
ザッ
TSH
ザッ
TSH

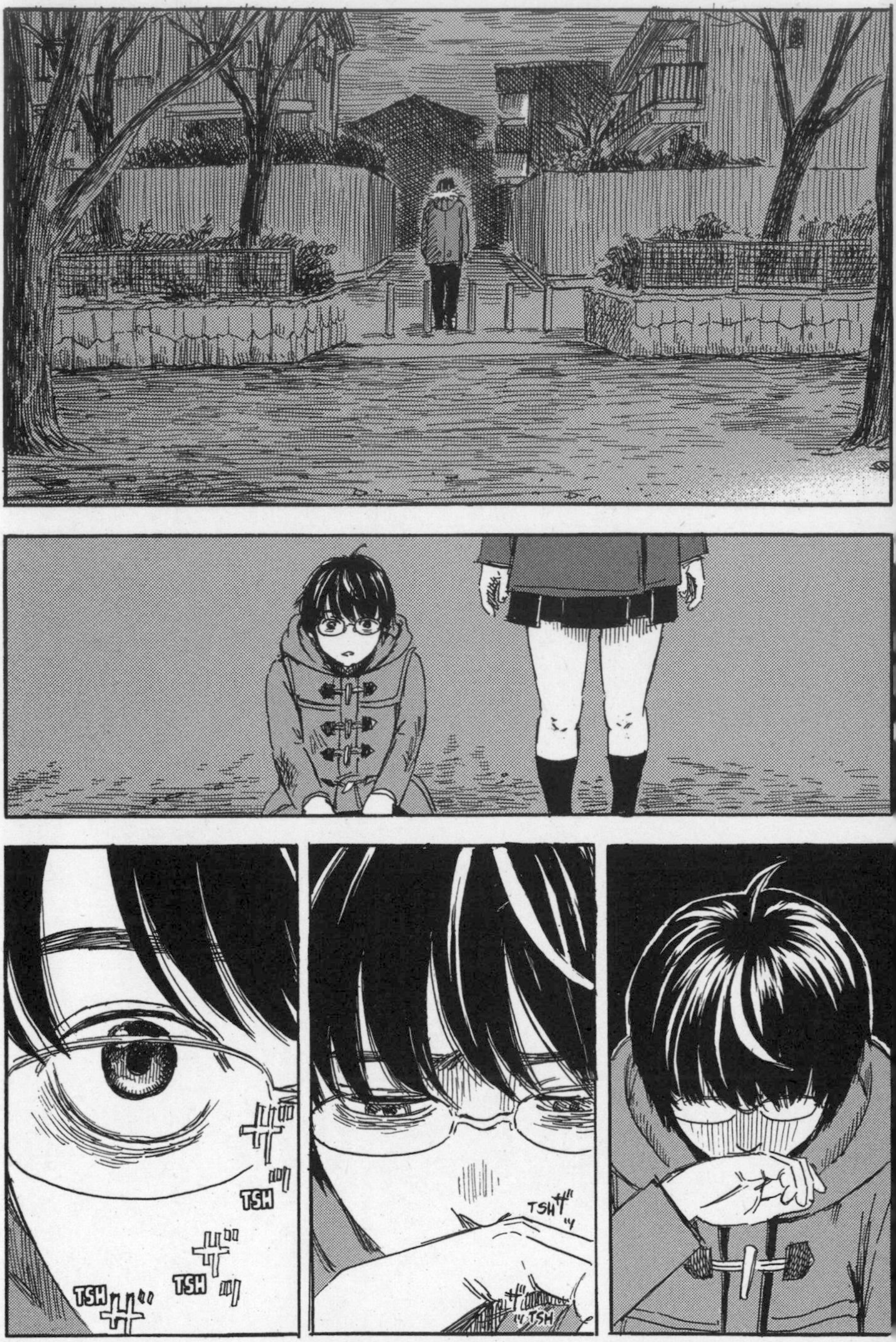
TSH
TSH
TSH
TSH
TSH

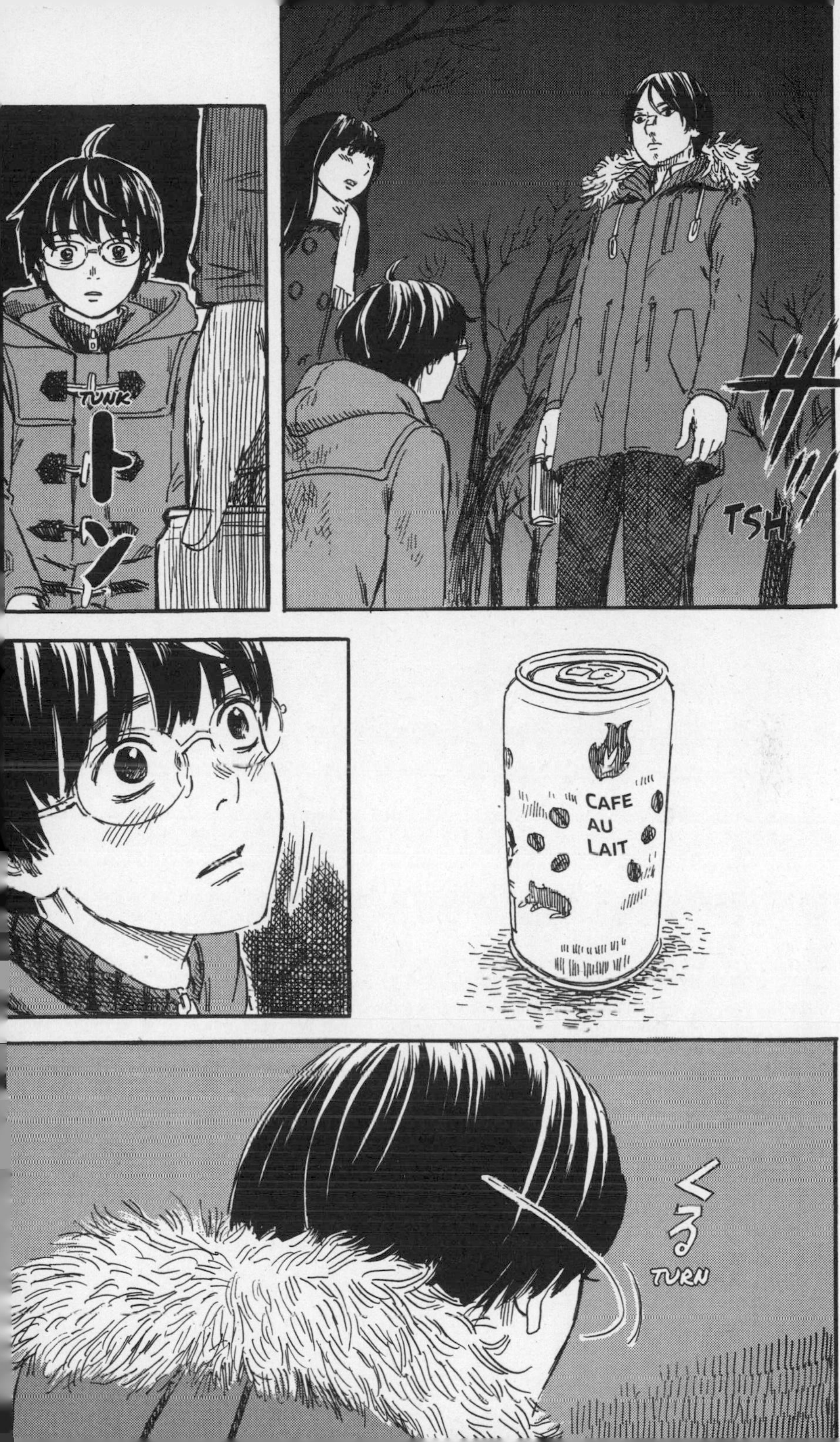
ザッ
TSH
トン
TUNK
CAFE AU LAIT
くる
TURN

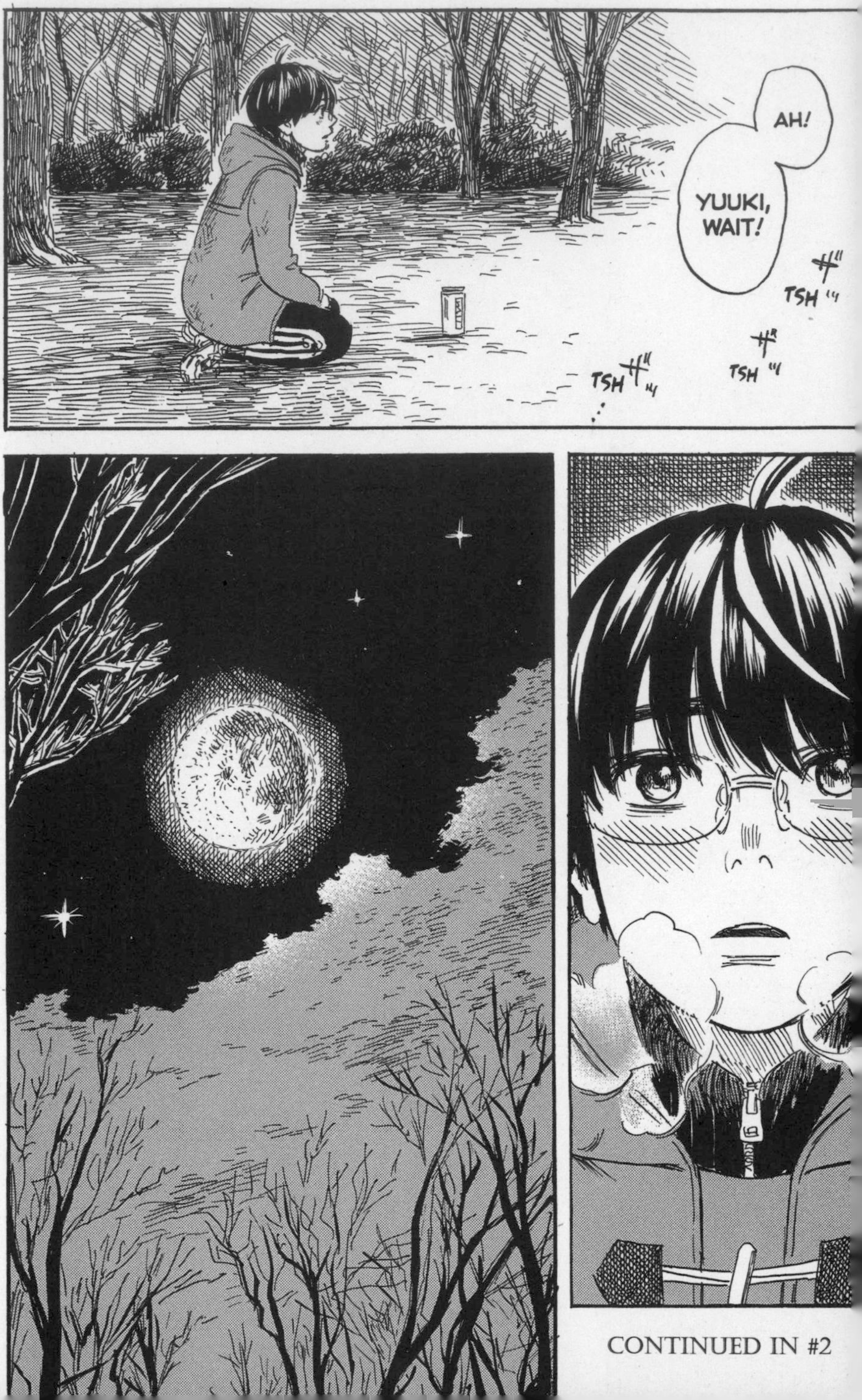
AH!
YUUKI, WAIT!
TSH
TSH
TSH

CONTINUED IN #2